Labeling
Pedagogy and Politics

Edited by
Glenn M. Hudak and Paul Kihn

RoutledgeFalmer

First published 2001 by RoutledgeFalmer
11 New Fetter Lane, London EC4P 4EE

Simultaneously published in the USA and Canada
by RoutledgeFalmer
29 West 35th Street, New York, NY 10001

Routledge is an imprint of the Taylor & Francis Group

© 2001 Glenn M Hudak and Paul Kihn.

Typeset in Baskerville by Bookcraft Ltd, Stroud, Gloucestershire
Printed and bound in Great Britain by TJ International Ltd, Padstow,
Cornwall

British Library Cataloguing in Publication Data
A catalogue record for this book is available from the British Library

Library of Congress Cataloging in Publication Data
Labeling : pedagogy and politics / [edited by] Glenn M. Hudak and
Paul Kihn
    p.   cm.
  Includes bibligraphical references and index.
  ISBN 0–415–23086–1 – ISBN 0–415–23087–X (pbk.)
  1. Critical pedagogy. 2. Stereotype (Psychology) 3. Stigma (Social
psychology) I. Hudak, Glenn M., 1951– II. Kihn, Paul, 1966–

LC196 .L33 2001
370.11'5–dc21   00–059187

ISBN 0–415–23086–1 – ISBN 0–415–23087–X (pbk.)

To Nicole and Ben (*Glenn Hudak*)
To my parents, the good doctors Kihn (*Paul Kihn*)

Contents

Knowing

Contributors

Michael W. Apple is the John Bascom Professor of Curriculum and Instruction and Educational Policy Studies at the University of Wisconsin, Madison. He has written extensively on the relationship between education and power. Among his many books are *Ideology And Curriculum, Education And Power, Teachers And Texts, Official Knowledge*, and *Cultural Politics And Education*. His newest book is *Educating The "Right" Way: Markets, Standards, God, and Inequality*.

Nina Asher is Assistant Professor in the Department of Curriculum and Instruction and a member of the Women's and Gender Studies faculty at Louisiana State University, Baton Rouge. Her work draws on postcolonial and feminist perspectives in education and critical, theoretical perspectives on identity and representation (with a focus on Asian American education). She is also working currently on a book project which engages multiculturalism from postcolonial perspectives to interrogate constructions of identity and the processes of negotiating self-representations in school (specificially among Indian American high school students in New York City).

Aimee Carrillo-Rowe is a Visiting Assistant Professor and the Acting Program Director of Gender and Women's Studies at Connecticut College (2000-2001). She recently completed her Ph.D. in Speech Communication and Women Studies at the University of Washington in Seattle (June, 2000). Her current research examines ideologies of race and whiteness, gender and sexuality. Her work is published in a variety of interdisciplinary outlets, including: *Our Voices: Essays in Culture, Ethnicity, and Communication* (Roxbury, 2000). She is currently working on a book manuscript and has essays under review with Signs, Genders, and Feminist Media Studies.

Warren Crichlow teaches cultural studies and education in the Faculty of Education at York University, Toronto, Canada. He is co-editor, along with Cameron McCarthy, of *Race Identity and Representation in Education* (1993).

Diane H. Dillon is a licensed psychologist and certified school psychologist who is currently on leave from the NYC Board of Education. She is an adjunct professor in the School Psychology Program in the Department of Health and Behavior Studies at Columbia University's Teachers College; she writes on the changing role of special education, AIDS, death, grief and social support in the context of loss. Diane is the proud mother of Kayla.

Peter W. Dillon is the Assistant Principal of The Heritage School, a New York City public high school located in East Harlem. He is a doctoral candidate in curriculum and teaching at Teachers College, Columbia University. Peter has taught English as a second language in Brooklyn (NY), the Bronx (NY), Massachusetts, and in the Republic of the Marshall Islands as a Peace Corps volunteer. Currently an IMPACT II National Teacher Policy Institute Fellow, Peter writes on teacher collaboration, professional development and the inclusion of teachers and students' voices in policy making.

Greg Dimitriadis is an assistant professor in the Department of Educational Leadership and Policy at the University at Buffalo, The State University of New York. He teaches in the sociology of education concentration. His work on popular culture, education, and the everyday lives of urban youth has appeared or is forthcoming in numerous books and journals both nationally and internationally. He has two books forthcoming: *Performing Identity/Performing Culture: Hip Hop as Text, Pedagogy, and Lived Practice* (Peter Lang) and *The Work of Art in the Postcolonial Imagination* co-authored with Cameron McCarthy (Teachers College Press).

Lee Fleischer began his academic career as a social studies high school teacher, received his doctorate at Teachers College, Columbia University, and currently teaches at Brooklyn College, City University of New York. His research interests include counter-hegemonic teaching, poststructuralism, and the politics of knowledge.

Hollyce C. (Sherry) Giles teaches in the School of Education at Brooklyn College, City University of New York. Dr. Giles has investigated and written about parents' efforts to reform public schools as Senior Research Fellow with the Institute for Education and Social Policy at New York University, the Public Education Association, and the Industrial Areas Foundation. Dr. Giles' current research interests and publications center on the social, psychological and political processes in family-school reform initiatives.

Glenn M. Hudak teaches in the Cultural Foundations of Education Program, University of North Carolina, Greensboro. Recently, he graduated from Union Theological Seminary, New York City with a Master of Divinity degree (M. Div.). He is also in a psychoanalytic residency at the Harlem Family Institute in New York City, where he has provided therapy to adolescents in economically poor communities. His research interests revolve around the intersections of liberation theology, critical pedagogy, and psychoanalytic thought, especially the work of D.W. Winnicott. He is co-editor of *Sound Identities : Youth Music and the Cultural Politics of Education* (Peter Lang, 1999).

Judith Kaufman teaches critical perspectives on human development in the Department of Currculum and Teaching at Hofstra University. She is part of a research collective that is using memory-work methodology as a tool for critically examining socialization. The collective is currently at work on a book describing their use of memory-work within the context of women and nature. The book will be published by Peter Lang and is due out by summer, 2001.

Paul Kihn is a middle school Language Arts teacher at the Beginning With Children School in New York City. He has taught in urban and rural schools in South Africa, and has been a community youth worker in Dublin, Ireland. Currently, he is a MetLife Fellow of the National Teachers' Policy Insitute, committed to including the voice of classroom teachers in the making of educational policy.

Cameron McCarthy teaches mass communications theory and cultural studies at the University of Illinois at Urbana. He is the author and co-author of *The Uses of Culture: Education and the Limits of Ethnic Affiliation* (Routledge, 1998) and *The Work of Art in the Post Colonial Imagination* (In Press, TCP, University of Columbia) and a co-editor of *Sound Identities: Youth Music and the Cultural Politics of Education* (Peter Lang, 1999). With Jack Bratich and Jeremy Packer, he is editing an anthology on Foucault and Cultural Studies entitled, *Governing the Present.* This book will be published by SUNY press next spring.

Jan McDonald is Professor and Dean in the School of Education at Pace University in New York. She lives in New Rochelle with her partner Judy Kaufman who teaches at Hofstra University. With her ex-husband and partner, she co-parents their teenage son Steven. Much of the rest of her life you will discover through reading her contribution to this volume.

Peter McLaren is Professor of Education in the Division of Urban Schooling, at UCLA's Graduate School of Education and Information Studies. He has written extensively on critical pedagogy, cultural studies, and multicultural education. His numerous books include, *Che Guevara, Paulo Freire, and the Pedagogy of Revolution* (2000), *Critical Pedagogy and Predatory Culture* (1999), *Schooling as Ritual Performance* (1999), and *Life in Schools* (1997).

Andrea Smith is a graduate of West Virginia University. She has a Bachelors of Science in education. She also attained her Masters Degree in Curriculum and Teaching from Teachers College, Columbia University. She is currently an educator for the Montclair Public school system in Montclair, New Jersey. She serves on several community based organizations and develops educational programs for students.

Randall Styers is assistant professor of the philosophy of religion at Union Theological Seminary in New York. His research and writing focus on modern Western religious thought, with particular focus on the application of contemporary critical philosophy and social theory to the study of Christianity.

Peter Taubman is an Associate Professor of Education and Head of Secondary Education in the School of Education at Brooklyn College in Brooklyn, New York. He is one of the co-editors of *Understanding Curriculum* (Peter Lang, 1995) and the author of several essays on identity, autobiography and teaching. He is currently working on a book about teaching and teacher education.

Acknowledgements

This project began as a conference organized at Teachers College, Columbia University. We acknowledge, with thanks, each of the initial conference organizers: Adé Faison, Lee Fleischer, Andrea Smith, and Ana Maroulis. In addition, Teachers College, and the Continuing Education Office, lent their support for that initial gathering on Labeling.

For her support of this volume, which added a wide range of contributors to the discussion, Anna Clarkson at RoutledgeFalmer Press deserves special thanks.

Finally, we also thank Chae Kihn for providing the photographs. Her ability to capture people's lives within a single moment exemplifies a primary purpose here: the process of critical looking, and listening, that demystifies labels.

Foreword

Maxine Greene

At a moment of expanding interest in the construction rather than the discovery of meanings, the problem of labeling takes on a significance that is more than pedagogical. There is a general agreement that what we call knowledge does not represent an independent, objective 'reality'; rather, knowledge arises from actions taking place in an environment and from our reflections on those actions. What we see, hear, and feel around us is known by means of perceptual and conceptual structures, constructs that we (as social beings) build for ourselves. Alfred Schutz (1967: 135) has written about the ways in which we learn to make sense of things through interpretations made by our predecessors and contemporaries. The very fact that we come to know by means of linguistic formulations emerging over time is what gives this book its peculiar importance.

There are many constructs, unreflected upon, that carry the messages of power: they demean; they exclude; they create stereotypes. There are problems having to do with ethnicity, with diversity, with difference that arise from the heartless and immoral manipulation of labels, perhaps particularly in schools. Not all labels function as stigmas; but stigmas, as Alan Peshkin writes, arise from 'a common sense of rejection, from a sense of being different, and needing to stand together in opposition to the notion of outsiders that what makes them different also makes them inferior' (1991: 25). One of the dramatic contributions of this text is that it moves readers to a new awareness of the immorality of stigmatization, as well as its irrationality. As important is the implicit reminder in so many of the following chapters that a new mode of thoughtfulness is needed, as is a new determination to stand together to oppose unwarranted mistreatment by means of language.

The chapters that follow are important too in the light they throw on the pursuit of identity in a media-dominated time, a time when 'celebrity politics' seem to have swept away whatever role models we have hoped for from the public space. This is a moment as well when we recognize that personal identity is and must be a function of participatory membership. The individual exists, we have come to realize, at intersections of class, ethnicity, gender, sexuality, and (more and more frequently) nationality. Given our realization of the insufficiency of theories geared to conceptions of autonomy, the issue of categorization calls for attention. The discussions that follow in this book derive, more often than not, from actual experiences in classrooms and community; and, whether the theme has to do with the impacts of popular culture or the practices in special education or the handling of parents, the opening of spaces in which each person can choose herself or himself remains crucial in each subtext.

There is no question but that the dissemination of power depends upon what the authors here think of as labeling. Distinctions have to be made, as these writers understand. When we think of Paulo Freire empowering peasants to 'name' their lived worlds, he too was denying that 'the world exists as a reality apart from men' (1970: 69). Linking subjectivity to objectivity, Freire realized that we come to understand through thematizing our experience by means of dialogue, the essence of which is the word. 'Within the word,' he wrote, 'we find two dimensions, reflection and action, in such radical interaction that if one is sacrificed – even in part – the other immediately suffers. There is no true word that is not at the same time a praxis. Thus, to speak a true word is to transform the world' (1970: 75).

For me, one of the purposes of this book is to move us to replace the label with the 'true word,' generated by lived experience. Another is to free people from what can be a cage brought into being by a stigma or a label. The hope expressed by Edward Said in *Culture and Imperialism* may well infuse this text, since it points beyond labeling and opens possibility. 'Labels,' wrote Said,

> like Indian, or woman, or Muslim, or American are not more than starting-points, which if followed into actual experience for only a moment are quickly left behind. Imperialism consolidated the mixture of culture and identities on a global scale. But its worst and most paradoxical gift was to allow people to believe that they were only, mainly, exclusively, White, or Black, or Western, or Oriental. Yet, just as human beings make their own history, they also make their cultures and ethnic identities.
>
> (Said 1993: 336)

The understanding this book makes accessible, the injustices it reveals are of human derivation, as are the ways of power. It challenges us to reflect, to stand together, and, at once to realize that labels, too, can be left behind.

References

Freire, P. (1970) *Pedagogy of the Oppressed*, New York: Herder and Herder.

Peshkin, A. (1991) *The Color of Strangers. The Color of Friends*, Chicago: University of Chicago Press.

Said, E. (1993) *Culture and Imperialism*, New York: Alfred A. Knopf.

Schutz, A. (1967) *Collected Papers: The Problem of Social Reality*, The Hague: Martinus Nijhoff.

Introduction

Glenn M. Hudak and Paul Kihn

A banner hanging from a lamppost on Park Avenue reads: 'New York City, Millennium Capital of the World' ...

One rainy evening beneath the banner a woman boarded a commuter-filled subway car. She squeezed in between the stoic and the work-weary people simply waiting for the doors to open on their station stops. She was in jovial spirits and, unusually for such a sullen journey, she spoke gregariously about herself and her son who must by now be wondering where she was. She had been out drinking, she declaimed with a chuckle. Her rasping voice grated; backs turned, faces turned to stone.

'Hey, Jewish boy,' she called out to a young man in a yarmulke. 'How you doin'?'

'Hey, Spanish man,' she said to the man on her left, a tired workman covered in paint. 'Como esta?' This she pronounced as comb-oh ee-stah while spitting out the final syllable.

'Hey, college boy,' she said to a bedraggled youngster with a voluminous backpack. 'You in college?' He nodded, and shifted his look away.

'Hey, sisters,' she cried out piercingly. The women in question were half-way down the carriage, and they giggled. 'You got kids? I got kids. I got a lot a' kids.' She laughed.

A shaggy man moving laboriously through the car did not acknowledge her. His eyes scanned the carriage floor. People parted to let him through. 'Watch it, here comes Mr Homeless-man,' she said, all seriousness. 'I can't help you today. Can barely get myself home.'

The moment was electric. People looked at each other, and looked away. Who would she name? How would she assign our labels? She made loud meaning of her fellow-travelers. She laid bare a common act of social understanding. In so doing, she humanized herself, and invited reflection. What had we thought of her? What meaning had we ascribed to her? Harmless old lady? Wretch, drunk, obnoxious loony?

She labeled loudly, and in so doing offered a bald statement about social meaning and the ways in which we commonly understand strangers. She reacted to visual clues, of course, and decoded these according to her schematic stereotypes. But once she had arrived at the 'appropriate' designation, her quest for meaning stopped. Her designations carried the weight of common sense within her world, and perhaps in many of ours as well. For her the labels existed, and she simply matched the people around her with pre-existing names.

We do not look for the label; it is affixed to us. Consider another story, this one of an aging elevator operator in New York City who spends a full forty hours a week transporting teachers from one floor to the next. The school in which he works is located on the fourth and fifth floors of an old building with extremely high ceilings. Students take the stairs, teachers and visitors the elevator. This elevator operator is a man who appears to be in his mid-fif-ties. As one enters, he sits on a small wooden stool to the right side of the door. He is dressed casually. It is easy to observe him in his sitting position, staring towards the control panel. Apparently the elevator is so outdated he has to turn a special key in order to make it stop at any floor. Silently he stares at the controls for eight hours a day turning a single key, first to the right then to the left. The elevator car is poorly ventilated; it is hot and stuffy and poorly lit by a bare 250-watt bulb. The walls of the elevator are a drab gray. There is nothing to look at, except the floor, as a means to shield one's eyes from the bulb – or perhaps from the operator.

It is not that he is growing old. Rather he looks 'beat.' He has deep lines in his forehead, his hair is thinning, and his body is puffy, bloated from sitting so long with so little fresh air or exercise. But most striking are his darkly cir-cled eyes; they look like they want to cry.

He does not initiate any conversation. Instead he politely nods his head upon hearing the floor request. 'Fifth floor please.' He nods. 'It must be a long day in here.' He nods. 'And hot.'

He slowly turns his head; his eyes connect to yours; eye-to-eye contact. Before you he slowly articulates his life. 'I never thought my life would come to this. I was employed for over thirty-five years as a printer here in the city. Then about five years ago I lost my job. I was out of work for over a year. A person my age, it's hard. They think because you're old, you're done in. It was rough, almost lost my wife. Then I got hired by the school board. They told me I would eventually get something in graphics, as positions opened. The elevator operator would be something temporary.'

He closes his eyes, and slowly shakes his head and continues. 'I've been here almost four years. I never thought I'd be sitting on some little stool in an elevator. I have eight more years before I retire. I never thought my life would come to this.' He looks up almost pleading. 'I always thought I'd do some-thing … be something more.'

You acknowledge that you've heard him with a knowing nod as you exit into the school corridor. Hearing the elevator door close behind you, a chill runs through your body.

Such crude renderings of others offer an unusual example of the agency of labelers. Labeling is an act; a label embodies both a product and a process. Labels are the tools – both blatant and sophisticated – of historical beings. Certainly we are in a time when the assumptions, beliefs and history embodied in particular nomenclature are often scrutinized to the point of reduction or abstraction. Meanwhile, we scan deeper into the human brain and move closer to a biology of labeling. From the words called out by a drunk woman on a New York subway, to the boxed-in history of an aging elevator operator, to the synaptic sparks within each of us, to the constellations of labels within which we work and live, labeling is indeed ubiquitous.

Labels. We are haunted at times by labels that surround and potentially condemn many due to societal prejudices, for example about age! Indeed, to unveil the label – before us, around us, living within us – is the project of this book. We live in a world saturated by labels. And it is truly difficult to distinguish, at times, our own inner thoughts, in our own inner voice, from the continuous barrage of media images that assault our consciousness daily. Of course life is not monolithic; and, given the daily stresses of modern life, it may be the case that we have arrived at a moment in history where the label is in fact what we are seeking – some quick linguistic cure to help us through the day. Sometimes, for instance, when feeling tired – too tired to carry on – we may be consoled by Nike's slogan – 'Just do it!' – as a way to ease the pressure and hence work through that tired state. What began as a slick advertisement slogan, a label for a brand of sneakers, becomes a prescription for momentary relief. In this sense, we are not presenting an anti-labeling diatribe, though we attempt to explicate some of labeling's harm. Rather, if this collection can be said to have a single focus it is this: the unveiling of labeling as a process. If it can be said to have a single purpose it is this: to provoke thoughtful, critical use of labels.

Our task in this book has been to bring together a community of scholars to investigate the label and to struggle against labels that oppress. Indeed, it is a community of dissonant voices whose common aim is serving humanity. As Cornel West argues in *Breaking Bread* (hooks and West, South End Press, 1991: 17):

> A rich life is fundamentally a life of serving others, a life of trying to leave the world a little better than you found it. That rich life comes into being in human relationships ... It has to do with what you see when you get up in the morning and look in the mirror and ask yourself whether you are simply wasting time on the planet or spending time in an enriching manner. We are talking fundamentally about the meaning of life and the place of struggle ... When we speak of commitment to a life of service we must also talk about the fact that such commitment goes against the grain, especially the foundations of our society.

Indeed one of the effects of labeling is to isolate us from each other. One form of resistance is to form communities, in solidarity. This edited book is one such community, searching and serving together in the hope, as Paulo Freire urges, of humanizing the world.

Given its ubiquity, we are not in any position to present an anatomy of labeling. Though our scope is broad, we are here primarily interested in individual unveilings of labels' contestations. The labeling under discussion by the diverse scholars assembled here is thus deeply political. Contributors here sound out against any spurious ideas about labeling's neutrality.

All of the essays recognize and foreground the effects of labeling on people. The individual voices are uniquely – in many cases courageously – personal. Each story lends insight into the activity and effects of labeling. The scholarly essays within this book reflect broad concerns about what labels hide, but also a profound hope about the possibilities inherent in labeling. Labels do not exist outside of human agency, as our labeler on the subway reminded us.

The voices here gathered are eclectic and have much to say, both to us and to one another. We have come to think of this volume about words, about naming, about labeling, as akin to a dinner table conversation in its best and fullest sense. Around the table people talk and agree or disagree and continue to talk. With this idea in mind, we have paired the writers into 'dissonant conversations.' A dissonant conversation is one in which there is critical listening and active engagement. There is room for disagreement, for divergent views. Each chapter speaks to its partner; the reading of one enriches our reading of the other.

We begin with 'Presumptions?' This first section seeks to problematize preconceived assumptions. Glenn Hudak, in Chapter 1, brings together Paulo Freire and D. W. Winnicott in a discussion of true words, the true self and labeling in education. Schooling constructs work and play as discrete, in the same ways in which the labels of true self and false self promote conformity and non-conformity. Diane Dillon then questions the presumptions of labeling from the perspective of the labeler. She articulates the dilemmas for all 'helping professionals' who must sort and select according to particular categories with attendant institutional responses.

From 'Presumptions?' we move into a specific focus on the young. In 'Youth' Judith Kaufman tells the story of being held back in first grade, and analyzes in poetic fashion the ramifications of that label on her, and thus labeling's influence on children generally. Paul Kihn assumes that such detrimental labeling occurs more and more in an age which is marked by the diminution of hope. He argues that current labels assigned to young people reflect the melancholy of liberal consumerism, and that hope, in its broad, ontological sense, provides an avenue for escaping the debilitating effects of such labeling.

Still with the young, the next section, 'Schooling,' examines labeling's influences on particular groups of young people in school settings. Nina Asher presents her research findings on young people labeled 'model minority.' This label, she argues, carries with it profound social and political consequences, and can be detrimental for a person so labeled despite the positive connotations of the category. Peter Dillon finds that the label of

'English language learner,' with its host of institutional repercussions, can equally be harmful if not handled in particularly humanistic ways. Exploring the world of labeling amongst recent immigrants, he discusses how particular acts of labeling exclude the very people they are intended to support.

Remaining in learning environments we next look at two experiences of the label 'special education,' in a section entitled 'Special-*izing*.' In Andrea Smith's essay, she sees both the humanity and the potential for harm beneath special education labels for African American boys. Lee Fleischer, too, adopts an innovative approach to exploring the label with those who have been labeled. He concludes that those students disempowered through an institutional act of labeling can not only find a voice, but can also articulate resistance to labels.

Young people and adults alike conform to 'Scripts,' the focus of the following section. Hollyce Giles, parent and activist, articulates a theoretical and personal understanding of the scripts schools impose on parents. She sees scripting as political, as does Warren Crichlow in his reflections on the institutionally imposed 'role model' labels prevalent in higher education. Such labeling, he thinks, serves more to obfuscate than to enlighten. These roles, he suggests, can benefit from a demystification of their flat imposition that allows room for real and complex role model relations to develop.

In our next section, 'Callings,' both Peter Taubman and Jan McDonald look at how sexual identity is constructed through labels. Taubman posits that we are called to our sexual identites; labels, he says, being static and imposed from without, inhibit our responses and deny us our humanity. McDonald charts labeling's hurtful and helpful aspects through her own personal and professional development as an administrator in higher education.

Carrying the theme of labeling on to a global political level, the two essays in 'Globalizing' are concerned with exploring the label of 'whiteness.' Peter McLaren, Aimee Carrillo-Roe, Rebecca Clark and Philip Craft argue that an exploration of this label allows for the decentering of the power and modes of analysis invested in the term. They argue in favor of unpacking the label of 'whiteness'. Naming, in this political sense, becomes a liberating act. Next, Cameron McCarthy and Greg Dimitriadis connect the label of 'whiteness' with a contemporary resentment; they take the idea of historically determined labelings into a racialized paradigm, arguing that resentment emerges from particular acts of labeling and itself prompts further detrimental labeling within our contemporary social framework.

The body of the book concludes with two essays on 'Knowing.' Randall Styers moves into the labeling of ideas. Understandings are organized within concrete descriptors that are historically constructed, he suggests, and he offers the profound case of the historically determined – and far from 'neutral' – notions of 'science' and 'magic', and the often blurred line of distinction between them. Glenn Hudak in this section suggests that the organization of knowledge, as in what constitutes 'science,' can and does become addictive in an unhealthy sense; we stop delving and come to accept particular ways of knowing as absolutes.

Michael Apple, in his Afterword, attempts to situate labeling within the current conservative restoration. In locating the various modes of labeling in this broad social and political context, he lays the ground for further exploration and political action.

This book, we hope, constitutes such action. As teachers and learners, we have long contemplated the complex acts of labeling in our institutions and our lives – many of which are reflected in these pages. It is our hope that this book provides a kind of collective wisdom about the nuanced complexities of labeling. We hope, indeed, that there is insight to be gained here. More particularly, we hope that these essays provide the kind of sustenance needed to engage and re-engage in cognizant, humanizing acts of labeling. For labeling will be with us always; we must attend carefully to the labels we use, and use them judiciously, and not conflate the label with the labeled.

Presumptions?

1 On what is labeled 'playing'

Locating the 'true' in education

Glenn M. Hudak

My way into this project on labeling began on a personal note: my son Ben had been labeled as needing 'special educational services.' The outcome of my struggles with a local school board over the 'appropriate label' for my son led me to write the essay 'A Suburban Tale' (Hudak 1996). From my experiences over Ben, I argued that the politics of labeling children and the attendant practices that segregate are hurtful to all and especially to the children. Further, I argued that our struggle as educators should be to break down the walls of segregation created by such practices as labeling. And that we, educators and parents, need to develop languages and practices of empathy and understanding that enable the whole child to be seen and appreciated. Finally, I urged parents to challenge school personnel's labeling of children by finding out the reasons for and consequences of such labeling.

As I reflect back upon Ben's experience, what lingers in my mind is the 'staying power' of labels, especially within the school context. Ben certainly needed assistance. But this was not the whole problem. One major difficulty, unfortunately, was teacher expectation. That is, prior to meeting Ben his new teachers often had a preconceived picture of his abilities. They focused on his labeled weaknesses, excluding other aspects of his personality. By tacitly relying on the label (and attendant information) these teachers often underestimated his capacities in class; some of them found it difficult to 'see' Ben as a whole child.

Fortunately, over time some aspects of this picture have changed. Ben has gradually been mainstreamed into a 'regular' classroom, and has succeeded academically, though he is accompanied by an aide and tests are modified to fit his particular handicapping condition. However, though the initial struggles with the school board have receded into memory, my point is that the label 'special needs student' still remains with him.

It is difficult to replace or remove a label, even as Maxine Greene urges us in her Foreword to this book 'to replace the label with the "true word."' What is of import in Greene's proposal is that labels become a part of our lived experiences; they can become a part of one's life, one's identity and hence, difficult to replace. Replacing a label with a true word, simply substituting one word for another, no matter how 'nice' the new term, will not do! Stigma is not removed by word substitutions, but is rather worked through in one's lived experience. This working through of stigma, of trauma, of the wounding associated with being labeled occurs at many levels of experience simultaneously: psychological, social, institutional, and spiritual. But more important for us is to take note of just how difficult the 'working through' of a label can be, assuming one is successful at all.

It would be irresponsible of us as educators to assume that this movement from labels to true words is a smooth, linear, orderly process. For this process of replacement is not a surface-level event – even, as will be explored in this essay, in the seemingly benign case of the kindergarten child learning the label 'student.' It would be irresponsible because those labeled, such as children, will over time internalize, live out their label as a prescription imposed by another. Damaged self-esteem – wounding of the spirit – can accompany a child in the process of living out other people's labels. Under these circumstances it is understandable if children set up defense mechanisms to guard against further pain and the wounding attendant upon being labeled. Moving beyond the label entails a complex therapeutic process at the clinical, psychological level, whereby the person must work with and through the label in a way that allows them to reconnect with what psychiatrist D. W. Winnicott (1996a) [1960] refers to as their 'true self.'

In this essay, then, I want to move toward locating the 'true self' in education, especially in the context of labeling. To this end, I want to circle back and start by discussing Freire's notion of 'true words' – what exactly are they? Next, I want to explore labeling in the context of schooling, especially that benign label of 'student.' And finally, I want to examine Winnicott's notion of the True Self–False Self dichotomy and its relationship to Freire's true words. Taken together I posit a matrix: the True, as the intersection of these two author's ideas. I end by focusing on Winnicott's very special formulation of 'playing' as a therapeutic activity, as a way of working with labels towards the True.

True words

How may we move beyond the label to the true words that express our lives, speak our existence? Educator Paulo Freire writes about the 'true word' in his seminal work *Pedagogy of the Oppressed* (1997) [1970]. In Chapter 3 of this text Freire stresses the central importance of dialogue in 'human phenomena', stating that the essence of dialogue is the word. He makes an analytic distinction between the true word on the one hand, and an 'unauthentic' word on the other. Unauthentic words may be likened to 'false' words, those linked to a kind of false generosity, a false charity towards others. Pedagogies, for instance, cloaked in false generosity begin with the egoistic interests of those in power and are used as 'an instrument of dehumanization' (Freire 1997: 36). In addition, unauthentic words are unable to transform reality, for they lack connectedness to the world and to the lived experiences within which they are spoken.

In contrast, Freire defines 'true' words as consisting of two constitutive elements: reflection, and action. These two elements are woven together 'in such radical interaction that if one is sacrificed – even in part – the other immediately suffers' (1997: 68). The relationship between reflection and action, which together constitute true words, exists as an 'ecological' balance between these two elements. If either of these two constitutive elements is missing or diminished from this ecological balance the true word is violated, and hence no longer able to be transformative in reality. That is, if the balance between reflection and action is altered, this ecological system falls in disarray reducing the true word to either empty verbalism (chatter) or activism (thoughtless acts). 'When a [true] word is deprived of its dimension of action, reflection automatically suffers as well; and the word is changed into clatter, into verbalism, into an alienating "blah"' (*ibid.* 68). Likewise when the true word is stripped of reflection the word is changed into activism – action for action's sake – which 'negates the true praxis and makes dialogue impossible' (*ibid.* 69).

Freire conceives the true word as praxis itself. 'There is no true word that is not at the same time praxis. Thus, to speak a true word is to transform the world; ... action+reflection=word=work=praxis' (*ibid.* 68). The true word provides concrete encounters between individuals in the act of transforming the world. This act, transforming the world, humanizing it, is our true vocation as human beings. The 'act' of transformation is initiated through the use of true words to name the world. 'To exist, humanly, is to name the world, to change it. Once named, the world in turn reappears to the namers as a problem and requires of them a new naming' (*ibid.* 69). The world – constructed out of true words – is identified in naming. What is named is, however, rendered problematic; the new name becomes a problem itself, to be built upon, acted upon and changed. This process of change and transformation is historical in nature, occurring over time and through the efforts of human beings working collectively.

Viewed from another perspective, the psychological aspect of naming through true words entails ego development and growth; of becoming an individual through a dialectical engagement with the world; an engagement of differentiation, of sorting, of separation from the world. This separation from the world is an aggressive action on our part as individuals, an aggressive moment of pulling away from the undifferentiated contents of our experiences in order to make sense of them. In naming, we differentiate ourselves from the world; as such, we become individuals in the very act of articulating our relationship with the world. Being an individual, here, does not mean we stand alone in the world. Rather, as individuals we are now able to act and relate, to 'use' the world in meaningful ways. But further, as therapist John Tarrant points out:

To name is to bring an attitude of wonder to the work of sorting ... When we can name what is happening to us, we are no longer wholly identified with it and have begun to separate from the grasping dark. If what we feel is known and named to be a tiger, then the whole world is not tiger. We can divide the compulsion and the image, action and the emotion. There is a landscape through which we move, trees casting their own stripes on the forest floor, places where the tiger is not ... Separation gives us being and world ... when we give names we devise an intimate link with what is named; we incur obligations that serve to establish us more stead-fastly.... *To name is to offer a piece of ourselves to the world ... Later what has been separated out may come to be seen as too solid and will need to be dissolved.*

(Tarrant 1998: 99–100, my emphasis)

To name the world through true words is to create an 'intimate link with what is named.' In this act of separation, between the naming and the named, we, as individuals, become a part of the world itself, for 'to name is to offer a piece of ourselves to the world'; a piece which if too solid 'will need to be dissolved.' The world is not us; rather, in naming we become a part of the world, connected to it in thought and action. When we name with true words, then we see ourselves *in* the world, and through this very action of naming, as we name the world we name ourselves. That is, through naming, the individual becomes a Subject who literally articulates and authors him- or herself into a world; and authoring oneself in this world affirms one's own existence: 'I am.'

This complex, multidimensional process of naming the world is never fixed, final or turned into an idol to be worshipped. Rather, the human-ization of reality, through praxis, is an ongoing dialectical process between reflection and action: thinking about the world critically, then acting to transform oppressive situations. Within this context, pedagogy becomes a vehicle for developing our problem-posing capacity; 'problem-posing educa-tion involves a constant unveiling of reality' (Freire 1997: 64). The process of humanizing the world is never settled, but is rather an ongoing project for humanity. Further, problem-posing – rendering problematic the name – is a dialogical encounter between people. In dialogue, we encounter each other in history as active Subjects, together naming our world. 'Consequently, no one can say a true word alone – nor can she say it for another, in a prescrip-tive act which robs others of their words' (*ibid.* 69). True words call to us of the existence of others in the world and the necessity of joining with them in the act of humanizing reality. This call – which acknowledges others and their importance – elicits hope in us, where 'hope is rooted in men's [*sic*] incompletion, from which they move in constant search – a search which can be carried out only in communion with others' (*ibid.* 72).

Our calling as human beings, then, is to find ourselves in the presence of others: 'a search which can be carried out only in communion with others.' True words elicit such communion with others. This communion is never a neutral enterprise; rather it is both political and moral – for the liberatory project is marked, in its effort to humanize the world by transforming oppressive structures and situations, by conflicting power relations between the oppressed and the oppressors. However, often left out of this picture of true words is a neglected dimension to Freire's thinking: his theology. Embedded in his conception of true words is a theological dimension where the communal aspect of dialogue is given shape. That is, in Freire's articulation of dialogue we find his close links with concepts adopted from liberation theology. He tells us that dialogue, the encounter of true words between people, cannot exist

> in the absence of a profound *love* for the world and the people ... cannot exist without *humility* ... requires an intense *faith* in humankind, faith in their power to make and remake, to create and recreate, faith in their vocation to be more fully human ... Founding itself upon love, humility, and faith, dialogue becomes a horizontal relationship of mutual *trust* between dialoguers ... Nor can dialogue exist without *hope* ... Finally, true dialogue cannot exist unless the dialoguers engage in *critical thinking*.
>
> (Freire 1997: 70–3, my emphasis)

This dialogical matrix – a communal holding environment within which dialogue is made possible – must include: love, humility, faith, trust, hope, and critical thinking. Notice how such a matrix embodies a moral, political, and theological stance in our undertakings to humanize reality through true words; a dimension in Freire's work that insists on our paying attention to our common lot, our humanity – the spiritual.[1]

Indeed, by placing the true word at the center of dialogue (and hence the liberatory project) Freire places the true word and our relation to it in a central, sacred light. Through dialogue – true words spoken together – we find ourselves and others. Being human entails, among other aspects of living, a spiritual dimension, a dimension deeply rooted in the flesh-and-blood reality of human existence. We attend to the spiritual each time we treat one another with humility and mutual respect in day-to-day living. The spiritual, which is grounded in faith and realized through love, provides us with a source of hope in the world by expanding our vision of self and society. This expanded awareness of life is a kind of nourishment for the soul; it feeds us when we are 'down.'

The spiritual affirms our presence in the world; it awakens us from the narrowing vision of injustice and offers a truly larger picture of life, namely: a more just world, a world that cares, a world that cherishes life as precious. Indeed, given the current play of power relations within capitalist North America – a society that thrives on competition, greed, and self over all others – the spiritual dimension suggested by Freire alerts us to the possibility that there can be more to all our lives – oppression can be transformed through collective struggle. Ultimately, this sense of the spiritual in Freire reminds us that we are not the center, but interconnected through dialogue, related to one another in a way where no one person has the 'whole' story, where we all have some partial truths to communicate to each other. The *spiritual* thus requires that we dialogue with each other in order collectively to construct our worlds and our sense of what it means to be alive. This is also *political*, especially within the current context which attempts to divide us, separate us into isolated individuals cut off from ourselves, from each other, and from the Universe. It is through true words that we find ourselves, and in finding ourselves that we come to discover our true vocation, our true work: to humanize the world.

Labeling

True words and labeling are related to each other, but not reducible to each other. That is to say, both true words and the process of labeling share a common characteristic: they both name aspects of the world through processes of separating, sorting, and differentiation; but while true words and labels share a common characteristic, they can hardly be said to be equivalent, the same. The social processes attendant with true words aim at affirming the Self in spiritual communion with others. The social processes of labeling do not affirm the Self, nor can they be classified as a spiritual communal effort.

Not all aspects of this complex process of labeling are necessarily immoral, unjust, or wrong. Labeling is a complex process of differentiation, identification, and separation, both of objects (such as commodities for purchase) and of people. As such, it might initially be useful to distinguish between 'benign' practices of labeling and those we may regard as 'toxic',[2] keeping in mind, of course, that these distinctions are purely metaphorical. The labeling and differentiating of various objects and products for consumption are not necessarily oppressive or toxic acts. For example, labeling a bottle of wine for sale and consumption is not an act of oppression. In this instance, the practice of labeling is benign: it does not affirm the Self, but neither does it negate it.

Needless to say, within the constellation of human affairs the process of labeling is a complex and often a contradictory practice; but here again, not all practices of labeling people are toxic or oppressive. For, as Freire writes, 'any situation in which "A" objectively exploits "B" or hinders his or her pursuit of self-affirmation as a responsible person is one of oppression. Such a situation in itself constitutes violence ... because it interferes with the individual's ontological and historical vocation to be more fully human' (1997: 37). For the labeling process to be oppressive, 'toxic,' it must demonstrate a moment of exploitation where one's ontological vocation – being fully human – is hindered.

Within modern capitalist societies, practices of labeling operate within complex historically-defined relations of power, systems of representation, and sites of identity formation; sites where those in power have the privilege

to frame the identity of those unable to name their own world collectively –
for Freire, this means the oppressed. As Cameron McCarthy and Warren
Crichlow (1993: xvi) point out, 'issues of identity and representation directly
raise questions about who has the power to define whom, and when and
how.' Here McCarthy and Crichlow want to emphasize that those who are
oppressed and marginalized in society – because of a number of factors,
including race, class, gender, sexual orientation, age and national origin –
often do not have control over the production of images of themselves.

Indeed, the issue is precisely: who labels whom and for what larger, political purpose. This is a knotty problem on many levels. For example, does
labeling children who are at high risk of developing osteoporosis entail an
act of oppression? Does it negate their sense of Self? Or, since they are unable
to name their bone ailment, is this act of labeling a moment of preventative
medicine – aimed at affirming the best interests of children's overall health –
or an oppressive act? Benign labeling, or toxic?

Here the analytic distinctions between benign and toxic become blurred as
we situate labeling practices within a concrete historic context. That is to say, the
answer to questions such as these can only be determined by making explicit the
concrete social, historical, and political conditions within which the diagnosis
(and its attendant label) are made. Historically, children living in poverty,[3] for
instance, were often identified with osteoporosis due to a lack of calcium in their
diets. However, the ways in which this situation was interpreted by early school
reformers suggest that the medical diagnosis was something much more than
merely alerting parents to their child's physical ailment. Being labeled 'poor'
already carried connotations about children's social locations, connotations
that prefigured, fixed and formulated their entire family into a stereotype.
Within this particular historic context, a child's label could become an indict-
ment of the family and its poverty, over which many immigrants had little control, especially within a system that was set against them.

The student

Within the context of contemporary schooling, Michael Apple's classic text
Ideology and Curriculum (1979) also investigates, in part, how children are
labeled through the hidden curriculum, through processes of sifting, sorting, and selecting to meet the demands of the larger economic order.
Expanding the scope of our investigation of labeling, Apple explores how
schools process not only people, but knowledge as well. Focusing on the kindergarten experience, Apple (with Nancy King) shows how learning to
become a 'student' entails not only learning attitudes and behaviors that
serve as a foundation for the years of schooling to follow, but further entails
learning social cate-gories, definitions that serve as organizing principles to
provide a foundation for one's success in school and subsequently in the
workplace. That is, something as seemingly benign as being labeled a 'student' entails a complex process – a complex fusion of knowledge and

behavior in the formation of a social identity such that 'the social definitions internalized during one's initial school life provide the constitutive rules for later life in the classroom. Thus, the elements needing examination are what is construed as work or play, "school knowledge" or merely "my knowledge," normality or deviance' (Apple 1979: 51). Notice that this socialization process includes the learning of norms as well as definitions of organizing categories, such as work and play. These categories come to define for the kindergartener what it means to be a student. The social identity of becoming a student is itself grounded upon socially accepted definitions that are woven into the classroom environment in ways that are congruent with teacher expectations.

In their classroom observations, Apple and Nancy King note that the assignment of meaning to various classroom activities for each child are linked to how that child 'uses' materials and the quality of their participation in classroom activities. Over time, for example, 'when asked about classroom objects, the children responded with remarkable agreement and uniformity. The children divided the materials into two categories: things to work with and things to play with. No child organized any material in violation of what seemed to be their guiding principle' (Apple 1979: 54). Apple and King report that the meaning of classroom objects and materials is linked with the use of such material in day-to-day activities.

Notice the process by which the child's experiences in school are separated, segregated and labeled into two broad social categories: work and play. 'Work includes any and all teacher-directed activities ... To work, then, is to do what one is *told* to do, no matter the nature of the activity involved ... All work activities, and only work activities, were compulsory' (*ibid.* 55). What is labeled 'work' includes school knowledge and all teacher-directed activities, and is compulsory.[4] Regarding the organizing category 'work', Apple observed, 'the point of work activities was to do them, not necessarily to do them well ... Diligence, perseverance, obedience, and participation were rewarded' (*ibid.* 56). That is, the child's relationship to work-defined activities is one of compliance. Work engenders compliance on the part of the child. The social identity of becoming a 'student' entails an aspect of compliance, of being externally motivated, externally regulated.

In contrast, play in Apple's study is a marginalized experience: the child's own free-flowing activity. The category of play is split off and segregated from the child's experience in the classroom. What is labeled 'play' is defined as 'only free-time activities.' Within this classroom context, the burgeoning student comes to understand normality as 'work'-related activities; and outside the norm, deviance is labeled 'play.'[5] Play is 'merely my knowledge.' Play-related activities – 'my' activities – are relegated to the margins of classroom life. Indeed, this dimension of the child's experience, play, suggests close connections with Freire's 'true words', in that both affirm the Self as free and internally regulated. Unfortunately in terms of their value in school, play activities hold little curricular status in relation to work activities.

To become a 'student,' then, means to learn and live out within the school context the social and epistemological distinctions between the organizing categories of work and play; between school knowledge and 'my' knowledge; between compliance and self-affirmation. This means that encountering what is labeled as 'work' and 'play' entails a complex social, psychological, and epistemological process, where children must

> learn and accept as natural the social distinctions schools both reinforce and teach between important and unimportant knowledge, between normality and deviance, between work and play, and the subtle ideological rules and norms that inhere in these distinctions; they also internalize visions of both the way institutions should be organized and their appropriate place in these institutions. These things are learned somewhat differently by different students, of course, and this is where the process of labeling becomes so important to social and economic class differentiation. The labeling of students ... has a strong impact on which students accept which particular distinction as natural.
>
> (Apple 1979: 142)

Becoming a student posits a life lived through what may seem to the child an endless series of compliant acts to meet the demands made by schooling. (To be sure, children do resist this process of compliance in contradictory fashions, yet the point here is that the demands on them are unending, and to a greater or lesser extent schooling becomes alienated labor.)

Even those labeled 'successful' students, those going on to college, experience some degree of alienation from the world and themselves. Educator Ira Shor, who works within a Freirian framework and teaches working-class college students, observed:

> Isolated from each other, and alienated from their own powers, students need *restoration* and *character-structure* awareness ... [for their] ego-damaged characters ... Years of processing through the institutions of mass society have left students divided, frustrated, and defensive about their own skills ... That is, the students need to appreciate each other as competent, effective and worthy human beings. They don't enter class feeling that way.
>
> (Shor 1987: 109)

Notice Shor's observation that students enter his class isolated, with damaged characters, in need of restoration and 'character-structure awareness.' Within Shor's context, it is difficult not to see the toxic elements attendant with the socialization process of studenthood. Indeed, Shor laments that 'from coast to coast, Monday morning fever grips the start of each school week. The old forms of discipline collapse under the weight of new alienation' (1987: 125). Under this weight, and with each new act of compliance, the student's ego is damaged. Feeling divided, frustrated and defensive about their abilities and skills, they ask, 'Why has my life become false?'

The False Self and the True Self

From a clinical, therapeutic perspective the 'false' – the imposed – is worked upon through processes that aim at healing the dislocated, fragmented elements of the Self. It is about the child-as-student again feeling 'real and alive,' not isolated and alienated, as Shor observed. Therapists Ann and Barry Ulanov note how

> being alive is more than being healthy. Feeling real involves more than functioning adequately. Believing life is worthwhile goes far beyond simply feeling able to cope with stresses and strains ... It is true that psychotherapy ... does two important things ... It strives to remove the blocks that obscure a person's vision of himself or herself as real, as fully alive, and it points the way to value ... It finds value in reality ... Healing has, properly enough, long been thought of as a way of recovering a sense of reality, not simply being restored to health ... Healing recovers a relationship between dislocated elements. It does not just paste them together, but rather establishes among them a new and conversant relationship.
>
> (Ulanov and Ulanov 1975: 171–3)

In the light of this passage, we ask again, what happens to the child's interior world as 'my knowledge' is split off, dislocated from the schooling experience? What happens to the child's inner world as it is cut off from the spiritual – knowledge that connects 'me' to my Self and others? Further, as the Ulanovs suggest, how do we establish among the dislocated elements of what are labeled 'work' and 'play' a new and conversant relationship? A healing relationship?

In an important paper, 'Ego Distortion in Terms of True and False Self,' child psychiatrist D. W. Winnicott describes how the ego defends against the dislocation of its inner being through the formation of a False Self.[6] Following the evolution of a number of cases, he notes, 'it was easy for me to see the defensive nature of the False Self. Its defensive function is to hide and protect the True Self' (1996a: 142 [1960]). Winnicott sketches out False Self organizations in terms of a spectrum of possible combinations between it and the True Self. The extremes are on the one end:

> the False Self sets up as real and it is this that observers tend to think is a real person ... In situations in which what is expected is a whole person the False Self has some essential lacking. At this extreme the True Self is hidden.
>
> More towards health: the False Self has as its main concern a search for the conditions which will make it possible for the True Self to come into

its own. If conditions cannot be found then there must be reorganized a new defence against exploitation of the True Self ... since its function is the protection of the True Self from insult.

In health: the False Self is represented by the whole organization ... the gain being the place in the society which can never be attained or maintained by the True Self alone.

(Winnicott 1996a: 142–3 [1960])

Notice that in this passage the movement from pathology to health is not one where the False Self is removed or eliminated. Rather this movement from pathology to health will entail a therapeutic intervention whereby the False Self becomes integrated into the 'whole organization' of the Self. For, as Winnicott points out, the False Self serves a necessary function – to protect the True Self from external threats. Indeed, his aim is to bring together, through therapy, these two otherwise dislocated elements of our inner world into an 'ecological' balance.

What is this True Self that needs defending? The True Self is the source of our feeling alive, of feeling real, of feeling accepted and a part of the surroundings within which we live. Further, in positing a True Self Winnicott does seem to suggest some kind of an essentialist Self, though this is neither fixed nor static at the core. Rather, at the core it is unknowable and unfound, for we are unable to communicate with it or grasp it directly. In almost mystical language Winnicott ponders:

> although healthy persons communicate and enjoy communicating, the other fact is equally true, that *each individual is an isolate, permanently non-communicating, permanently unknown, in fact unfound.*
>
> In life and living this hard fact is softened by the sharing that belongs to the whole range of cultural experience. At the center of each person is an incommunicado element, and this is sacred and most worthy of preservation ... [Its] defense consists in a further hiding of the secret self ... Rape, and being eaten by cannibals, these are mere bagatelles as compared with the violation of the self's core, the alteration of the self's central elements by communication seeping through the defenses.
>
> (1996b [1963]: 187)

This passage is reminiscent of the Taoist saying regarding the nature of the Self – 'those who know don't speak.' For at the core of the Self is a secret Silence, permanently non-communicating, unfound, beneath the Word itself. Further note that the core is named as sacred, and most worthy of preservation. The True Self is spiritual and creative. 'Only the True Self can be creative and only the True Self can feel real. Whereas a True Self feels real, the existence of a False Self results in a feeling unreal or a sense of futility' (Winnicott 1996b: 148). The core of the Self cannot be labeled, named, or communicated to by an external source without some traumatic violation occurring at the center of one's being. Since it is permanently unknown and unfound, the core cannot be named or labeled by ourselves, either, without violation of our being. This attempt at self-labeling for Winnicott 'would be the sin against the self' (an act grounded, in Freire's and Shor's language, in false consciousness). Indeed, it is in defense of this precious core, the sacred, that the False Self is organized.

The False Self protects the True Self both from internal leaks – self-communications that betray oneself – and from external damage. As Winnicott observes, 'the False Self has one positive and very important function: to hide the true Self, which it does by compliance with external demands.' He then refers to 'the point of origin of the False Self, which can now be a defense against that which is unthinkable, the exploitation of the True Self, which would result in annihilation' (1996b: 147). In the healthy relationship between child and caregiver there is a compliant aspect to living: 'the ability to compromise is an achievement ... In health this social manner represents compromise. At the same time, in health, the compromise ceases to become allowable when the issues become crucial. When this happens the True Self is able to override the compliant self' (*ibid.* 150). As these characteristics are woven into our adult capacities, compromise yields to the ability to negotiate and dialogue with others in the world.

In pathology, however, the True Self, in a defensive action, becomes buried. Reality is harsh; the child, and later the adult, must shield him- or herself from these continued assaults. Within an academic environment, for instance, such as the school or university, the intellect is often used as an instrument of the False Self, as a means of protection from assault. In these instances, where

> a False Self becomes organized in an individual who has a high intellectual potential there is a tendency for the mind to become the location of the False Self ... the world may observe academic success of a high degree, and may find it hard to believe in the very real distress of the individual concerned, who feels 'phoney' the more he is successful.
>
> (Winnicott 1996b: 144 [1963])

For the student whose False Self has assumed dominance in its efforts to hide the True Self, the world becomes deadened. It is no wonder that as the intellect acquires more prominence, students become literally out of touch, both with themselves and with reality. They no longer fully feel either themselves or the world; they become numb. In such a situation, as Shor observed, students feel isolated and alone – disconnected from others and from themselves. They begin to feel empty, hollow, shallow – 'phoney'. This means the spoken word is no longer connected with the core of the True Self – connected with the spiritual, the sacred. Actions become disconnected from thoughts; words no longer link up with actions in the world. And here, as Freire observed, disconnected words become so much 'blah' (verbalism), and disconnected actions are reduced to mere activism.

In contrast, 'the True Self comes from the aliveness of the body tissues and the working of body-functions, including the heart's action and breathing' (Winnicott 1996b: 148). In health, the head and the heart, the whole body, including the intellect, work together in each breath we take. Aliveness, spontaneity, and creativity are associated with the capacities of the True.

The True

For Winnicott and Freire the center of our being is a sacred, precious place; it is a spiritual dimension which serves as the ground of our life. It provides us with hope; it proves to us that life is worth living, even in our most despairing moments. For Winnicott the sacred is located in the True Self. For Freire the sacred is defined through True Words. The True Self and True Words, while related to each other, are not reducible to each other. Rather, when placed together they form a spiritual matrix: 'the True.' The True grounds us in ways that make us feel alive, real, and affirmed in the world.

And yet it is foolish to ignore the world of power and politics and labeling. Embedded within the True – the spiritual – is also the political. That is, while 'true' education[7] refers to the search for the meaning of life, 'schooling' refers to the political and historic realities that accompany the institutionalization of learning to meet the demands of society. Schooling has a history: schooling is about helping to create and maintain a workforce. Schooling is about power relations and the ways in which schools sift, sort, and select students through testing and evaluation. Schooling is about certification and credentialing students for various professions in society. Schooling is about labeling children as students.

While education and schooling are related to each other, they are not reducible to each other. But notice further: schooling creates and labels the child's experiences as work and play. Regarding work and play, notice: work-related activities are associated with compliance, with teacher-directed activities, with the school itself, and hence are complicitous in the formation of a school-based False Self. Play-related activities are associated with 'my' knowledge, 'my' internal world, with spontaneity and freedom, with the spirit, and hence in the affirmation of the True Self. It is interesting here that the False and the True Selves, work and play, label and True Word, schooling and education, are all brought together under the umbrella label: student!

Imposed from the outside, living the label 'student' serves a purpose: to provide boundaries – it limits and defines the learning realities children must face in school. Indeed both Freire and Winnicott are aware of the necessity of external forces pressing upon us – as limit-situations or through the 'reality principle'[8] – which have the capacity to negate or impinge on our lives in ways that oppress. Paradoxically, they argue that it is through our very engagements with the world and its pressures that we come to realize that we are not the whole picture; we are not alone, others do exist. Confronted by others, we begin to understand that compromise and negotiation are necessary for dialogue to proceed and from this dialogue with others springs forth the possibility of replacing labels with true words. For it is by confronting the concrete conditions within which the label is constructed, that we can begin to transform it.

At issue, then, is the historically lopsided emphasis in schools on work – school-related activities – at the cost of marginalizing play, how do we create an ecology, a balance, between the 'spirit' of education, on the one hand, and the demands of society and schooling on the other? Another way of thinking about this is: how do we balance the scales of learning to reintegrate the spiritual, the True Self, into the student's world? Given the often nasty debates over the separation of church and state, any talk of the spiritual is likely to be considered suspicious.

Playing

Labeling is about politics and power and representation. It raises questions of who has the power to define whom, when and how. Amid the fields of power and representation – labeling – we (children and adults) struggle to find meaning in our lives, though work, through relationships, through searching for ourselves. In his classic book *Playing and Reality* (1996c) [1971] Winnicott explores the therapeutic search for ourselves and others through the complex and multilayered activity of playing. I will draw on some of the more salient aspects of playing as a way to bring this essay to closure, keeping in mind that my discussion here is but an opening caveat to such a rich domain.

Winnicott writes: 'it is in playing and only in playing that the individual child or adult is able to be creative and to use the whole personality, and it is only in being creative that the individual discovers the self' (1996c: 54). Through playing the whole personality is used. For the student the categories of work and play become reintegrated through the activity of playing. This activity, however, is not primarily pedagogical; rather it is itself therapy, in that playing does not necessarily have a goal, nor a product attached to it. Instead, in our search for the Self, creative play emerges as we begin to reconnect, to communicate with the True Self. 'In the search for the self the person concerned may have produced something valuable in terms of art, but a successful artist may be universally acclaimed and yet have failed to find the self that he or she is looking for … The finished creation never heals the underlying lack of sense of self' (*ibid.* 55). For Winnicott playing is about healing, not about becoming a creative artist, producing a product for the world.

Indeed, rather than with producing artifacts, playing is associated with relaxation and trust; hence its therapeutic capacity. Relaxation refers to free association, where the subject is 'allowed to communicate a succession of ideas, thoughts, impulses, sensations that are not linked' to any specific purpose beyond activity itself. Playing is to be relaxed, like the child in the sandbox; playing is a creative outlet for communicating with oneself. For the child in this context, playing is an end in itself. Playing is relaxing despite being active. It is relaxation in the sense of the child at rest and at peace in the world, secure enough, trusting enough in their environment to let go of their defensive postures. Within such a facilitating, trusting environment – an environment that 'holds' child or student safe – this resting state produces a 'creative reaching out' whereby in the act of using external objects (for infants) or naming the world (for children and adults) through playing, we offer the world pieces of ourselves. As we see ourselves, find ourselves once again in the world, we lower our defenses. Playing is both restful and energizing. Through it we feel at home in the world. Hence it makes us once again feel real and alive. It restores our hope and faith and opens us to the larger world. Winnicott writes: 'cultural experience begins with creative living first manifested in play' (1996c: 100).

Finally, Winnicott views playing as a third space, a transitional space, in between inner reality and external environment 'which expands into creative living and into the whole cultural life of man [*sic*].'

> The potential space between baby and mother, between child and family, between individual and society or the world, depends on the experience which leads to trust. It can be looked upon as sacred to the individual in that it is here that the individual experiences creative living.
>
> In contrast, exploitation of this area leads to a pathological condition in which the individual is cluttered up with persecutory elements of which he has no means of ridding himself.
>
> (1996c: 102–3)

Along similar lines of thinking, Paulo Freire writes,

> Perhaps it was during my distant childhood that I developed the habit that I still carry today of occasionally surrendering myself to profound contemplation, as if I am isolated from everything else, the people and things that surround me. I like to think I find myself in the play of losing myself. I often find myself in this contemplative state while doing research or in my office.
>
> (1996: 14)

Indeed, playing can be looked upon as a sacred, True space. A space of rest and activity, a place where one can trust in the world as oneself – acting without pretense or compliance. Through playing, the student locates that space in between the categories of play ('my world') and work (external reality).

What is labeled 'playing' is not the solution to all the problems attendant with schooling or living. Through playing one doesn't remove labels such as 'student,' or in Ben's case 'special needs student.' Through playing, however, it is possible to recommunicate with ourselves beyond the label, and to realize that beneath the label there is something more: a place where we can once again feel alive and real, feel at home and once again trust in ourselves. And perhaps we may begin to feel the courage to live our lives to the fullest, the courage to live our lives as authentically as possible, the courage to once again trust in others, so that 'we' may continue the struggle together to humanize the school and the world.

Notes

1   Few scholars have noted the strong theological dimension in Freire's work. Among those who have recognized Freire's spirituality is historian and educator James W. Fraser. I quote Fraser at length here, for he captures eloquently the spiritual dimension embedded in Freire as well as the politics attached to using religious notions within educational discourse. He writes (1997: 175):

> There is in Paulo Freire, in his writing, his speaking, and his personal presence, a profound sense of love, humility, and rootedness in life and in the present historical moment. In other times and traditions, Paulo Freire would be seen as not only a great teacher but also a spiritual guide.
>
> For very understandable reasons, most North American educators ignore this aspect of Freire's life and work. We are uncomfortable with 'religious' language, we have fought too many battles to keep a range of religious dogma out of the schools, and we have seen escapism and the sheer meanspiritedness of what passes for religiosity in this country, whether of the fundamentalist, mainstream, or the New Age type. But ignoring spirituality, ignoring Freire's own power as a 'spiritual guide' is both a distortion of his work and an unnecessary impoverishment of our understanding of the world.

2   The terms 'benign' and 'toxic' were suggested to me in a conversation with Hollyce Giles.

3   Further, as historian of education Joel Spring notes (1997: 201), the urban kindergarten in 1873 was created for a specific purpose: to deal with increasing urban poverty among newly arriving poor immigrants:

> the kindergarten was to be a substitute for habits of living and moral training formerly taught by the family organization that supposedly has been lost in the slums of the new urban areas ... Emphasis was placed on teaching morals, cleanliness, politeness, obedience, regularity, and self-control ... a major goal of the early kindergarten movement was to teach children habits that would reform the home. In other words, the early kindergarten was viewed as a method of educating the parents, particularly the mother.

Thus the labeling of an immigrant child living in urban poverty – as, for example, being in a high risk category to develop osteoporosis – was not just a simple act of preventative medicine. Embedded within the medical diagnosis and the attendant preventative measures were moral and political strictures: the child labeled as poor and at high risk of osteoporosis was smothered under the weight of societal prejudice against the poor. Though the overt focus was the child, social reformers proposed the urban kindergarten precisely as a preventative measure: to 'educate' the parents, hence 'cure' a family in poverty. Unfortunately, as Spring goes on to point out, it achieved neither; it merely reproduced social class differences.

4   The term 'work' used in Apple's study is *not* to be confused with Freire's usage of this term. For Freire, 'work' refers to our 'true vocation' – to humanize the world; work is linked to modes of self-affirmation. David Hansen writes (1995: 3): 'vocation describes work that is fulfilling and meaningful to the individual, such that it helps provide a sense of self, of personal identity ... it is work that results in service to

others and personal satisfaction in rendering of that service.' For Freire our true work is our vocation, and our vocation is to humanize the world for everybody.

5   Apple's usage of the term 'play' as 'my knowledge,' is not to be confused with the formation of urban kindergartens and the attendant 'play movement' of the late 1800s. As Joel Spring found (1997: 202): 'The play movement, and the resulting changes it led to in the school, was another product of the desire among educational reformers to protect children ... and to provide a mechanism for controlling the process of socialization.' As we have discussed, within the formation of the urban kindergarten, the play movement utilized play as a means of social control, i.e. a mode of external compliance. Here we see historical connections, a selective tradition at work, between the former play movement and the current usage of the category of 'work' observed in Apple's study.

6   It is beyond the scope of this essay to elaborate fully the complex development of the True and False Self. For a wonderfully written summary and critical commentary see Adam Phillips (1988), *Winnicott*, especially Chapter 5, 'Real-making.'

7   Further, the matrix of the True includes an educational dimension: what might be defined as 'true education.' Indian philosopher J. Krishnamurti wrote (1951: 17): 'to understand life is to understand ourselves, and that is both the beginning and end of education ... Thus education, in the true sense, is the understanding of oneself, for it is within each of us that the whole of existence is gathered.' True education aims at naming the world as a creative act of self-affirmation in the search for the Self.

8   Freire refers to the boundaries created by an external reality as 'limit-situations.' Such situations limit our humanity, but in the process of engagement within a limit-situation we also learn about ourselves and our world; we come to define the boundaries of our capacities as well as tacitly affirming the existence of an external reality.

The limit-situation, then, is not seen as necessarily negative; rather it is a wall that must be overcome if we are to mature as individuals and grow collectively as humans. For, as Freire argues (1997: 80), humans,

> because they are aware of themselves and thus of the world – because they are conscious beings – exist in a dialectical relationship between the determination of limits and their own freedom ... it is not the limit-situations in and of themselves which create a climate of hopelessness, but rather how they are perceived by women and men at a given historical moment: whether they appear as fetters or as insurmountable barriers.

Limit-situations refer to social, political, and historic encounters with the world; they are revolutionary moments in confronting oppressive situations. No less revolutionary are the small daily struggles that children face in their confrontations with the demanding reality of schooling. Here the clash between the child's personal impulses and the external demands of schooling constitutes an example of the 'Reality Principle,' the psychological correlate to the limit-situation. The Reality Principle, writes Winnicott (1990 [1970]: 40, 46, 49)

> is just too bad ... for the Reality Principle is an insult ... We are happy enough, and can be creative, but we do realize that there is inherently some kind of clash between the personal impulse and the compromises that belong to any kind of relationship that has reliable features. In other words, we are once more talking about the Reality Principle ... Every moment I have my little experience of omnipotence ... then the Reality Principle may be introduced, and the child who has known omnipotence experiences the limitations that the world imposes.

Children in kindergarten, confronted with the reality of schooling, are 'insulted' by the reality principle: they must now comply with social norms. Failure to do so is labeled deviant. This clash is an awakening. For children, as well as for us adults, clashing against an outside reality awakens us to other people; we do not exist alone. This awakening is a profound pedagogical moment, in that we learn through our struggles (and the compromises, and the negotiations) with others the boundaries and limits of ourselves, as well as of the world. Further, Winnicott's thinking suggests, no matter how we define our classroom situations, students must inevitably clash with the reality of there being a force that lies 'outside'; a force that has the capacity to impinge (to a greater or lesser degree) upon their private world.

Following the logic of Winnicott and Freire's thinking we see that both the reality principle and limit-situations signify for them the existence of an external world, a world that is 'not-me.' And regardless of the fact that this world is historically contingent, it nonetheless exists. As such, it has an ontological status independent of our awareness of it. In the best of all possible worlds, then, we would still have to confront both: the reality principle, and limit-situations.

References

Apple, M. (1979) *Ideology and Curriculum*, London: Routledge & Kegan Paul.

Fraser, J. W. (1997) 'Love and History in the Work of Paulo Freire' in Paulo Freire (ed.) *Mentoring the Mentor*, New York: Peter Lang.

Freire, P. (1996) *Letters to Christina: Reflections on My Life and Work*. New York: Routledge Press.

——, (1997) [1970] *Pedagogy of the Oppressed*, New York: Continuum.

Hanson, D. (1995) *The Call to Teach*, New York: Teachers College Press.

Hudak, G. (1996) 'A Suburban Tale: Representation and Segregation in Special Needs Education' in J. Kincheloe, S. Steinberg and A. Gresson (eds) *Measured Lies: The Bell Curve Examined*, New York: St Martin's Press.

Krishnamurti, J. (1951) *Education and the Significance of Life*, New York: Harper & Row.

McCarthy, C. and Crichlow, W. (eds) (1993) *Race, Identity, and Representation in Education*, New York: Routledge.

Phillips, A. (1988) *Winnicott*, Cambridge: Harvard University Press.

Shor, I. (1987) *Critical Teaching and Everyday Life*, Chicago: University of Chicago Press.

Spring, J. (1997) *The American School: 1642–1996*, Fourth Edition, New York: McGraw-Hill.

Tarrant, J. (1998) *The Light inside the Dark*, New York: HarperCollins.

Ulanov, A. and Ulanov, B. (1975) *Religion and the Unconscious*, Philadelphia: Westminster Press.

Winnicott, D. W. (1996a) [1960] 'Ego Distortion in Terms of the True and False Self' in *The Maturational Processes and the Facilitating Environment*, Madison: International Universities Press.

—— (1996b) [1963] 'Communicating and Not Communicating Leading to a Study of Certain Opposites' in *The Maturational Processes and the Facilitating Environment*, Madison: International Universities Press.

—— (1996c) [1971] *Playing and Reality*, New York: Routledge.

—— (1990) [1970] 'Living Creatively' in *Home is Where We Start from*, New York: W. W. Norton & Co.

2 On being a labeler

Diane H. Dillon

> Children with disabilities are entitled to a free, appropriate public education.
>
> Public Law 94–142

As a school psychologist working for the Committee on Special Education (CSE) in New York City, I spend much of my time trying to ensure that children with disabilities are placed in appropriate educational settings in least restrictive environments (LREs). In theory, LRE means being educated with other children who do not have disabilities; children are removed from the general education classroom only when they cannot benefit there even with the provision of necessary supports and services. In practice, there are limited resources for supplementary aids and services. As Hudak (1996) poignantly describes in his 'Suburban Tale,' scheduling difficulties and limited resources prevented his son Ben from receiving all of the needed services in his regular classroom. Instead, Ben was 'pulled out' of class to receive services. There are many children in Ben's situation who are pulled out of their class to receive needed supports such as speech and language therapy, occupational therapy, or resource room. When the amount of time a child must be pulled from class to receive needed help becomes excessive, such a child falls further behind classmates. Eventually, it is more efficient for the system to place students in a different class with similarly abled students receiving special help. Thus begins the segregation of special needs children.

I am on a CSE review team which consists of myself, a social worker, an educational evaluator (former classroom teacher), and a parent advocate (parent with a child currently in special education). Together, along with the input of their parents and teachers, we review the needs of children referred for special education and recommend appropriate services and programs to address those needs.

The review and placement process can be lengthy and complex. Based on a number of court decisions, there are many laws and regulations which govern the actions of the CSE. For example, an evaluation and recommendation must occur within forty school days from the receipt of the referral, or thirty school days from the date of the parent's consent to have their child evaluated (whichever is earlier). Implementation of the recommendation can take up to an additional thirty days. Thus, from the time a child is referred for possible special education to the time that child receives any services may be as long as sixty school days (three months!).

The review process entails reviewing a child's social and developmental history, reading anecdotes and observations from teachers; analyzing evaluations from psychologists, educational evaluators, and other professionals, listening to parents and other school personnel, and, on occasion, meeting the student. We attempt to integrate all this information in order to have a full picture of the student we are considering – a child with strengths and weaknesses, successes and disappointments, with or without many friends or much family support, a child with hobbies and interests, with his or her own way of interacting and thinking about the world, of thinking about him- or herself ... a unique, developing individual. And, because this child has been referred to the CSE, we suspect there is some difficulty in school and maybe an intellectual, emotional or physical disability which is interfering with learning.

Our job is to assess the child's difficulty, the possible causes and potential modifications which will mitigate the problem and increase the chances of success in school. Unfortunately, in order to navigate through the special educational system and access needed services, children and programs are classified. Thus, I am a 'labeler' of children. I use the word 'unfortunately' because I do not believe anybody likes to be labeled or categorized, least of all by their weaknesses. Fat. Tall. Skinny. Short. Individuals are far more than any one label or category into which they might fall. Labeling someone tends to magnify the label and can mean that their many other unique aspects are minimized. Whilst naming a disability does not create the condition, it can contribute to a host of other problems.

There are negative connotations associated with having a labeled disability and, often, to being in special education. Children sense this. Unkind comments from other children or simply their own observations can lead those who are receiving special education services to feel that they are not only different from, but worse than their 'mainstream' peers. Just having a disability can in itself lower one's self-esteem; I believe a label can further contribute to a lack of self-worth. Labels can limit how children see themselves and how others see them. Thus, instead of being viewed as someone with special needs and a myriad of other strengths and characteristics, such children may begin to see themselves as deficient – as 'learning disabled,' or perhaps 'emotionally disturbed.'

At other times, both parents and children are relieved to have a label or 'name' for a student's difficulty. Often, he or she has been struggling in silence or avoiding the work altogether. Behavioral problems may have resulted from frustrations with classwork. Once a disability is identified, parents, educators and children can speak about the disability as the problem and look for specific ways to mitigate it. Thus, modifications or solutions can be sought or 'named'.

I have very mixed feelings about my job. On a good day, I am instrumental in pinpointing the specific cause of a child's difficulty in school and finding the services and/or program which help the child learn and thrive. On a great day, I help find modifications which improve a child's functioning in the world and reduce his or her suffering. At these times, any stigma attached to a label seems worth enduring as a means to a very positive end.

For example, Jonathan (I have used pseudonyms throughout this essay) had a history of extreme impulsivity and inattentiveness. His parents and teachers were in desperate need of support. Under ordinary circumstances, Jonathan's pediatrician felt that medication would have best addressed his attention deficit/hyperactivity disorder, but due to other physical conditions Jonathan was not a good candidate for medication. A very small, highly structured class with a low student–teacher ratio was recommended for him. Within several weeks of his entrance to this class his academic performance and behavior markedly improved. His mother expressed relief that her son was adjusting and that he seemed happier than he had ever been in his previous class. In order to meet the Board of Education's criteria for placement in this class, Jonathan had to be labeled 'other health impaired' before such a positive remediation could be suggested.

However, a bad day is filled with unanswered questions and less positive outcomes. Why is a child having so much difficulty and, more importantly, what can be done to help? Specific answers to these questions are often elusive.

Victor, aged 8, was acting out repeatedly in his general education classroom. Teacher reports and evaluations indicated that he had a high average IQ but was below grade level in reading and math, suggesting a learning disability. Counseling and a temporary crisis management paraprofessional were doing little to address his needs while other placements were being considered. His mother had refused the few program placements offered, stating that she felt his behavior might be controlled in the placements but that he would not be challenged academically. Finally, it was determined that the NYC public schools did not have an appropriate class for Victor and a recommendation for non-public school was made. No seats were available in the appropriate non-public schools and he continues to await placement in a class which will address his complex needs. Meanwhile, he is in a class that has been determined inappropriate for him and continues to disrupt learning for others.

There are many children for whom the current available classes or services are not effective. Special education programs have proven unhelpful for some children. For instance, programs need to be developed for bright children with attentional difficulties or mild learning disabilities. Seven per cent of the 1997–8 New York City public education budget went to approved private schools that educate children for whom the Board of Education has no program (Educational Priorities Panel 1997). While that 7 per cent includes textbooks and programs as diverse as, for example, those of the Fashion Institute of Technology, the lion's share pays for tuition at non-public schools. NYC's public schools serve 1.1 million students. They should be able to offer a broader range of alternatives. Some parents are rightfully frustrated and angry that their children's needs are not being met. The system is failing these students.

Regarding the process of using clinical, psychological, and therapeutic perspectives and evaluations in schools, Apple states (1990: 126):

> They're not helping devices, but more critically mechanisms by which schools engage in anonymizing and sorting out abstract individuals into preordained social, economic, and educational slots. The labeling process thus tends to function as a form of social control ... to use supposedly therapeutic means to create moral, valuative, and intellectual consensus.

The dominant culture forms a consensus and chooses what knowledge, skills and behaviors are valued and should be taught in its schools. Educational standards are based on attaining these goals. Students who have difficulty are often singled out for help – for services, or for redirection into programs with goals or teaching approaches that better match their abilities – but unfortunately the disability and service categories are overly broad, which means that they are intrinsically not very useful. (What *are* useful are specific descriptions of skills and specific recommendations for mitigating difficulties and building on strengths.) And the labeling process functions in some ways as a form of social control. Acting out and disruptive students are often not tolerated for long in the mainstream.

However, I do believe that psychological and educational interventions can be very helpful devices in schools. They are not simply 'mechanisms for anonymizing and sorting out abstract individuals'; at times, they are real lifesavers. For students who are having difficulty attaining the educational standards, assessments can identify specific weaknesses which can be addressed and identify areas of strengths which can be further nurtured and built upon. The actions of the psychologist do not create a child's strengths or weaknesses – rather they identify existing skills and attempt to ameliorate problems by directly addressing them. Early interventions can make a tremendous impact in a child's future learning.

As a conscientious professional and human being, I strive to treat others with the sensitivity and dignity with which I want to be treated. I work with many other principled professionals who attempt to do the same. While I maintain that special education can be a tremendous benefit for children with specific difficulties that are well suited for certain programs, there are children whose needs are not well met by the existing 'educational slots.' As I describe aspects of the process by which children are classified for special education, I will address some of the shortcomings of the NYC special education system and process in the following pages. (For a complete description of the classification process in special education, please refer to 'A Parent's Guide to Special Education for Children Ages 5–21' written by and available through the Board of Education of the City of New York.)

Referring a child for an evaluation

The act of referring and diagnosing a child for special education is a powerful one. Early diagnosis can prevent school failure and mitigate the effects of handicapping conditions. By evaluating a child, a difficulty is documented and appropriate services can be found. By law and intent, we (psychologists, educators, parents, related professionals) want to move in the direction of less restrictive educational settings, meaning closer to general education when possible and, for some, the return to general education.

A child first becomes involved with special education when a parent or teacher notices a problem which is impeding that child's learning. Others who may make a referral include school or district staff, a physician, a court officer, an agency responsible for the health and welfare of the child, or, if 18 years of age or older, an individual on his or her own behalf. Schools are required to provide alternative services in general education prior to a referral to the CSE. Ideally, many attempts to remediate the learning difficulty in the general education class will have been attempted and exhausted before a referral is made. Alternatives to special education may include: bilingual education, ESL, educationally related support services, guidance services, and speech and language services.

This first step – the act of referring a child to special education – begins a process with many potential social, economic, and educational consequences. For some children with severe handicapping conditions such as autism or severe mental retardation, their needs may best be served in small, highly structured classroom settings which specifically address their skills and abilities and exist apart from the general education program. For others, the goal is to remediate the student's difficulty and then return the child to general education. However, according to Trachtman (1997), over 85 per cent of referred children end up in special education and 98 per cent never leave!

Initial referrals demand careful consideration. There is the potential for personal biases and prejudice to set the special education process in motion for a child who in fact has the potential to achieve in general education. Thus, as professionals, we must continually ask who is making a referral, and why. We must also question who is being overlooked and not being referred. Certainly, children with behavior problems stand out more than those with more subtle difficulties. There are educational and other long-term consequences of classifying and (often) segregating children who do not behave in school. What does it mean, that more and more students are classified into special education? More importantly, what does it say about the kind of learning environments we are creating in which some children cannot behave appropriately?

The diagnostic process

Psychologists rely on observations, projective tests, other relevant assessment instruments, interviews, and a review of the records to complete their evaluations. According to Anastasi (1988), 'psychological tests are designed to be objective and standardized measures of a sample of behavior'. The behaviors selected for measurement are frequently those that are highly valued in middle-class Western cultures. Thus, it is imperative that a psychologist consider the cultural and educational history of the person being tested. Test scores are not useful in isolation and always reflect the competence and integrity of the person administering the tests.

Other information which is crucial to the decision-making process includes the student's scores on achievement tests. These tests reveal how much a child has learned in specific academic areas, primarily reading and math. If a student's achievement scores are much lower than his or her intelligence scores would predict, then a learning or emotional problem may be present. The social history may provide clues about developmental delays, relevant emotional and family issues, as well as important educational history. Finally, a teacher's observations and report supply specific important details about how the child functions in the classroom and what might help him or her to function better.

Once a referral is made, the law requires that consent be obtained from a parent or legal guardian in order for an assessment to be conducted by the school-based support team (SBST). The team consists of a psychologist, educational evaluator, and a social worker. Assessments from other professionals (speech and language therapists, occupational therapists, physical therapists, psychiatrists) are solicited as needed. Thus, the assessment instruments include: a social history, psychological and educational evaluations, other relevant evaluations, classroom observations, teacher reports, incident reports (if applicable) and information from outside agencies if relevant. The findings are discussed at an educational planning committee (EPC) meeting which the parents and teachers are invited to attend, together with the SBST. At this meeting, the child's strengths and weaknesses are discussed and the team determines whether any special education services are needed. Thus, both the problem and the need for a special education intervention are 'named' at the EPC meeting.

When a recommendation for a self-contained special education class is made for the first time, the child's case is submitted to the CSE for a review meeting. Ideally, a time is selected that is convenient for the parents so that they may participate. At the CSE review meeting, a determination is made whether services are needed and if so, what services will meet the child's educational needs. Thus, the needed interventions and special education services are 'named' at the CSE meeting.

When psychologists assess the intelligence of children, they are generally referring to a composite of levels of cognitive functioning in several domains. These domains include verbal abilities and spatial–perceptual skills which often require abstract and analytical thinking. An intelligence score is expressed as an intelligence quotient or IQ.

The most commonly used intelligence tests include the Wechsler intelligence scales and the Stanford-Binet. These tests assess present functioning and can measure change. While the results can offer valuable information about an individual's strengths and weaknesses, they must be interpreted carefully. Cognitive functioning is very sensitive to emotional and environmental changes.

There are many important considerations that must be taken into account when referring to IQ scores. Since intelligence tests are not culture-free, results must be interpreted cautiously when given to non-Westerners. Scores reflect past educational experiences as well as serving as predictors of future educational performance. Thus, a child who has not received an age-appropriate education would not be expected to perform well on general or school-learned information questions. An IQ score may be an expression of an individual's ability at a given point in time relative to available age norms. In addition, because cognitive functioning is sensitive to emotional and environmental factors, scores can be inconsistent. IQ scores do not measure innate intelligence. Rather, heredity and environmental factors operate jointly from conception.

There is a great deal that is not known about intelligence. The word itself has a diversity of meanings to the general public, to different disciplines and even within disciplines. In conversations with Goleman, Gardner spoke extensively about multiple intelligences:

> The single most important contribution education can make to a child's development is to help him toward a field where his talents best suit him, where he will be satisfied and competent ... We should spend less time ranking children and more time helping them to identify their natural competencies and gifts, and cultivate those. There are hundreds and hundreds of ways to succeed, and many, many different abilities that will help you get there.
>
> (Goleman 1995: 37)

Goleman describes aspects of emotional intelligence. He suggests that too often tests ignore other important aspects of our lives. 'Yet even though a high IQ is no guarantee of prosperity, prestige, or happiness in life, our schools and our culture fixate on academic abilities, ignoring emotional intelligence, a set of traits – some might call it character – that also matters immensely for our personal destiny' (*ibid.* 36).

So, given their limitations, why use intelligence tests? Primarily because they provide a great deal of useful information in a relatively short amount of time. By comparing performances on intelligence tests with those on achievement tests, learning disabilities can be identified and then further explored. In addition to information gleaned about specific verbal and spatial–perceptual abilities, attentional and motivational factors can be assessed. Emotional issues surface and grapho-motor problems can be noted. Intelligence tests are most useful when used in conjunction with a variety of other educational and developmental information.

Outcomes: recommendations and classifications

As a school psychologist on a CSE review team, I am relying on the professional judgment and skills of my colleagues in the schools and the information they have provided for the review. I assume they have spent sufficient time and energy conducting their assessments and collecting all relevant information about a child. More often than not, I do not actually meet the child I am making crucial decisions about. For approximately a quarter of the students, I do not meet their parents because they do not attend the CSE meeting. My fellow review team members and I make many phone calls to parents and other professionals to clarify any questions we have and to discuss various issues. While this is not an ideal situation, we do attempt to understand the various aspects of each unique child.

However, for every wonderfully unique and developing child with special needs, there are a limited number of programs and services available. This is clearly problematic. Regardless of how well we understand a child's abilities, the least restrictive setting to meet the child's needs may have overly broad admission criteria.

A child who is found to have a disability must be classified according to the thirteen disabilities specified in the New York State Commissioner of Education's Regulations in order to receive special educational services. Classifications include: autistic, deaf, deaf-blindness, emotionally disturbed, hard of hearing, learning disabled, mentally retarded, multiply-disabled, orthopedically impaired, other health impaired, speech impaired, traumatic brain injury, or visually impaired. Clearly, these are very broad classifications which allow for a great deal of variation among the students within each category.

In addition, various classifications serve to organize the NYC special education system. Large divisions such as Supplemental Instructional Services (SIS), Modified Instructional Services (MIS), and Special Instructional Environments (SIE) indicate the type of special assistance provided – whether a child remains in general education for the majority of the day and is pulled out for resource room for one period only (SIS), whether a child is in a self-contained special education class throughout the day (MIS), or in a special class in a special school (SIE). These classifications are further divided by a number indicating what disabilities the children in the class may have. For example, MIS I is for learning disabled students while MIS II is for children with emotional and social difficulties.

An obvious limitation of these categories is that, like the admission criteria, they too are overly broad. Children within the same classifications have many differences. While they may share a common disability, they have varying abilities, learning styles, temperaments and cultural backgrounds. Specific recommendations which address a student's learning must be determined and implemented. This requires more individualized attention – more teachers, and more time.

Strategies for change

By focusing on the individual student's specific behavioral, educational, or emotional 'problems,' 'there is a strong inclination to divert attention from the inadequacies of the educational system itself and what bureaucratic, cultural, and economic conditions caused the necessity of applying these constructs originally' (Apple 1990: 135).

Apple makes a compelling argument for the problematic nature of blaming students for their circumstances. Real reform needs to be more about reworking systems than about fitting students into slots. Given the size and complexities of the special education system, there are no simple solutions for improving it. More resources should be directed toward prevention and early intervention with young children. And there are steps which educators, parents, and students can take which might enhance the education of children identified as having special needs. These changes must occur simultaneously in classrooms and school districts.

Repeatedly I have heard from classroom teachers, and witnessed firsthand, their need for additional support to work with differently abled children. One general education high school teacher reported that he had thirty-four students in a class: five had been identified as special education students, another four were disruptive and five more were having problems keeping up. He stated that there simply was not enough time in a 40-minute class with that many students to give each of the special education students the sort of attention they really needed. His situation is far too common. Too many students, too little time, and not enough support. If given the support of a comprehensive education and perhaps another teacher to work with the class, more learning could be happening for more students.

Inclusion programs offer one possibility, in which children with and without learning disabilities are taught in one classroom by two teachers working together. The students do not know who has been identified as needing special education and who is in general education. There is no segregation of special needs students. All the children have the opportunity to interact, socialize and learn alongside peers with varying abilities. The inclusion program is highly desirable for parents of children with mild enough learning ties to qualify for this type of class. The inclusion classrooms fill up quickly and there is generally not enough space to accommodate all the special needs kids that could qualify for one.

Why not create more inclusion programs? Clearly, there is a need and desire for students who require special education services to be included in general education classes with support services. Unfortunately, many parents of general education students do not want their children in these classes. Some parents state that they do not want their own children's learning rate slowed.

When a current CSE review team member was asked how he felt about the inclusion of differently abled children in the same class, he recounted his own experience with his child. His son started in a homogeneous first grade class in which all the children were high achievers. The next year, the principal made the classes heterogeneous. When he went to observe his son's class he saw that the students were poorly behaved and that his son was acting out. His son was not being challenged enough academically and was playing with students who weren't doing their work. The next year his son was back in a homogeneous class and his progress improved. The CSE review team member concluded by saying, 'No parent wants their child experimented on.'

While it seems that children of varying abilities would benefit from learning together and socializing with one another, there is strong resistance against it. Implicit assumptions about how schools sift, sort and select children encourage parents to do what is best, in a limited sense of academic progress, for their own children. The broader implications of creating diverse communities of learners are too often ignored. Little changes in practice could foster big changes in attitude. Perhaps students who learn more quickly could deepen their understanding of material by helping classmates. Additional assignments could also be given to students who are higher functioning so that they would continue to be challenged.

Clearly, additional supports would be needed to accommodate the different learning rates and styles of the children in the class. These supports might include a paraprofessional as well as scheduled time for the teachers to collaborate and determine how best to work with the special needs kids.

Parents vary in their understanding of their rights and of the system. Some feel disempowered, while others feel entitled. All parents should learn to be better advocates for their own children. They have their children's best interests at heart and know their children better than anyone. To improve special education, parents must become more aware and involved in their children's education. Although a social worker reviews parental and children's rights with every single parent who has a child in special education, too few choose to exercise those rights.

The most basic right is that every child has a right to a free, appropriate education in a least restrictive setting. Sadly, not all special educators and staff members conscientiously work to uphold this right for every child. Parents should be able to expect excellence in all classrooms. More attention needs to be paid and more resources need to be invested in how we prepare, recruit, and retain professional teachers. As this is accomplished, more parents need to visit schools and classrooms to determine for themselves whether their children's needs are being met. As with every profession, special educators vary in their experience and skill. Parents have a right to accept or reject classes or programs proposed by the placement officer.

Each year many parents take their cases to 'impartial hearings.' As with any system, there are those parents who manipulate the system by dragging out deadlines and winning cases on technicalities. It is easy to fault these parents, who are often affluent and take money away from public education by having the Board of Education pay for their children's private school. However, there are many parents who legitimately win the right to send their children to a New York State-approved private school because no appropriate program can be found within the Board of Education. They, too, are taking money away from public education. But should they be faulted because they have the wherewithal and persistence to fight for the most appropriate education for their child? No: the Board of Education must provide more appropriate services for children with different needs.

Personal commitment and interest in one's own children can easily replace one's commitment to the broader ideals of public education. While few would say that they would support the segregation of students with special needs, many more would consider it, or even support it, if they perceived a direct connection to their own child's level of academic achievement. Educators should work on raising consciousness about the range of benefits of inclusion. Even if academic achievement might suffer, there are other benefits to be gained that are valuable but less emphasized. In a democratic society, isn't it important that we care about each other's children along with our own children?

Special education, something that has great potential, is problematic. We are at a point where litigation is the driving force behind change. Relationships that should function to foster students' development have become adversarial. Many teachers, parents, and support team members have come to no longer trust each other. In the end, though, however tired we adults may individually be of paperwork, long meetings, or contentious battles, the ones who are really cheated are the children.

Among many other things, I am a 'labeler.' I have mixed feelings about that. I hope that by demystifying a complex process and creating opportunities to question my professional role, I can invite dialogue across groups. We must continue to find ways to meet students' needs by addressing individual differences and re-examining systems that are all too willing to cast out or cage in students who do not fit a narrowly defined label of 'normal.' Special education was intended for students whose needs were not being met in regular education. Its labels were intended to be usefully descriptive, rather than dangerously prescriptive. Our challenge is to create learning environments which celebrate a range of talents and abilities, and thereby to ensure that we do not conflate the label with the person.

References

Anastasi, A. (1988) *Psychological Testing* (6th edn), New York: Macmillan.

Apple, M. (1990) *Ideology and Curriculum* (2nd edn), New York: Routledge.

Board of Education (1997) 'A Parent's Guide to Special Education for Children Ages 5–21: Your Child's Right to an Education in New York State', University of the State of New York, State Education Department, Office for Special Education Services, Albany, New York 12234.

Goleman, D. (1995). *Emotional Intelligence: Why It Can Matter More Than IQ*, New York: Bantam Books.

Hudak, G. (1996). 'A Suburban Tale: Representation and Segregation in Special Needs Education' in J. L. Kincheloe, S. Steinberg and A. Gresson (eds) *Measured Lies: The Bell Curve Examined*, New York: St Martin's Press.

Trachtman, G. M. (1997) 'The Road Less Traveled, Part II: Forty Years in School Psychology,' *Communiqué*, 26(4): 8.

Youth

3 The classroom and labeling

'The girl who stayed back'

Judith S. Kaufman

The school was not a far walk from the house. When she is older she can remember walking there in about 15 minutes. She doesn't remember if she walked to school when she was 5 and 6, but she always walked home. There was a military ritual to walking home. The whole school queued up in patrol lines. Each class was their own patrol and you lined up two by two in the corridors outside the classroom. Each patrol had a patrol leader, someone who was lucky enough to wear an adjustable glow-orange plastic belt that angled down from one shoulder and wrapped around the waist. It was secured with a silver metal clasp. It always took a bit of finagling to work the clasp, something that made her nervous when she was finally selected to be a patrol leader in fourth grade. She didn't want to look stupid in front of her patrol line. Their teachers selected the patrol leaders. They were given the prized patrol belts if they had 'leadership qualities,' and if they were deemed 'responsible enough' to lead the patrol line safely away from the school. That meant keeping the kids quiet and orderly as they passed by the modest homes surrounding the school.

Park Street School [I have used pseudonyms for the school, teachers and students] in Worcester, Massachusetts, was a square brick building that reached three floors including the basement. The brick was a light blonde color. A huge flat lawn framed the front of the school. A wide cement walkway bisected the lawn and led from the center front door out to the sidewalk. There was a large driveway off to the left if you were facing the school. The driveway led to a paved schoolyard in back of the school. It was never called a playground, though there was a gray metal jungle gym tucked away in the back corner of the yard. It was the place they filed out to for recess, the boys going out one side of the building and the girls the other side. They played dodgeball or kickball and picked teams that made some kids feel bad for being picked last. The pavement was unyielding to the kids who fell and bloodied their knees and hands and elbows. There were woods right behind the yard and an old cyclone fence with lots of wire cut away. The students were forbidden from going into those woods, except if they were lucky enough to get Mr

Scully for fourth grade. He took his kids out almost every day during the spring and fall for nature walks in those woods. She got Mr Scully in fourth grade.

She doesn't remember the first day in Mrs Garrett's first grade, but she can remember her first day in Mrs Flaherty's first grade class a year later. Maybe it was true what they said, that she was just too immature to go on to second grade. If she had been mature enough, she would have a clear recollection of that first day in Mrs Garrett's class. She can remember the classroom, though. It was a dark room that got its character from the mammoth blackboards on three sides of the room and the black linoleum tiles on the floor. The tiles had flecks of lighter colors, but the overall effect was to make the room very dark. As if to spite the darkness, the back wall of the classroom was mostly windows, the kinds of window that went all the way up to the ceiling. To a 5-year-old, that ceiling seemed very far away. You used a long pole with a hook on the end to raise and lower the windows and to raise and lower the blackout shades. This was 1961 and, though she'd never experienced a duck-and-cover drill, evidence of the fears still permeated the school. She remembers the signs in front that designated the school basement as a shelter from nuclear fallout.

The class never looked out those windows. They faced the opposite way, staring at the blackboard and the big and small letters on cardboard hanging from taut wire strung across the top. Mrs Garrett's desk was off to the left side, angled for a view of the whole class. She doesn't remember a bathroom in the classroom. Mrs Flaherty's first grade had their own bathroom, as she learned a year later. In Mrs Garrett's class, you had to raise your hand and ask to go to the basement. That's where the bathrooms were. The students never asked to go to the bathroom.

The desks were square with wooden tops that had an indentation for holding a pencil and off to the right, a hole for an inkwell. During art, they sometimes used glasses filled with paint that fit right into the inkwells. The rest of the desk was metal painted light brown. A metal compartment right under the wood top held papers and books, and metal legs extended down. Wooden chairs were paired with the desks. The desks and chairs varied in size, but for a while there was not a desk that was big enough for her. She was the tallest student in the class. Sitting at the largest desk, her knees rubbed against the bottom and she'd have to balance the desk on her knees to maneuver her feet out in front. If she got up too quickly from the desk, it would tip over and crash to the floor. The class would laugh, but not Mrs Garrett who always thought she did it on purpose.

Her memories of that class do not center on the expected learning. She remembers feeling separate from that, an outsider at the margins. There are memories of letters and numbers, but no memories that they fit together to make other kinds of meaning. She sat at her desk and when she tried hard to attend, she would stare at those symbols on the board. Maybe if she stared hard enough, they would start to make sense. The symbols meant nothing to her and she felt lonely and stupid in the classroom that she spent so much time in. Those symbols were a part of a world that she could not access no matter how hard she tried. It was a world that Mrs Garrett belonged to and a world that many of her classmates belonged to. Mrs Garrett never made fun of her, though she could sense the teacher's frustration. The other kids in the class didn't make fun of her, though she could sense they felt smarter. And perhaps they didn't say anything because in the emerging hierarchy of the classroom her marginality reminded them of the tenuous nature of their insider status and privilege (Sapon-Shevin 1994).

She can visualize Mrs Garrett. She was tall and thin, and had short black curly hair with some gray that she probably had 'done' once every few weeks. Mrs Garrett's face was stern when she wanted it to be and gentle when she wanted it to be. She remembers the gentleness of that face when her parents and Mrs Garrett finally decided that it would be best to keep her back for one more year. Mrs Garrett seemed much older than her parents; she was probably in her forties.

Her memories of that class center on her friends and getting into trouble with Mrs Garrett. Her best friend was Susie who lived on June Street just at the edge of her neighborhood. They talked all the time in class and Mrs Garrett had to separate them. One time, when Mrs Garrett wasn't looking, she picked up her desk and moved it right next to Susie's. Mrs Garrett was irate. Now it's not clear whether the rest of the story is a memory of an experience, or a memory of a story, because she has told these stories a lot. They form the narrative that justifies why she was held back. It wasn't that she was 'stupid.' She was held back because she was immature, a 'hellion' who would be unable to handle the expectations of second grade. What she remembers is that Mrs Garrett picked up the yardstick laying in the chalk tray. She angrily walked over to her desk and told her to hold out her hands and lay them palms down on the desk. As Mrs Garrett swung the yardstick down toward her hands, she flinched and her too small desk fell over on the toes of Mrs Garrett's shiny black pumps. Mrs Garrett was too horrified to continue and walked away.

On another day she was again talking with her 'neighbors,' and not responding to the warnings. Mrs Garrett put the dunce-cap on her head and ordered her to sit in the corner by the piano. It was time for art and everyone in class was given a slab of gray clay on brown folded paper towels. Her memory is that a friend slipped her a piece of clay to play with behind the piano. The piano was an upright and the front was open exposing the hammers. She took bits of clay and stuck them on the ends of the hammers. The story she often told to her friends in school is that later that day during music time, Mrs Garrett began to play and pieces of clay began flying everywhere amid deadened notes. Mrs Garrett was very angry. The teacher didn't accuse her, but she felt sure Mrs Garrett knew.

There are no clear memories of when the discussions started. Her mother and sometimes her father were coming to school a lot to talk to Mrs Garrett. It was probably her mother who talked to her daughter first. 'Staying back' and 'repeating the year' were the phrases combined with 'you're just not ready,' 'you're too young,' 'you need another year,' and 'it's the best thing for you.' She was compared to her brother. He was four years older, but they were both November babies and just turning six in first grade. They thought about keeping him back, but decided not to. He was struggling with school, and maybe she wouldn't have to struggle if they kept her back.

Mrs Garrett didn't ask her parents for their opinion, and they didn't have a choice. Young working-class parents didn't have a sense of entitlement that could have prompted scrutiny of a teacher's judgment. Mrs Garrett had power and authority and so didn't consult with her parents. She simply explained why she had decided to hold her back and that lots of famous people repeated first grade. It did not mean that she would continue to have problems. She would probably do well, just like Einstein had succeeded even though, as Mrs Garrett suggested, he was held back in first grade. It was Mrs Garrett's decision, and she had decided that it would be the best thing.

There are two narratives that can serve to explain why I was held back. One is overt and centers on being too young, the other is unspoken and centers on conformity to the institution. In the overt narrative, my 'developmental immaturity' was causing an academic and a social delay and if I was not given time to mature, I would always be behind and struggling to catch up. I was a young first-grader and, according to Mrs Garrett, not ready for the social rules and structural expectations that define relationships between student and teacher and student and student. I was not 'able' or willing to conform to expectations such as not playing with friends in the classroom, sitting in one place for long periods of time, or focusing my attention on the teacher. Much to Mrs Garrett's dismay, I did not even seem to notice that there was a set of rules and expectations for how to 'do' first grade. What I did notice were my classmates, and in particular Susie on whom I probably had a young crush. As a 5-year-old, my energy was focused on establishing relationships with other kids in a newly forming community.

The unspoken narrative, the unconscious motivation behind Mrs Garrett's decision was that I had not acquiesced and I was not yet impressed by the importance of conformity to the institutional community. She did not question the intractability of the institution. This was a given, as well as the demand for conformity. Mrs Garrett internalized this hegemony and, powerless to challenge it, instead challenged a 5-year-old who moved amid the structure of a first grade classroom, seemingly untouched by rigid expectations. I had, in Alison Jaggar's (1989) terms, taken on an outlaw identity that signified a critique of the institution. I had to be restrained, 'held back' from challenging the institution. If Mrs Garrett allowed me to continue to challenge the institution by advancing to the next grade, my nonconformity might intensify and the institution's ability to control my behaviors would be weakened. The analogy to a straightjacket is not extreme. Such a device functions to 'hold' an individual 'back' until he or she is calm enough to be controlled more passively. Retention in grade one, much like the straightjacket, would hold me back and make me pliant and submissive. A second year in first grade would help me to understand and notice the structural expectations of the classroom. However, it is not simply the action of being 'held back' that brings about this change; it is the stigma associated with the label 'held back.'

> Mrs Garrett's decision to hold her back was finalized by the school administration and there were immediate consequences. Along with public school, she was also in Hebrew school. Her parents consulted with administrators at the temple, and they decided to retain her there as well. It would not be workable for her to be a grade ahead in Hebrew school. That would complicate matters; consistency was best. She had hoped they would leave Hebrew school alone. If she was in the 'right' grade in Hebrew school, that would be a place where she was still with her friends and perhaps a place where she could feel smart. Until they made the decision to retain her there as well, Hebrew school, for a short time, had been a place where she could feel herself.
>
> Toward the end of the school year, she began to mourn the loss of her friends who would move on to second grade without her. What would she do without them? What would they think when she wasn't with them in second grade? What would the first-graders in Mrs Flaherty's class think? She thought they would think she was stupid. She was already big for her age and perhaps understood she would be even bigger next year, especially next to students who were in first grade for the first time.
>
> Mrs Flaherty was a large woman, at least a hundred pounds too many for her frame. She seemed younger and gentler than Mrs Garrett. She could be stern and raise her voice, but those were exceptions to a much gentler demeanor. The classroom was much brighter, with green chalkboards instead of black ones. The students were seated with the windows to their sides, instead of to their backs, and the floors were wood, shined to a high gloss for the beginning of the school year.
>
> She felt very big on that first day. Even though she had a desk that fit her, it was the biggest desk and she seemed to tower over everybody in the classroom. She didn't read Steinbeck's *Of Mice and Men* until junior high, but Lenny was a character she came to identify with. He epitomized big and stupid: the way she felt and the way she felt she was perceived. She was consumed with having stayed back and felt different from everyone else in the class. Mrs Flaherty was having everyone say

their names. When it came to her, she said her name and announced to everyone that she had stayed back. She wasn't sure why she did it.

I was so inside myself, and so disconnected from everyone on that first day of school that telling the class I had stayed back was a release and at the same time a connection. Self-identifying with the label was also a way of controlling how I would be perceived. My classmates and the teacher would see that I was okay with it; it wasn't a big deal. Inside, though, it was a big deal; I didn't *feel* a release or a connection. I worried that they saw me as big and dumb.

In that moment when I told them I had stayed back, an exchange occurred: the complexity of my being was traded for the simplicity of a label. In Mrs Garrett's class I was a complex being. I lived at the margins in that classroom, and though I didn't 'get it' in the same way my classmates got it, I could live with not feeling as smart, I could live with Mrs Garrett's frustration. There was a sense that I would get there eventually – not that I hoped for it, but a sense that it would happen – in the same way that it happened to my peers. I had no experience in the world that told me it would be any different for me. The idea that one individual can be compared to another according to some characteristic was entirely foreign to my emerging sense of identity. I still thrived in the privilege that comes with a lack of experience, and in that privilege was power and possibility.

From a social constructivist perspective, the way that we come to know who we are in the world is in the social space constructed by community (see Rogoff 1990; Lave and Wenger 1993). Some of the ways that we interact in these social spaces arise out of potentialities that are with us at birth. Despite the best efforts of sociobiologists, we cannot predict the outcomes of these potentialities. By definition they are infinite; they variously manifest themselves in interaction with environments, and with infinite arrangements of influences and factors within those environments. Thus it is impossible to draw any causal connections between human potentialities and the ways in which these become manifest in particular communities. Retrospectively, potentialities can explain our differences, while communities can explain our similarities. So in the social space between our potentialities and their manifestations, our identities begin to take form. In the complex interplay between the self and community, we draw and at the same time notice the edges of who we are becoming. Labels employed by members of our communities often shape these edges. We are labeled as males or females, black or white, poor or rich, straight or gay, and so on. Some of these labels, such as gender and race, are more rigidly applied than others and the degree of rigidity usually corresponds to benefits accrued by those in power. Such labels, once applied, fix us in time and space. For example, gender is a label rigidly applied in our patriarchal culture and once assigned, we are always male or female unless we opt for surgical and/or hormonal alterations. If we feel, despite outward manifestations, that we have been wrongly labeled, we must change. The possibility that a binary conception of gender is flawed is not considered. This is the power of labeling – the label itself takes on more reality than the person to whom it is affixed.

Before I went to public school, the space between who I was becoming and my community was large, with lots of room for exploration. As a white, working-class, Jewish kid in a similarly labeled community I accrued benefits from the labels ascribed to me. Surely, restrictions, impositions, and cultural expectations defined the space I traveled in, but prior to first grade there was still a sense of openness. Interactions with caregivers, relatives and other adults were almost always marked by validation. Adults remarked on how tall I was, how beautiful, how smart, how funny, and what a fine young lady I was becoming. These labels imposed definition on the shape of my identity. They left covert markers, but still there was freedom and possibility. Early on I was a tomboy and so I tried to take some of the cultural capital that was bestowed on males. Within the world of a preschooler, it seemed as if I could do anything, go anywhere, and be whatever I wanted to be. Much like the pre-adolescent girls whose powerful voices have been captured by Gilligan and her colleagues (Gilligan *et al.* 1990; Taylor *et al.* 1995), I was confident, powerful, and ready to take on the world. These feelings stayed with me in first grade even after they told me I was staying back. At that moment, my reality didn't shift; it was the same world, the same social space. But that first day in Mrs Flaherty's class contained the moment when it all changed, when my reality shifted. The idea of being held back suddenly had power – the space between self and community had shifted. It was a violent shift; my burgeoning sense of who I was had been altered. I lost my power, my sense of control.

Alan Block (1997) uses object relations theory to analyze the violence inflicted on children by educational institutions. Much like social constructivist theory, object relations theory describes how our interactions with objects (read actual objects, events, and people) in the world come to define who we are as individuals. We choose objects to interact with, and objects also come to us by virtue of our increasing participation in the communities of which we are members. The relationships with these objects, not the objects themselves, comprise the stuff of our being; in those relationships, the self is formed. Block explains that at home, we are provided with a frame that facilitates our search for and use of objects. Within the constraints of this frame we freely and creatively evoke and construct ourselves in the world. I did this at home and carried those habits into the frame provided by Mrs Garrett. I didn't notice that the frame was far more structured and much less facilitating, and because I didn't notice, the self that I had constructed thus far no longer worked. It became a 'bad' self, and so the predictability and safety I felt in the world that enabled me to explore and create was suddenly taken away. The violence I experienced resides with this loss of self. I also knew that it was all my fault and ironically it is this consciousness of agency that made me feel powerless. How could I know that anything I did in the future would not lead to similar circumstances?

She did not know the kids in Mrs Flaherty's class and they didn't know her. In Mrs Garrett's class there had been a lot of kids from her neighborhood. The kids in this new class didn't have familiar faces; they were from other streets in neighborhoods nearby. The violent shift she experienced occurred not only in school but in her neighborhood as well. When she got home from school, the kids from Mrs Garrett's class were still on the street, but they were also absent to her; they were now in second grade. The kids in Mrs Flaherty's class only knew her as the 'girl who stayed back.' This label set within the frame of that first day in Mrs Flaherty's class was what she related to, and in that relationship another self was evoked. On that day, no one had any knowledge of her year with Mrs Garrett and so the complexity of her being was diminished.

Beyond that first day, there are few clear memories of the year. In later grades, her repertoire of stories did not include any from her second year in first grade. She doesn't remember getting into trouble or engaging in pranks. One memory that speaks to her changing identity is a memory of extreme emotion. Perhaps it was after she announced to the class that she had stayed back. She felt tears welling up inside her and she had to get away. She made an excuse to go to the coat closet to get something out of her coat. She walked to the back of the classroom, slid the folding doors to the side, clutched a brass hook with all her might, held her face as close to the hook as she possibly could and tried to muffle and contain her sobs. The idea that she should contain herself marked the shift in her identity. All that was familiar about the context of schooling had been taken away. The community that reflected her, that had helped her shape her identity in the last year was gone, along with the expectation that her actions would lead to familiar results. She didn't know how to act in this new community; perhaps she would have tried the familiar, but it was familiar ways of being that had held her back. Familiar ways of being reflected that she was big and stupid. The stigma, the label that signified her retention, now contained her. It exerted an incredible power that kept her from experimenting with who she was and what she did. She waited for the cues that would tell her what was the right thing to say, the right thing to do. She held herself in check.

After Mrs Flaherty's class, she stopped announcing that she had stayed back. Most of the kids knew anyway. It was a small neighborhood school and they stayed with each other year after year. There were always new kids, however, and eventually she would have to tell them, especially around her birthday. Until November she was the same age as everyone else, but then she suddenly became a year older, and kids would always ask her how old she was on her birthday. And when she told them, they always asked how come she was older, and she would have to 'come out' to them. There was a silence when she told them; they were stunned and didn't know what to say. In those moments, a gulf formed that separated her from those kids. She would immediately fill the silence and explain

that they had kept her back because she was immature, smoothly imply-
ing, she thought, that it was not because she was stupid. Then she told
the stories of her antics and pranks in Mrs Garrett's class. She would tell
them about the desk falling on her teacher's toes and clay that flew out of
the piano during music. They always laughed, but she never felt like the
stories bridged the gulf between them or transformed their perceptions.
She felt separate from them and stupid, and she felt like they thought
she was stupid.

In the late winter and early spring, other kids started having birthdays
and some of them reached her age. It gave her some comfort that now
there were at least a few kids who were the same age as her. She, along
with her classmates, had thoroughly internalized the institution's definition of age. Age signified that you belonged, that you were the same as
everyone else. When a kid was new, age was one of the first things classmates inquired about. Her own age signified her failure. It had a power
that bestowed comfort at the beginning and end of the school year, and
bestowed feelings of inadequacy during the year when her age indicated
that she had been held back.

There was no overt tracking in her elementary school, but students
were inevitably compared to each other in a system where an external
standard was used to measure progress. The teachers adopted the institutional values of comparison, and ultimately students adopted these
values. Students began to see with the eyes of the institution; they began
to notice the differences among themselves. As this paradigm became a
reality, she felt less alone. She was no longer the only one who was
different.

By third grade, she had found a place in the middle of the rapidly developing classroom hierarchy. There were the few students, four or five
out of a class of twenty-five, who seemed very confident about schoolwork and about how smart they were. She was friendly to but distant
from those kids. They never really accepted her into their group. They
would joke around with her, but when it came time to talk about schoolwork they only talked to each other. She was not as confident as they
were; they intimidated her and she felt insecure around them. John and
Debbie in particular were too sure of themselves, or so it seemed to her.
The kids in the middle did not really think about school or how smart
they were; school was just something you did. Then there were the kids
on the bottom, the ones who just did not seem to get it. The students all
saw them as the 'dumb' kids and/or the 'troublemakers.' The boys were
usually both 'dumb' and 'troublemakers.' The girls were for the most
part just 'dumb,' except for Pam. She made trouble in a covert way. She
would say things about other kids that were not true, things that would
get those kids into trouble. Cathy was also in the bottom group. She was
very sweet, and generous to a fault. Her demeanor helped her cover her
lack of understanding in class, but when the teacher pressed her, Cathy

would become silent and somewhat vacant in response to a curriculum that seemed to mean nothing to her. Carol was another member in their group who had a very hard time. She was socially very awkward and often wet her pants because it seemed she was too shy to ask to go to the 'basement.'

She never teased the kids in the lower group. She did not see herself as a part of this group, and that was a comfort. She was in the middle group, the largest and most boisterous in the class. They joked around in class, occasionally acted out, and played together after school. Being in the middle group, she still felt dumb, but she was not as dumb as the kids in the low group. Ironically, though, those kids were a constant reminder of how others perceived her. They never said anything to reinforce her assumptions, but she thought that the teachers and the smart kids saw her the way she saw the kids in the dumb group.

She did well in school after being held back: mostly As and some Bs. She was not struggling with schoolwork and so it seemed to everyone that being held back had done wonders. She got messages from her parents and teachers that she was smart and doing well. However, she did not feel smart, and in fact was very insecure about her abilities. These feelings of insecurity – predictable in a system that compares one individual to another – were magnified through the lens of being held back. No matter how she did in her work, no matter what others said about her, she had been held back and that defined and shaped a place of insecurity within her identity. She could never really win the comparison contest in school because she had been held back; she could never really be smart because she had been held back. She could never really be equal among her peers because she had been held back. Being held back was an immutable aspect of who she was in a world where being at grade level was highly valued.

There was nothing I could change about being held back, but I could potentially change how others viewed me. I assumed, despite messages from my parents and teachers, that others perceived me as 'average,' which I translated as 'dumb.' Controlling these perceptions, along with containing my feelings of insecurity, became driving forces in my life. Learning and information are commodified in schools. Students acquire information (as opposed to knowledge) in order to acquire grades, not to participate increasingly in the larger communities of which they are members. I took this process a step further. I learned and acquired information to try to prove to others that I was smarter than they thought.

These efforts at controlling perceptions, trying to show others that I was smart, demonstrate how successful labeling is for the institution. In Mrs Garrett's class my behaviors challenged institutional structures and expectations. I was not behaving or learning like everyone else, and the system is structured around this expectation of uniformity. When behavior lies outside tolerated variations, there are two alternatives. The first is that the institution changes to accommodate the behavior; given the immutable character of institutions, this is highly unlikely. The second and much more likely alternative is that the institution applies a label that functions to alter the behavior. In my case, being held back and labeled as such successfully altered my behavior. My intellectual insecurity and my efforts at controlling others' perceptions meant that I engaged in behaviors that served the interests of the institution. First, I engaged in school-like behaviors to try to show my teachers and peers I was smart. In my second grade class I learned how to focus my eyes and furrow my brow to demonstrate to the teacher that I was engaged. I internalized these behaviors so thoroughly that most of my teachers thought I was puzzled by something and would often ask me if I had a question.

A second behavior that served the interests of the institution had to do with acquiring information rather than with producing knowledge. Children come to school with an expansive sense of reality gained from inter-acting with objects in a frame that imposes limits but offers lots of possibility and exploration. Within this frame, children produce knowledge about events, interactions, people, and about themselves in relation to these objects. In school, a frame whose contents are wholly visible and strictly defined gradually displaces that expansive reality (Block 1997). The school frame cannot allow for knowledge production, because such productions would expand the frame. Knowledge productions are not visible until they are produced, and such productions elude definition because they are unpredictable. Children learn rather quickly that their knowledge has little value in the classroom and many forget how to produce knowledge on their own. They learn that what is valued is information that is visible, defined, and transmitted, and once they demonstrate that they have 'learned' the infor-mation, they can trade that learning for a grade. I 'learned' not only to get a good grade, but also to control perceptions. I also forgot how to produce knowledge. I was, in a sense, consumed by the institution. I had lost the power I brought with me to Mrs Garrett's class. That power was independent of the institution of the school. The only power I had now was power that served school interests and this had been achieved through labeling me as someone who had been held back.

> She continued to do good work through her years at Park Street School. There was the science fair project she did for Mr Scully in fourth grade. He taught them all about weather that year and she has vivid memories of learning how to identify stratus, nimbus and cumulus clouds. For her science project, she built weather instruments: a rain gauge, a barometer, a thermometer, and a wind vane. She took readings for a month and compared the accuracy of her instruments with those of the national weather service. In sixth grade, she wrote a twenty-page paper (typed) on the trial of Julius and Ethel Rosenberg. In this work and in other

projects, though, she only learned how to reproduce and she was good at it. Staying back had taught her a lesson in compliance. She stayed on the visible paths circumscribed by the institution of the school. As a result, she never learned how to take ideas and make them her own. In all of her time in public school, she never discovered the power of her own thinking.

She never told anyone about feeling stupid. It was a piece of her identity that she thought about every day and revealing it would make her vulnerability apparent. She could never admit she felt insecure, because that would unravel the identity she was constructing in order to try to change how she felt and to change how others saw her. She worked hard on building an identity that cloaked the insecurity. She worked on her humor, memorizing joke books and clowning around in class. She got very good at projecting an image of being calm and in control. 'Everything is copacetic' was a saying she used a great deal.

She was separate from herself in those years. Her energies were spent on hiding who she was and trying to control other's perceptions. She continued to do well in school and continued to feel inadequate relative to her peers who were labeled as the smartest in her class. She took most of her classes with them, but she stayed away from courses where there was a risk of getting anything less than an A. She didn't take physics or calculus, and took only one Advanced Placement course, in history. She never gained acceptance with her 'smartest' peers as they advanced through junior high and high school. They continued to tolerate her presence, but never engaged her in their serious discussions about schoolwork or plans to apply to Ivy League institutions. She lived on the margins of this group and it was clear to her and to them that she had little to offer.

When I came to Mrs Garrett's class at the age of 5, I had been operating in a world where those around me reacted to me, reacted to who I was in the world. In my second time in first grade, that was all changed. I had been labeled and that label functioned as a clear, soundproof wall that violently separated me from the world. People around me were no longer reacting to me, they were reacting to the wall. I was imprisoned, and I could yell and bang on the wall, but no one would hear me. The label wrested all sense of control over who I was in the world. This is the insidious and violent act of labeling.

My teachers and classmates saw a label and formed a set of expectations about who I was and responded to it, not to me. I, in turn, responded to the way in which I was reflected in their eyes. The school community expected that I was average and not among the smartest students. I internalized this image and spent the rest of my school career trying to present an image that I was smart, while simultaneously trying to keep myself from doing or saying anything that validated the expectations of others. I never felt successful at these tasks, and so I remained in a constant state of insecurity. This insecurity is, in a sense, toxic runoff from the label and it shaped what I did and how I came to know the world. It kept me from taking any risks in school for fear that I would be exposed as average or 'stupid' to my peers and teachers. It kept me on the outside of knowledge, passively looking in and reproducing, but never on the inside producing knowledge.

Thinking about where I am now, it is easy to argue that the experience of staying back did not irreparably harm me. Despite the demons of anxiety and insecurity, I made it and succeeded and perhaps would not have driven myself as hard as I did if not for those demons. However, I am white, and though my parents were working class when I was young, they aspired to and tried to live a middle-class existence. Privilege can account for a great deal of my seeming resilience to the effects of being held back. But is this really the point of school? Should school be something to overcome?

The practice of labeling by an institution signifies that the institution has taken on far more importance than the clients it serves. It signifies, in relation to education, that we teach school, not children, and when children cannot or will not conform to the expectations of school, it is they who are altered – not the school. The school, as an institution, is preserved at the expense of children. The alterations or costs that children incur are labels that imprison them and thus keep them from challenging the school. Children spend their time defending themselves against the toxic effects of labeling, or else they opt out altogether and either spiritually or physically withdraw. In all cases, the threat of change that these children pose to the institution is neutralized.

There is a vision of schooling that extends from the European romantics of the eighteenth century through the reformers of the twentieth century. In this vision, schools are broad and open places where children learn the values of their adult community, and at the same time are given space to explore, create, and construct who they are in relation to and apart from those values. In this vision, the school resists institutionalization. It is responsive to the difference and sameness that children bring with them as they enter the community of the school. In this vision, the school is hardly a test of children's resilience or their ability to overcome the effects of imprisonment within an institutional label. It is a place that supports children as they learn skills and construct knowledge that will move them, in Lave and Wenger's (1993) terms, from legitimate peripheral participation to more central participation in the life of their respective and shared communities. This school is also a place that recognizes that it, as well as the community it is a part of, will ultimately be challenged and changed by children as they become more central participants in their communities. However, until we begin to value our children more than our schools, 'we will continue to practice extreme violence upon the child, denying him/her growth, health, and experience' (Block 1997: 173).

References

Block, A. A. (1997) *I'm Only Bleeding: Education as the Practice of Violence against Children*, New York: Peter Lang.

Gilligan, C., Lyons, N. P. and Hanmer, T. J. (1990) *Making Connections: The Relational Worlds of Adolescent Girls at Emma Willard School*, Cambridge, MA: Harvard University Press.

Jaggar, Alison (1989) 'Love and Knowledge: Emotion in Feminist Epistemology' in A. M. Jaggar and S. R. Bordo (eds) *Gender/Body/Knowledge: Feminist Reconstructions of Being and Knowing*, New Brunswick: Rutgers University Press.

Lave, Jean and Wenger, Etienne (1993) *Situated Learning: Legitimate Peripheral Participation*, Cambridge: Cambridge University Press.

Rogoff, Barbara (1990) *Apprenticeship in Thinking: Cognitive Development in Social Context*, New York: Oxford University Press.

Sapon-Shevin, M. (1994) *Playing Favorites: Gifted Education and Disruption of Community*, Albany, NY: SUNY Press.

Steinbeck, John (1937) *Of Mice and Men*, New York: Covici-Friede.

Taylor, J. McClean, Gilligan, Carol and Sullivan, A. M. (1995) *Between Voice and Silence: Women and Girls, Race and Relationship*, Cambridge, MA: Harvard University Press.

4   Labeling the young

Hope and contemporary childhood

Paul Kihn

It is a Friday morning in winter. Snow carpets the roads and sidewalks, calming this Bronx neighborhood, slowing traffic, precipitating quiet. At a small intermediate school, four adults sit huddled around an 11-year-old child. We sit in the principal's office talking about disruption and safety. The boy's elderly mother is on a sofa next to her child. She is weary, and wears a resigned expression. The boy's adult brother watches the principal carefully. The boy watches me, his teacher.

It is hot in the room and we shift in the heat. The boy is failing all of his classes. He is disruptive. Yesterday, he repeatedly kicked another student. He used a teacher's manual to strike a classmate over the head. He stood on a chair in a classroom and performed a strange dance, making obscene gestures towards his teacher. Now we begin to speak the labels. Surely he knows his reputation will continue to cause him grief. He is a troublemaker. He is defiant. Is he on medication? Does he take it consistently? He is at an age when certain behaviors are expected. By calling him an early adolescent, we will excuse many things. But this? We might have to refer him for evaluation. He will earn a label, there, which will allow access to a smaller, more appropriate setting. Meanwhile, he is being suspended. His mother places her face in her soft hands. It is a melancholy gesture. It is a gesture appropriate for the melancholy litany.

The principal softens her tone. This is all about you, she says to the boy. These are people who care about you. This is all about your future. The boy, small for his age, meets the principal's gaze without expression. We are silent for a moment, in the heat of the room. Yes, that is right. This is all about the future of the boy. In some small way, our meeting is an attempt to raise hope amidst melancholy. Schools are, after all, poignant symbols of the future, and places of dreaming. The opprobrium in the room on this winter Friday thus feels both anachronistic and truthful. 'Nothing,' writes literary scholar Andrew Delbanco (1999: 98), 'is more alarming than the impoverishment of our children's capacity to imagine the future.' Can this boy envision a future for himself? Do the adults around him – powerful shadows – possess a collective, sustainable hope?

Hope matters because it reflects a collective commitment to the future, and thus to young people. Hope is an abiding faith that there is some meaning outside of ourselves, that some greater purpose underlies the quotidian comings and goings of our lives. Delbanco says that hope emerges from the inevitable story which organizes 'the inchoate sensations amid which we pass our days – pain, desire, pleasure, fear.' The story provides hope if it 'leads somewhere and thereby helps us navigate through life' (1999: 1). Hope is a sustaining vision. It is both impetus and guide. It provides the necessary feeling that we are on a road that leads somewhere, and not simply into oblivion. Hope thus creates the opportunity to move beyond the realms of material desire, immediate gratification, and the stupor of a present mired in meaninglessness.

Apart from supplying a sustaining narrative and lending meaning, hope is of critical importance for the transformation of a world replete with injustice and oppression. It is a necessary aspect of being and becoming fully human, of living up to our existential potential. For Paulo Freire it is hence an 'ontological need': 'I do not understand human existence,' he writes, 'and the struggle needed to improve it, apart from hope and dream' (1994: 8). Hope is the utopian force which enables the possibility of political change. In Freire's vision, it resides within each of us as an aspect of our selves. It is this hope which allows people to envision the possibilities of change and an end to oppression and injustice.

Extending this argument, it becomes clear that the absence of hope denies the possibility of change. Without hope, contemporary dehumanization and oppression continue unabated. Freire allows that people can and do lose sight of hope. 'Hopelessness,' he writes, 'is but hope that has lost its bearings' (*ibid.*). It is hopelessness that leads to inaction and to the acceptance of an iniquitous status quo.

Delbanco, on the other hand, claims a more substantial alternative. The absence of hope, he writes (1999: 3), is its 'dogged companion,' melancholy. Melancholy expresses hope's absence. They are thus twinned, poised in a significant social balance. In the absence of any sustaining, hopeful story – at the level of nation or community – melancholy governs. Melancholy in this sense reflects a feeling of purposelessness, a grand cry of 'Why bother?' It is, according to Delbanco, 'the lurking suspicion that all our getting and spending amounts to nothing more than fidgeting while we wait for death' (*ibid.*). It is not sadness or despair; it is, rather, a profound uncertainty about meaning in our lives.

Hope would lift the boy and his four adult companions out of the heat and opprobrium of that office, and invest their meeting with meaning and possibility. Dante chose to place the words 'abandon all hope' at the gateway to his *Inferno*. In Robert Pinsky's translation, this reads:

> Through me you enter into the city of woes,
> Through me you enter into eternal pain,
> Through me you enter the population of loss.
> ...

Abandon all hope you who enter here.
These words I saw inscribed in some dark color
Over a portal

(Dante 1994: 25)

What more severe circumstance could exist than the abandonment of meaning, and relinquishing of any narrative which we might tell to provide comfort and purpose in our lives? We stand, perhaps unwittingly, at Dante's dark
portal not as passage from one world into hell, but as transition from one way
of living to another.

Hope's importance becomes clearer once we accept that the four adults in
the principal's office are raising the child into a world of their own making.
For psychologist Robert Coles, the interactions between adults and children
facilitate hope's growth or its diminution. Coles sees hope within the complex interplay of parent and child. He writes (1998: 187) of 'the grounding
of hope':

> its genesis is in a faithfulness of parents that plants and tends and nour-
> ishes faith in the child – a faith that time builds, a faith for which space
> offers itself so that there can be experiments, play, the testing and teas-
> ing that go with life, come to terms with matter, with floors and objects,
> and porches and steps and the waiting ground below: the incarnation of
> hope in the daily explorations, the rhythms of curiosity, discovery that go
> with (indeed, constitute) childhood.

Coles, like Freire, sees hope as ontological. Hope lives within the fabric of
childhood. The adult context sustains this, or diminishes it. The faith of the
adults becomes the faith of the children. We are raising the boy into a world
of faith and meaning and possibility, or alternatively into a world which
denies the importance of human agency. We are providing a hopeful context in which the boy understands his life in relation to a sustaining narrative – a narrative which provides a touchstone and a guide – or a context
which isolates him and locates him firmly in the present making what
meaning he can from whimsy and desire. We provide the context for the
actualization of his ontological vocation, his becoming fully human, or we
deny him his humanity and repress his ability to question and problematize
his world.

I believe that given these options we have fallen into a pattern of hopelessness. I believe that the melancholy room reflects melancholy times. Or,
put another way, I believe that American society has experienced a diminution of hope with profound and disturbing consequences for youth. Hopelessness has played a prominent role in shaping our social and political
behavior, and our institutions. Freire regards hopelessness 'as a concrete
entity,' and underscores the 'historical, economic, and social reasons that
explain' it.

We are distracted away from hope in what amount to melancholy times. The labels we use in relation to young people manifest these distractions. The labels reflect and foster a new perspective on young people, kids, youth, children. The perspective, antagonistic and baffled, amounts to an assault on youth, both in the ways in which we perceive young people – constructing 'youth' – and the ways in which we treat them. The central premise here is that a contemporary, prevailing melancholy provides the context for our current assault on youth. This assault is manifested in the changing labels we apply to young people, and in our social and political treatment of them. It will be necessary to begin, then, with an overview of the historical nature of hope in America. How did we arrive in these melancholy times, and what do they look like?

Hope's diminution

The 11-year-old sits within a melancholy that extends far beyond his mother's weary gesture, his principal's troubled gaze. He is not so much a victim of an individual or psychological despair, but rather of a deeply rooted cultural melancholy. The balance between hope and melancholy expresses the relative strength or weakness of narratives which lend meaning to our lives. The adults around the boy have lost the thread of any hopeful narrative and given in to Freire's dehumanizing hopelessness.

Hope's and melancholy's cultural manifestations are historical. That is, the conditions which foster one or the other are made through time by people. Delbanco provides a schematic account of hope in American history. He proposes three eras of hope. The first era took place from the early colonization to roughly 1800. During this time, hope was provided by a puritan faith in God. In this phase, writes Delbanco (1999: 4–5), 'hope was chiefly expressed through a Christian story that gave meaning to suffering and pleasure alike and promised deliverance from death.' This hope built within a sacred community was supplanted, in the second era, by Enlightenment rationality. Abraham Lincoln serves as a harbinger for this phase, which ran roughly until the Vietnam War. During this time, writes Delbanco, 'the promise of self-realization was transformed into the idea of citizenship in a sacred union' (*ibid.* 5). Hope's sustaining narrative transferred from the sacred community of puritan faith to the omnipotent, benevolent, secular state.

Today, with the boy in the principal's office, we find ourselves in the third era. Beginning in approximately the 1960s, hope's underpinning has shifted from the nation to the less certain terrain of the self. The story we tell ourselves as a way of making meaning no longer incorporates sacred communities, or secular nationhood. Rather, it courses its incoherent way through corporate advertising and the prospect of consumable, individual happiness. In the contemporary era, a number of forces 'cooperated in installing instant gratification as the hallmark of the good life, and in repudiating the interventionist state as a source of hope' (Delbanco 1999: 96–7). Corporate logos predominate in our symbolic landscape. As a solid foundation of meaning, however, such symbols lack coherence and sustained narrative force: 'Though vivid and ubiquitous, such symbols will never deliver the indispensable feeling that the world does not end with the borders of the self' (*ibid.* 5). The replacement for the state as a symbolic locus of hope has been the 'vanishing point of the self alone' (*ibid.* 103).

This replacement marks hope's diminution. Personal consumption, buying and owning, desires governed by profit-driven marketing, hardly suffice to assuage our existential quest for meaning. So why have we shifted? Why have we entered here, and abandoned hope? The intrusions of profit-driven media have profoundly influenced desire. Writing thirty-five years ago, Michael Harrington (1966: 28) described it thus:

> Through one of society's most important educators, the advertising industry, all of the techniques of science are used for the private socialization of the public taste. The consumer's 'free' choice is thus engineered and calculated as far as is possible so that it will coincide with the highest profitability to the producer.

Hope diminishes as our visions narrow. It is ironic that we laud our current age as a time of enhanced choice, opting to construe choice within the marketplace as personal choice, ignoring the virtual denial of choice over whether or not to consume. Meaning built upon ownership and consumption is not the faith of hope; it is rather the fractured sense of desire and entitlement. The ubiquity of advertising is the prime culprit. According to John Berger (1972: 131), the advertising which has become ubiquitous 'proposes to each of us that we transform ourselves, or our lives, by buying something more.' The possibilities of this transformation become the governing possibilities as we narrow our focus to our own personal consumption.

Such a focus has been famously described by Christopher Lasch (1979) as the 'culture of narcissism.' For Lasch, as for Delbanco, we drift away from a sense of community, from a sense of the significance of others in our civic society, as we move towards a cultural understanding of a world centered around us as individuals. This is not a world centered around a god, or a world centered around political leaders, or village elders, or even around family. It is a world premised on the importance of immediate gratification, and immediate gratification contradicts a civic life foregrounding responsibility and collective well-being. This narcissistic way of being, built on desire for possession, manipulated by image-makers and representations of 'better lives', interferes with the possibility of hope within civic life. The bombardment by 'the mass culture of romantic escape' pacifies with its distractions and possibilities. Lasch writes (1979: 96):

> The disparity between romance and reality, the world of the beautiful people and the workaday world, gives rise to an ironic detachment that

> dulls pain but also cripples the will to change social conditions, to make even modest improvements in work and play, and to restore meaning and dignity to everyday life.

There is, for Lasch, a difference between what we have and what we want. There is a difference between who we are and who we want to be. The way we cope with these distinctions, through 'ironic detachment,' stifles the desire to alter our lives and better our world. Without the 'will to change' and 'to restore meaning,' hope falters.

Many aspects of the seemingly chaotic organization of contemporary society diminish hope and our 'will to change,' perhaps none so profoundly as the interference with and manipulation of desire. Hope is vocational, and we seek, find, and create foundations for hope as we build meaning and stories and reflect this meaning in symbols. The meaning and attendant symbols reflect, in turn, our understanding of our identities. We attach the symbols to ourselves – the cross or the Star of David on a chain, the flag tattoo – and look to our understandings to provide daily meaning, to help us find answers to the ponderous questions of life and death. We are, currently, bombarded by corporate symbols; we are pulled towards identities of the present, not of the future – and in many cases they are identities we can never inhabit (because they are identities constructed to shape our desire, and our continuous re-desiring). In the controversial film *American Beauty*, Kevin Spacey says to his wife, in effect, as she interrupts a potentially passionate moment with worries about beer spilling on her expensive sofa, 'This is stuff, this isn't life.' He touches on the dilemma of hope and melancholy: in an age when stuff is offered up as meaning in our lives, it is hard to live beyond detachment – whether ironic or not – hard to sustain collective hope outside of consumer aspirations, many of which are shaped to remain unattainable.

This culture of narcissism, and its attendant focus on personal gratification, is multidetermined. And, while its growth is historical and thus caused by human agency, the agency may have been unwitting. In examining his own variation on the theme of Delbanco's era of the self, Harrington describes what he calls the 'Accidental Revolution.' According to Harrington, the technological revolution outpaced civic society's readiness and willingness to harness it for the good of all and for the good of tomorrow. At the same time, the technological revolution created a social revolution uninformed by any thoughtful, democratic process. The advancement of technology has been under private control, and manipulated for private profit. 'This accidental revolution,' Harrington writes (1966: 16), 'is the sweeping and unprecedented technological transformation of the Western environment which has been, and is being, carried out in a casual way … In following their individual aims, industrialists blundered into a social revolution.' The social upheaval bred a new, profound uncertainty; there was no democratic or consensual decision about the changes afoot being promulgated by private entities. 'The accidental revolution,' says Harrington, 'has resulted not in this or that loss of faith, but in introducing doubt and contradiction into every Western creed, secular or religious' (*ibid.* 36). The West 'has lost its utopia to come ... the present decadence is the corruption of a dream rather than of a reality' (*ibid.*17).

This revolution created what Steinberg and Kincheloe refer to as 'hyperreality': 'The information explosion, the media saturation of the late twentieth century with its access to private realms of human consciousness, has created a social vertigo' (Steinberg and Kincheloe 1997: 9); the 'average' American youth has seen more than 380,000 television commercials by the time she or he has graduated from high school (Finnegan 1999: xxi). One trillion dollars a year are spent on marketing in the United States: that is, 'one-sixth of gross domestic product, much of it tax-deductible, so that people pay for the privilege of being subjected to manipulation of their attitudes and behavior' (Chomsky 1999: 58). Hyperreality offers a sensory bombardment in which the meanings, particulary large-scale meanings such as hope, become lost. Steinberg and Kincheloe write (1997: 9):

> Hyperreality's flood of signifiers in everything from megabytes to TV advertising diminishes our ability to either find meaning or engender passion for commitment. With so much power-generated information bombarding the senses, adults and children lose the faith that they can make sense of anything.

People cannot 'make sense of anything,' one assumes, on their own terms. In other words, hyperreality causes less a sense of being overwhelmed – though this may be literally true – and more an abstract sense of powerlessness. Given the power, and money, behind the information overload, what can I do to influence anything? I am simply a consumer of information. My epistemology is receptive, not constructive.[1]

Hyperreality, and the flood of corporate symbols, advertising images, and popular culture stereotypes and icons, are but aspects of the cultural, political and economic ideology known as neo-liberalism. The ideological foundation of neo-liberalism presents perhaps the greatest obstacle to any deeply rooted hope. Neo-liberal ideology assumes the good of a 'neutral' market. It obfuscates power relations and assumes a neutral, technical rationalism which eulogizes private companies while eschewing political analysis and intervention. Large multinational corporations range with reasonable impunity over the globe, finding cheap labor and low rates of taxation – existing beyond the arm of civic control. Neo-liberal assumptions include the good of the market, the 'common sense' of privatization, and the benefits of state disengagement from economic and (many) social structures. The effects of neo-liberalism have been to bolster the wealth of the wealthy, while diminishing the real wages of most working Americans: '... young people and males and those with no advanced degrees ... ' (Finnegan 1999: xiii). 'Neo-liberal doctrines,' writes Noam Chomsky (1999: 32), 'undermine education and health, increase inequality, and reduce labor's share in income.' It is the country's most powerless people, including those people of color living in increasingly entrenched inner-city poverty (Wilson 1996), and the nation's youth, who have experienced the detrimental effects of neo-liberal policies most severely. This is what Finnegan (1999: xvii) calls the 'official and political neglect of children, particularly poor children.'

In a moment, we shall turn to some of the specific effects – on the labeling of youth and on their lives – of the current melancholy, bred in part by the 'self'-centered ideology of neo-liberalism. Here, though, it is important to ask, why we have allowed the inequalities and what I am terming the assault on young people to grow. The answer lies partly within the doctrine of neo-liberalism itself. Neo-liberalism manifests as what John Kenneth Galbraith calls 'the culture of contentment.' This culture describes a social system designed to promote political apathy. 'Central to the economics of contentment,' writes Galbraith (1992: 51), 'is the general commitment to *laissez-faire* … It is an attitude, the belief that it is in the nature of things, and especially of economic life, that all works out for the best in the end.' This false 'optimism' is a way of disguising a myopic focus on short-term personal gain. According to Galbraith (*ibid.* 6): 'the fortunate and the favored, it is more than evident, do not contemplate and respond to their own longer-run well-being. Rather, they respond, and powerfully, to immediate comfort and contentment. This is the controlling mood.' This mood is 'controlling' because the current democracy is, due to polling demographics, a democracy of the contented. Galbraith continues (*ibid.* 10):

> the controlling contentment and resulting belief is now that of the many, not just of the few. It operates under the compelling cover of democracy, albeit a democracy not of all citizens but of those who, in defense of their social and economic advantage, actually go to the polls.

While contentment now belongs to the 'many,' it does not belong to the 'most.' But the many are powerful, and their economic and political actions contribute to hope's diminution by – among other tools of disingenuous 'progress' – sustaining inequality and promoting hyperreality

The 'controlling mood' of contentment, within a neo-liberal ideology, thus limits choice. It allows the profiteers free rein while simultaneously reining in the state; it prioritizes the enhanced wealth of those already invested with political and economic power, at the expense of the longer-run well-being of all citizens. Neo-liberalism, infused as it is with short-term, profit-oriented business interests, is by definition melancholic. And the diminution of choice within it is deeply political. It is only through the active seeking and making of choices, through the recognition of the fundamental, human imperative to engage in thoughtful action, that people avoid falling into hopelessness, and sustain what Freire (1994) calls the 'ontological imperative' of hope.

Labeling the young

The diminution of hope – caused by contentment and by hyperreality, in part – affects the lives of youth; our 11-year-old boy thus becomes a symbol of loss. The short-sighted, profit-driven, media-saturated world inhabited by kids is akin to Dante's 'city of woes.' For many have, albeit unwittingly, 'abandoned' hope – meaning that the surrounding adults have accidentally abandoned the narrative and symbols which provided meaning beyond immediate lives.

This abandonment is reflected and expressed, and in turn influenced, by the language we use. Our labels and our ways of labeling emerge from the controlling mood. The ways in which we name the young, the meanings we invest in labels for kids, both express the predominant melancholy and contribute to it. More pointedly, the ways in which we name the boy in the principal's office first reflect and then influence our understanding, both of the boy and of ourselves. Naming has constructive potential, but in this instance is primarily destructive. Those who impose static, dehumanizing labels born of melancholy cannot live in hope.[2] Sartre, in his essay 'Portrait of the Antisemite,' has written about the ways in which particular forms of naming prohibit thought, development, critical engagement and, implicitly, hope. In Sartre's rendering, the act of naming someone as 'other', of dehumanizing and crudely labeling, is a self-destructive act. 'By adhering to antisemitism,' he writes of the archetypal Antisemite, 'he is not only adopting an opinion, he is choosing himself as a person. He is choosing the permanence and the impenetrability of rock' (Sartre 1975: 345). To label others according to stereotype is to deny one's own humanity, one's own historical place within the world. Such acts of denial are common in relation to young people – one recent commentator, for example, referred to teenagers as 'a tribe apart' (Hersch 1999) – and common in our melancholy age. In short, the way in which we use labels influences us. Further, the ways in which we 'construct' childhood, and treat children, reflect our collective state of being.

Childhood is a social construction, manipulated by those forces and ideologies – particularly popular culture, and the world of work – which powerfully influence social conventions. Historically, the construction of childhood has been relatively recent. The idea of childhood began to emerge in its present form in the Renaissance (Postman 1982: xii; Ariès 1962; Jenks 1996). It has proven particularly malleable, and subsequent ages have conceptualized and re-conceptualized childhood, youth and adolescence – according to technological growth, employment exigencies, the development of psychology, the passing of wars, and so on. The twentieth century, according to Phillipe Ariès, was the age of adolescence, which gradually encroached on both childhood and maturity. As our understandings shifted, so did our definitions, and so did our resulting social behaviors. 'It is as if,' writes Ariès, 'to every period of history, there corresponded a

ge and a particular division of human life: "youth" is the privi-
' the seventeenth century, childhood of the nineteenth, adoles-
twentieth' (1962: 32). This is why, with its child protection and
labor laws, with the expansion of educational provision, and with a
heavy investment in 'adolescence' as a developmental stage, our most recent
century came to be known as the century of the child.

As the century closed, however, the 'privilege' of adolescence or, more
loosely, childhood, was questionable, and unquestionably changing once
again. These shifts – which I am arguing resulted in large part due to the rise
of melancholy, and which in turn have profoundly influenced the lives of
young people – are both reflected within and in turn influenced by the labels
used to describe people between the dependency of infancy and the maturity
of adulthood.

The label 'youth,' for example, reflects a fear of social disorder and a
desire for social control. As a term, it appeared from within the field of sociology near the beginning of this past century. The early understandings of
youth, according to Dick Hebdige, elaborated an 'equation ... between adolescence as a social and psychological problem of particular intensity and the
juvenile offender as the victim of material, cultural, psychological or moral
deprivation' (1988: 27). It is from within this framework that contemporary
elaborations of youth emerged. Youth remains 'youth-as-trouble, youth-in-
trouble' (ibid.) and refers almost exclusively to inner-city kids. The young are
portrayed in the media, including the omnipresent popular cultural media,
as overly sexualized, as slackers or as predators. This is particularly true for
children of color. Mike Males (1999; 1996), in two recent books, has pains-
takingly accumulated evidence of current political (and adult) attacks on
'youth,' and also of the corrupt and dishonest bases for those attacks. Despite
the litany of concerns about rising youth violence, for example, Males demonstrates how there is 'no measure (or honest combination of measures) for
which the statement, "crime is down, but youth violence is up" can be made'
(1999: 32). He shows that the rate of serious offences committed by youths
has gone down by between five and ten per cent over the past twenty years
(ibid. 7), and that 'the average teenager of the mid-1990s is 0.00025 times
more likely to commit murder than the average teen of the 1950s' (ibid. 4).
Nevertheless, images of violent, crime-prone youth persist in our media,
both in that which comprises the news media and in popular culture. The
assaultive labeling of youth is an exemplar of social melancholy.

Hebdige, following on from the 'youth-as-trouble' image, offers a second
conception of youth which emerged in the 1950s. Youth-as-fun neatly
embodies the label 'teenager.' This word, like 'youth,' represents an act of
labeling promoted by a particular ideology, in this case neo-liberal consumerism. The term teenager emerged as a powerful social construction after
the Second World War. This emergence shows the interplay between the
label and the labeled. The label in this instance served as the definition of a
target market. Young people, with new disposable income, responded and

filled out the social category. 'The word "teenager,"' writes Hebdige, 'establishes a permanent wedge between childhood and adulthood. The wedge means money. The invention of the teenager is intimately bound up with the creation of the youth market' (1988: 29–30). Harrington, too, ascribes the birth and growth of teenagers to political and economic forces. 'As a result of Megalopolis and the technological culture which it incarnated, there appeared a generation of adolescents with leisure, money, and mobility,' he writes. 'They constituted a huge market, and tastes were duly fabricated for them' (1966: 20). The accidental revolution thus created the teenager as one element of the new social terrain. The teenager is the embodiment of the commodification of childhood. It is a corporate creation, and thus born into a social space whose symbols and 'story' are more about the self than the world outside the self, more about desire for stuff than fulfilling Freire's ontological need with hope.

This development has since the 1950s been extended into the realm of all children, as childhood has become increasingly commodified. It is now a social construction which Shirley Steinberg and Joe Kincheloe (1997) have usefully contextualized within 'kinderculture.' Kinderculture is that popular 'culture' targeted directly at kids and is produced by profit-seeking corporations. It includes toys, and the ways in which toys are advertised. It includes music, and videos, and films. Kinderculture is a phenomenon, now, because of the large amounts of money spent on marketing and production for children. Drawing a comparison with both teachers and national policy-makers, Steinberg and Kincheloe go so far as to say, 'America's corporate producers of kinderculture are the most influential pedagogues and policymakers' (1997: 10). The education and policy offered by kinderculture is influential, and is racist and classist. Not only does it promote a 'consumption theology' (*ibid*. 11) similar to that described by Berger (1972) above – kinderculture categorizes kids, labels them as particular consumers, imposes on the ways kids understand themselves and their world, and thus alters what it means to be a 'child.' 'Contemporary children's access to commercial kinderculture and popular culture,' write Steinberg and Kincheloe, 'not only motivates them to become hedonistic consumers but also undermines the innocence, the protected status from the tribulations of adult existence' (1997: 16). Kinderculture endangers the very idea of childhood.

Lamentations about the end of childhood are not new. In 1982, Neil Postman wrote of childhood's 'disappearance.'[3] Such ideas are speculative and, in many popular renderings, bewildered. But they all argue essentially that the more we treat kids like adults, the less like kids they remain. According to sociologist Chris Jenks (1996: 117):

> new forms of media are now systematically undermining that distinction
> between child and adult due to an indifference to difference generated
> through economies in production or the drive to create new and

uniform categories of consumer. As a consequence, childhood is disappearing. A child, subject to a diet of violence, sexuality, exploitation and a persistent invitation to consume cannot sustain an autonomous realm of being.

There are profound consequences to this blurring of social identities. As the ideologies of social control and neo-liberalism shape ideas of 'youth' and 'teenager,' they shape the people who inhabit these categories. Childhood's disappearance refers to changing behaviors, desires, and circumstances. The disappearance of childhood both influences and results from melancholy.

Melancholy's consequences

The diminution of hope is our cold-hearted legacy. It is the melancholic underside of affluent times. It is the dark cousin of the immediate gratification of which we are all so enamoured. Finnegan has called this our 'cold new world':

> We jail the poor in their multitudes, abandon the dream of equality, cede more and more of public life to private interests, let lobbyists run government. Those who can afford to do so lock themselves inside gated communities and send their children to private schools. And then we wonder why the world at large has become harsher and more cynical, why our kids have become strange to us. What young people show us is simply the world we have made for them.
>
> (Finnegan 1999: 351)

Males goes even further, suggesting that contemporary adults purposefully target youth, using them as scapegoats:

> What is transpiring today is new and ominous. A particular danger attends older generations indulging 'they-deserve-it' myths to justify enriching ourselves at the expense of younger ones. The message Nineties American adults have spent two decades sending to youths is: *You are not our kids. We don't care about you.*
>
> (Males 1996: 43).

Giroux concurs. 'Put bluntly,' he writes (1997: 37), 'American society at present exudes both a deep-rooted hostility and chilling indifference toward youth, reinforcing the dismal conditions under which young people increasingly are living.' What Finnegan – and Males, and Giroux – attempt to explain is that our children are 'strange to us' because adults have separated kids by entrenching poverty, falling into contentment, and turning up the volume of hyperreality. Our 11-year-old friend in the principal's office confronts a complicated world replete with challenges to hope. Specifically then, what are the immediate consequences of hope's diminution for the young?

Youth is being demonized as possessing adult traits, is being administered as adult, without being proffered any of the rewards of adulthood. In short, youth is being accorded the responsibilities of adult life, without any of the concomitant rights. Young people are thereby easily oppressed, and live within a social domination. In the United States in 1996, 14.5 million children (or 20.5 per cent of the total) were living in poverty, up from 14.4 per cent of all children in 1973 (Children's Defense Fund 1998: 3–4). Marian Wright Edelman claims that 50,000 children were killed by gunfire between 1979 and 1996 (Edelman 1996). Mike Males claims that *most* 'sexually active' girls under the age of 15 were initiated into sex through rape by older males (Males 1996). Child abuse – reported and confirmed cases – is increasing (Preston 1996).

Our current domination of the young also includes the variety of public measures designed to physically confine young people, from mandatory sentencing to boot camps to curfews. Fearful of social disorder – a fear bolstered by contrived and often racialized stereotypes of 'predators' and alienated youth – we have responded with tougher juvenile crime laws, more prisons, and exclusive educational provision. As youth plays out as recalcitrant and uncooperative and fiendish, so we find 'appropriate' institutional pathways and placements. Institutions such as schools and juvenile detention facilities manifest the 'sense' we make of young people. When the sense changes, as it did at the beginning of the century when child labor laws were enacted, institutional responses change; just as now, in an age of receding hope, institutions treat youth differently. Jerome Miller, writing in *Phi Delta Kappan*, elaborates the startling growth of such arrangements across the whole of society:

> As the government investment in social and employment programs in the inner cities was held stable or cut back during the 1980s, the criminal justice system was ratcheted up to fill the void. Federal, state, and local expenditures for police grew 416%; for courts, 585%; for prosecution of legal services, 1,019%; for public defence, 1,255%; and for corrections, 989.5%. Federal spending for justice grew 668%; county spending increased 710.9%; state spending surged 848%.
>
> (Miller 1997: K1)

It is for such reasons, given that so much funding is being channeled into the punishment of juvenile crime, that Giroux writes, 'This is a dangerous time for youth in the United States' (1996: 117). The contemporary mood is one which encourages treating children as adults within the criminal justice system; America is one of the few countries which still executes youth. The conservative cry that such toughening is a response to rising rates of violent juvenile crime is misdirected. 'How surprising,' ask Steinberg and

Kincheloe (1977: 21), 'can child violence figures be when we learn that kids in 60 percent of American homes confront child abuse yearly, including sexual abuse, hitting, and battering – not to mention emotional violence?' And Males offers evidence that our heavy-handed response to 'super-predators' is fostered by political expediency rather than by an honest response to a familiar social problem. Males' point, well proven, is that adult society scapegoats youth, focusing on the behavior of young people, holding it up for vilification and fear and stigmatization, whereas in fact the 'most important predictor of youth behavior is the behavior of adults around them' (1999: 25).

Conclusion

We live in a time when the Children's Defense Fund (CDF) titles a report on young people *Wasting America's Future* (1994). In the introduction to a subsequent CDF yearbook, Marian Wright Edelman acknowledges the progress made in improving the material conditions of many children's lives. 'But shamefully,' she continues, 'high child poverty rates persist, and children are the poorest group of Americans. The gap between America's poor and rich has grown into a chasm, the wages of young families with children have eroded, and many middle-class families are treading economic water' (Children's Defense Fund 1998: xi). This historical moment contains contradictions – volunteerism is up, as is prison-building – but such are the indices of a people in search of meaning beyond consumerism; such are the grand fissures of a society without a sustaining hope. W. B. Yeats, in *The Second Coming*, wrote: 'The best lack all conviction/The worst are full of passionate intensity.' He was writing of Ireland during the merciless civil war of 1921–2, but the sentiment is universal. We are again in the throes of a passion born of melancholy; it is an intensity wrought from troubled, meandering times.

Youth depression and suicide are on the increase. These are symptoms, and not the only ones. By focusing our negative and melancholy attention on youth, shifting its meaning, prescribing its contexts, we are merely attacking such symptoms while the mortification of our society continues unchecked. Our understanding of and treatment of young people can be an expression of our hope, or of its opposite, melancholy. A society targeting its youth as 'a tribe apart' is deeply troubled. It is at war, so to speak, with itself. How telling are our descriptive words, relational words used in isolation: if youth is alienated, it is alienated from something; if young people are marginalized, they are on the periphery of something. In a melancholy age, the vulnerable suffer most. Like adults, like the young people we all were, we respond to our contexts. The young are not a tribe apart, but a group within and among.

It is strange to witness devastation amidst plenty. It is difficult to make sense of the miseries of poverty during affluent times. It is terrible indeed to experience the stone-cold hardness of young people reacting to a hard, cold world. Hyperbole? Perhaps not, as seen in the faces of so many children. Why the American fascination with Frank McCourt's Irish poverty? Does this not suggest some kind of displacement? The political mythology of childhood allows scant room for children these days – so I have focused on our melancholy assault. The assault is both devastating in the present, and ominous for the future. As Giroux points out (1997: 37), 'children and teenagers are losing ground in securing a decent present and future for themselves and others.'

Given the assault how can we pull back? Much of the oppression of the young could be alleviated through lessening poverty. The Children's Defense Fund offers a blatant recommendation. 'If we are truly concerned,' it writes, 'about preventing welfare, teen pregnancy, youth violence, school drop-outs, and crime, then we need to start first by preventing child poverty and ensuring every child a fair start in life' (1998: xii). In order to accomplish this, or any, goal, we need to build a will to change. Such a will is only possible within a context of profound hope. Building hope is thus a political act of tremendous contemporary import.

How do we build hope? By working with young people, not against them. 'A student's hope,' write the Sizers, 'and sense of agency is often dependent on her sense that there is something she can do which is valued by others. Not just other kids, but adults as well' (Sizer and Sizer 1999: 22). We value young people when we refuse to label them, and refuse to accept them as merely markets or stereotypes produced by the mass media or policy 'experts' with hidden agendas. A healthy response to melancholy requires a rejection of official shorthand and an unmasking of kinderculture and the other damaging consequences of neo-liberalism and contentment.

Hope grows within environments created and cultivated by adults – be they parents or teachers or company directors. In the principal's office, we continue to look at the 11-year-old child. And he looks back at us. His gaze is steady, and questioning. What world will we work with him to create? Will we maintain our will to change? Will we look for sustained, narrative meaning within the story we can tell about the building of a more equitable, less melancholy world?

Notes

1 Douglas Rushkoff, a self-styled social critic, calls the current cohort of US kids the 'children of chaos.' He believes that kids today – whom he quaintly describes as 'screenagers' – are several steps ahead of adults. 'We are afraid,' he writes, 'of the universal wash of our media ocean because, unlike our children, we can't recognize the bigger patterns in its overall structure' (1997: 194). By this he means that the unregulated expansion of media, and particularly computer media, has created a disjuncture between parents and kids. Of kids he says, 'Chaos is their natural environment' (*ibid.* 269). Adults look across this divide and panic, it seems, and label as Sartre's antisemite labeled: thoughtlessly, perilously, and self-destructively. But their labeling is not appropriated, for the children of chaos are learning to build their own meanings within the flood of

signifiers. There is potential, Rushkoff argues, for hope. Here, however, we are concerned with the adult response, which labels and dismisses in fear.

2   Freire (1990) talks about this process when he suggests that the act of naming is a political act in that it is undertaken by people who live in the world and who create and re-create that world. He thus warns against the static objectification of the kind leveled at young people through melancholy naming. He writes (1994: 99):

> the oppressor is dehumanized in dehumanizing the oppressed. No matter that the oppressor eat well, be well regarded, or sleep well. It would be impossible to dehumanize without being dehumanized … I am not, I do not be, unless you are, unless you be. Above all, I am not if I forbid you to be.

It is impossible to deny a person's humanity without in some way denying one's own.

3   By now, such theories have entered popular discourse. In 1998, for example, *The Nation* published an essay by Annette Fuentes entitled 'The Crackdown on Kids,' in which she wrote: 'In the past two decades our collective attitude toward children and youth has undergone a profound change that's reflected in the educational and criminal justice systems as well as in our daily discourse … to be young is to be suspect' (Fuentes 1998: 20).

References

Apple, Michael (1990) *Ideology and Curriculum* (2nd edn), New York: Routledge.

Ariès, Philippe (1962) *Centuries of Childhood: A Social History of Family Life* tr. Robert Baldick, New York: Vintage Books.

Berger, John (1972) *Ways of Seeing*, London: Penguin.

Children's Defense Fund (1994) *Wasting America's Future: The Children's Defense Fund on the Costs of Child Poverty*, Boston: Beacon Press.

—— (1998) *The State of America's Children: Yearbook 1998*, Boston: Beacon Press.

Chomsky, Noam (1999) *Profit over People: Neoliberalism and Global Order*, New York: Seven Stories Press.

Coles, Robert (1998) 'Steps, Leaps' in Alice Ross, George Marks and Lee Marks (eds) *Hope Photographs*, New York: Thames and Hudson.

Dante (1994) *The Inferno of Dante* tr. Robert Pinsky, New York: Farrar, Straus and Giroux.

Delbanco, Andrew (1999) *The Real American Dream: A Meditation on Hope*, Cambridge, MA: Harvard University Press.

Edelman, Marian Wright (1996) 'Taking a Stand,' *Emerge*, June 1996: 59–63.

Finnegan, William (1999) *Cold New World: Growing up in a Harder Country*, New York: The Modern Library.

Freire, Paulo (1990) [1970] *Pedagogy of the Oppressed*, New York: Continuum.

—— (1994) *Pedagogy of Hope: Reliving Pedagogy of the Oppressed*, New York: Continuum.

Fuentes, Annette (1998) 'The Crackdown on Kids,' *The Nation*, 15–22 June 1998: 20–22.

Galbraith, John Kenneth (1992) *The Culture of Contentment*, Boston: Houghton Mifflin Co.

Giroux, Henry A. (1996) *Fugitive Cultures: Race, Violence and Youth*, New York: Routledge.

—— (1997) *Channel Surfing: Race Talk and the Destruction of Today's Youth*, New York: St Martin's Press.

Harrington, Michael (1966) *The Accidental Century*, Baltimore: Penguin.

Hebdige, Dick (1988) *Hiding in the Light: On Images and Things*, London: Routledge.

Hersch, Patricia (1999) *A Tribe Apart: A Journey into the Heart of American Adolescence*, New York: Ballantine.

Jenks, Chris (1996) *Childhood*, London: Routledge.

Lasch, Christopher (1979) *The Culture of Narcissism: American Life in an Age of Diminishing Expectations*, New York: W. W. Norton & Co.

Males, Mike A. (1999) *Framing Youth: 10 Myths about the Next Generation*, Monroe, ME: Common Courage Press.

—— (1996) *The Scapegoat Generation: America's War on Adolescents*, Monroe, ME: Common Courage Press.

McCourt, Frank (1996) *Angela's Ashes*, New York: Scribner.

Miller, Jerome G. (1997) 'African American Males in the Criminal Justice System,' *Phi Delta Kappan*, June 1997: K1–K5, K9–K12.

Postman, Neil (1982) *The Disappearance of Childhood*, New York: Vintage Books.

Preston, Samuel H. (1996) 'Children Will Pay,' *New York Times*, 29 September 1996, Magazine: 96–7.

Rushkoff, Douglas (1997) *Children of Chaos: Surviving the End of the World As We Know It*, London: Flamingo.

Sartre, Jean-Paul (1975) 'Portrait of the Antisemite' in Walter Kaufmann (ed.) *Existentialism from Dostoevsky to Sartre* (revised edn), New York: Meridian.

Sizer, Theodore R. and Nancy (1999) *The Students are Watching: Schools and the Moral Contract* Boston: Beacon Press.

Steinberg, Shirley and Kincheloe, Joe L. (1997) *Kinderculture: The Corporate Construction of Childhood*, Boulder, CO: Westview Press.

Wilson, William Julius (1996) *When Work Disappears: The World of the New Urban Poor*, New York: Alfred A. Knopf.

Yeats, W.B. (1996) *The Collected Poems of W.B. Yeats*, second edition, New York: Simon and Schuster.

Schooling

5 Checking the box

The label of 'model minority'

Nina Asher

Umm yeah, my parents expect me to do very well in school. They don't mind if I do badly in one subject ... minor subject like shop or drafting but I should be doing well in stuff like math and sciences ... But, just get good grades and do well because we are smart people, we are Indians, and we should do well.[1]

Anita,[2] an eleventh-grader in a New York City high school

Umm, like, we've like, now there are a lot of Indian gangs too. Like Malayalee Hit Squad, Punjabi By Nature, Madina. Things like that.

Nitin, a twelfth-grader in a New York City high school

Labeling: a way of life

The need to identify, classify, categorize – in other words, create order in one's world – is, very likely, a universal human trait. Labeling is one way of achieving this sense of order: it allows us to create common parameters in order to make recognizable what is around us and find shared bases for our judgments. Labels inform us and carry a wealth of connotative knowledge – in a word or two (for instance, an 'Ivy League' education as opposed to just any higher education) they convey critical information which contributes to our sense-making and decision-making within our larger social context.

The democratic desire to ensure that a free society has an informed citizenry is, perhaps, one reason why we rely on labeling as we do – often, even in the most mundane, quotidian aspects of our lives. For instance, it was here in the United States that I first bought individually labeled pieces of fruit – 'Chiquita' bananas, 'Dole' pineapples, 'Sunkist' oranges and so on. Over the years, I have not been able to overcome my bafflement at this practice of labeling each piece of fruit. (Besides, I find that when I am peeling off the label, I have to be extra careful not to damage the fruit.) I have never understood how this practice benefits society and its members, and am troubled by the utter normalcy of such labeling. Labeling, it appears, is so much a part of life that we scarcely notice how all-pervasive it is, much less question its apparent usefulness, purpose, and effects on the social and individual psyche.

The meanings and (ab)uses of labels such as 'mentally retarded,' 'learning disabled,' and 'dyslexic' have been much debated in education, particularly in the areas of special education and bilingual education. The exclusionary politics and problematic nature of such widely used labels are generally recognized and hotly contested (see, for instance, Brantlinger 1997). By contrast, labels which appear benevolent, positive, and affirming can be seductive even for those labeled, and thus present subtler challenges – for instance, the label of 'model minority,' under which Asian American students have been popularly packaged, is generally perceived as good, attractive, worth having. This apparently positive representation effectively overshadows more problematic considerations such as 'who has the power to define whom and when and how' (McCarthy and Crichlow 1993: xvi).

In this essay I discuss the epistemological and sociopolitical implications of labeling, focusing in particular on the construct of Asian American students as a 'model minority' and the role of this perception in the development of their identities. I argue that the model minority construct is hegemonic (Lee 1996) and succeeds in co-opting those thus labeled. I analyze the narratives of South Asian American high school students in an attempt to understand the process by which this label becomes reified and how this contributes to the oversight of the contradictions and complexities of their lives. I focus here on identifying those forces operating in the lives of these young Asian Americans which shape their academic and career choices. To that end, I consider the influences and interaction of such broad social forces as the desire for middle-class status and the need for financial security, as well as realities specific to the home and school contexts of particular students.

Epistemological implications of labels: inscribing the 'other'

Just as unconsciously as we use (or get used to) labels, we come to see these signifiers as 'true' in and of themselves. Labels get reified, become ways of knowing. They serve as identifiers that help us to know and situate ourselves in relation to others (and vice versa) in the larger social context. Labels become boxes, representing categories and criteria that we can check off to define ourselves and others. Thus they allow us to inscribe an 'other' (Fine 1994).

Labels, then, are a convenience. They offer us a framework which lets us believe that we can know or understand, with a degree of confidence, an individual who appears to be different from us. They allow us to arrive at conclusions about someone on the basis of their race, culture, appearance or name, without having to process any information specific to them. The individual or institution being categorized – 'person of color,' 'immigrant,' 'urban school' – can automatically be assumed to possess certain characteristics generic to that group, *sans* variation. In other words, labels 'pre-package' the individual for us and justify any assumptions we might make about them. They frame and limit our vision, saving us from having to see the complexity of and rethink the 'other.'

For instance, I know myself to be seen primarily as 'Indian' rather than as 'colleague,' or 'faculty member' when – as has happened a number of times – a fellow academic makes a point of weaving 'karma,' or 'Indian' food or music, or even the name of another Indian colleague into the *very first* conversation I happen to have with her, or him. I experience then how it feels to be construed within the frame of 'Indian,' or 'Asian American,' or 'Asian,' or simply 'Other.' I find myself wondering once again if I have been summarily classified and labeled – reduced in that instant to one more check-mark in one more box.

Labels further simplify diversity and difference by enabling the labeler to represent those who are the 'not-me' as a mass of comfortingly blurred 'others.' In an earlier article (Asher 1997: 105) I noted 'the casualness with which various peoples of color get lumped together, labeled as "minorities," and "immigrants" and so on, and treated as mutually interchangeable, thereby rendering their particular identities inconsequential.' That such categorical labeling gets reified into social and historical knowledge is borne out by Spivak's (1993: 54) comment on the mistaken labeling of Native Americans as Asian Indians: 'Subterfuges of nomenclature that are by now standard have almost … obliterated the fact that that name [Indian] lost some specificity in the first American genocide.' Labels, then, enable those in power to maintain the status quo by identifying themselves as distinct from that blurred mass of interchangeable 'others.' They are a device of social control, depicting 'others' in ways most easily or popularly understood and eliminating nuances of complexity, contradiction and variation. Labels do not admit departure. Over time, they become reified, transformed into 'knowledge.'

Under the label of 'model minority' Asian Americans are 'known' to be 'better educated, to be earning as much as any group, to be well assimilated, and to manifest low rates of social deviance' (Chun 1995: 95). Further, the media have portrayed this population as having succeeded, despite past discrimination, in becoming 'a hardworking, uncomplaining minority deserving to serve as a model for other minorities' (*ibid.* 96). Asian American students are defined as hardworking 'whiz kids,' excelling at math and science, high achievers overall in terms of academic performance, and, unlike other students of color, not educationally disadvantaged (Lee 1996; Nakanishi 1995). This popular inscription of Asian Americans as a monolithic model minority ignores the diverse ethnicities, histories, socioeconomic realities and academic concerns of this population.

Recent writings on the education of Asian Americans note the need to document the diversity within this population (Goodwin *et al.* 1996; Nakanishi 1995; Pang 1995). Issues such as the educational achievement levels of Asian Americans (see Nakanishi 1995), their representation in teaching and teacher education (see Goodwin *et al.* 1997; Rong and Preissle 1997), and the inclusion of the voices and concerns of Asian American students (see Lee 1996) are some of the areas in which researchers are unearthing diverse and, at times, troubling realities. However, even as such findings emerge, the notion persists within the larger social context that Asian Americans are, uniformly, a 'model minority.'

Lee, referring to the 'absent voice(s) of Asian America,' notes that Asian Americans have been 'simultaneously ignored and exalted in the US imagination,' and are typically left out of the discourse on diversity:

> perhaps the most insidious reason given for excluding Asian voices from the discourse on race is the stereotype that Asians do not have any problems (i.e., they are model minorities). In the minds of most Americans, minorities like African Americans, Latinos, and Native Americans are minorities precisely because they experience disproportionate levels of poverty and educational underachievement. The model minority stereotype suggests that Asian Americans are 'outwhiting whites' and have overcome discrimination to be more successful than whites ... when Asians are included in the discourse on race it is usually to talk about their 'success.' Asian Americans are described as hardworking entrepreneurs who are doing well economically (e.g., Korean merchants), and they are described as hardworking students who excel in math and science (e.g., Asian American whiz kids). While Asian Americans are stereotyped as model minorities, other racial minorities are stereotyped in overtly negative ways.
>
> (Lee 1996: 5)

This 'insidiousness' of the 'model minority' label is a seductive force which can lure those labeled into contributing to its reification, because, after all, which one of us would not want to know ourselves as 'successful' and be recognized, particularly by those wielding power, as such? It is also seductive because it allows the 'labelers' to recognize themselves as willing to acknowledge, able to accept, indeed open to the success of a 'minority' population. Questions as to who is labeling whom and to what end can then be ignored. And this insidiousness is dangerous – it makes those who come under the label complicit in the oversight of their own struggles, allowing these to remain unaddressed. It is also dangerous because it serves to pit one minority community against others, thereby allowing those in power to 'divide and rule.' Ultimately, then, the seductive nature of this label is dangerous because it first puts into circulation the notion that Asian Americans are 'the model minority,' and then *invites them to realize it – making them known for and, in fact, identified only by their achievements.*

The politics of labeling and the construction of a 'model minority'

In discussing 'the politics of location, positionality, or enunciation' in relation to rethinking identity and difference in a postmodern multicultural context, McLaren (1994) notes the contested character of the signifiers used in the process of constructing identities. The fact that the model minority construct has been created by those of the dominant culture in order to situate and define Asian Americans as a minority community is overshadowed by the apparent desirability of the preferred status and identification it affords them. Lee (1996) contends that the model minority stereotype is a hegemonic device which serves to hide the diverse and complex experiences of Asian Americans, lumping diverse Asian ethnicities into one racial/panethnic group, silencing their multiple voices, and creating a 'monolithic monotone.' Furthermore, by imposing the categorical label of 'model minority' on Asian Americans, the dominant group has denied their experiences of poverty, illiteracy and racism (Lee 1996) and has engendered a 'restricted self-definition' and a 'sense of lost identity' among Asian Americans (Chun 1995).

In their desire to be accepted by the dominant group, Asian Americans may be tempted to live up to the model minority stereotype because this seems 'positive and even flattering when compared with the stereotypes of other racial minorities' (Lee 1996: 7). Therefore, as a hegemonic device, 'the model minority stereotype maintains the dominance of whites in the racial hierarchy by diverting attention away from racial inequality and by setting standards for how minorities should behave' (*ibid.* 6). Thus, more generally, it may be argued that the co-optive dynamics of the process by which such social constructions are shaped can also be understood in terms of communities and individuals who 'participate in discourse in local, often idiosyncratic ways, both resisting and becoming complicit in their own moral regulation' (Luke 1995: 9). In other words, both the specific individual and the larger community are implicated in internalizing the oppression of the label.

Given this analysis of the label of 'model minority' as a social and political device which effectively reifies the marginalization of Asians in the United States, I turn now to the stories of ten South Asian American high school students[3] in order to illuminate further this process of reification. In particular, I focus on those aspects of their stories which factor directly into the model minority construct – for instance, negotiations around academic achievement and career choice. I problematize and examine the apparent academic competence and proclivity for financially secure, and, typically, science- or business-related careers on the part of these students in the context of the broader social forces which shape the expectations they encounter at home and in school, as well as their own particular educational realities and concerns. Their stories reveal the process by which they make choices about their academic and career paths and bring to light the struggles and contestations which shape their identities and their visions of their future selves. For purposes of clarity I must point out here that, throughout the study, the participants were simply talking about themselves in relation to the four areas raised in the interviews and not in terms of the model minority construct. (In fact, as I write, I find myself wondering if any of them might even have been aware, at that time, that a label exists which thus defines them – tidily wrapping up all their struggles in just two words.)

In the sections that follow, I focus on the following questions in order to examine closely the model minority construct as it relates to the lives of these young South Asian Americans. What kinds of messages do these students receive regarding their career options and choices? What kind of academic preparation is considered necessary? Why? How do these students process these messages? And what kinds of decisions do they make in terms of attending college and choosing careers?

If indeed the lived experiences of Asian American students are more complex and nuanced than conveyed by the simple characterization of 'model minority,' what aspects get marginalized? Finally, how does the label itself operate as a social force – at the broad and local level – in this process?

Constructing the Asian American self as an academic and professional success story

Common to the stories of all ten participants in my study was the expectation from those at home and at school that they would excel academically, make 'good grades,' and work towards getting into a 'good college.' All the participants expected to earn at least one degree and to work at jobs which ensured their financial security. In the paragraphs that follow I share the voices of these South Asian American high school students as they discussed: their experience and negotiation of the external and internal pressures they encountered in the course of learning to excel at academics; the long-range planning and preparation, particularly within the home context, for financially viable careers; and their experiences as Asian Americans within the school context.

People at home consistently expected excellent grades and usually encouraged (sometimes to the point of insistence) the participants to prepare for professional occupations, often in science-related fields. For instance, as Sharmila put it:

> [My parents] want what's best for me, like most parents do. But I think they expect, like, a lot more than most parents ... Y'know, I'll come home and say, 'Oh, I got a ninety-six on my test,' and, I don't know if they are joking or they're serious, but they'll say, 'Where'd the other four points go?'

In contrast, the school context generally allowed them a greater degree of flexibility and was more supportive of any diversity in academic and career interests on their part. For example, according to Nitin the teachers and guidance counselors at school encouraged students to explore different options in terms of the curricular offerings:

Yeah. Like that's why they've different types classes required, so if you are interested in some other things, then you can always try everything out. And then pick, like, you know, decide what you like ... what you want to do.

Another student, Poonam, talked about people at school recognizing effort on the part of students, '[People at school] say that if you are working very hard at an AP class and you are getting a B plus that's very good, cuz they rarely give out As in AP class.' However, despite the greater openness within the school context, overall these young South Asian Americans experienced pressure in terms of working hard to meet the high standards expected by those at home and at school.

At the same time, they talked about their attempts to rationalize this pressure to excel by either questioning or dismissing their experience, or recognizing their internalization of it in terms of working hard to achieve. This was illustrated by the following exchange with Vijay:

VIJAY: [My parents] want me to perform at my highest level. Make very good grades. I mean they don't necessarily say anything to pressure me, but ... I know they expect me to do very well.

NA: Right. So you don't feel any obvious, stated pressure?

VIJAY: Well, it's weird, I suppose. Because I am saying that they don't put the pressure on me and yet I feel it, so then I guess they do. I know that if I did not do well academically they would not like it, and so, I guess, I put the pressure on myself.

NA: Well, how d'you mean?

VIJAY: I mean I know that they expect that I will make very good grades, even if they don't say it in as many words. And so, then I don't want to disappoint them, so I make myself work harder. So, I feel the pressure, their expectation, and try to meet it. I know that as long as I try to do my best, they won't have a major fit.

In addition, these students were aware that they were constructed as high achievers both within and without the home, particularly because they are Asian – witness Anita's words at the beginning of this essay. Thus, their very Asianness was seen as sufficient reason by those at home and at school to expect academic excellence. As Anita elaborated:

Like, especially Asian – Indians, Chinese everybody – they expect to do well. Because that is our persona ... And we expect ourselves to do well ... But a lot of others, like the Black people and White people and the Spanish, they either wanta do well, or they don't ... And that's accepted.

It appears then that this expectation to excel academically is embodied in Asian American students and recognized as their particular identity, distinguishing them from students of other racial backgrounds. This expectation also colored their involvement in extra-curricular activities at school.

To the extent that the parents of these students realized that extra-curricular activities are an integral part of schooling in the United States, they accepted that some involvement in them is necessary for their children to develop a competitive college profile. If the particular extra-curricular activity was seen as helpful in developing a competitive profile for college – for example a Westinghouse research project in biology for those aiming for a pre-med program – or if it was seen as having 'prestige value,' then it was more likely to meet with parental approval. According to Mary,

> [My parents] both agree that leadership in school or in clubs and stuff like that equals kind of like leadership in later life, which is what they'd like for me. It's just, you know, the status thing again … they do respect that I have a job at [this highly reputed] medical school.

Such expectations in relation to extra-curricular activities, underpinned by a general achievement-oriented attitude to school, prescribed the involvement of these young South Asian Americans in their schooling and did not always allow them to partake of all the opportunities that school offered them.

A rather obvious factor within the larger social context which influences this expectation of success at school is the desire to ensure future economic and professional success. To that end, the people at home typically expected these students to 'take relevant courses' which would help them prepare for college and to follow appropriate career paths such as medicine or business which would guarantee financial success. For instance, Poonam's parents expected her to take classes that 'challenge [her] a lot,' and her father wished for her to 'take lots of science classes and do well at them,' so that she could 'be a doctor.' Poonam was aware that her parents were motivated by their concern for her future happiness:

> [My parents] want the best for me. And they see that – you see – that some of the most prosperous people in this country are doctors and, like, I know a lot of them, a lot of kids in this school, their parents are doctors and so they see that doctors have a good income. So they figure that if I am a doctor, I'll make money and I won't be needing anything, I won't be lacking anything in my life.

Messages regarding the need to focus on future economic success were systematically delivered to these young Asian Americans in various ways, and reflected long-range planning on the part of their parents. For instance, these students received specific suggestions and detailed directions from their parents – their fathers in most cases – with regard to planning for future academic and professional pursuits. According to Poonam,

Yeah [my parents] want very good grades. Like they want A plus for every-thing. If not A plus then A. But my average is about an A minus and I am happy with it because I am working hard and I know I am doing well. But my dad's very strict with this, he thinks I might not get into a good pro-gram – he wants me to get into a … six- or seven-year program at some college, so I don't have to do eight years for med. school.

Similarly, Mary's mother was already planning to babysit for Mary when, years hence, she was going to be a very busy doctor. And although Mohan's 'B' average indicated that he had held out against expectations of academic excellence, he was aware that he had given in to and, in fact, internalized parental demands when it came to career choice:

All right, with my parents, my father's a doctor, my mother's a doctor, most of my aunts and uncles are doctors. So, ever since I was a kid, I was raised to understand that I'd be a doctor. Know what I'm sayin'? I was never really given the option of searching around, 'OK, do whatever you want.' Like, they had, they had accounts ready for me to go to med. school, y'know … So, I mean, it's not my goal, it's what I was given. And I mean, now it is sort of ingrained, cuz I have been brainwashed. D'you know I wanta be a doctor [*with a wry laugh*]. You know, it wasn't really my goal.

Mohan's words reflected his sophisticated understanding of how, in spite of himself, he ended up believing that he did want to pursue medicine. Ironically, he was also aware that his self-knowledge was to no avail when it came to resisting parental demands regarding career choice, because by this point in his life he had internalized the expectations which had infused the context of his home from his formative years.

One of the thrusts regarding career choice was the push from home for science-related fields, particularly medicine, over humanities and the social sciences. For instance, Mohan traced the evolution of his career plans, begin-ning with his wanting to be a cop when he was a kid:

I switched to veterinary medicine, which I really like a lot. And then I switched to animal behaviorology, and then to psychology. But, er, then, er, I guess I matured. [My parents'] expectations to go to medicine, you know, sort of, came down to me. So, I switched. I don't know if it's to sat-isfy them, but I still want to experience psycho[logy], behaviorology – that's why I am thinking psychiatrist.

Here, although Mohan abandoned the idea of veterinary work, he struggled to marry his own interests and those of his parents. And Mary's mother, although proud of her daughter's talent in art, relegated it to the margin as 'only a side hobby,' not to be confused with serious professional pursuits.

Similarly, when Poonam had expressed interest in psychiatry, her father informed her that 'psychiatrists are crazy, crazier than their patients.' And with regard to a career as a journalist or a writer – 'something different,' according to Poonam – her father said such activities were meant for one's 'spare time.' Poonam was given the choice of becoming a doctor or a lawyer, and came to know herself as a future doctor. She said: 'I accept it. It's a set thing. Part of being an Indian family – you have to, like, accept certain things. So, like, that's one of the things I have accepted.'

The above segments from the participants' stories reveal how they encountered messages, particularly from those at home, to excel academically and succeed financially. It can be argued that the parents of these students, as immigrants to the United States, had to work to establish themselves, and therefore desired financial security and middle-class status for their children. However, this material or socioeconomic desire, understandable though it may be, serves to eliminate a range of career options and interests, including the profession of teaching, thus, unwittingly, reifying the model minority stereotype.

Parental expectations and preferences, then, shaped by socioeconomic forces and considerations, serve to guide these students down 'safe,' 'respectable,' and tried-and-true career paths and to prevent their own personal explorations and expressions of difference. Cultural factors also contribute to the students' compliance – sooner or later, and to varying degrees – with parental wishes. Ironically, while the model minority label highlights the 'end result'– the Asian American whiz kid – what gets lost are the negotiations these young Asian Americans engage in, their efforts to resist being railroaded into careers which may not appeal to them, and the gradual process by which they end up accepting or at least falling in with parental wishes.

Further, the fact that Asians in America are generally perceived as compliant, hardworking, and successful contributes to the image of them as a desirable minority which can be incorporated into existing socioeconomic structures without the risk of repercussions. Such apparently benign characterizations become part of the self-knowledge of Asian Americans and, in effect, ensure that they do live by the label in order to continue being accepted within the mainstream context. Thus, Asian Americans internalize the oppressor (Freire 1982; hooks 1990) and remain on the margins in a number of fields such as 'social sciences, humanities, and arts, whose primary vehicle for professional activities is either linguistic communication or interpersonal contacts' (Chun 1995: 105). Therefore, in terms of 'story,' 'representation' and 'voice,' Asian American narratives are generally absent in the very arenas which offer opportunities to focus on these issues.

The profession of teaching provides a clear example. Although the field of education could serve as a site of self-representation, such intersecting socioeconomic forces as financial security and prestige operate to draw Asian Americans away from teaching, co-opting them in their own marginalization. For instance, according to Sanjoy it was because of 'the money issue' that his parents were not supportive of his interest in becoming a teacher. Anita had a similar story. Her parents, she said, had no arguments with her choosing accounting as a career: 'They don't care what I do, as long as I am happy.' However, practically in the same breath she continued:

> But I'd always wanted to be a teacher, but, my mother is like, 'No!' ... because they don't think it's a high ... high enough paying job. They think if I want to be a college professor it is fine – that pays well. But kindergarten ... I want to teach, like, children, but they don't like that because it's not like high, like, well paying enough.

Although Anita's parents 'think all the fields respectable,' it appears that they were indeed making assumptions about prestige when they endorsed a career as a college professor but vetoed teaching young children. Further, Anita expressed prestige as a consideration in terms of 'skilled' and 'unskilled' jobs:

NA: Are there other fields that they rule out, other than teaching?

ANITA: They like law, medicine, anything to do with math. They like most topics, except for teaching, social work and stuff like that.

NA: So, teaching, and social work and stuff like that because again ... ?

ANITA: It's not high paying enough. They don't like anything that's, like, sanitation work. They don't like that because it's like non ... It's not really a skilled job. They don't mind anything that's in the skilled areas, except for teaching and anything that is not well paying.

So here Anita, who knew of her interest and ability as a teacher – 'I like teaching kids, I am good at it ... I am a pretty good teacher' – ended up focusing on accounting as a career choice, and equating teaching with such apparently unskilled jobs as 'sanitation work.'

As young Asian Americans, Mohan, Mary, Poonam, Sanjoy, and Anita internalized messages from home and learned to stay on the straight and narrow path in terms of their academic and career choices. Their stories reveal the parental and familial expectations conveyed to them both verbally and non-verbally from their earliest days, and their resultant efforts to resist these expectations and to negotiate alternatives even as they found themselves giving in. As these Asian American high school students yielded to parental wishes, they ended up rethinking themselves, modifying their hopes and dreams. They came to know themselves as future doctors and business-people rather than as psychiatrists, social workers, teachers, writers, and artists. They ended up fitting into the frame of the 'successful' model minority, thereby unwittingly contributing to their own marginalization and the reification of the construct.

By contrast, the school context generally offered these students greater flexibility and choice regarding their academic and career options, and encouraged their involvement in extra-curricular activities. In particular the messages from their teachers and guidance counselors at school differed from those they got from parents, in that they allowed for a 'greater degree of openness.' In Nitin's words, the approach of people at school was 'Just do as much as you can. Participate as much as you can. Experience as much as you can. Try different things.' And according to Mary, in terms of how best to prepare for one's career, her teachers and guidance counselors encouraged students to be well rounded by diversifying their experiences and exploring their options:

> So, they're trying to let you see what, what that environment looks like and see if your perspective changes. I mean because, like, again, every experience changes you and you might decide, 'Wow! I really don't like that.' So, I think that's what your teachers and guidance counselors try to encourage. That you actually go, and, like, look at what they do, and then think for yourself whether that's something that you would want.

However, this greater openness within the school context was partially offset for these young Asian Americans by other expectations based on popular images and constructions of Asians in America. As the following conversation with Vijay illustrates, the school context also conveyed messages which prescribed and limited their options:

VIJAY: You know, one thing is that people expect that if you are Asian you'll be a doctor. They'll say, 'Oh, you're Asian, so you'll want to be a doctor.' And you do see a lot of Asian doctors around.

NA: Right … Expectation … And what about things like prestige, respectability, only option for men – do these come into the minds of school people?

VIJAY: Even this thing about Asian doctors, it is particularly expected of Asian males. If you are an Asian male you are going to be a doctor. It is connected with making enough money, security.

NA: OK. Asian males in particular.

VIJAY: There are so many Asian doctors around – mostly men, and so many Asian students opt for medicine …

NA: So you are thinking of Asian males in medicine, hah?

VIJAY: It's a fact but also it is an invented fact or truth.

NA: How d'you mean?

VIJAY: I mean people say that there are lots of Asian doctors and that Asians mostly go for medicine, but that's an invented fact, kind of, because it's not true that only Asians are doctors. They just notice them. There are other [non-Asian] doctors around but somehow they don't get noticed as much as the Asians.

According to Vijay's analysis above, it appears that students of Asian descent – particularly males – were automatically expected to opt for the medical field and were highlighted as such, although there were students of other racial backgrounds who also went to medical school. The contradictions and dynamic tensions in deconstructing such perceived social realities are evident in the above dialectic as Vijay moves from describing the presence of 'many Asian doctors' as 'a fact' to 'an invented fact.' Such stereotypical representations of Asian American students serve automatically not only to direct them towards certain career paths, but also to eliminate other options for them, thus belying the apparent openness within the school context.

A related image the participants frequently confronted within the school context was that students of Asian descent are 'smart': academically competent. Despite the 'greater degree of openness' – the encouragement to explore their options and diversify their interests – within the school context, as Asian Americans these students were expected by their teachers to earn consistently high grades. Mohan, the exception with a 'B' average, was aware that his teachers wished for him to emulate his South Asian American peers and improve his academic performance:

> [My teachers] tell me that I am really smart, but, er, I mean, I'll admit it, I am sort of lazy … I'm not laaazy, I'm not, like, spoilt or anything. I just don't find myself motivated. So, for them, they expect out of me, not to work harder, but to keep me awake … And most of the students you find here, the South Asian [American] kids, they're getting As, I'm sure. But most of them are like, er, their parents are really strict. My parents are too. I just don't find myself motivated.

Mohan's stated 'laziness' and 'lack of motivation' can be interpreted as expressions of resistance which allow a departure from the frame of being a 'model' Asian American student. Ironically, this very resistance, and Mohan's stated exceptionality, served to underscore the 'norm' of South Asian American and other Asian American students excelling academically – once again reifying the model minority stereotype.

Sharmila, the participant who distanced herself the most from sources of Indian identification, observed how students of Indian descent are generally perceived as 'quiet' at school. In fact, her words reveal her own complicity with this notion:

> Like, I think some people have a certain view, they have, like, a pre-set notion of what, like, an Indian person, like, an Indian student, or child, or whatever would be like. They usually tend to be more quiet and whatever, like, and very smart and whatever. And sometimes, like, I don't know, like, most of the Indian students in this school they are, like, quiet, and, like, you know, most of them are very smart kids. So, I think, you know, that that makes the thing believable … Like, I know myself, I'm not quiet and, like, I've been friends with a lot of people in my grade since fifth grade, so I don't think they see me as any different from themselves.

The external and internal perception of 'Indian' students generally being 'quiet' and 'very smart' can be examined in relation to the 'greater degree of openness' at school in terms of the options that these students were, in fact, able to explore and develop. Such characterizations, along with popular notions – within and outside the school context – of Asian American students as future doctors, served to reify the model minority construct, thereby creating a subtext which contradicted the apparent openness of the school context.

Once again, both Mohan and Sharmila, like Vijay, point to the tension between fact and perception, which, to cite Sharmila's astute observation, 'makes the thing believable.' Such is the insidiousness of the label. Further, the school context can be understood as the site at which representations from the larger social context translate into the particular expectations that Asian American students encounter. These representations seem to be further reified as they intersect with the expectations from home which the students attempt so hard to meet. Through a different lens, the Asian American student embodies a contested site where expectations from parents and school, social fact and perception, and the student's own participation in and resistance to being boxed in criss-cross one another, creating a paradoxical pattern of validation and contestation, making it difficult to peel off the label.

Discussion

Given the unrelenting push for academic achievement and the career-driven messages from home, it is not surprising that Asian American students learn to work hard, strive for excellence and identify themselves as 'smart.' As the messages from home and school reinforce each other, these young South Asian Americans internalize them to make their way along traditionally 'safe' career paths and are seen as success stories, thereby reifying the model minority construct. However, despite this obvious 'success,' they are in fact multiply marginalized by the label: their status as a model minority is defined by those within the dominant context; the focus on academic success and financially viable careers ignores the fact that their representation in the social sciences and humanities is curtailed; their struggles to represent themselves and realize their interests remain submerged; and they are sectioned off from students from other minority communities.

The internalized desire to ensure financial security, social respectability and acceptability as part of the middle class drives these students to comply with parental expectations and pursue science- and business-related academic and career paths instead of developing their particular talents and doing 'something different,' as Poonam would say. This echoes Lee's (1996) conclusions that issues of social class and perception of future opportunities are significant variables in the identity formation of Asian American students, influencing their perception of their positionality in society. Even as these students critique popular constructions of Asian Americans they contribute to their realization, recognizing such traits as 'being quiet,' 'being smart,' and 'achieving high grades' as characteristic of and integral to the persona of Asian American students. Thus they participate in their own labeling and marginalization.

However, expressions of difference on the part of young South Asian Americans are becoming increasingly evident today – witness Nitin's words at the beginning of this essay. Similarly, Sengupta's (1996) article in the *New York Times*, 'To be young, Indian and hip: Hip-hop meets Hindi pop as a new generation of South Asians finds its own groove,' describes how young South Asian Americans are locating themselves in new, hybrid cultural spaces, through such forms of expression as music and dance. In her 1996 study Lee found that those students of Asian descent who systematically rejected the model minority stereotype critiqued it as a racist device, 'inaccurate and harmful to interracial relationships between Asian Americans and other racial minorities.'

Despite these contrasting realities and identifications, the model minority stereotype endures. As Lee (1996: 125) documented:

> As I sit talking to Mr Engen, the teacher in charge of the computer room, the subject of Asian American student achievement surfaces. Mr Engen is bubbling over with praise for his Asian American students. After listening for some minutes, I decide to question his understanding of Asian Americans as model minorities. Mr Engen understands that I am critical of the stereotype, but before I can complete my thought, he stops me and says, 'Please don't ruin my stereotype. It is such a nice one.' Thus, once again, I learn one of the secrets to the endurance of the model minority stereotype.

Mr Engen's words indicate that the label no longer needs to operate insidiously – it is legitimated as a rather pleasant, complimentary perception of Asian Americans, making it so easy to affix and so difficult to relinquish or resist.

In order to deconstruct the label of 'model minority' and bring to light the diverse educational realities of Asian Americans, educational researchers need to continue documenting the stories of Asian American students and sharing them within the field of education – in the curriculum of the school as well as in teacher education (Goodwin *et al.* 1997). Further, the lived realities of Asian American students need to be shared beyond the educational context so that they are no longer depicted as an uncomplaining and problem-free minority community in the public imagination. And, finally, if we are to arrest further reification of the model minority stereotype, we need to inform and engage in dialogue with the parents and communities of these students (as well as other minority students) regarding their lives at school and the range of academic and career options available to them. If we make it more possible for Asian American students to depart from traditionally 'safe' academic and career paths, they will be able to participate more fully in their educational and social contexts and move beyond the confines of the box marked 'model minority,' into new spaces of re-presentation.

Notes

1   These two opening quotes are segments of raw data from the study on which this essay draws.
2   Pseudonyms have been used for all the participants and are matched for regional and religious background.
3   I draw on data gathered for my dissertation study, during which I conducted a series of three in-depth interviews with ten female and male seniors and juniors in two schools in New York City about messages from home and school regarding academic achievement and career choice, and social behavior and identity.

References

Asher, N. (1997) 'Apache Indian's Syncretic Music and the Representation of South Asian Identities: A Case Study of a Minority Artist,' *Taboo: The Journal of Culture and Education*, Spring 1997: 99–118.

Brantlinger, E. (1997) 'Using Ideology: Cases of Nonrecognition of the Politics of Research and Practice in Special Education,' *Review of Educational Research*, 67(4): 425–59.

Chun, K. (1995) 'The Myth of Asian American Success and Its Educational Ramifications' in D. T. Nakanishi and T. Y. Nishida (eds) *The Asian American Educational Experience: A Source Book for Teachers and Students* (95–112), New York: Routledge.

Fine, M. (1994) 'Working the Hyphens: Reinventing Self and Other in Qualitative Research' in N. K. Denzin and Y. S. Lincoln (eds) *Handbook of Qualitative Research* (70–82), Thousand Oaks, CA: Sage.

Freire, P. (1982) *Pedagogy of the Oppressed*, New York: Continuum.

Genishi, C. S., Goodwin, A. L., Asher, N. and Woo, K. A. (1997) 'Voices from the Margins: Asian American Teachers' Experiences in the Profession' in D. M. Byrd and D. J. McIntyre (eds) *Research on the Education of our Nation's Teachers: Teacher Education Yearbook V* (219–41), Thousand Oaks, CA: Corwin Press.

Goodwin, A. L., Genishi, C. S., Woo, K. A. and Asher, N. (1996) *Growing up Asian in America: The Role of Social Context and Education in Shaping Racial and Personal Identity*, paper presented at the annual meeting of the American Educational Research Association, April 1996, New York.

hooks, b. (1990) *Yearning: Race, gender, and cultural politics*, Boston, South End.

Lee, S. J. (1996) *Unraveling the 'Model Minority' Stereotype: Listening to Asian American Youth*, New York: Teachers College Press.

Luke, A. (1995) 'Text and Discourse in Education: An Introduction to Critical Discourse Analysis' in M. W. Apple (ed.) *Review of Research in Education*, 21: 3–48, Washington, DC: AERA.

McCarthy, C. and Crichlow, W. (1993) 'Introduction: Theories of Identity, Theories of Representation, Theories of Race' in C. McCarthy and W. Crichlow (eds) *Race, Identity, and Representation in Education* (xiii–xxix), New York: Routledge.

McLaren, P. (1994) 'Multiculturalism and the Post-modern Critique: Toward a Pedagogy of Resistance and Transformation' in H. A. Giroux and P. McLaren (eds) *Between Borders: Pedagogy and the Politics of Cultural Studies* (192–222), New York: Routledge.

Nakanishi, D. T. (1995) 'Growth and Diversity: The Education of Asian/Pacific Americans' in D. T. Nakanishi and T. Y. Nishida (eds) *The Asian American Educational Experience: A Source Book for Teachers and Students* (xi–xx), New York: Routledge.

Pang, V. O. (1995) 'Asian American Children: A Diverse Population' in D. T. Nakanishi and T. Y. Nishida (eds) *The Asian American Educational Experience: A Source Book for Teachers and Students* (167–79), New York: Routledge.

Rong, X. L. and Preissle, J. (1997) 'The Continuing Decline of Asian American Teachers,' *American Educational Research Journal*, 34(2), 267–93.

Sengupta, S. (1996) 'To Be Young, Indian and Hip: Hip-hop Meets Hindi Pop as a New Generation of South Asians Finds Its Own Groove,' *New York Times*, 30 June 1996: CY1, CY11.

Spivak, G. C. (1993) *Outside in the Teaching Machine*, New York: Routledge.

6   Labeling and English language learners

Hearing recent immigrants' needs

Peter W. Dillon

Labels can be used by those in power to control or marginalize the powerless. Occasionally when the disenfranchized come to power, they use labels, often with good intentions, in a similar way. Inadvertently, as Freire (1970) writes, the formerly oppressed can easily slip into the role of oppressor.

The recent history of bilingual education in the New York City public schools, especially the development of policies and the administration of English as a second language (ESL) programs, exemplifies such displacement in power and leadership, as well as the contradictions of newly imposed 'beneficial' labels. Those once on the edge have come to rule a portion of a tremendous bureaucracy, serving in total more than 1.1 million students. Their decisions directly impact on hundreds of thousands of students, parents, teachers, and administrators, and indirectly influence textbook publishers, colleges, and the city's economy.

Systems initially intended to empower recent immigrants have had a range of unexpected results. Combating traditional and conservative notions of forced assimilation has created wonderful nurturing learning environments and affirmed cultural identities, but has simultaneously labeled students out of the educational mainstream (Dentler and Hafner 1997). In turn, while ESL students have been granted access to specialized teaching and learning intended to meet their needs, they have been denied access to knowledge and power from other contexts.

Such contradictions are not unique to New York; similar policies and programs exist around the country and the world. The New York City public schools, however, offer a startlingly unambiguous portrait of the consequences of a purportedly empowering educational program – particularly when viewed from the perspective of students.

As a teacher and administrator working within the ESL system, I shall examine in this essay the complexities of labeling in relation to how the 'labeled' feel about their labels. Initially I shall explore historical trends in ESL policies and the implications of these for teaching and learning in the New York City public schools. Then I shall examine how those policies are implemented in two divergent school contexts. Finally, I shall explore the importance of labeling from students' perspectives. Perhaps through listening to students' voices, transformative opportunities – in the spirit of Doll (1993) – may be created to encourage dialogue across polarized ideological, curricular, and political camps. Asking and then really listening to students, a seemingly simple and obvious task, may enable us to break out of traditional ruts and rethink how to use labels in our students' – and not our systems' or our own – best interests.

The means of labeling

In thinking about what contributes to and what comes from labeling English language learner (ELL) students, it's easy to get caught up in pointing fingers at what is wrong with the system. My initial interest in this topic was stirred five years ago when, as a high school teacher in the Bronx, I was asked by a Dominican student when we would be taking the language assessment battery (LAB) test. She wanted to go to college and hoped to get out of ESL.

I quickly found out that the LAB test is something unique to New York City that is used to determine whether ESL programs are making progress. Each year this test is ritualistically given, taking up many hours of class and administrative time. I also came to learn that the test may not measure what it purports to assess. As a teacher, I thus became responsible for administering a mediocre assessment that influences the lives of all my students and many hundreds of thousands of students throughout the system. Few students pass it. Students with strong communicative skills often do not do well. Students with weak skills might end up with higher scores than proficient students. Perhaps most alarmingly, the test simply is not fair. It is composed of four sections: reading, reading comprehension, listening, and speaking. The first three sections are multiple-choice and based on peculiar jargon-filled topics such as trigger fish and shell collecting. The speaking section, which is open-ended and more authentic, is not included in the scoring. On the basis of its content, many native English-speaking students would not pass this test and would be mandated to take ESL.

As I grew as a teacher and gained confidence, I started asking questions. Why did we have to give the LAB test? What did it measure? Could we change it? I approached the test coordinator, my assistant principal, colleagues in other schools, staff developers, and even a member of the Board of Education. Again and again I was told to focus on my teaching, give the test, and encourage students to do well. It became clear that the system had created a measure, a culture around it, and a reluctance to reconsider its purpose and consequences. The LAB test had become an effective and efficient means to separate a group of students out of the mainstream.

One illustration of the marginalizing intent concerns the passing point, which was raised from 21 per cent to 41 per cent. I was told that too many students were leaving ESL and that they were unsuccessful in regular English classes. Rather than looking at what was happening in regular English classes, perhaps adjusting curriculum and instruction to better serve all students, a decision was made to raise 'standards' for a traditionally disenfranchised group. I wondered if there were other reasons for raising the passing percentile. How might funding and turf issues come into play? Did the decision have a connection to students' needs, or was it driven by other forces?

As a teacher, my reactions to the test were not seen as important or even valid. While I kept on asking questions and not getting responses, I was continually being asked by my students about what was happening to them. 'When will we get the results?' 'When will I get out of ESL?'

I had and continue to have mixed feelings. While I was not willing to let an inappropriate measure undermine my teaching and my students' learning, together we had to confront the reality that that measure would influence their academic careers and the range of possibilities open to them. I compromised, and spent most of each semester engaged in meaningful student-driven work around posing, analyzing, and addressing societal problems such as racism, pollution, and inequity. We used those problems to frame intensive work in writing, reading, and presenting ideas. Each semester, though, we also spent time preparing for the LAB test. Each year more and more students would pass and leave my ESL classes. In helping them achieve their goal of getting out of ESL, I wondered how they were served in regular English classes. Did larger mainstream English classes with more of a focus on literature than on writing or collegial interactions really help them grow as students, communicators, and people? Was it naive to think that in smaller ESL classes we could better meet their needs? What did the students want and why? How could their voices be included in these decisions? It became clear that in students' eyes policy mattered less than how it was implemented.

Contexts for labeling

The contradictions inherent in ESL labeling are played out in different ways in different settings. In a system as large as New York City, it can become difficult to speak broadly about policy. While ESL policies have been set for the entire city, how they play out in specific schools is often what matters most. Policies come to life in how they are enacted. Looking at how policies are implemented reveals much about the assumptions and belief systems of the implementors – teachers and administrators. By contrasting two schools, it becomes easier to see how students are treated, what is behind their treatment, and how they feel about it. The students I've been speaking with are recent immigrants from Bangladesh, China, the Dominican Republic, Haiti, Iraq, Malaysia, Poland, and Russia. While I have chosen to describe actual schools, I have used pseudonyms for the names of schools, teachers and students.

Hillview High School

Hillview High School[1] is a large comprehensive school. It comprises 2,200 students and 120 faculty. Students take up to nine classes a day, each 40 minutes long. Teachers work within academic departments. Their experiences at the school vary widely based on how their supervisor interacts with them. In some departments, teachers exchange ideas regularly and visit each other's classes; in other departments teachers mostly keep to themselves. Typically teachers are responsible for five classes. They have one preparation period, one lunch period, and one period of administrative duty. Most of the collaboration that takes place among staff occurs at the beginning and end of each semester, often over books, materials, and students' grades. During the rest of the year, teachers exchange ideas in the lunchroom, while copying assignments, or after school. Teachers are encouraged to keep their classroom doors locked for safety reasons. The prevailing culture and structure of the school encourages teachers not to engage in a professional dialogue, though many see that dialogue as important.

The school has a focus on tests. The current political climate and the State Commissioner's initiatives emphasize the newly revised Regents exams (students need to pass seven Regents exams to earn a Regents diploma, which is necessary to gain access into a competitive four-year college). The prevailing model of instruction often encourages the one-way transmission of knowledge. The curriculum and, in turn, the teachers treat students as deficient.

Gateway High School

Gateway High School is a small alternative school. It comprises 460 students and thirty faculty. The school only serves recent immigrants. These students have a need to develop their communicative and academic competence in English. The school is structured to meet the students' needs. Students learn English not in separate ESL classes, but through content areas. Those content areas are not separated into distinct disciplines, but revolve around interdisciplinary themes. Students take four classes, each 70 minutes, a day. Teachers work in five-member interdisciplinary teams. Each team works with a limited number of students, currently about seventy-five. The curriculum itself encourages collaboration. A theme such as 'American Dream' is addressed from different perspectives in all four classes. Teams of teachers collaborate in and across those groups. Students also work in a variety of groups. The prevailing philosophy of education values students' diverse lives and linguistic experiences. Much of the learning is not about teacher–student interactions, but student–student interactions (González and Darling-Hammond 1995). Student work is evaluated by performance-based assessments, including portfolios and presentations.

Assumptions and orientations

Each institution sets its own priorities and adheres to an existing belief system. At Hillview, these appear to be by default. At Gateway, they seem intentionally and carefully chosen. For the purposes of framing my thoughts about how ELL students are treated, I've focused on the different approaches taken by these two high schools. While at times the differences may appear gross, they generally seem to hold true. As I dig deeper into the realities of each school, I'm struck by the assumptions that the schools are founded upon. Each school reveals its beliefs through how it establishes organizational structure, in learning relationships, and in its treatment of students and staff. Do respect and trust prevail?

Organizational structures set the boundaries for how individuals interact. While teachers at Gateway work in interdisciplinary clusters with five members, teachers at Hillview work in departments with as many as thirty members. Gateway rather intentionally mimics an elementary school model where teachers are expected to be generalists who share ideas. Hillview upholds a high school model where teachers are experts in academic disciplines and often then specialize in particular subjects – be they earth science or Shakespeare.

Gateway, strongly influenced by the social constructivist philosophy of Vygotsky, is concerned about how learners grow in relation to other learners (Ancess and Darling-Hammond 1994). Just as students are asked to work in groups and construct meaning, so are teachers. A common sight is a classroom filled with several spirited discussions. Students, teachers, and administrators are evaluated by their peers and through portfolios. A strong sense of parallelism exists. At Hillview, students are likely to be seen sitting in rows, facing the teacher, and listening to information. In this conception of learning an ideal classroom might be quiet. Interestingly enough, a faculty meeting at Hillview with teachers half-heartedly listening to a principal, is nearly parallel to classroom interactions.

Clearly, besides a sense of organization and a conception of learning, a school's functioning is deeply connected to how it approaches the people in it. Schools that do not trust students tend not to trust teachers. Schools that really value a range of perspectives tend to do this on a number of different levels. How immigrants, or indeed how any groups of students are treated in schools has much to do with how they are valued.

How students are labeled offers a clear indication of how they are valued, and creates or limits their opportunities.

Students' voices

Schools are or should be about helping students grow. While a variety of approaches may prove successful, success is often measured too narrowly.

Too often we inhibit real success by ignoring students' reactions to their own learning (Carger 1997; González and Huerta-Macias 1997; Gantner 1997).

I hope that by sharing students' voices we can come to a better understanding of the impact of labeling. By looking at specific students, we can come to realize the importance of reconsidering ESL programs and ESL testing practices in New York. The first two students are from Hillview High School and the next two from Gateway. Their stories help to illustrate all the complexities of labeling for ELL students and its effects on them.

Louise

Louise is a 19-year-old Haitian immigrant. Louise came to New York four years ago with little English, though she had attended school in Haiti. She was enrolled in the ESL and bilingual Haitian Creole programs. She placed out of Haitian Creole and by end of year had completed the sequence of ESL courses. She did not pass the LAB test. She graduated from Hillview last June, passing the requisite Regents competency test in English (the less rigorous and soon to be phased out version of the State Regents exam). She is currently a student at a private college in New York.

Louise was an extremely sophisticated student. While at Hillview she completed several internships and took college courses at two local universities. She was a finalist for a prestigious bank scholarship and received a number of smaller scholarships.

Louise appreciated the attention she got in her ESL classes and approached the work with a sense of humor, but often asked, 'When can I get out of ESL?' Her predicament is not uncommon. Her score on the LAB test would have made her eligible for entering mainstream English classes when the passing score was 21 per cent, as it was originally. As a senior, on the new scale, it became nearly impossible for her to pass out.

Louise commented, in a letter to a younger sister:

> I know you like the guys that you are hanging out with, don't get me wrong because I'm not criticizing them or anything but what they are doing is not my style and it's certainly not yours. I am the oldest. I'm supposed to watch you guys and you guys are supposed to look after me. I am not saying that I am perfect and I don't have the right to judge anyone and that's not what I'm doing. If you could just stop hanging out with them for only two or three days every week I think it will help you a lot. As your big sister I don't want to see you suffering later on. I'm just warning you try to be aware of the stakes. I don't want to see you stuck where I am. Take the classes and get out of ESL. It's fun now, but it gives you problems later on. I hope you will take my advice it will help a lot.

Ironically, Louise, a 'successful product' of the ESL program, urges her sister to get out of ESL. Underlying Louise's comments are a nagging sense of disconnection from the rest of the school. While Louise might have been able to use her high status in a low status group to get attention and advance her own education, she did that at the cost of access to other learning that might serve her well in college, and at the cost of socialization. Louise sensed that she didn't need to be where she was placed. She had little redress about that placement. And while colleagues and I tried to create environments that were challenging for her, she was inevitably short-changed as we simultaneously responded to pressure to address the needs of more challenged students.

Richard

Richard is also a 19-year-old Haitian immigrant. Richard attended junior high school in Brooklyn. He had little formal schooling in Haiti. He too was enrolled in the ESL and bilingual Haitian Creole programs. He has not graduated, and will likely never graduate, as he has only accumulated a fraction of the necessary credits. He is functionally illiterate. He is, however, quite sophisticated verbally. He speaks English like a native speaker.

Richard finds ESL unchallenging. He cannot connect with written texts. But although he cannot write, he can express sophisticated ideas. He feels out of place in advanced classes with students his own age because of the content, and in more suitable beginner classes because of the younger students. As a result he is unengaged, disruptive, and frequently absent.

Last year we piloted a special program for students like Richard. We were tired of seeing students programmed for failure. One teacher said:

> It became obvious why certain students were failing and why they were acting out. There didn't seem much that we could do. You can't make up for years of not reading or writing in one period or even after school. These students need a special program that is more like an elementary school. These students need a self-contained classroom where they can grow as readers and writers.

Because these students were still expected to take the State examination, and thus had to prepare seven subjects, we were only able to work with them one period a day. A system that asks students who do not read or write to complete complex State tests is not confronting reality. Our band-aid approach was expected to address needs that arose out of years of ineffective teaching and learning. Not surprisingly, Richard made little progress in developing literacy – he never had the time – or in passing tests – he never acquired the skills or knowledge.

When I asked Richard about ESL class he said:

> There are some things to watch out for. Either they get mad at you 'cause

it's boring or they play me 'cause I know too much. I don't need to do that kid stuff. I like the presentation, but I want something real.

Richard is served in an even worse way than Louise. While Louise was able to make the best of a less than challenging situation, Richard is caught in a vicious cycle. He acts out because he is not given an opportunity to succeed. He cannot succeed because he lacks the skills. He can't develop the skills because the system lacks the patience and the courage to accept where he is and to address his needs.

Omar

Omar is a 17-year-old Iraqi immigrant. His spoken English is strong. He has struggled in school both in his native country and in the US. In particular, he has problems with reading and writing and staying focused. He often complains of distracting noises. He easily gets flustered. One day he lost his camera and was unable to work for days until a friend found it. He often misplaces work.

The staff at Gateway are well aware of Omar's struggles. Teachers have worked with a qualified psychologist and trainees from a nearby college to assess his needs and to develop appropriate responses. In team meetings he is often a topic of discussion. Teams of teachers have devised a number of strategies to help him be successful. One year one cluster group let him work in blocks of time on individual subjects. Another year four teachers decided to have him work in two combined areas – history/English and science/professional and career development. Pairs of teachers meet with him before class twice weekly. A paraprofessional meets with him daily to check on his progress, and tutors him regularly. He is starting to become more focused, to accomplish more, and to contribute to his group.

In an American studies class, students were working in groups on research papers about immigration. Omar's contribution was to develop a number of graphs detailing the influx of Chinese immigrants over 150 years. He did them on a computer. After class he asked his teacher for help. Though he spelled 'year' incorrectly, his teacher Jane let him dictate how he would like to title his graphs. She carefully wrote what he said and then corrected each phrase with him. She introduced 'decade' as a possibility. Omar replied that he didn't want to use big words, so that his friends could understand his work. He settled on 'ten-year period'.

As they rechecked his percentage calculations, each worked individually. Jane asked, 'How much did you get?' Omar replied, 'You write it, I'll write it too.' After some laughter and talk about buying a used car, they each explained their process to the other. While both had originally made mistakes, they both demonstrated their understanding through discussion. Omar left the room understanding the mathematical concept and ready to apply it to the rest of his graph.

A week or two later at an open school afternoon, the entire team of teachers met with Omar and his mother. With the help of a translator, the group discussed Omar's schedule in exhaustive detail. One teacher is concerned that Omar is not completing assignments. She says, 'If Omar gave us work, even if it wasn't all correct he would not be getting an "incomplete". The problem is, it isn't wrong, but he doesn't give us all the work.'

More probing leads to some interesting realizations. In addition to his high school classes, Omar is taking a college class in photography. He likes to – and feels he needs to – spend about three hours every day in the darkroom. He then comes home exhausted and unable to do his other schoolwork. Neither the teachers nor Omar's mother have realized how busy Omar actually is. Another teacher proposes that Omar spend just two days a week in the darkroom. He reacts strongly, citing his desire to get credit and develop as a photographer. The group compromises on three days.

Jane wrote the following statement about Omar in a journal reflecting on her teaching practice:

> Later, I sat down with Omar to write up a weekly schedule for doing his work, meeting with his tutor, and turning in assignments. In light of his learning disability, I modified some assignments but the list was still daunting. Copies were made for his mother, his friend, his teachers, a student teacher who tutors him individually and a helpful LaGuardia Community College professor who speaks his first language. The next Thursday, I met with Omar after school to go over the list, see how he had done and write up a new one for the next week. Anything he had not completed got carried over to the new week, marked with an asterisk. Copies were made for the same people. We have been following this procedure every Thursday and the improvement in his attendance and turning in of work is dramatic.

Omar is making progress. He enjoys school, contributes to discussions, works well in groups, and excels at photography. While it is still unclear if or when he will graduate, the possibility of his doing so is greatly strengthened by the teachers' collective concern and collaborative response. Much of what makes school work for Omar is in the relationships he develops with adults in the building. The size of classes, the interdependence of teachers, the strong sense of community all keep him from slipping through the cracks and enable him to really succeed, both as a learner and as a person.

Alex

Alex is a 17-year-old Russian immigrant who also attends Gateway. He is very bright. He is a senior and hopes to attend SUNY New Paltz. He wants to be a doctor. In addition to his studies at Gateway, Alex is enrolled in a college class and is doing very well. He excels in school.

Alex sometimes wonders if school is challenging enough. He can become impatient with his peers. He often twists his assignments to make them more interesting and challenging. In a class doing research on French immigrants where most students looked at concrete concepts such as reasons for leaving, adjusting to the US, and immigration laws, he decided to focus on cultural theory. He developed a hypothesis about why French Americans are more closely connected to their culture than are other immigrants. He incorporated geographical, political, religious, and economic considerations. In his part of his group's presentation, he raised issues that the entire class mulled over. He set a standard for making broader connections.

His understanding of English is sophisticated. During an activity related to the immigration research projects, students were asked to look at and write captions for a variety of cartoons. Reacting to a cartoon from 1870 portraying Uncle Sam mobbed by hordes of small and seemingly deranged immigrants, Alex wrote, 'Yankee doodle came to town riding on a pony, get the heck out of here you immigrant phony.'

Alex is undertaking an additional research project as part of a nationwide contest sponsored by a large Wall Street firm. He is working with two other advanced students under the supervision of a teacher with a strong background in research and a PhD in education. He consults additionally with two science teachers. Potential topics include studying traffic flow in a busy section of the Brooklyn–Queens Expressway and developing a spray that would keep gum from sticking to the bottom of tables. Alex and his research team are selecting their final topic by comparing the amount and quality of information they can get. They have contacted the Department of Transportation and Police for accident reports, and paint companies for samples of Teflon-based paints.

For all his occasional griping, Alex is satisfied with his education. He enjoys the variety of topics he studies and the opportunities to interact with adults and other advanced students. While he sometimes wishes he was challenged more, he is willing to accommodate the needs of recent arrivals. He is satisfied with the personal attention he is able to get from his teachers.

Implications for practice

These student stories illustrate the contradictions of being labeled an ESL student. Recent immigrants are not served as well as they might be, due to a number of factors. These factors are apparent on the broadest policy levels in the forms of mandates and inappropriate assessments. They are apparent on the school level in terms of curriculum, scheduling, and class size. And finally they become apparent on the classroom level in terms of how teachers interact with classes and individual students.

Unfortunately, highly successful students like Louise and Alex succeed not so much due to what happens in their classes, as because of the opportunities they are able to access outside of the regular curriculum. Less successful students like Omar manage to barely get by only through the enormous commitment and time of dedicated teachers. Even less successfully, in spite of the commitment of his teachers, Richard fails. The size and complexity of his school context make it nearly impossible for his needs to be met.

In each school and with each individual it seems that students have the greatest opportunities to grow when they are met where they *are*, as opposed to where they are not. Meaningful connections with students are most likely to occur in smaller contexts, either in individual relationships or in groups of teachers working with groups of students. Though bigger contexts may prove more efficient at sifting, sorting, and selecting, they do not meet the individual needs of students. Labeling does not need to be a dirty word; but labels do need to be grounded in thoughtful interactions.

Students are calling out for attention. They want to connect with adults. They want help to grow as learners. They want their work to be challenging and relevant. They also want to be part of their larger school communities. English language learner students are tired of being segregated from other students because of where they were born or how they speak and write in English. They have compelling thoughts that they want to share.

As educators, our challenge is to rethink some of our practices and reconnect to the needs of the students we are serving. Originally, labels were intended to help us better meet the needs of ELL students. Unfortunately, labeling has come to take on a life of its own. We need to revisit how we can adjust our practices to help our students. We need to incorporate asking students for their opinions into the very fabric of our ongoing evaluation and program planning. Initial areas for consideration should include class and school size, what drives the curriculum, where students fit into programs – or rather how programs can fit students, what skills they have, and how students can be helped to connect with each other and with adults.

Through carefully looking at how ELL students are treated in two different school contexts, and at how these students perceive how they are treated, this essay has brought to the surface a variety of concerns. ELL students do indeed have a range of individual needs, from becoming literate to refining writing skills, but they are tired of being segregated from broader school populations. Often they feel that they can be successful with only minimum additional support in traditional English classes. They enjoy opportunities to connect with adults in their schools. Finally, they express frustration with the LAB test. They see it as an unfair measure.

Looking at how students' concerns can be translated into policy and practice can do much to rejuvenate a lethargic and insensitive system. These needs can first be addressed on the school level, though they have implications for many educational systems.

Recommendations

1 Encourage discussion among ESL and other content area teachers   Research on second language acquisition, begun some thirty years ago, supported a movement of ESL teachers and classes from English departments to foreign language departments (Hakuta 1986). While this meant that ESL teachers were able to develop practices supportive of ESL students, it widened the gap between ESL and English curriculum and teachers. In turn, ELL students have often found the transition from ESL into English classes difficult.

ESL and English teachers need opportunities to collaborate, exchange pedagogical ideas, and develop strategies to better meet the needs of ELL students (Smith 1996). ESL teachers often have specific training and experience in language acquisition, vocabulary building, spoken English, grammar, and writing process; English teachers often have specific training and experience in literature, formal writing, and writing process. When both approaches can be integrated they complement one another, better meet the needs of ELL students, and better meet the needs of other students.

Additionally, when ESL is grounded in academic content areas – history, biology and math, for example – students and teachers have more opportunities to use language for authentic communication in realistic contexts.

2 Increase opportunities for students and teachers to interact   Students who get personal attention tend to learn, grow, and not act out. Unfortunately, too many high schools are structured for failure. Students have few opportunities for meaningful connection with adults in their schools. Interactions take place in crowded classes or in unmanageable situations such as lunchrooms or auditoriums. As English learners, ELL students may have few opportunities to practice using English. In both cases, less really can be more.

Classes and schools should be restructured so that students and teachers can interact with each other on a manageable level. Personal attention influences achievement and attitude by chipping away at anonymity.

3 Rework assessments   In an age of constantly rising standards, the LAB test, or whatever test your school system uses, can easily become misused. Tests often ignore current research on language acquisition and competence. The LAB test is flawed as a multiple-choice test because it does not include any writing. More shocking still, the spoken section of the test is not counted in the scoring.

Language assessments need to be reworked to include authentic written and spoken English. They also need to be normed again on the basis of student success in both transitional and traditional English classes, so that the largest numbers of students are given the widest range of opportunities. While no one is against high standards, assessments need to be created that measure a range of competencies.

Note

1 I have disguised the names of schools and students used in this essay.

References

Ancess, J. and Darling-Hammond, L. (1994) *Authentic Teaching, Learning, and Assessment with New English Learners at International High School,* New York: NCREST.

Carger, Chris Liska (1997) 'Attending to New Voices,' *Educational Leadership* 54(7): 39–43.

Dentler, R. and Hafner, A. (1997) *Hosting Newcomers: Structuring Educational Opportunities for Children,* New York: Teachers College Press.

Doll, W. E. (1993) *A Post-modern Perspective on Curriculum,* New York: Teachers College Press.

Freire, P. (1970) *Pedagogy of the Oppressed,* New York: Continuum.

Gantner, M. (1997) 'Lessons Learned from My Students in the Barrio.' *Educational Leadership,* 54(7): 44–5.

González, J. and Darling-Hammond, L. (1995) *Professional Development for Teachers of Immigrant Youth: New Concepts for New Challenges,* unpublished manuscript.

González, M. L. and Huerta-Macias, A. (1997) 'Mi casa es su casa,' *Educational Leadership,* 55(2): 39-43.

Hakuta, K. (1986) *Mirror of Language: The Debate on Bilingualism,* New York: Basic Books.

Smith, L. (1996) *Professional Development through Teacher Collaboration: The Experiences of a Co-teaching Triad in an Intensive ESL Program,* unpublished doctoral proposal, Teachers College, Columbia University.

Special-*izing*

7 The labeling of African American boys in special education

A case study

Andrea Smith

In this chapter I shall be examining the formation of an African American male's identity within special education classes through a case study of 'Jessie,' an African American schoolboy.[1] My overall aim is to generate a 'grounded theory' to explain the dynamics of identity formation. First I shall present Jessie's narratives; then I shall generate a hypothesis grounded within a specific context (Hudak 1993).

Before we begin, we must adequately define the concept of identity formation. Peter Taubman writes of 'registers' of identity formation. In the first register, identity emerges as a construct of language, thus as a kind of fiction that can alienate one from the complex interplay of differences within oneself and between oneself and others. Identity can also be viewed from a psychoanalytical perspective as a product of the Lacanian 'mirror stage.' In isolation this fictional register functions through a self-essentializing movement in which boundaries between self and not-self, margin and center, are rigidly drawn and assumed stable, while contradictorily at the same time a kind of fusion is sought (i.e. 'the other is the same as me'). In this register the site of resistance to knowledge can be found in the boundaries between a dominant and an unauthorized discourse (Taubman, in Edgerton 1993).

The second register, which Taubman calls the 'communal as an identity-in-motion,' involves group membership and all that that implies for identity as it emerges in the relations among and between individual, group, and society. The term 'identity-in-motion' derives from Henry Louis Gates Jr's explanation of the 'mask-in-motion,' exemplified by the Yoruba mask which only produces meaning when worn in front of an audience it initiates. This production of meaning evokes a sense of interior cohesion for the group involved in the process. Taubman explains: 'Within the communal register identity is made the ground for action. The identity is not taken as a formation of language but as an identity-in-motion ... In such a world only those who are members can explore the meaning of identity' (Taubman, in Edgerton 1993: 221). The socially marginalized stand to benefit from the solidarity that such identity formation generates. It is through this register that multicultural education is approached, as in for example an Afrocentric curriculum. However, this register also risks essentializing identity, freezing it into mere group membership, if its relationship to other registers is lost.

Now, with an insight into the politics of identity formation, I can begin to answer the question of Why? Why would the public be concerned with the formation of an African American male's identity in special education?

Research has shown there is a persistent and pervasive problem in the education of African American male students in special education classes (Artiles 1992). The problem is manifested in patterns of passivity and apathy. African American males develop low self-esteem, low self-perception, poor self-image, and possess negative attitudes toward self. African American males in Special Education are often inclined to think they are dumb, stupid, or useless and tend to give up. They demonstrate feelings of 'I can't' and 'It's too hard' (Reglin 1992). Once an African American male is labeled 'special education child,' teachers create a stereotype, causing a blurring of focus that results in the child feeling intimidated and often psychically destroyed (Kunjufu 1986).

Jessie

Jessie is labeled and has been psychically destroyed on many occasions. He is a 16-year-old African American, a Jehovah's Witness, and grew up in Windale, New Jersey. Windale is a predominantly African American community largely made up committed working people. Windale represents a community of strength, struggle and survival. It is a place of cultural pride and unity: African American parades, local mosques, the great Reverend Peters, gospel music, and double dutch rope-jumping all add to the essence of the town. Although this community gave Jessie his roots – his inner being – his mother wanted more. She wanted a house, not an apartment. She wanted diversity, not separation. She wanted more for her family, more for Jessie.

So they moved from Windale to Gate Hills. Gate Hills is the yuppie's dream – a diverse, multicultural community. However, within the community the term Upper Gate Hills (a community with its own zip code) is also recognized. Jessie thinks of Upper Gate Hills as this rich white neighborhood in which, unfortunately, his mother has chosen to live: seclusion, parks, recreation and million-dollar homes.

Jessie is a sophomore at Gate Hills High School. He radiates an intense level of energy as he strives for voice in the classroom. This attempt is often silenced. A sea of social bias – special education – causes his silence. Jessie has been in special education since second grade and has been classified as perceptionally impaired. He claims he has been erroneously diagnosed. He wants to get out but no one is listening: 'I want out! Get me outta' here!'

How it began

JESSIE: It began in second grade. I was in another school and my teacher asked me if my father was an alcoholic ... I said, 'He drinks sometimes' ... She then asked me where I live and how many people live in the house ... I told her I live with my mother, my baby sister, and my two brothers in an apartment building on Eland Avenue.

(Jessie's second grade teacher asked him these questions because he had been misbehaving in class. He would talk back and fail to complete classwork. The teacher's inquiry was based on 'getting to the root' of the problem. The teacher's final diagnosis: Unsafe Living Conditions ... Alcoholic Father ... Special Education!!!!!)

INTERVIEWER: What is special education?

JESSIE: I have no idea to this day ... I don't get it. The guidance counselor told me it was a place that was going to help me. They said it was a place that would control my temper. They also said my basic skills were low and this would help me.

INTERVIEWER: Why do you think you're in special education?

JESSIE: I'm here because of my temper ... I have a really bad temper ... and anything sets it off ... Because I challenged my teachers the wrong way they put me in special education ... I'm mad. They put me in special education because of my environment, and my attitude. They said my learning level wasn't up to par.

(Jessie has been told his temper is the reason for special education. He sees special education as a place that causes frustration and 'attitude.' Why? Where is this frustration coming from?)

INTERVIEWER: What do you do in your special education classes?

JESSIE: Basically nothin' ... We did worksheets, that's it ... it was really boring ... The only reason I was really there is because I challenged my teachers and they couldn't take it ... Actually, they didn't know how to deal with my challenge so they put me in the resource room ... Those teachers make me sick anyway ... this proves they really can't do their job ... they don't know how to handle students ... so they throw them in special education ... and those teachers make you feel as though a Black man is not supposed to challenge their teachers ... I was always taught to not be afraid to challenge.

(Jessie's experience in the resource room left him with feelings of humiliation, sadness and confusion.)

INTERVIEWER: You mentioned the resource room, what is the resource room?

JESSIE: The resource room is for kids who are in special education. Special ed ... they make you feel like ... I mean ... when you in special ed ... they like put you around basically the stupidest kids in the school. When you in the resource room you got the kids that's recovering like ... like ... they some type of addicts or something. The kids that are in special education ain't gettin' an education. White kids get the better education ... they get a better chance in life. When you're in there you ain't doin' nothin'. You're doin' basics ... for example, when I was in fifth grade I was doin' first grade work. When you're in special ed, they don't put you in a grade

... so when you get out of special ed, they don't know what grade to put you in.

The acrostic

The terms 'special education' and 'resource room' have marked Jessie as a kid with a 'bad temper.' This labeling has damaged his self-concept and motivation to learn. 'Special education' conveyed powerful meanings, causing Jessie to become frustrated and at times psychically destroyed. For this reason I decided to present him with an acrostic of the phrase. An acrostic is a series of lines in which certain letters, usually the first in each line, form a name, motto, or message when read in sequence. I wanted to know how he thinks and feels.

S illy
P lain
E ducation
C aution
I mmature
A musement
L ong

E xit
D umb
U nusual
C onfusion
A ction
T eaching
I llogical
O dd
N ekeema

INTERVIEWER: What made you choose these words to describe the term 'special education'?

JESSIE: I chose 'silly' because it's silly being here. I chose 'plain' because we do plain stuff in here. I chose 'education' because we're not gettin' one. I chose 'caution' because I have to be cautious with my attitude and temper. I chose 'immature' because they can't control the immature students. I chose 'long' because I've been there since second grade. I chose 'exit' because Jessie wants out. I chose 'dumb' because the special education system is dumb. I chose 'unusual' because we get a lower education than the student body. I chose 'confusion' because you sometimes think you're a good student than you think you're a bad student. I chose 'action' because what it takes that to get out of here. I chose 'teaching' because it teaches you nothing. I chose 'illogical' because special education is not logical, it's confusing. I chose 'odd' because you're considered the odd person out. I chose 'Nekeema,' my girlfriend, because she's the only one who can keep my temper down.

(I wanted to continue with an idea similar to an acrostic by adding some color.)

INTERVIEWER: What color would you use to describe the resource room?

JESSIE: Black ... because it's predominantly Black. All you see is Black faces.

The formation of Jessie's identity is grounded in his description of the term 'special education.' His anger is apparent in every word and phrase. Jessie has developed a complicated inner being that describes his oppressive environment. In each word we get a sense of the anxiety, fear, pain, struggle, and lack of power within him. Why this lack of power? Is the pain being heard?

Quest for voice

Jessie developed a 'quest for voice' based on years of oppression and a label marked 'special education child.'

INTERVIEWER: Why do you think you are being silenced?

JESSIE: Because of my age ... they think I know nothing. They think I don't know what I'm talkin' about. They are the teachers. My resource room teacher doesn't listen to what I have to say ... she doesn't hear me. She never lets me say anything. They push me aside ... they say 'You don't know what you're talking about.' She says she can't help my past but she wants the future better for me ... but I'm saying ... there is only two years left of my school ... Ten years of my life has been wasted in special education.

(Jessie continues his speech. It is apparent Jessie feels he has not had a fair deal. He wants people to listen to his story. Are people not listening because of his youth? Is there more to this silencing?)

JESSIE: I want Ms Sacofa *(the resource room teacher)* to sit down and just listen because I know what I'm talkin' about. If teachers are faced with children who have attitude problems they should pull them aside and talk ... or go to the guidance counselor or something. They should not put the student in special education, like they did with me.

Jessie's 'quest for voice' is grounded in his struggles and fears in special education. His identity within the frame of Taubman's 'communal' register emerges as a construct of individuals placing him in an oppressive situation. More broadly, identity emerges as a construct of *language*, thus as a kind of fiction that can alienate one from the complex interplay of differences within oneself and others (Edgerton 1993). The language created by the individuals who classified Jessie as 'perceptionally impaired' constructed his identity. His identity became that of a frustrated African American male with a vision of voice and a yearning for empowerment.

Final thought

What I have attempted here is to conduct a narrative study. In narrative, we weave the fabric of others' lives, connecting information with experience to construct knowledge (Brunner 1994). With that in mind, I have attempted to include questions about knowledge, power, voices, and position. This was an opportunity to look through my own perspective, to problematize that perspective, to see it in the light of 'constructed knowledge.'

Jessie's story is framed within a special educational experience. He acknowledges and critiques this by challenging the system. Jessie's search is challenged through a quest to be heard. He has acknowledged that being in the resource room – i.e. special education – has not prepared him for what he wants out of life. Special education is working against him instead of for him. He challenges his teachers, to be heard, seen, and noticed. He has no fear of challenging, for that is how the system has made him.

A school is designed to nurture, comfort, praise, encourage, build self-esteem, and offer guidance; so why are such strategies for coping with pain and suffering an integral part of an African American male's school experience?

Note

1   I have changed his name, and the names of places discussed in this essay.

References

Artiles, A.J. and Trent, S.C. (1992) 'Over-representation of minority students in special education: a continuing debate.' *Journal of Special Education.* 27:4. pp. 410–37.

Brunner, D. (1994) *Inquiry and Reflection: Framing Narrative Practice in Education*, New York: SUNY Press.

Edgerton, S. (1993) 'Toni Morrison Teaching the Interminable' in C. McCarthy and W. Crichlow (eds) *Race Identity and Representation in Education.* New York: Routledge.

Hudak, G. (1993) 'Technologies of Marginality' in C. McCarthy and W. Crichlow (eds) *Race Identity and Representation in Education.* New York: Routledge.

Kunjufu, J. (1985) *Countering the Conspiracy to Destroy Black Boys*, Chicago: African American Images.

Reglin, G. (1992) *Bound for Failure*, Charlotte, NC: Department of Curriculum and Instruction, University of North Carolina.

8 Special education students as counter-hegemonic theorizers

Lee Elliott Fleischer

Can special education students in the public high school theorize? Recently I was engaged with four special education students in a New York City high school while completing my doctoral research project (Fleischer 1998). I discovered that a trusting environment, supplemented by literature that is critical of and calls attention to hegemony, can be a catalyst, igniting both the researcher and the researched of special education to theorize, imagine, and act. In particular, the students in my study were able to illustrate their theorizing ability, constructing frameworks that speak to the many ways they are stigmatized, marginalized, and labeled in their special education school program.

'How do they know we are special?'

In the initial interviews,[1] the students clearly expressed feelings about being labeled. Zena turned to all of us and said: 'How do they know we are special – do we have a sign around our necks, or something?' Gregory enjoined: 'Yeah, sometimes I feel the regular students are going to turn on me.' Lisa said: 'When they call out my number in homeroom, the other students turn around and stare at me.' Randy added: 'Yeah, it's that look, that look can make you snap. It makes you feel that they think you don't have any intelligence.' 'It's like when rumors spread,' added Zena, 'it tells everybody who is special and who is a loser.' Zena further insisted, 'They make us feel down and disrespect us.'

From this starting point, the students, through our working together, came to a wider perspective. It has been noted by Freire (1970) that constructing themes that 'limit situations' or recognize contradictory circumstances as a problem is one method by which those within the underclass or the oppressed can become critically conscious of their schools and societal surroundings. It has also been noted in special education research that to 'have an adequate understanding of wider social structures ... [in order to] understand how people interact within these structures' (Barton and Tomlinson 1984), theorizing should occur from the 'ground up' (Stainback and Stainback 1984).

In the present study, the students' theorizing elucidated a perspective from which to understand why and how the label 'special' positions them in often contradictory ways. Although they believed their special education program was necessary for them to get 'help,' they felt that they were 'looked at the wrong way.' They also felt powerless, stuck in this trade-off. Yet if given the hypothetical choice to return to regular education, they immediately declined this option. Why?

A theoretical proposition grounded the present study: while special education students struggled in their contradictory circumstances, their struggle, rather than being productive, was triggering self-defeating and divisive relations – within themselves, among the special education peer group, with the regular education population, and with school personnel. The students, rather than recognizing the divisive nature of these relations, perceived some of them as being to their benefit.

One such relation was 'cutting deals' with teachers and deans, in which students would agree to remain silent, trading this accommodation for various 'privileges' in the school, such as coming in late or getting entry to the cafeteria without a pass. Another involved the appeal mechanism whereby students and teachers went to the deans to resolve their disputes. Although this action appeared to be productive, a dean's response was merely palliative ('Why don't you write this down in your journal?') and stopped the students from taking their grievances further. Productive student–teacher negotiation and communication were thereby circumvented by the intervention of the dean, who sided with one or the other, minimizing the possibility of shared student–teacher decision-making. A third relation, and perhaps the most important, was the 'one-downing' effect that the students named as a theme in their stories, in which a student would appropriate a derisive label, such as 'slow,' often one heard as a 'put down' from regular education students or teachers. Randy, for example, looked at Gregory and, mimicking his teachers, said: 'What are you, slow? Don't you get it?'

Breaking the chains and 'one-downing'

It was further discovered in focus groups[2] that 'breaking the chains,' or just the image of 'chains,' was, for the students, a metaphor of their special education school program, which was analogous to being in bondage. Yet it also became clear that this image represented other actions in speech that tied the students to each other and the school institution metonymically.[3] When Randy called Gregory 'slow,' Randy took on the image of the school's dominant others – whom Randy perceived as 'the Teacher, the Man, the White Man, the Enemy' – as if on another link in an oppressive chain. This same student, once he feels he is 'looked at the wrong way,' is triggered into disrespectful actions which contribute to an environment of mistrust. In such an environment, his perception of the teacher cannot be developed on a mutual basis through critical dialogue. Rather, he sees the teacher in several guises: the teacher as an Other, defined on administrative and hierarchical chains; the teacher as the Man, defined on authoritarian chains; the teacher as the White Man, defined on racial chains; and the teacher as the Enemy, defined on class-dominated chains. Randy sees his hegemonic world as contained within an intricate web of chains: a complex of discourses in a formation that do not allow him entry. In these chains and webs of discursive formations, Randy begins to identify a hegemonic 'system' of violence comprising name-calling, blaming, reversing, and 'one-downing'. He further mis-recognizes his position as a resistant, deal-cutting student, as he slides into a set of positions which align him with the dominant group norms of the school's cultures.

An abundance of theoretical and historical examples illustrate these moments of reversing or 'one-downing' or, in Randy's terms, seeing others and oneself on a series of labeling chains. To Fromm (1961), these reversal moments explain why 'the led' identify their frustration and resistance to higher authority by adoring 'the leader,' as the lower middle classes of Germany did in supporting the rise of Hitler and fascism. Genovese illustrates how pre-civil war plantation owners in the southern states of America selected 'drivers' from the general slave population who managed the other slaves and exacted production and discipline from them. When a driver became overbearing to the slaves, they 'appealed' to their more benevolent masters and, by their resistance, forced the driver out of power. By this action, however, the slaves 'found their dependence on the whites reinforced and the solidarity of their own ranks undermined' (Genovese 1976: 373).

Foucault describes the reversal of the trade unions' support of student movements in Paris in the 'Days of May, 1968.' He reveals not only how the 'historical fascism of Hitler and Mussolini was … able to mobilize and use the desire of the masses so effectively,' but, more contemporarily, how 'the fascism in all of us, in our heads and in our everyday behavior, the fascism that causes us to love power, to desire the very thing that dominates and exploits us' (1972: xiii), can lend itself to a fracturing of social or class unity.

In noting how the oppressed live out their existence in an 'existential duality,' being at the same time the oppressed and the oppressor – the latter an image they have internalized – Freire seeks to reveal to the masses the process of their identification with their masters. The oppressed discover in their own consciousness a submersion that is often manifested as a 'type of horizontal violence, striking out at their own comrades for the pettiest reasons' (1970: 48). According to Freire, the oppressed will continue to do two things: first, 'because the oppressor exists within their oppressed comrades, when they attack those comrades they [think they] are indirectly attacking the oppressor'; second, the oppressed 'feel an irresistible attraction towards the oppressors and their ways of life,' and so 'resemble,' 'imitate,' and 'follow them' (*ibid.* 49).

To fight those moments in which individuals become contained and immobilized in hegemony, as, in Foucault's words, 'hierarchized individuals'

(1972: xiv), may require a theory and methodology for analyzing labeling within moments of hegemonic discourse. Such discourse can be seen as a capillary system embedded in discourse as chains, or metonymic micro-units making up the 'multiplicity of force relations' (Foucault 1980: 92). These structures are often referred to by Foucault as the most 'insignificant aspects of hierarchy and [its] forms of control, surveillance, prohibition, and constraint' (in Bouchard 1977: 213).

Flying rumors

Just such a theory and methodology as Foucault describes were developed by the students and the researcher in the present study, as they told stories and developed themes from their stories in focus groups. As the focus groups developed throughout the year of the study, the students came to see how they themselves were part of the problem, in maintaining themselves in positions of subjugation that acted as forces in silencing and stigmatizing them. In these discussions the students theorized by retelling their stories to each other. For example, Lisa stated, 'Everybody knows quickly by rumors being spread around who is slow or low functioning.' 'Yeah,' responded Gregory, 'rumors fly, rumors fly.' Continuing, Gregory insisted, 'We got to break the chains between us and them.'

Such remarks caused the emergence of salient themes, such as the 'culture of respect,' 'flying rumors,' 'repression,' 'dependency,' 'playing the game of exchanging their silence for respect,' 'one-downing,' 'appealing to the administrator,' 'administrative chains and carriers,' 'breaking the chains,' and 'the system.' The students also checked and rechecked each others' stories and, unsatisfied with tentative results, pushed each other to further examine how their themes might be expanded into a way to 'see through' the system. They were propelled to examine how the 'system' produced perceptions in them that made it difficult to 'see through' and 'penetrate' how they embroiled themselves in self-defeating behaviors.

Emerging with a counter-hegemonic framework

Through many stories recounted and shared with one another, the students emerged with a counter-hegemonic framework, further informed by literature that interacted with the themes of their stories. The literature presented to the students, largely grounded in critical, feminist, and post-structural linguistic theories, allowed both the students and the researcher to theorize and take counter-hegemonic actions. Ultimately, the group formed a counter-hegemonic criterion of validity, which laid the groundwork for their coming together to talk 'the truth,' to discuss whose truth and knowledge counted in their school. The literature further provided the groundwork necessary to form a group committed to discussing how students were being 'hegemonized.' Within this theorizing, the students were able to examine

Randy's struggle with authority in the school as constituting several discourses within metonymic chains of images which, in turn, occurred within discursive processes, which, in turn, the researcher introduced to the students as 'discursive formations' and 'signifiers.'

When these concepts were used as analytical devices, the students were able to connect their notion of 'flying rumors' to 'flying signifiers,' and later, 'flying truths' to 'flying labels,' circulating in and through their discourse. The chains of meaning linking words like 'special' to 'slow' were further re-examined within different contexts, relative to larger structures, as discursive formations, which changed these meanings of the words. This meant that when positioned by their talk, the student's sense of themselves evoked a larger chain or complex of discursive formations that linked them not only to their immediate setting but, as a part of a larger setting, to the bigger picture. For example, the word 'special' changed its meaning from 'slow' to 'different' or 'oppositional,' depending on which discourses were linked to which discursive formations, as constructed by which groups. These juxtapositions of the various meanings to the word 'slow' enabled one student, Zena, to define equality as the respect of others despite their differences; another student, Gregory, cited a contradiction of school tracking: 'Those who need the most help, get the least; but, those who get the most help, need it the least!'

The students theorized further by drawing diagrams of how power in these discursive formations circulated through sliding signifiers. Randy went to the chalkboard and began to illustrate chains, one overlying the other, illustrating how several groups of chains are linked together through sliding signifiers (see note 3). If one or two chains are broken, neither the whole system nor the other chains fall apart.

The structure of chains that Randy had drawn was grounded in several diagrams being displayed on an overhead projector. These included diagrams produced by the researcher to illustrate Williams's (1977) theory of hegemony, Pecheux's (1982) concept of discursive formations, and Lacan's (1977) role of the signifier in language as understanding the subject as a signifier for another signifier. These diagrams provided a theoretical base for understanding language as making up discourse as a capillary system of power, and for understanding how hegemony is fought out in language.

As we moved through the discussion, the researcher pointed out to the students how group action and interaction occurred within a complex of discursive formations, further made up of chains, signifiers, subject-positions, and group norms. Based on these diagrammatic examples, Randy expanded his images to include chains of wealthy and poor: wealthy Blacks–wealthy Whites/poor Blacks–poor Whites. He thereby theorized a correlation between one chain of positions (Full Respect–Disrespect) and other chains of positions (e.g. Wealthy–Poor, White–Black) as they slide together. This sliding, however, is subjugated or held down by a cross-over chain of positions and signifiers. Randy thus concluded that a wealthy Black person, when aligned by a cross-over chain of positions, may feel for neither a poor Black nor a poor White person, because the latter are connected to another chain linked to 'Disrespect,' low achievement, and low-functioning status.

After the students and the researcher added other chains of positions and signifiers, penetrating into the deeper levels of the capillary world of special education and its labels, a counter-hegemonic moment of theorizing occurred. This moment emerged when the researcher indicated images of self with the words 'I' and 'We.' There was a continuum between the 'I' and 'We' selves. One end depicted selfish and individual selves, 'I.' The other end showed the unselfish and collective selves of 'We'.

To Randy, the signifiers 'I' and 'We' were not as important as 'Selfish' and 'Unselfish,' the former aligned to 'Disrespect' and the latter to 'Full Respect.' Then suddenly, as if a second thought had crossed his mind, Randy also pointed out how 'once a Black or White person become wealthy, they never see or understand the point of view of the poor person, whether Black or White.' It was at this point that Randy broke from the values he had previously outlined, and realigned respect and full control – no longer with the attainment of wealth, high achievement in school, and 'high functioning,' but with unselfish caring for others.

Special education students as counter-hegemonic theorizers

After their theorizing and diagram construction, the students came to see the significance of the 'flying rumors,' another theme articulated in their stories. The construct of 'flying rumors' was seen as a positioning and repositioning mechanism affecting the students' perceptions according to two or more conflicting and overlapping value systems. 'Flying rumors' also acted as expressions of the circulation of chains and signifiers constituting and crossing over one another, producing a discursive consciousness that maintained the students in hegemonic and potentially counter-hegemonic subject-positions.

Understanding 'flying rumors' within these contexts, then, helped Randy to clarify the meanings of the metonymic images that flashed across his mind every time he felt 'disrespected' or 'looked at the wrong way.' In this way, the students began to discover how 'flying rumors,' serving as a positioning mechanism within several discursive formations, may have accounted for their metonymic experiences as they recounted self-defeating and divisive relations with each other and their teachers. The students named these formations as invading their 'culture of respect'; administrative, hierarchical, and hegemonic discursive formations that made up the culture of the school overlapped and intruded into their own 'culture of respect.'

The students began to understand their hegemonic subject-positions by using theoretical constructs to integrate their themes with relevant literature, as presented by the researcher. The thrust of this literature was taken from Pecheux's (1982) notion of discursive formations, and in particular his notion of counter-identifying. In counter-identification, the oppressed and labeled subject mis-recognizes the position he or she slides into as favorable, simultaneously assuming positions that maintain the dominant group norms. What the subject opposes as a hierarchical and discriminatory policy is the very policy that he or she, at the same time, confirms.

This reversal of positions was further examined by the researcher and the students in looking at other literature related to student resistance, in particular, the Willis study of working-class youth in England (1977). The students wanted to know why and how the resistance of the students in Willis's study, the 'Lads,' was short-circuited or stopped. They also wanted to know how, by questioning the system, the 'Lads' could have taken resistant positions that were not self-defeating and reversing.

As a result of these discussions, the present students responded by insisting that they could do better than the Lads. They could construct, with the researcher, a counter-hegemonic framework by which to expose the unequal practices of the special/regular education programs in their high school. By applying their frameworks, the students began to understand the shifts of meaning of words that labeled them in their special education program, along with the shifting movements of signifiers and their chains within several aligning and realigning discursive formations. In these formations of discourse, the students described how 'flying rumors' positioned them on the different meanings the label 'special' had for them, ranging from 'slow' and 'stupid' to 'misunderstood,' to 'oppositional.' By doing this, the students were able to see how the seemingly contradictory natures of their labeled experiences were not, in fact, contradictory, irreconcilable forces but instead represented the shifting of discursive formations which aligned, dis-aligned, and realigned them with others, whether on administrative and anti-administrative, hierarchical and anti-hierarchical, or hegemonic and counter-hegemonic chains of positions. They further learned that this positioning was the result of a process in which words, gestures, expressions, and even moments of silence become signifiers communicating subject-positions.

With the use of the framework they had developed, the students could begin to see how the circulation of rumors also provided a way to circulate 'flying truths,' informing the remainder of the school population that although they were different, they were of value precisely because of their marginalized and oppositional viewpoint. Assisted by oppositional literature (hooks 1984, 1991; Hall 1997), the students contended that their viewpoint, one from the margins of school life, allowed them to see through and penetrate the system of hegemony more effectively than did the viewpoint of the regular school population. Hence, their definition of being 'special' revised the pejorative meaning of the label and made the word a vehicle for their potential acceptance, respect, and, if they chose, reconciliation with the regular school population.

By applying an understanding of language as a discursive formation or system, the students came to understand how, whenever they appealed to the administrators rather than themselves to resolve their differences, or 'one-downed' each other, or exchanged their voices for artificial respect, they were triggered into self-defeating positions, all of these behaviors merely reproducing the administrative, hierarchical, and hegemonic chains of meanings. They were able to see how power alignments play a role in positioning not just regular and special education students, but also faculty and administrators, as each is triggered into self-defeating and divisive behaviors that then produce counter-reactive behaviors among 'Them' – precisely those who might be potential allies rather than enemies.

By naming the various discursive formations, the students were able to show how their struggles within and against school administrative authority got hegemonized on different levels, ranging from anti-administrative action, which co-opted their resistance; to anti-hierarchical levels, which began to provide penetrating glimpses of the system of school administrative and hierarchical authority; to counter-hegemonic levels, which provided them with a base upon which to identify themselves as their own support group, with their own criteria of truth and knowledge, and the will to fight as 'analyzers.'

With these insights the students re-examined why they appealed to higher authority, falsely made assumptions of their own powers to 'cut deals' with their teachers, and, finally, why they displaced their anger by 'one-downing' each other. They began to see that communication can be constructed by the use of signifiers rather than by their hands in fits of anger and violence. One student asserted: 'While I still put my alerts, I now think of the other as a signifier.' Still another student, usually shy and afraid to talk, broke her silence: 'Now we have a system to counter stigma!' Most important, they began to realize that they could think and theorize in making their grievances known.

In this way, the students theorized that their school, as part of a complex of discursive formations, controlled by administrators and other 'higher-ups,' aligned according to hierarchical chains of positions related to race, class, gender, and authority, precluded them from seeing further through the system. With such penetration, the students imagined defining their own discursive formation within this complex, repositioning students, teachers, parents, and administrators, so all would share decision-making in running and governing their school.

Implications for future storytelling research as a counter-hegemonic community

Special education student theorizing thus demonstrably implies a counter-hegemonic perspective for further qualitative story research, in which the subject of the story is not seen as unified, but rather as as a multiplicity of subjects distributed across a complex of discursive formations and constructed in the chains and signifiers of language and labels. Special education student theorizing further implies an appeal for egalitarian structures of authority and shared decision-making. Before these structures can be built, however, special education student theorizing offers a way in which the recent calls for inclusion may be criticized by those themselves most affected by these changes, the students labeled as 'special.'

Whether this label provides these students with some relief from the larger forces that would otherwise overtake them if not insulated by it, or whether it serves to subjugate them to the institution that has so sorted them, remains a highly controversial issue. It may finally be clarified by acknowledging special education students as theorists in their own right who, when organized into a counter-hegemonic storytelling community, can examine the label 'special' as a collectivizing act of critical consciousness in a self-determining discursive formation.

Notes

1   Permission to use the names of the students involved in the study has been obtained.
2   After individual and smaller joint interviews, the students and researcher regularly came together as a group of five, reviewing and revising each other's stories and the themes that emerged in the previous interviews.
3   The notion of metonymy as a chain in language is a post-structuralist concept. Lacan uses the construct of chains in at least two contexts in which he radicalizes Saussure's relationship between the signifier (spoken word) and the signified (meaning of the word spoken). In the first context, the one-to-one relationship between signifier and signified is altered as a meaning-making arrangement. The 'sliding' of one signifier replaces the position of another signifier (as opposed to a simple one-to-one correspondence of word-sound to word-meaning), suturing for the moment the meaning articulated that was in motion. Hence 'a signifier represents a subject for another signifier' (Lacan 1977: 208, 214, 236). To Sarap, the signifying chain does not refer to the object of representation but, rather, 'to other signifiers ... [and when] the signified seems finally to be within reach, it dissolves into yet more signifiers.' Therefore 'the subject is nothing more than that which slides in a chain (or chains) of signifiers' (Sarap 1992: 47).

In this metonymic form, the relations to meaning and the meaning-maker in discourse reveal parts of a whole and other wholes while, simultaneously, taking on meanings that become intermediary subject-positions. These meanings, in turn, may reveal larger wholes and, in the process of suturing, cross over other meanings, revealing yet larger or intruding meanings emanating from society's institutions and their ideological apparatuses. Metaphorically speaking, Lacan's notion of a chain constitutes sliding or circulating signifiers which become at a certain point a link or bridge to one another in yet another, larger, or 'mobile' chain. To Sarap, while 'the chain is what limits one's freedom, the chain is mobile; any one of its links can provide a point of attachment to other chains' (1992: 47). In this moment, meaning(s) are brought into place, *condensed*, and interpellated, at the moment of speech (Althusser 1971; see also Heath 1977: 55).

Interpreting Lacan, Pecheux (1982) maintains that the signifier circulates and becomes *displaced* within several discourses, 'passing through' several discursive formations and their subject-forms. These discourses and forms make up a complex of subject-positions (including perceptions, feelings, senses), one overlaying and/or imbricating the other. Metonymically, to Pecheux, these discourses may be a part of a larger complex of forces and/or institutions, linked together via intra-discourses, inter-discourses, and trans-discourses. These discourses may cross over their own and other chains of meanings and signifiers of other discourses, producing conflicting as well as contradictory meanings, while momentarily, as one discourse crosses over the other, positioning the subject within coherent states and/or chains. This positioning is not static, however: as new thoughts enter into discourse the speaker may be moved to experience the sudden flashing of second thoughts; conversely, after these experiences, a forgetfulness may result and 'things return to normal.'

References

Althusser, Louis (1971) *Lenin and Philosophy*, New York: Monthly Press.

Barton, Len and Tomlinson, Sally (1984) *Special Education and Social Interests* (1–12), London: Croom-Helm.

Fleischer, Lee (1998) *Living in Contradiction: Stories of Special Education Students*, unpublished doctoral dissertation, Teachers College, Columbia University.

Foucault, Michel (1972) 'Preface' in Gilles Deleuze and Felix Guattari *Anti-Oedipus: Capitalism and Schizophrenia* tr. Robert Hurley, Mark Seem and Helen Lane, New York: Viking Press.

—— (1980) *The History of Sexuality* vol. 1 tr. Robert Hurley, New York: Vintage Press.

Foucault, Michel and Deleuze, Gilles (1977) 'Intellectuals and Power' in Donald Bouchard (ed.) *Language, Counter-Memory, Practice: Selected Essays and Interviews by Michel Foucault* (205–17), Ithaca, New York: Cornell University Press.

Freire, Paulo (1970) *Pedagogy of the Oppressed* (20th edn), New York: Herder and Herder.

Fromm, Erich (1961) *Escape from Freedom* (22nd edn), New York: Holt, Rinehardt, and Winston.

Genovese, Eugene (1976) *Roll, Jordan, Roll: The World the Slaves Made*, New York: Vintage Books.

Hall, Stuart (1997) 'The Goldsmith Lectures' in *Race, The Floating Signifier*, VHS Tape, Northampton, MA: Media Education Foundation.

Heath, Stephen (1977) 'Notes on Suture,' *Screen*, 18(4): 47–76.

hooks, bell (1984) *Feminist Theory: From Margin to Center*, Boston: South End Press.

—— (1991) 'Talking Back' in Russell Ferguson, Martha Gever, Trinh T. Minh-ha and Cornel West (eds) *Out There: Marginalization Contemporary Culture* (337–40), Cambridge, MA: MIT Press.

Lacan, Jacques (1977) *The Four Fundamental Concepts of Psycho-Analysis* tr. Alan Sheridan, London: Hogarth Press.

Pecheux, Michel (1982) *Language, Semantics, and Ideology* tr. Harbans Nagpal, New York: St Martin's Press.

Sarap, Madam (1992) *Jacques Lacan*, Toronto, Canada: Toronto University Press.

Stainback, Susan and Stainback, William (1984) 'Broadening the Research Perspective in Special Education,' *Exceptional Children*, February 1984, 50(5): 400–8.

Weedon, Chris (1997) *Feminist Practice and Poststructuralist Theory* (2nd edn), London: Blackwell Publishers.

Williams, Raymond (1977) *Marxism and Literature*, New York: Oxford University Press.

Willis, Paul (1977) *Learning to Labor: How Working Class Kids Get Working Class Jobs*, New York: Columbia University Press.

Scripts

9 A word in hand

The scripted labeling of parents by schools

Hollyce C. Giles

[A]t one time ... the poet ... reaches the place of the ancient goddess of fate, and demands the name of the rich and frail prize that lies there plain in his hand ... The goddess searches long, but in vain ... There is nothing in these depths that is like the prize so rich and frail which is plainly there in his hand ... such a word would have to well up out of the secure depths.

(Martin Heidegger 1971: 68–9)

When we cannot find the names or the words to describe the treasures which we have in hand, these are not transformed into the cultural values of our cultural 'land' or era. And if we take willing risks at this moment of extreme importance, in which we are brought face to face with the tremendous negativity of not being able to express the value of what we have in hand, or 'inside,' ... if we are able to avoid running away from it, a more genuine experience of language will be disclosed to us ... [we] assent to an act of learning.

(Gemma Fiumara 1990: 163)

For me, these passages from Heidegger and Fiumara bring to mind a kindly yet demanding teacher who, through patient listening and astute questioning, coaches another through the trying labor of giving birth to her own language (meaning) for her experiences in the world. Such a teacher resists offering her own words for her laborer's 'treasure,' even encouraging her to renounce naming/labeling what she has in hand until she has a fuller, deeper relationship with it. This teacher is also *political*, for she nurtures the wellsprings of social action, her pupil's visceral experience of her life in specific, concrete situations, and her own powerful naming and understanding of that experience. She awakens and affirms her student's epistemic potential, her interest and belief in her ability to make meaning of her life, necessary for taking action to change it.

In my travels in schools as a psychologist, counselor and researcher, and as a parent myself, I have seen few teachers/educators of this kind. Over the past several years I have worked in various professional capacities with economically poor parents[1] of school-age children, most recently as a researcher and advocate. I have visited and talked with parents who are trying to reform failing public schools in their neighborhoods, to learn which educational experiences or 'training' best engage and equip them for their Herculean task. I have observed educators communicate to parents in subtle and direct ways what they should do, how they should act, even what it is acceptable for them to say and think – essentially 'scripting' their participation in schools.

Though I began my own career 'telling' parents how to raise their children in parenting workshops in schools, at some point I began to identify with parents who I felt were being silenced in their children's schools. I shifted into a role of midwife to parents' expression of their perceptions and experiences of their children's education. Indeed, one of the most powerful moments of my professional experience occurred when I helped to create the conditions for parents in a low-income school to 'find their voices.' Parents confronted educators, police precinct officials, and public housing managers with their thoughts about what was important to them in their children's education and care (Giles 2000). On reflection, I realize now that what was so powerful for me was helping parents to break free from the school's scripts for them, scripts that were constraining them from challenging those practices that were harmful to them and to their children.

Creating conditions for parents to find their own language for their experiences was significant for me personally – I too struggled with naming my experiences. Parents' desire to name their experiences resonated with mine, and I felt deeply moved when I witnessed their realization that their perceptions and opinions counted in the world, that they had agency.

In this essay, I consider how the labels and scripts that parents receive from schools may impair their ability to know and name their own experience, and to create knowledge grounded in their subjective experience of their children's education. As a professional in schools, I have observed educators interact with parents in ways that channel and manipulate their participation. I have seen educators 'offer' parents cues for scripts that call for an epistemology with little of parents' 'selves' in the process of knowing. These scripts do not involve their selves/inner voices/creative spirits – that is, a perspective that can think outside of the existing system. And thinking outside the existing system is essential if failing schools are to change.

As a parent myself, and as a white woman, I have come to understand the psychological consequences of scripts, the defenses required to cope with them, and the possibilities for thinking outside of them. As a parent I have struggled to hold on to my self, to what I knew 'in my gut' about my child's experience in school in the face of eight 'experts' at a school meeting telling me to take an action that I knew would be disastrous for my child. The meta-message from the school's experts was 'we have experience, we know what we are talking about, we know what's best for your child. Trust us, we care about your child. We have no other agendas – we can see more clearly than you can at this point. You are too emotional and biased as a parent to see what's best.' I wanted to trust them, but my gut would not let me. I left the meeting feeling powerless, practically invisible, in an arena where a crucial aspect of my child's life was at stake. I had tried to balance carefully saying what I truly thought, with preserving relations with these powerful people at whom I felt very, very angry. I weave this knowledge of my own epistemology into the essay – the ways in which labels and scripts that I have absorbed from the various social contexts in my life have affected my ability to create knowledge grounded in my subjective experience of the world.

I draw upon the work of the Italian philosopher and psychoanalyst, Gemma Fiumara (1990), and the 'script theory' developed by the late psychologist Sylvan Tomkins (1995) to consider the ways in which social scripts may influence our ways of knowing and naming our own experience in the contexts of institutions such as schools. The epistemological categories for women documented in *Women's Ways of Knowing* (Belenky *et al.* 1986, 1997) have also shed light on the issues I explore in this essay. These categories ring true for my own 'epistemological journey' and for what I have observed of the (mostly female) parents in the schools where I have worked. The evolution of my own way of knowing can be described within their paradigm as a movement toward an epistemology in which I allow my self 'back into the process of knowing' (*ibid.* 136).

In the next section, I explore the psychological processes through which labels and scripts have influenced the evolution of my own epistemology, and the epistemologies of parents in the context of schools. I then describe in detail a few of the scripted labels for parents that I have observed in my field research.

Scripts and ways of knowing

The first several times I read the passages by Heidegger and Fiumara I was moved deeply, sometimes to tears. I begin my reflections on the poetry and politics of language and community from this point, going back up the stream of tears, starting from something that is for me unexplained, mysterious and concrete. I am grateful to Helene Cixous (Cixous and Calle-Gruber 1994) for describing this way of knowing that picks up a trail subjectively important to the knower, following where it leads.

One of the stories often told in my family was how a caregiver would cover my face with a pillow when I was an infant to make me stop seemingly interminable and loud crying. The story goes that I stopped crying when I could not breathe any more, and the pillow would be lifted.

In college, when friends were horsing around someone began screaming into a pillow, and soon the pillow was passed around so everyone could have a turn. My heart raced, and embarrassed, I had to decline. I could not bring myself to scream into the pillow – I felt a sort of terror at the thought.

In my family we talked a lot. Yet there were topics that we knew not to talk about, and they were topics at the heart of my family's life. I learned in many ways, now deeply encoded/enscripted into my being, not to talk of certain essential matters. As an infant my most prolonged and intense cries of pain, anger, and discomfort were met at times with a disruption of my air supply. Though now I can scream into a pillow, it still sometimes feels subversive and dangerous to express my deepest feelings and thoughts – to name my 'treasures inside.'

This early, pre-linguistic experience of others literally stifling my expression of strong negative feelings (my voice) was followed up and reinforced over and over once I had language, as I learned to be first a white girl, and then a white woman in Texas in the late 1950s through the 1970s. I often heard 'Pretty is as pretty does,' and 'pretty' definitely did not include being angry or in any way disrupting the status quo.

Fortunately, I received some mixed messages – cracks through which the light shone in – from people important to me. My maternal grandmother, 'Mimi,' often asked me as a child, 'Have you been Mimi's good girl?' and drove home the importance of being a 'lady' in a hundred different ways. Yet I knew (and loved) that she herself was not always ladylike. Under her picture in her 1920s small-town Texas college yearbook was the caption 'Most likely to become a Bolshevik.' I had to laugh when I recently read a description of the approach to education reform with which I have been involved. Henderson and Berla (1994) write, 'Schools don't know anything about community organizing. It terrifies them. It sounds Bolshevik.'

I witnessed my grandmother struggle to allow her creative spirit, her self, to express itself in her context, where the predominant social script for a white woman was to 'be a lady.' Knowing that she struggled helped me to hold on to the possibility that my creative spirit/self could survive the expectations of a context requiring me to be polite, smooth things over, and ignore what my gut was trying to tell me.

In my work, I have seen evidence of parents' struggles to preserve their selves or inner voices. At a parents' meeting, a mother in the South Bronx eloquently expressed the desire to protect the 'treasure inside' in speaking of her hopes for her daughter. Parents were identifying the one thing they wanted their children to take to college to help them succeed. 'Good SAT scores, being prepared for college work, confidence,' they suggested. Toward the end of the sharing, a Latina mother offered, 'I want my daughter to *think her own thoughts.*' This powerful statement sent a small tremor of recognition and assent through the parents in the room, including me – recognition of the importance and the difficulty of thinking one's own thoughts, bombarded as we are by the thoughts of others.

Those memories and associations evoked for me by Heidegger's passage about the unnamed prize in the poet's hand suggest the possible origins of my concern for our creative spirits, or *daemons*, 'messages from within which inspire, advise and direct' (Fiumara 1990: 127). The 'rich and frail prize' lying in the poet's hand can be seen as metaphor for his daemon. I am moved by the great value that the goddess attaches to this prize ('there is nothing in these depths that is like the prize,' Heidegger 1971: 68), and her guidance to the poet that he should look inside to find a name for it ('such a word would have to well up out of the secure depths,' *ibid.* 69). She does *not* suggest that he ask his friends, or the local experts, to name it.

The goddess, aware of the frailty of the poet's prize and its vulnerability to being 'transformed into the cultural values of [the] cultural "land" or era' (Fiumara 1990: 163) through the very act of naming, advises that even the poet renounce naming it for a while. In his commentary on the story of the goddess and the poet, Heidegger (1971: 69) suggests that in the renunciation of its naming, the prize will not become 'a poetically secured possession of the land,' and the poet will have a more immediate experience of 'the relation of word to thing.'

Protecting the daemon: warding off others' words and rhythms

That the daemon or inner voice is indeed frail is reflected in descriptions of others' efforts to protect theirs from being diluted or altered by external, incompatible influence. Three stories follow, from people – two artists and two parents – who describe their strategies to protect what essentially are their daemons/creative spirits/voices.

Georgia O'Keefe, the painter, spoke of having a 'queer feeling of being invaded' (Cowart and Hamilton 1987: 171) by the words of critics who she felt wrote their own autobiographies into her work. 'The things they write sound so strange and far removed from what I feel of myself' (*ibid.* 170). At one point she solicited reviews from several women in the hope that women would critique her work from a perspective closer to her own. In a letter requesting such a review, she wrote, 'a woman who has lived many things and who sees lines and colors as an expression of living – might say something a man cant [*sic*] – I feel there is something unexplored about woman that only a woman can explore' (*ibid.*: 180).

Petah Coyne, an artist working in a different medium, sculpting and installations, calls her work her 'girls' (Dobrzynski 1998). She devises strategies to protect her girls from the altering influence of others. Speaking of her requirement that her assistants, art students, work in silence while listening to books on tape, she says, 'I asked them not to comment on my work. I'd get very insecure. You're so vulnerable in your studio unless you're braced for it and ask for an opinion. It may change what you're doing' (*ibid.* E3).

Two parent leaders in a public school in Queens, Marjorie and Elaine, do not have the privilege of choosing the voices they will listen to, or of arranging silent collaboration from those around them. Yet along with O'Keefe and Coyne they are skilled at the art of preserving their inner voices, of thinking their own thoughts. In the fray of local school politics these women hold their own amidst a chorus of voices challenging and criticizing their perspectives. As members of the leadership team and parents' association at their school, they have questioned several harmful practices and attitudes, including low expectations for their children and graft offered to some parents in exchange for their silence about unethical situations.

According to Marjorie and Elaine, the school responds to their independent voices by closing them out of important meetings and ignoring them whenever possible. Elaine describes their situation succinctly: 'As long as you have a mind or a mouth, you're blacklisted.' These women find crucial support for their inner voices in meetings with like-minded parents and education activists.

My resonance with these stories comes from my own vulnerability to the words of others. I fear that others' words will 'change what I'm doing,' that they will displace my own words for my experience, wedging in between my inner life and the world, estranging me from the thing that makes me who I am, the thing that enables me to think my own thoughts.

Fiumara describes a strategy used to avoid such a state of estrangement as *benumbment*. She suggests that the benumbed person 'does not seem capable of listening vigilantly to our resounding culture, but only of becoming its victim' (1990: 83). Assuming that human beings have a natural inclination to make meaning out of our relation to the world, rather than have false words shape our experiences, we may seek ways of simply not thinking. We may avoid thinking by losing ourselves in work, drinking too much, doing anything too much, to crowd out the false words. So, a person enters benumbment, probably unwittingly and gradually, as if she were tacitly saying to herself, 'I am trying to find a way of not thinking because I no longer want to think the thoughts of others' (*ibid*. 82).

Community organizers who listen to economically poor parents talking about their children's schools often report that it is difficult initially to engage parents in conversations about their concerns. Such reticence is probably multi-determined, but one cause may be a psychic withdrawal from such conversations, a withdrawal caused by powerful educators who *tell* them about their children. They are benumbed.

The antidote to benumbment, the silver bullet that pierces through the torpor and passivity of such a state, is 'radical listening.' Inner listening to oneself and careful listening by others can help one to become 'aware of the undertow dragging us towards benumbment' (Fiumara 1990: 86). Once one has cultivated a listening self, and has a visceral sense of the danger of benumbment, one 'trembles when faced by ... being engulfed once more; and it is exclusively because of this terror that the whirlpool can be avoided' (*ibid*. 91). O'Keefe, Coyne, Marjorie and Elaine, aware of the encroaching whirlpool of others' words and rhythms, devised strategies to protect their daemons. I too have felt the undertow of benumbment, and have been heartened by others' stories of avoiding the whirlpool, their ways of preserving space for their own inner listening.

To conceive of strategies for fending off threats to one's inner listening, it helps to have a way to think of 'the enemy.' That is, how exactly do the words of others intrude upon our ability to listen to ourselves? Through what social and psychological processes does one become vulnerable to drowning or suffocating epistemologically in the words and rhythms of others? How do words, phrases, and constellations of words with their attendant meanings become attached to our experiences in our own thinking? A consideration of the ways in which language enters our thinking through names, labels and scripts offers avenues for reflection upon these questions.

Names, labels and scripts

> Our needs are made of words: they come to us in speech, and they can die for lack of expression. Without a public language to help us find our words, our needs will dry up in silence. Without a language adequate to this moment we risk losing ourselves in resignation to the portion of life which has been assigned to us.
>
> (Michael Ignatieff 1985: 142)

> The impulse to enter, with other humans, through language, into the order and disorder of the world, is poetic at its root as surely as it is political at its root. Poetry and politics both have to do with description and with power.
>
> (Adrienne Rich 1993: 6)

The 'portion of life which has been assigned to us' is conveyed and reinforced through language, through the labels and scripts 'assigned' to us by the expectations others communicate in our everyday conversations and interactions. The public language in institutions often does not 'help us to find our words' attached to our needs, but rather dictates acceptable needs to us, through embedded labels and scripts.

It is important to distinguish naming from labeling, and to clarify the relationship between labels and scripts, as I am defining these concepts in this chapter. Whereas 'naming' a thing or a person usually is intended to reflect its essence or uniqueness in some way (as in poetry), 'labeling' appears to be related more to society's needs and uses regarding the thing or person, to the utility for others of identifying it in a particular manner. We might say, 'They *named* their baby "Joshua," after his uncle,' but we would not say, 'They *labeled* the baby "Joshua."' Labels are anonymous, not personal, and locate a person or thing in a class of persons or things. Labels give information about how to deal with or respond to classes or groups of others. Rather than evoke the uniqueness of something or someone, a label renders uniqueness invisible in favor of similarity with others of its kind – making the person or thing easier to handle, contain, or diagnose.

In common with Heidegger and Fiumara, Rich's use of the terms 'name' and 'label' suggests that the *labeling* of our experience by others robs us of the opportunity to *name* and thereby *know* our own desires. She writes of 'an alleged triumph of corporate capitalism in which our experience – our desire itself – is taken from us, processed and *labeled*, and sold back to us before we have had a chance to *name* it for ourselves (what do we really want and fear?)' (Rich 1993: 6, my emphases).

A script can be seen as an extension of labeling. A script expands out from the identification conferred by a label to encompass, indeed to order, whole constellations of perceptions and behaviors. If a label is an identification, or a role, a script conveys how to see the world and how to behave in that role or with that particular label.

Tomkins' script theory suggests that a person's internal world is largely shaped by scripts. An individual's script is their 'rules for predicting, responding to, and controlling a magnified set of scenes' in their life (Tomkins 1995: 180). The series of scenes, happenings with perceived beginnings and ends, constitute the plot of a person's life. Tomkins distinguishes between *nuclear* scripts, that emerge from significant early relationships in our lives, which we unwittingly insert over and over in various scenes, and *non-nuclear* scripts that we use in a more instrumental, less driven way to accomplish our purposes. Examples of non-nuclear scripts would be *power* scripts, concerning rules around being powerful, *resignation* scripts, offering particular responses to perceived limitations, and *affluence* scripts, which address the sources of an individual's zest for life.

Tomkins' theory concerns scripts for scenes from the perspective of the individual, not society. Yet he observes that society's definition of a scene will be related to the individual's definition of a scene – that they will sometimes conflict and sometimes support each other. We draw upon shared social scripts for the individual scripts that furnish our internal worlds.

Applying Tomkins' theory to my own experience, I believe that I developed a nuclear script early in life that goes something like this: 'I would like to express strong feelings, angry feelings. However, if I express these feelings then people I love and depend upon will deprive me of oxygen, both real oxygen and the oxygen of their human presence in my life.' I have imported this script into many later scenes in my life. Shared social scripts for white girls and women have reinforced this nuclear script for me – scripts that offer strong cues to mediate, to 'soothe the savage beast,' and to avoid 'rocking the boat.'

According to Tomkins, scripts do not order all of our experiences. Scripts offer 'incomplete rules, even within scenes they attempt to order' (1995: 181). What concerns me in this essay is a person's relation or connection to the world, the grounding of his or her knowledge, and how institutional and social scripts – sets of rules – affect this connection. Why is this concern important in the politics of community? If we lose the ability or desire to name our own experience, we will live out 'the lot assigned to us,' the lot

conveyed by the scripts we absorb from our everyday conversations and interactions, the scripts such as those assigned to parents by schools.

Scripts are not all bad. Scripts help us to know how to live in the world.
Mindy Fullilove (1999), who spent much of her childhood alone, reading
and creating a rich fantasy world, writes of how watching other adolescents
do improvizations in acting class helped her to learn the 'scripts' of adolescence. I, myself, have had experiences where I had no script to convey meaning
that I urgently needed to express. In these instances close colleagues and
friends have given me words, scripts, which transported me across rough
spots where my own words failed me. In these instances, I improvized scripts
to accomplish important ends.

The word 'improvization' is derived from the Latin for 'unforeseen.' In
improvization we are always 'working off of' one script or another, but we
bring more of ourselves to the script when we allow the unforeseen, the
unplanned, to well up from inside ourselves. I see the improvizational space
as a space occupied by one's daemon, unforeseen, vibrant, alive and kicking.

Thus, one can bring more or less of one's self to a script that one is performing – consider a gifted actress such as Emma Thompson who one
assumes draws deeply on her connection to the world in her performance of
a script. The interior problem occurs only when we mindlessly follow a script,
not having chosen it, or perhaps not even aware that we are performing it.
We have no, or little, psychic space between ourselves and the scripts we are
called to play. We cannot then improvize or change the rules guiding our
actions, for we are unwittingly locked into a script.

I am suggesting, however, that we can improvize scripts and, in the improvization, experience a different relationship between language and the 'treasure' inside. But first the scripts that we are living, or that are living us, must
be made visible.

A social script made visible: entredeux

Two years ago, a social script central to my own life was made visible to me by
a colleague – it felt to me as if she had thrown the script in my face. Though
she was simply telling a story about her workplace, the implications of her
words jarred me deeply. Her words catapulted me out of benumbment and
into what Cixous has called *entredeux*, 'a true in-between – between a life
which is ending and a life which is beginning ... an event arrives which evicts
us from ourselves ... we are launched into a space-time whose coordinates
are all different from those we have always been accustomed to ... we are
thrown into strangeness' (Cixous and Calle-Gruber 1997: 9–10).

The story-event that threw me into strangeness and plunged me into an
unsettling anger was about white women. At a conference on culture and psychology this colleague, a woman of color, was chatting with another colleague, a white woman, and myself. She recounted how as the director of
psychology interns at a counseling center she had had difficulty supervising

the interns the previous year. She noted that the intern group that year had consisted mostly of people of color, and that they had been very critical of their training program in a way that had created serious problems for the administrators of the program. She laughed and said that the following year, she and her colleagues had purposely selected a group of interns consisting entirely of white women, and that they had had an easy, conflict-free year.

This experience jarred me into a renewed awareness of the power of others' implicit expectations, their scripts, to shape the behavior and thoughts of those around them. I also wondered about the extent to which powerful others rely on subordinates following these scripts to sustain their institutions.

My colleague's story about the compliant white female psychology interns provided the catalyst for the beginning of a shift in my epistemology from a reliance upon received knowledge and procedural knowledge (Belenky *et al.* 1997) to a way of knowing in which my self/daemon/inner voice has become more central to what I know. The influence of social scripts upon my own epistemology as a white woman and a parent parallels the experiences of other parents with whom I have met and worked. In the last section of this essay, I consider parents' responses to schools' expectations and scripts for them – the phenomenon that first led me to wonder about social scripting's influence on my own ways of knowing.

Schools' scripts and parents' ways of knowing

In the United States and several other Western countries, schools are in the midst of a wave of financial and rhetorical support for partnerships between themselves and the communities around them – to reform schools, and to govern them (Davies 1994; Giles 1998). Yet not many of these partnerships have succeeded in substantially improving school climates or more traditional indicators of achievement such as scores on standardized tests. The few schools that have changed have found ways to engage and use parents' knowledge about their children's education (Murnane and Levy 1996). Typically, however, such partnerships do not alter the status quo, and relationships between educators and parents remain unchanged; educators are much more powerful, and continue to 'call the shots' (Vincent 1996).

Many partnership efforts are what British scholar Carol Vincent (1996) has called 'statist reforms.' In these kinds of partnership, schools invite parents to participate in working toward goals that educators have already decided upon; parents are *not* invited in any significant way into the conversation that shapes the goals (even if a small number of them are included on 'leadership teams' or the like). In these ersatz partnerships, parents take on various roles (labels), all essentially geared to support the existing power relations in the school and community. The roles and their accompanying scripts that I have observed in many failing schools reflect this approach to parent involvement.

Evidence for the relationship between parents' experience in schools and the emergence of their epistemological perspectives exists in the research of Lynne Bond and her colleagues (Bond *et al.* 1996). In discussing their participants' responses about the 'people and experiences that have been important in shaping their understanding of themselves as thinkers and knowers,' they write (1996: 493):

> As children, many remember a school system and a peer culture that demeaned the way they dressed, the way they lived, and the way they talked; many describe being treated as outcasts, condemned to the margins of the school and peer cultures because they did not have the economic resources or the social 'know-how' to be accepted.

Bond and her fellow authors also report that mothers describe the roots of their ways of knowing by 'pointing to the degree to which they have felt truly heard and felt they have witnessed the power and/or impotence of their own minds and voices' (*ibid.*). These findings are in accord with Fiumara's (1990) description of the importance of radical listening to developing one's inner voice or daemon.

In this last part of the essay, I lay out several snapshots of the 'scripts' I have observed for parents in schools from my field research over the past four years in three American cities: a large city in the Northeast, one in the Mid-west, and a medium-sized city in the Southwest.[2] The data I offer in support of the existence of these scripts and their influence on parents' epistemologies are partial. The portrayals are intended to be heuristic and to evoke further reflection on parents' ways of knowing about their children's education in the context of their schools.

The welfare parent

In a session training parents to become leaders in the reformation of failing schools I met with a father, whom I shall call Jose, to get to know each other and to share why we were involved in this particular community-organizing initiative to reform schools. I was a researcher for the organization sponsoring the training, and Jose was a parent leader in his daughter's public school, a school with very low reading and math scores. Our task was to share our personal 'stories' with each other, with the larger goal of building a relationship that would become part of the foundation for working together to change schools and education policy in this large city. Pairs of parents were talking quietly in the same kind of meeting in various corners of the large room where the training was being held.

As the leader of a parent group that had made significant improvements in the physical plant of their children's school, Jose reflected back on a conversation he had had with the principal early in his experience at the school. With anger and indignation he recalled:

> I went to the principal to tell her that a group of us parents wanted to talk
> with her about some ideas about how to make the school better. She told
> me, 'Look, I'll give you letters for welfare.' I couldn't believe it! I told her
> I had a job, I wasn't there for a handout.

The principal mistook these parents who wanted to take action to improve
the school for parents who were trying to comply with welfare requirements.
The principal was deaf to Jose's request to help improve the school, evoking
instead an image of parents as dependent and needy, simply seeking the
'handout' of a letter for welfare.

The parents pushed past the principal's low expectations of them and
went on to make significant improvements in the school, with her eventual
collaboration. Fortunately, community organizers had coached parents to
talk as equals with school officials, even in the face of such demeaning
responses.

The principal's assumption that parents simply wanted letters for welfare is
evidence for one of the labels economically poor parents face in schools –
that of *welfare parent*. The stereotype of welfare parents is that they do not
want to work, though they may be able. A sense of passivity and shame accompanies this label. A parent labeled in this way would not be expected to have
important knowledge to contribute to the conversation about the nature and
quality of education their children are receiving at their school.

The parent in recovery

A colleague and I observed and interviewed parents and staff at an elementary school in a large Mid-western city that had received an award from an
advocacy organization for 'outstanding parent involvement.' We had
explained to staff and parents that we were interested in learning about successful approaches to engaging parents that we could take back to share with
parents in our city.

Located in a low-income neighborhood, the school had received grants
and significant publicity for developing programs to engage parents and
members of the local community in projects to improve the school and the
neighborhood. A governance committee composed of parents, teachers,
one local business owner, and the principal in an *ex officio* role, met regularly to make decisions about the school budget, curriculum, and the principal's performance. Some parents participated in a program in which
each parent helped a classroom teacher for a period of several weeks doing
tasks that a paraprofessional typically might do, such as reading with children and doing clerical tasks when necessary. Parents had also conducted a
door-to-door needs assessment of residents in the surrounding community,
and had developed a community center that offered programs to help residents to continue their education, learn English, and develop job-hunting
skills.

My colleague and I observed a meeting of the governance council, toured the school with the assistant principal, and met with a group of eight parents (all women) who had gathered to talk with us at the request of the teacher-coordinator of the parent program. At this meeting, after the coordinator had given a general introduction to the parents, one by one each parent stood, introduced herself, and told the story of her involvement in the school. Each person's story included a description of how her self-esteem had been very low because of the stresses and trauma she had experienced in her life, and how her self-esteem had improved through her involvement with the school. During the presentations the teacher-coordinator leaned over and whispered to me that a couple of the parents were former substance abusers, and that one had been battered by her husband. Each parent expressed gratitude for the positive changes in her life resulting from her experience with the school.

I began to feel uncomfortable as I listened to the parents. I felt grateful that the school had responded to our request for the meeting, yet I also felt voyeuristic, as if I were at a Twelve Step meeting of some kind, as a curious outsider. My experience was of the teacher-coordinator parading parents in front of us to display the school's good work as reflected in these parents. After the meeting I expressed my discomfort indirectly by asking the coordinator whether the self-esteem of the teachers had been improved through the programs. She looked puzzled and then a bit defeated when I shared my observation that the program seemed to view only the parents as having problems and the teachers as having none.

I see this school as having an implicit label and script for parents as being 'in recovery.' The school worked with parents from a social services perspective: staff helped parents to recover from low self-esteem, to further their education, and to find jobs – all very important goals – but they did not make an ongoing place for parents in the life of the school as *fellow thinkers*, or producers of knowledge about their children's education. The parents were seen as *in recovery*. Those I heard seemed to have learned their role and the accompanying script well. I noted that the school had not made any significant progress in academic achievement since the project began several years earlier, and the program's leaders were having difficulty engaging a larger group of parents.

Parent as bureaucrat

In the same large Mid-western city, my colleague and I interviewed two parent leaders of a predominantly African American elementary school in a working-class and low-income community. We also toured the school and observed a meeting of the school governance committee. The parents, both men, had been members of the school committee at various times. One of the men, Charles, was still on the committee and had also been active in lobbying and advocacy for education reform at the state level for several years.

The other father, Ian, had been on the governance committee in the past, and was currently the president of the parent–teacher association.

As we sat in the comfortable teachers' lounge, Charles and Ian talked about their experiences as parent leaders at the school. They cracked jokes with two teachers who came into the lounge to get a snack from the vending machine during our conversation. In the context of his description of the work of the governance committee, I asked Charles whether many parents attended the meetings of the committee which were open to the public. He laughed and said,

> The meetings are open, but not too many people show up for them. We're talking about a lot of details that are boring to most people, you know, budgets and things like that. I tell my wife that watching one of our meetings is like watching paint dry.

This description of the governance meetings as boring conveyed the surprising message that parents would not be interested in the decisions being made about how well the principal was doing at leading the school, the best curriculum for their children, or how to spend the school's money. Charles' portrayal evoked an image of the committee's work as bureaucratic, draining this work of its significance for the lives of the children in the school.

Ian, on the other hand, told of how he had resigned from the governance committee largely because he felt that his participation distanced him from other parents who were his friends. He recalled that when he was on the committee other parents called him by his last name, Mr Alford, and that they did not 'joke around' with him. As the PTA president, though, he said that they again called him by his nickname, 'Rocky', and he felt much more comfortable. He saw the PTA as 'social,' as compared to the governance committee which was 'about doing business.'

Charles' and Ian's description of the governance committee, and the role of the parent on that committee, evokes a script of *parent as bureaucrat*. Such a script would not seem to call on the parent's inner voice or spirit, or his gut, in his way of knowing about the school. The committee seemed to be about business as usual, not calling on parents to reach into the 'secure depths' of their inner lives to name and possibly transform their children's experience in the school. As with the other school in the city with outstanding parent involvement, this school had not improved in academic achievement in the past several years.

Parent as citizen

Just before our visit to the Mid-western city, my colleague and I had been in the Southwest interviewing and observing parents, school administrators, and staff who were part of a community-organizing initiative to reform schools in a city of several hundred thousand people. On our visit to one of the schools we spoke with the principal and assistant principal about their efforts to involve parents to improve the quality of education for children in the school. Located in a working-class and low-income community, the school's test scores were below the average for city schools. Our visit was in February and the administrators had just arrived at the school the previous September, so they were relatively new. They told a very different story about parent involvement from the stories we would hear in the Mid-western city.

The assistant principal, Maria, described how she and the principal, Cheryl, learned that parents only became involved when they chose issues *they* were interested in:

> because we are a school, we wanted them to get involved with educational issues, which is good. But when you don't have the passion and the history of parent involvement and you want to get the ball rolling – what we learned from them is that it has to be an issue that's in their interest, and test scores are not in their interest.

Maria and Cheryl went on to tell how at a parents' association meeting only three parents signed up for a committee to plan a workshop on improving their children's test scores, while twelve parents signed up to work on a project to get rats out of the school. School administrators had filed reports and requests to exterminate the rats with the central education bureaucracy for years, with no results. So, at the prompting of a community organizer, Maria and Cheryl told parents about the rats and enlisted their help.

A core group of twenty-two parents, coached by the organizer, met at 7:30 a.m. one day at the school with an operations manager from the central office of the city's school district to address the issue of the rats. Later that same day, crews from the central office were at the school, filling holes, putting up screens by air-conditioning units, and taking other measures to prevent the rats from entering the school.

Maria reported that after these initial preventive actions, the parents pushed the district to eliminate the source of the rat problem by removing the old heating units where the rats were nesting. Though the district balked at the expense of removing the units, saying that that funds would not be appropriated for this work until a couple of years later, parents persisted and the heating units were removed within a week.

I was struck by Maria and Cheryl's excitement about the parents' role in improving the school, and how they spread this image of parents as powerful to the teachers. When describing parents' initial morning meeting with the operations manager, Maria reported:

> the teachers weren't involved, and the teachers wondered, 'What's going on? Why are all these parents here so early? Are we in trouble? What did we do? Oh my gosh, it's a riot.' And the next day at the faculty meeting, we told them and we shared the story with them, and they were clapping

and they got all excited. It was an example of these parents advocating for their kids, maybe not in the traditional educational way that we expect, but they are.

A persistent theme in our interview with Maria and Cheryl was their interest, as administrators, in communicating to the teachers that parents are powerful and can help the school. They did not seem to be afraid of the potential power of the parents. Maria told us:

> These are the examples that we bring to the teachers. Making sure that the teachers know that these things are happening because they need to understand that these parents have a lot of power. And that we need to be working with them and inviting them in, in order that they can help us because there are things we cannot do.

In contrast to the story that we heard later in the Mid-western city about how parents had improved their self-esteem, that is, how their 'recovery' was going well, here in the Southwest administrators were emphasizing parents' *power* to change harmful conditions at the school. Also, attending meetings at this school was certainly not 'like watching paint dry.' I got the impression that parents made important decisions about how to change conditions at the school. Their knowledge counted.

One of the administrators, Maria, had participated as a teacher in a community organizing initiative in another school in which parents and teachers had collaborated to start a health clinic in the school. She brought her concept of parents' role in schools from that experience to her work as assistant principal in her current school. She described how ideas about parents' roles had evolved at her previous school:

> You know at Kingston, we used to talk about would you pay for a new bulletin board, yeah they can come in and laminate, yeah come in and run off papers and that was parent involvement five years ago. And today it is not; it's about a parent on a school board; it's about parents on task-forces all over the district from Kingston, and developing a health clinic from a grant.

Maria's description reflects an expectation, or a script, for parents to participate in creating knowledge about their children's education in a school. This particular social/institutional script, or set of rules, allows for and encourages their passion, including their anger, about their children's education. I call this script *parent as citizen.*

Forces do exist though in their district that would silence parents' voices to the extent that they disrupt the status quo. Maria gave a telling description of her district colleagues' responses when they heard about parents' success at ridding the school of rats:

They said, 'We know you must be under a lot of stress with those parents at that school … I mean, I cannot believe these parents, oh bless your heart. I know you need a break from this office.' And I am looking at them like, 'What?' Now, finally, I am seeing what I wanted to see in the school. I mean, we want parents to be angry about things when it is not going right … I think what the district sees as good is quiet. When it is quiet, it's okay, and apparently that was the situation with the administration last year.

In this school the administrators, Cheryl and Maria, were changing the prevailing script for parents in the school. In the new script, parents' selves, their feelings, including their anger, appeared to be more involved in the process of knowing. The staff with the greatest power in the school, the principal and assistant principal, repeatedly identified parents as powerful and lauded their anger about conditions that interfered with their children's education. Parents were asked to name the issues most important to them, and were encouraged to take action to address these issues. Their subjective knowledge of their children's education was valued.

The temptation to tell/script others

One last 'snapshot' depicts the temptation for professionals to script parents' thinking about their children's education, even within an organization that explicitly affirms, as central to their work, parents' own naming/defining of issues important to them. In this 'scene,' parent leaders had gathered with two education advocates, Martha and Tom, to prepare for their impending interview with a reporter from the local newspaper. The parents and advocates had worked together as part of an initiative to reform failing schools in their city. The reporter requested to interview parents for an article she was writing about the politics surrounding education reform in this city.

A parent leader suggested that they role-play the interview to help to prepare them for what they would say to the reporter. Martha and Tom took on the role of the reporter, and posed questions to the parents, one by one, and then everyone gave feedback to the parent being interviewed as to how he or she was coming across.

Carmen, a Latina mother in her mid-twenties, stumbled over her answer in response to one of Tom's questions. She said that she did not know what to say. Martha told her, 'You don't have to think up your own ideas – you can use the ideas in Tom's handout.' Before the mother could refer to the handout, which outlined the key policy positions of the organization, Tom jumped in and asked her, 'What do *you* think about how the commissioner [of education] is doing?' She began to speak about her own experience of her child's school in a passionate way, though she still seemed a little unsure of her course. Tom followed up with another question that resulted in the mother speaking even more strongly about the poor quality of education in the schools in her neighborhood. One of the other parents, Oscar, said, 'I think you have a good story; *tell your story!* The more we sound like parents, the better off we are.'

The irony is that though these participants *are* parents, all with rich, first-hand knowledge about schools, they have to work at *sounding like* parents in the context of this interview. In this context the pressure is intense for parents to say the 'right words,' even if they are not their own words or ideas, to have an impact on public policy through the media.

Listening to the role-playing, I was startled and intrigued to hear one organizer tell the mother that she could use the words and ideas of the other organizer. I felt the pressure on everyone to 'get it right' for the interview. I silently cheered when Tom redirected the parent to her own experience by asking her a question that led her back to 'the treasure in her hand,' to her own inner experience of the schools in her neighborhood.

The non-profit group that has trained these parent leaders and coordinated this meeting with the reporter intentionally prepares, or scripts, if you will, public events or actions where parents aim to have an impact on public policy. The challenge, as I see it, for this organization and other similar organizations is to continue to evoke and honor parents' perspectives and knowledge about their children's education, and to create scripts for public consumption that are grounded in parents' knowledge. The temptation, though, is to trump parents' firsthand, grass-roots knowledge with 'higher-level' analyses of policy developed by the advocates who have more formal education and interact more regularly with high-level public officials.

Conclusion

Though Heidegger's allegory about the treasure in the poet's hand is no longer new to me, I continue to be moved deeply by the recognition he gives in this passage to the individual's inner life. I am moved because I am more aware than ever of the grave challenges to the preservation of this inner life, challenges to the possibility of 'thinking one's own thoughts.' In this essay, I have tried to articulate the importance of parents being able to think their own thoughts about their children's education, and the ways in which schools' labels and scripts for parents cut off the oxygen needed for these thoughts to be born.

The practical implications of these issues are reflected in reports from community organizers about how hard it is to engage parents in voicing their concerns about the quality of their children's education. There are many reasons for this difficulty, including the pull for individual parents to accept the perquisites – the best teachers for their children, even jobs – offered by some schools in exchange for silence about school problems. From my own experience as a parent I know that I sometimes hold my tongue because I fear the consequences for my child if I anger his teachers or the administrators of his school by voicing my concerns. I believe that schools, especially poorly-performing schools, are often aware of parents' fears and they count on them to ensure silence. Indeed, when parents step outside the schools' scripts for them, when they improvize, schools let them know that they are out of line and often out in the cold.

Thus, our fear may lead us as parents to deny or ignore what we see, what we know, to *benumb* ourselves. The result is often that our children suffer. Our choice is to give voice to what we see, what we feel in our guts, to keep our *selves* in the process of knowing and take action based on that knowledge. We can engage educators in dialogue and create new knowledge, constructive knowledge.

It is a rare educator who is prepared to engage in a true dialogue with parents, particularly economically poor parents. As an educator I have some insight into the barriers that prevent educators from becoming the 'kindly challenging' teacher/mentor that I describe earlier. If I, the educator, cannot allow myself to think my own thoughts then how can I midwife the thoughts of others? Also, I am anxious about listening to what others know, about helping their knowledge to be born, because it could conflict with my knowledge. Parents with whom I enter into relationship as equal, fellow thinkers destroy the myth alive in most schools that I, the educator, as the expert, am superior.

We need schools that will allow parents and educators to develop relationships that enable us to create new knowledge together. We need schools that can create improvizational spaces where we can meet each other as fellow thinkers, as co-creators of the best schools possible for our children. We need spaces where we can break free of the scripts that constrain our imagination and our deepest knowledge. Since few schools exist that can do this, we must create these schools at the same time as trying to give birth to ourselves as creative thinkers. Though this is a daunting task, if we do not take it on we will continue to accept others' words, false words, for our experience. Our 'treasures inside' will wither and die, and we will continue to function merely as instruments, participating in reproducing the same problems in our children's education from one generation to the next.

Notes

1 By 'parents' I mean caregivers who have primary responsibility for raising children. This includes grandparents, aunts, uncles, foster parents, and other caregivers who may or may not be kin to the children.
2 To preserve participants' anonymity, I do not identify cities or the actual names of people I observed and interviewed. I use pseudonyms when referring to participants.

References

Belenky, M. F., Clinchy, B. M., Goldberger, N. R. and Tarule, J. M. (1986, 1997) *Women's Ways of Knowing: The Development of Self, Voice, and Mind*, New York: Basic Books.

Bond, L. A., Belenky, M. F., Weinstock, J. S. and Cook, T. (1996) *Imagining and Engaging One's Children: Lessons from Poor, Rural New England Mothers.*

Cixous, H. and Calle-Gruber, M. (1997) *Helene Cixous Rootprints: Memory and Life Writing*, London: Routledge.

Cortes, E. (1996). 'Organizing Communities and Constituencies for Change' in S. L. Kagan and N. E. Cohen (eds) *Reinventing Early Care and Education: A Vision for a Quality System* (247–66), San Francisco: Jossey Bass.

Cowart, J. and Hamilton, J. (1987) *Georgia O'Keefe: Arts and Letters*, Washington, DC: National Gallery of Art.

Davies, D. (1994). 'Partnership for reform: Change happens at the local level and must link family, community and schools,' *Education Week*, 12 October 1994.

Dobrzynski, J. H. (1998) 'Steadily weaving toward her goal: Petah Coyne's art strategy has its scary moments,' *New York Times*, 6 October 1998.

Fiumara, G. C. (1990) *The Other Side of Language: A Philosophy of Listening*, London: Routledge.

Fullilove, M. (1999) *The House of Joshua: Meditations on Family and Place*, Lincoln and London: University of Nebraska Press.

Giles, H.C. (1998). ERIC Digest: Parent engagement as a reform strategy. New York: ERIC Clearinghouse on Urban Education.

Giles, H.C. (2000). Transforming the deficit narrative: Race, class and social capital in parent-school relations, In C. Korn and A. Bursztyn, Case studies in cultural transitions: Rethinking multicultural education. CT: Greenwood Press. In Press.

Heidegger, M. (1971) *On the Way to Language*, New York: Harper & Row.

Henderson, A. and Berla, N. (1994) *A New Generation of Evidence: The Family Is Critical to Student Achievement*, Washington, DC: National Commission for Citizens in Education.

Ignatieff, M. (1985) *The Needs of Strangers*, New York: Viking.

Murnane, R.J. and Levy, F. (1996). *Teaching the new basic skills: Principles for educating children in a changing economy.* New York: The Free Press.

Rich, A. (1993) *What Is Found There: Notebooks on Poetry and Politics*, New York: W. W. Norton & Co.

Tomkins, S. (1995) 'Script Theory and Nuclear Scripts' in E. K. Sedgwick and A. F. Frank (eds) *Shame and Its Sisters: A Sylvan Tomkins Reader* (179–95), Durham, NC: Duke University Press.

Vincent, C. (1996) *Parents and Teachers: Power and Participation*, London: Falmer Press.

10 Labeling heroes

Role models in higher education[1]

Warren Crichlow

> One person's desire can bring a role model into being. In this respect, the
> process of taking and making role models is like falling in love.
>
> (Bernice Fisher 1988)

> We were in love at first sight.
>
> (Hilton Als 1996)

In the wake of persistent demands for social justice and equality, the label
'role model' has become ubiquitous within university affairs. Glib responses
to equity such as the institutionalization of cultural diversity programs, affirmative action and multicultural curricula have produced a narrow educational prescription for real or imagined role models. While critical
theorizing has challenged innocent notions of the essential raced, classed or
gendered subject, bureaucratic equity achievement in the university tacitly
requires 'positive images' of success within these same 'naturally' binding
categories. Despite recognition that identities are partial and contradictory –
and do not fit into neatly labeled classifications – 'role models' are politically
and culturally constituted along racial and gender lines, and other socially
and historically articulated lines of difference. In this context, role model
positions function as idealized identity boxes where ascribed characteristics
become literally employable. Blacks, gays, women, physically challenged persons and so on are positioned (or im-position themselves) as representatives
of success. They doubly serve as fixed images of achievement and pedagogues of 'academic' (or conversely ideologues of 'politically correct')
socialization. Here the institutional 'role' function and the primacy of physical or imagined identity attributes of individuals are artificially fused. The
role model thus performs an officially designated expectation which takes
on a pedagogical life of its own.[2]

In performing the authorized role, however, the 'model' can come perilously close to losing his or her sense of identity and individuality. That is,
both are subject to displacement by irresistible illusions of institutional

power, authority, legitimacy and job mobility. Vested with normative institutional identifications, expectations of 'role' conformity consequently structure university and classroom protocol in forced and often alienating ways. The results are usually disastrous for the process of teaching and learning, both for the subjected student and the person who carries the burden of *perfect* model expectation.

This conundrum, which invariably attends role modeling in the university – in curriculum, administration, teaching, advising and supervision – lies with the cynical illusion that primary lines of difference determine, as Mary Helen Washington notes, who can have something in common with whom: that diversity 'is like having so-many crayons in your crayon box ... their color is their identity, their substance, their uniqueness' (Washington 1985: 228). Within this dubious economy of likeness, students are blithely provided with role models whom they resemble or with whom they are assumed to intrinsically share a collective interest and which they will therefore automatically 'be-like.'

Fortunately, this simplistic 'be-like' scenario is more complicated than first meets the eye. On the one hand, the institutionalized nature of role models cannot ensure identifications along rigid lines of race, sex or any other presumption of essentialized difference. The premise of automatic conformity to legitimated role models is also countered by extant forms of dissent and resistance observed in the classroom and in the everyday environment. On the other, the restricted availability of models of behavior accepted within narrowly construed narrative of university culture represses possibilities for the open-ended communication and fluid identifications that are essential to realizing more substantive academic goals of intellectual exchange and knowledge production.[3]

Rescuing role modeling from confining labels, cliché and narrow preconceptions requires a more complex awareness of its machinations. Role model processes involve, of course, interrelationality. How such relations are made and unmade, however, derives from both conscious and unconscious motivations and life choices. In this view, even the willing role model is not in charge! These processes are not fixed or natural in any strict consensual sense, since a role model is not a person who simply models or impersonates an abstract role.[4] Rather, a role model is a person chosen and created by another, a relationship which emerges from spoken and unspoken forms of fantasy, pleasure, and desire. The non-linear processes of relationship formation endemic to role model choosing are open-ended and can arouse unexpected forms of identification and meaning. Contrary to the obligatory institutional mandate for linear identificatory or 'become like' arrangements, role modeling is conceived here as a dynamic process which fosters the exercise of individual agency. Indeed, role model processes share in the vitality of everyday life. That is, a striving for productive self-fashioning is integral to multifarious forms of problem-solving, creative endeavors and cultural resistance struggles. Rather than restricting agency, the conflict and change embodied in role model relationships should ideally open individuals to the possibilities of the unimagined.

The role model process I posit is one that escapes normative university categorization. To more fully approximate this departure, in part from restrictive and untenable labeling processes, I turn to the two juxtaposed epigraphs which began this text. Read together, they indicate the possible complexity of role model relationships, constituted both formally and informally. The first is from feminist scholar Bernice Fisher. In 'Wandering in the Wilderness: The Search for Women Role Models,' Fisher explores her considered ambivalence toward idealistic enthusiasm among liberal feminist professionals for role models: 'if women merely follow the lead of so-called role models, we all, every one of us, can succeed.' Eschewing these reductive, celebratory prescriptions for university models, she meditates instead on the multiplicity of 'meanings of role models as personal heroes' (1988: 213).[5] Fisher's analysis is striking because she intently embraces the slippery contradictions of model-making and model-taking to open up consideration of those more complicated yearnings that bring individuals together despite social realities of difference and conflict. For Fisher, taking and making role models is akin to the process of falling in love. Role model relationships entail a feeling of longing which, she contends, 'comes from ... not only what has not been given but also for what can be – the kind of passions we need to carry us over into the future, to the realization of vaguely perceived ideals' (*ibid.* 220).[6]

The second epigraph, from writer Hilton Als's recent collection of memoirist essays *The Women*, emphatically underscores the importance of Fisher's analysis: that desire can bring another into being as a role model. His first-person narrative implicitly interrelates the fraught and fragile nature of falling in love with the workings of private, unpredictable desires. He endeavors to show that choosing, loving, criticizing and ultimately 'moving on' from a role model is a significant, though painful, process of self-discovery. To explore the contradictory truths revealed by the love/role model relationship, Als deploys the caustic trope 'Negress' – a metaphor for the price paid for living life in an intolerable condition of puritanical self-sacrifice and self-denigration. Throughout his slim study, Als insistently offers a critical reading of the consequence of modeling roles that disable individuality (Lee 1997); relational situations that, as Barbara Houston puts it, 'prevent other more useful identifications' (1996: 155). In Als's hands, retrospective portraiture serves as a critical device for unpacking the stultifying and tragic ways role models are labeled – trapped and often trap themselves in a role performance defined outside the self.

Each of the role models on whom Als meditates serves to reveal moments of both significance and dread, passion and commitment, desire and betrayal (of self and other) in the struggle against conformity to externally defined expectations of behavior. He reflects forthrightly to define his voice as a writer and as an individual. He writes, in fact, to remember joys and tragic despairs in the lives of three role models. He writes also to expunge the self-imposed limits each lived so self-destructively. Working through vulnerabilities of self–other disclosure, Als provocatively models what he has learned from the implication of denial and loss in each of their lives and, in turn, acknowledges what these role models collectively contributed to his own intellectual formation. At the same time, his melancholic defense of his individuality must be understood as a performance of both his deep connection to and autonomy from these models. He is eager to demonstrate how he finally resolved their contradictions in his own life. Central to Als's project is a personal (if political) act of writing beyond the reflexive politics of socially circumscribed identity.

It is significant that Als's depictions render role models who are enigmatic, difficult and lamentable but who nevertheless remain complexly influential through the instabilities and tragic contradictions of their identities. Contrary to the popular 'simple version' of the role model idea (Britzman 1993), a desire for a perfect example of whom, how and what to become like, I recognize in Als's portraits a mutable view of the role model process. This perspective takes seriously the workings of passion, identification and love as vital categories through which to understand the ways role models are complexly taken and made, both in and outside of the university context.

Indeed, the overlap between Als and Fisher confirms the contravening notion that role model relations do not work simply through mimesis: 'the process of model making approaches copying or imitation ... [but never] exactly' (Fisher 1988: 220).[7] As Fisher points out, role models can neither provide 'neat, uncontradictory selves [nor guarantee] a nonproblematic relation to the world.' Examining how the specifically untidy processes of discovery engendered by role model relationships reveal serviceable yet 'unpalatable and contradictory truths about the world and ourselves' (*ibid.* 227–8) is relevant here. Before returning to Fisher's useful reconsideration of models and heroes, I shall probe Hilton Als's account of his first encounter and subsequent friendship with the poet, novelist, dramatist and professor Owen Dodson.[8]

In the third and final essay of his collection, Als reflects on the strong residual effect Dodson had on his earlier life. Through both intellectual history and literary criticism, he pensively maps the intimate construction and highly contested nature of a role model relationship. The contentious contradictions at play in Als's melancholic portrait of Dodson indicate the imprecise character of the label 'role model.' He demonstrates how extraordinary role model relationships result from complex, difficult and uncertain experiences, rather than from the standardized, linear and predictable emulations assumed in university press to service diversity, affirmative action and multiculturalism.

Als and Dodson first met in 1974 in Dodson's Brooklyn home, not in a customary site of higher learning. The 13-year-old Als was under the tutelage of a long-time woman friend of Dodson's. This woman taught poetry and piano to 'gifted' initiates who were either self-interested or had parents like Als's mother who, with upward mobility in mind, deemed exposure to extracurricular arts important.

Als recalls that he received a scholarship to study with this teacher. But instead of learning poetry, he remembers that he studied her dishevelment, her 'intractable bewilderment.' It was a bewilderment that, Als thinks, was as much about her own ruffled life as it was about 'young people like myself, whose ambition would consume what she had to offer and carry them on to the next person they would need to consume in order to become something other than themselves' (1996: 121–2). Recognizing that Als's ambition required something greater than she could impart, the teacher sent him on to that next person, her friend Owen Dodson.

Als does not use the term 'role model' to describe the formative yet ultimately failed intellectual and sexual liaison he claims as an adolescent to have shared for six years with the older man.[9] In fact he states, curiously, that neither was Dodson a 'father' figure, nor was his literary work 'an immense liberation for me' (1996: 130).[10] The Dodson that emerges from Als's cool, irreverent and unsentimental analysis is a rather impulsive nurturer and a pedantic teacher who nevertheless 'made the world less common through exposing people to many things they had never known before' (*ibid.* 139). Als says that Dodson made it possible for him to come close to a 'curiously shaped' world of literary personalities, gossip and the history of the Harlem Renaissance at a time when 'I had just begun to be confused by my attraction to reflection (writing) and to being social' (*ibid.* 122). With Dodson as a conduit, Als temporarily moved beyond the thrall of his mother and sisters: he traversed further, into parts of the world and of himself that he had only begun to imagine possible.

Making the strange approachable and the familiar again difficult is perhaps the more common adage for what transpired between Dodson and Als. Providing access to a larger world of idiosyncratic people and ideas is the implicit task a role model performs in relation to the inchoate desires of an inquisitive and ordinarily ambitious student. The afternoon Als first encountered Dodson was marked by immediate recognition and identification. Each immediately recognized in the other flirtatious skills in dissembling, the ability to mask and falsely charm. Talk of books and looking at old photographs, finding shared resemblances, discovering cross-cutting interests and curiosities combined to unleash fluid psychological needs and suppressed desires. Seduced and energized in a mutual pedagogical gaze, Als says he and Dodson fell in love.

I am concerned here neither with the truth of Als's vogue tell-all details of intimacies gained and lost, nor with his critical assertions that 'reflexive, sentimental race consciousness' and victim status-for-aesthetics stymied the creative possibilities of Dodson and other black American writers following the Harlem Renaissance (Als 1996: 119).[11] Als's waspish literary criticisms and generational dissent notwithstanding, his portrayal of Dodson is of interest because it is paradoxical: Dodson is represented as both a seminal influence on and as an inappropriate role model for the writer that Hilton Als is today. What fascinates is how Als's desire, like falling in love, brought Dodson into being as a role model.

The relationship eventually failed, eroded in fact by the very desire that initiated it: the passionate need to fulfil ambition and love. Als's ambition was to learn about literature and writing. He was intrigued by the marvelously close association Dodson's experience provided to that larger world of language and culture. Despite the admiration which initially mediated this relationship, the dangerous lesson learned by the ambitious student was how to think in ways perhaps unintended by his teacher. As Als states (1996: 133–4):

> our relationship was that of the pedant and his student consumed with ambition. What the pedant knows: his ambitious student will stop at nothing in order to learn to be himself ... to become a self without the burden of the pedant's influence.

Thinking led Als to recognize the frailties of his mentor; that social pressures to conform to hackneyed respectability had already moved Dodson 'away from the expansive interior places writing could have taken him to' (*ibid.* 127). In one sense, the linked life of the mind and writing that Als's ambition preciously sought outgrew what Dodson, in his senior years, was capable of giving. At 19, Als left his aging teacher and lover in order to find the next person who would help him to accept his right to individual vision – a right whose ambitious possibilities he had only momentarily glimpsed in the chic literary world of Dodson's archaic memory. In another, perhaps more telling sense, Als confesses that he too betrayed the friendship (and his own vision) by succumbing to a terror of the individuality he had so hoped to vacate: that place where kinship and fear 'had the power to displace my love and confusion for men like Owen' (*ibid.* 143).

Reading Hilton Als's essays foregrounds tensions that are often suppressed in role model arguments, especially those in higher education where the label 'role model' typically refers to a rather contrived and often disingenuous sense of what constitutes relationships between students and faculty of the same race or gender (Allen 1994). Although generated through reflexive literary means, Als's insights into the limits of the joined terms 'role' and 'model' illuminate knotty issues about race, gender and difference that university-based discussions often evade. His reflections suggest questions generally held in abeyance by institutional quests for positive role models: roles filled by persons who are expected to both conform to and piously reflect social standards and conventions of success authored by the dominant group. From the university viewpoint, queries that challenge such idealized desires for model behavior and attendant assumptions of piety include: what roles are role models supposed to model? Are there fragilities that role models cannot *not* avoid modeling? What fascinations, desires, needs draw the young person, the student to take and make a role model? What aspects of the positive role model's narrative are impor- tant/unimportant to what that role model might mean for different stu- dents in changing times? And where and when do shifting aspects of biographical narrative produce the 'negative role model'? (See Austin 1989.) What do we covet, admire and deny in the role model label? And finally, can role models assure gender and race equity in the university in the new millennium?

In a variety of ways critics of the role model argument have com- mented on similar questions, from fields as diverse as women's studies, critical legal studies, critical race theory, multicultural education, black studies and queer studies.[12] Though there are important theoretical and pedagogical differences among critical scholars, their common point of contestation clusters around the problematic nature of the positive role model idea. Writing at the intersection of multicultural education and gender, for example, Deborah Britzman argues that a desire for an ideal- ized, stable and positive role model displaces the contradictions and controversies which actually construct and set individual identity into perpetual motion and change. Britzman's analysis problematizes the assumption that the role model can serve as the guaranteed 'transitional object' to unique gendered (or normatively 'successful') identities. Given that role models are also fashioned through existing circuits of dominant–subordinate social relations, Britzman asks whether, in fact, 'a copy can be unique.' Her inquiry does not suggest that role models should not be offered in educational settings. Rather, she specifically pushes for an account of gender that understands its contextual particu- larities, and for a radical conception of role modeling practices beyond normative frameworks of labeling that occlude power and domination (Britzman 1993).[13]

As I have suggested above, neither gender nor race, nor other stable constructions of social difference, can be the final arbiter in choosing a role model. While consciously chosen practices of oppositional 'differ- ence' are important and demand careful contextual consideration, I argue that conceptualizing radical role modeling requires an engage- ment with the more complex ways individuals achieve such relation- ships. Specifically, the larger question concerns the conscious and unconscious search for role models and what this reveals about self- fashioning desire. I consider Hilton Als's portrait of Dodson as but one of the myriad instances in which role model relationships are experi- enced. Passion, identification and love are vital to the creation of role models. And, as Als poignantly writes, role models can also be con- sumed by a creator's ambition. The need for role models is not simply about binding identificatory expectations. Rather, the powerfully felt desire to become 'something more,' albeit only vaguely envisioned, is the dynamic factor that urges a person to go in search of what another might offer.

Bernice Fisher's explication of role models and heroes also foregrounds the individual's search for the adoption of another as a role model. Most significant is the individual's quest to forge a new life that markedly differs from the present: to redefine the self in a way that is (or will become) at odds with kin, community or dominant modes of thought. Often there is no known precedent for the life one imagines (say, the dual inconceivability of a viable life as a gay man and writer that Als recalls in his own immediate familial context). In fact, such a life, as mere fantasy, may constitute a threat to traditional sustaining social supports. Taking on a new life necessitates change – and the tensions of change 'rend' the self. Fisher argues that this process, the 'rending' of the self and of the intricate social fabric in which we participate, constitutes 'the [meaningful] context for our quest for role models and heroes' (1988: 217).

At issue is the transition from the present imagined self (lack and all), to the future self only vaguely perceived. For Fisher, this anxious search for role models – the creation of idealized persons – 'is an attempt to find support, validation and guidance in changing historical circumstances.' In a volatile social context, Fisher observes, the inadequacies of selected role models may have less to do with individual imperfections than with the fact that 'no authority figure can provide definitive answers or solutions to the problems that change poses.' Neither the individual nor the corporate role model can impart definitive guidance; no one can guarantee a contradiction-free transition to an imagined future. Crossing borderlands of change is indeed lonely work, as the destination is elusive, and assurance that the immense struggle to arrive is worth the price of the ticket similarly escapes foreknowledge (1988: 217–18).

Change in uncertain times manufactures powerful longing for guidance through the historical contradictions that mark everyday life. I think Fisher is correct in pointing out that 'the people we find to help us in this struggle, and the models we [subsequently] make of them are not the same.' Role models, as Fisher puts it, can be anyone alive or dead whose voice (spoken or written) speaks 'to ways of acting not yet [generally] embodied in our social realities' (1988: 219–20). In this sense then, the role model simultaneously arouses passion and helps to clarify a vision through an arduous transitional period. But as Als's account vividly demonstrates, the accumulation of deepening insights wrought by change brings about an attendant disappointment: the irreconcilable difference between the model's fragilities (as well as the sloppiness in our own life) and the idealized features that once made that model's life so compelling to follow. Perhaps the role relationship's end is that untenable moment of dissatisfaction when illusion painfully unravels. Als's portrait articulates both an unnerving will to move on and the awful cost of suppressing creative ambition.

Fisher is critical of feminists who unproblematically view the role model process as simply choosing 'images of women who have survived and who therefore in some sense negate [historical and political] contradictions.' In order to formulate an alternative to this rigid 'be like' idealism she questions memories of her own encounters with role models and their larger-than-life representations. The valuable lessons Fisher draws from rethinking her experiences serve to confirm that a radical conception of role modeling must be sought in the context of the commitments it entails and the passions it expresses (1988: 217, 225). Relatedly, Als's transgressive act of memoir interrogates the problematic of role modeling, particularly the debilitating costs individuality pays for modeling externally defined values. Als's 'raced' Negress figures are destroyed by self-sacrifice. To exorcise this tragic inheritance, Als sifts through the ruins of his mentors' silenced lives. He finds salvation only in the public exhumation of their failures and, in so doing, surmounts socially imposed limits antithetical to individual agency and artistic freedom.

Despite their distinct critical strategies, both Als and Fisher valorize the passion and elements of individual choice that should ideally inform role model practices. Within the context of the narrow norm-laden prescriptions that dominate hierarchical educational and political institutions, this commitment to the passionate and selective nature of role model-making reasserts a radical respect for the various choices and desires individuals may express in forming these relationships. Of course, as Fisher reminds us, role model-taking is 'rarely, if ever, a solely individual or completely social matter ... [W]hat seems to be a deeply personal act takes place in a profoundly political environment' (1988: 221). Inequality in material conditions and social justice within and across communities profoundly differentiates access to role models and other kinds of supportive social relationships. Clearly racism, sexism and other exclusionary practices require redress through ongoing political struggle and collective action. In community and university contexts, however, where social and political demands for solidarity with a specific identity position are so pervasive, sustaining individuals' capacities to choose and shape their own political values is a necessary interventional measure for radical role model practices.

My reading of Fisher and Als suggests that role model relationships must be evaluated by their capacity to model practices of living and thinking beyond reflexive identity politics and ideological confines. Hilton Als finally rejected the style of literary celebration to which he felt Owen Dodson had eventually succumbed. He did not, however, relinquish his own ambitions to engage the larger world of intellectual pursuits so dramatically opened by Dodson. I have utilized Als's reflections to extend the criteria of responsibility in role model relationships: the nurturance, sustenance and extension of individuality. In this sense, then, the ethos of role model relationships is to 'model' disciplined self-reflection that enables complex judgements and critical action independent of larger social pressures. I imagine that this commitment to the multiple ambitions, desires and pleasures that inform agency can only be supported in those interpersonal spaces that consciously and cognitively resist those coercive forms of authority and conformity that are all too pervasive in the politics of universities.

Can role models assure gender and race equity in the university in the new millennium? My immediate response is a negative one, particularly if the goal of equity is dependent upon role models understood within the banal administrative discourses of cultural diversity, multiculturalism, and affirmative action. Inscribed in these institutional arguments for role models lie question-able premises of 'race' and 'gender' labeling. This produces an odd tension, given that we can no longer believe (at least within some intellectual work on the complexities of identity categories) in consensual categories of race and gender. Under the rubric of institutional rhetoric, inequalities will be repro-duced, modeled in a ghettoized matrix of endless difference and politically rigid identity.

Of course this is dangerous territory. On the one hand I agree with Anita L. Allen, who correctly argues that raising critical questions about role models is not meant 'to cripple activism' for equity – it is a given that this fight is ongoing. On the other, it is politically important to contest the assumption that 'role model capacity' is specifically reducible to a race or gender determination (Allen 1994: 195). That is, the contribution a person can make as a role model is simply incommensurable with such socially con-structed labels. Moreover, role modeling is certainly not the only reason for diversifying university faculties, or the only tactic in the struggle to achieve equity. Professors, teachers and other professionals are traditionally held up as role models, but this elevation does not reflexively mean that all professors and teachers are good role models, nor should they be expected to be. 'Raced' professors have the right to pursue their commitment to scholarship and teaching duties as 'cosmopolitan intellectuals,' who, as Phillip Richards puts it, necessarily engage in university politics with an 'outsider's detach-ment' (1998: 75, 80). And students of any identity or persuasion have the right to adopt non-traditional commitments to a life of the mind beyond a limiting 'be like' scenario.

I have asserted the individual here as the center of a radical conception of role model practice. Obviously this view does not solve the complex prob-lems that surround role modeling as pedagogy or as strategy for equity in the university. As Bernice Fisher (1988: 223) insightfully points out:

> contradictions surface as we try to embody values like equality, justice, compassion, and freedom in our ongoing relationships. Because our so-cial order systematically undermines these relationships by destroying connections necessary to realize them, experience often teaches us to go it alone.

Despite this paradox, in its deepest sense, I believe the search for role models is about the need for relationships that can help us become something more, creatively and productively. Beyond the compulsion to label, role modeling in the university has the unrealized capacity to engender new vitalized ways of relating, both individually and collectively, to thinking differently and living differently in a world of difference. But like matters of love, to institutionalize this highly idiomatic attachment will foreclose insight into the more difficult work we do in the name of finding something more.

Notes

1 An earlier version of this essay was prepared for the conference on 'Rescuing Graduate Studies: Equity and How to Get It' sponsored by the Graduate Collaborative Program in Women's Studies, University of Toronto, February 1997 and subsequently published in Kay Armatage (ed.) (1999) *Equity and How to Get It: Rescuing Graduate Studies*, Toronto: Innna Publication and Education Inc. I am grateful to Kass Banning, Winston Smith, Deborah Britzman, Rinaldo Walcott and Kay Armatage for their invaluable insights and suggestions on this essay.

2 This does not deny any commitment to political redress of existing inequities, expansion of multicultural democracy access and access to economic opportunity. I am committed to interesting and provacative role model relationships in the university that cannot be predicted in advance. With other critics, however, I affirm the need to sustain critical dialogue on the institutional presumptions and discourses surrounding this term – especially in the present atmosphere of intense public and governmental conflict over the future of 'diversity' efforts in higher education. Along with Bernice Fisher, I want to claim 'the possibility but also the importance of criticizing the role-modelling process, not despite, but because ... [it is] so powerful and meaningful' (Fisher 1988: 227).

3 For example, see Barbara Houston's reading (1996: 154–5) of Mary Helen Washington's acount of the tensions of interracial co-teaching in a women's literature classroom. In addition, Valerie Smith (1998) interprets Washington's discussion to focus on the difficulties and possibilities of building an academic community in a racially diverse classroom.

4 Recently, studies of impersonation and performativity have advanced important insights into the processes of pedagogy, teacher/student relations and performance practices in everyday life and academic disciplines. Relevant to the examination of role models, these studies expand understanding of the ways identities are constructed through complex human relations known as 'performance.' See Gallop (1995) and Parker and Sedgwick (1995).

5 Fisher's title is in part inspired by the phrase 'wandering in the wilderness,' written by Alice Walker in her meditation on Zora Neale Hurston. See Walker (1983).

6 See also Fisher (1980) and Fisher (1981).

7 Fisher's critical analysis identifies celebratory role model discourses as 'forked' because the real conditions that have produced these relationships are elided. Role model discourse works well because it obscures a context of inequality that refuses to change. 'Capitalist or patriarchal structures prevent us all from succeeding, no matter how many role models or heroes we acquire. Success cannot be attained by everyone: it depends on access to social, economic and

political resources' (1988 212). Fisher's blunt critique of role modelling as mimesis has its parallel in the analyses of difference in colonial discourse illuminated by Homi K. Bhabha. The concept of mimicry in colonial discourse, like role model mimesis, operates as a strategic compromise. Both occupy an unstable place between what Bhabha (addressing limitations in Said's analysis of 'orientalism') describes as 'the demand for identity, stasis ... and the counter pressure of ... change, difference' (Bhabha 1994: 86). Mimicry in this sense works through tensions of ambivalence. I suggest that mimesis in role modelling also works through ambivalence. Here role modeling can be understood as an illusionary vehicle of reform and equity: there is the appearance of leveling the playing field, but only through the production of a 'recognizable Other,' *as a subject of difference that is almost the same but not quite.* To quote Bhabha at length here, 'mimicry is constructed around ambivalence; in order to be effective, [it] must continually produce its slippage, its excess, its difference ... an indeterminacy ... the representation of difference that is itself a process of disavowal ... a complex strategy of reform, regulation and discipline, which appropriates the other as it visualizes power' (*ibid.* my emphasis). I will not pursue the implications of this line of thought now. Rather, I suggest it as a critical method for further examination not only of how conventional role model discourse helps to sustain inequity, but also of how its limitations may reveal subversive possibilities in role model relationships. For a useful critique of Bhabha see Young (1990).

8   Als unsparingly portrays two other significants in his life. First his mother, Marie, a proud immigrant from Barbados and resourceful single mother who nevertheless yearned hopelessly for love, always just beyond her reach. Second Dorothy Dean, the unfulfilled 1950s Radcliffe/Harvard educated black American woman mostly known for her social impetuousness in the heady world of New York's gay white elites during the 1960s and 1970s. For Als, Dodson shared with Marie and Dorothy a commitment to 'the experience of pain' and to the tragedy pain affords. The three are also marked by important differences. Dodson's life and his relationship to Als is as different from both women's as Marie's is from Dorothy's. They are linked, however, in a stoic Negress stance Als describes as living 'while trying not to experience' (1996: 15).

9   *The Women* may be considered an eclectic work of memoir. The reader might usefully heed Samuel Delany's insightful caution regarding the autobiographer and, more so, the would-be memoirist: 'I hope to sketch, as honestly and as effectively as I can, something I can recognize as my own, aware as I do so that even as I work after honesty and accuracy, memory will make this only one possible fiction among the myriad ... anyone might write of any of us, as convinced as any other what he or she wrote was the truth' (Delany 1993: 14).

10   Here Als makes a rather presumptuous attempt to differentiate his relationship to Dodson from James Baldwin's famous relationship with his 'mentor' Richard Wright. Als writes, I think, to settle accounts and to emphasize his own trajectory from Dodson that, in an unwarranted manner, thematically parallels Baldwin's troubled essays on Wright. Nonetheless, I read Dodson as a role model for Als. In a sense by no means 'metaphysical,' the typical 'role' Dodson played for Als is similar to the example Wright initially provided Baldwin: 'he was a writer. He proved it could be done – proved it to me, and gave me an arm against all those who assured me it could *not* be done.' See e.g. Baldwin's 'Eight Men,' 'The Exile,' and 'Alas, Poor Richard' (1998: 247–68).

11   To be sure, Als forthrightly makes critical allusions to 'victim status,' which is informed by Orlando Patterson (1973). Sociology aside, however, he does not make explicit his analytic criteria for rendering assessments of 'writers and writing. In a cavalier way that is both acontextual and ahistorical, the 'Negress' trope is deployed to skewer a range of black female and male writers as diverse as

Zora Neale Hurston, John Edgar Wideman and Toni Morrison. In Als's view, black writers constitute an undifferentiated mass whom he characteristically chides: 'The Negress in literature ... a nearly dead construct who does not exist independent of her creator's need to fulfill his or her audience's expectations of performing "black" writing' (1996: 48). In his quest to valorize an intellectual and literary approach to producing and sustaining himself as an autonomous (black) writer, Als may be subject to the same kinds of criticism he levels. In particular, note the belletristic school of genteel writing whose *gemütlich* feel Als has aspired to, assimilated and now uncritically performs for *The New Yorker*. For a different assessment of twentieth-century black American literary and intellectual culture (including Dodson) see e.g. Brown (1996) and Watts (1994).

12   In addition to authors cited above, see Dyson (1993), Lopez (1993), Morgan (1996), Munoz (1996) and Richards (1998).

13   Other critics, like Morgan (1996), address contradictions in authority and norm-ladened behavior inscribed in role model-mediated socialization in feminist pedagogy. Conversely, Houston (1996) adopts a view of role modeling as a more active and contingent process, focusing on possibilities cultivated in relationships rather than on what might be jeopardized.

References

Als, Hilton (1996) *The Women*, New York: Farrar, Straus and Giroux.

Allen, Anita L. (1994) 'On being a role model,' in *Critical Multiculturalism: A Critical Reader*, edited by David Theo Goldberg, Cambridge, Mass: Basil Blackwell, pp. 180-99.

Austin, Regina (1989) 'Saphire bound,' *Wisconsin Law Review* 3, 539–78.

Baldwin, James (1998) *Collected Essays*, New York: Library Classics of the United States.

Bhabha, Homi K. (1994) 'Of Mimicry and Man: The Ambivalence of Colonial Discourse' in *The Location of Culture* (85–92), New York: Routledge.

Britzman, Deborah (1993) 'Beyond Rolling Models: Gender and Multicultural Education' in Sari Knopp Bliken and Diane Pollard (eds) *Gender and Education: Ninety-second Yearbook of the National Society for the Study of Education* (25–42), Chicago: University of Chicago Press.

Brown, Sterling A. (1996) in Mark A. Sanders (ed.) *A Son's Return: Selected Essays of Sterling A. Brown*, Boston: North Eastern University Press.

Delany, Samuel (1993) *The Motion of Light in Water: Sex and Science Fiction Writing in the East Village: 1960–1965*, New York: Richard Kasak Book Edition.

Dyson, Michael Eric. (1993) '"Be Like Mike": Michael Jordan and the Pedagogy of Desire' in *Reflecting Black: African-American Cultural Criticism* (64–77), Minneapolis: University of Minnesota Press.

Fisher, Bernice (1980) 'Who Needs Woman Heroes?', *Heresies*, 3(1): 10–13.

—— (1981) 'The Models among Us: Social Authority and Political Activism,' *Feminist Studies*, Spring 1981, 7(1): 100-112.

—— (1988) 'Wandering in the Wilderness: The Search for Women Role Models,' *Signs: Journal and Women in Culture and Society*, 13(13): 211–33.

Gallop, Jane (ed.) (1995) *Pedagogy: The Question of Impersonation*, Bloomington: University of Indiana Press.

Houston, Barbara (1996) 'Role Models: Help or Hindrance in the Pursuit of Autonomy?' in A. Diller, B. Houston, K. Pauly Morgan and M. Ayim (eds) *The Gender Question in Education: Theory, Pedagogy, and Politics* (144–60), Boulder, CO: Westview Press.

Lee, Andrea (1997) 'Fatal Limitations,' *New York Times*, Book Review, 5 January 1997: 7.

Lopez, Ian Haney (1993) 'Community Ties and Law School Faculty Hiring: The Case for Professors Who Don't Think White' in Becky W.Thompson and Sangeeta Tyagi (eds) *Beyond a Dream Deferred: Multicultural Education and the Politics of Excellence* (100–30), Minneapolis: University of Minnesota Press.

Morgan, Kathryn Pauly (1996) 'The Perils and Paradoxes of the Bearded Mother' in A. Diller, B. Houston, K. Pauly Morgan and M. Ayim (eds) *The Gender Question in Education: Theory, Pedagogy, and Politics* (124–34), Boulder, CO: Westview Press.

Munoz, Jose Esteban (1996) 'Famous and Dandy Like B. 'n' Andy: Race, Pop and Basquiat' in J. Doyle, J. Flately and J. E. Munoz (eds) *Pop Out: Queer Warhol* (140-179), Durham: Duke University Press.

Parker, Andrew, and Sedgwick, Eve Kosofsky (eds) (1995) *Performativity and Performance*, New York: Routledge.

Patterson, Orlando (1973) 'The Moral Crisis of the Black American,' *Public Interest*, Summer 1973, 32.

Pauly Morgan, Katheryn (1996) 'The Perils and paradoxes of the Bearded Mother,' in A. Diller, B. Houston, K. Pauly Morgan and M. Ayim (eds) *The Gender Question in Education: Theory, Pedagogy, and Politics* (124–34), Boulder, CO: Westview Press.

Richards, Phillip M. (1998) 'A Stranger in the Village: Coming of Age in a White College,' *Dissent*, Summer 1998: 75–80.

Smith, Valerie (1998) 'Split Affinities: Representing Interracial Rape,' in *Not Just Race, Not Just Gender: Black Feminist Readings*. New York: Routledge. pp. 1–34.

Walker, Alice (1983) 'Saving the Life That Is Your Own: The Importance of Role Models in the Artist's Life' in *In Search of Our Mothers' Gardens* (3–14), San Diego: Harcourt Brace Javonovich.

Washington, Mary Helen (1985) 'How Racial Differences Helped Us Discover Our Common Ground' in Margo Cully and Catherine Portuges (eds) *The Dynamics of Feminist Teaching*, Boston: Routledge & Kegan Paul.

Watts, Jerry Gafio (1994) *Heroism and the Black Intellectual: Ralph Ellison, Politics, and Afro-American Intellectual Life*, Chapel Hill: University of North Carolina Press.

Young, Robert (1990) *White Mythologies: Writing History in the West*, London: Routledge.

Callings

11 Connecting with the lesbian label

A personal and professional evolution

Jan McDonald

As a lesbian, my connection with the label 'lesbian' has been a complex, evolutionary, and often difficult process. I have known all of my life that I was somehow 'different' from others. But the homophobic and heterosexist world in which we live provided me with few cues or models to help me understand that difference or to connect it with the label *lesbian*.

My first connection with the label came with an awareness of its existence. For those of us who came of age twenty to thirty years ago, the label was forbidden discourse and so our 'discovery' of it was often an event in itself (Morris *et al.* 1995). We may have first excitedly encountered the lesbian label in a dime-store novel, or by scanning the dictionary. We may have first heard it screamed as an epithet against us by someone who recognized who we were before we recognized this ourselves (see a variety of initial encounters with the label in stories collected by, among others, Barber and Holmes 1994; Jay 1995; Jay and Glasgow 1990; Jay and Young 1992; Penelope 1994; Stanley and Wolfe 1980).

Like many others whose stories are noted above, my discovery of the label had a negative connotation. Even absent any explicit homophobic sense of the label, when I was growing up its relative invisibility alone carried a negative meaning. Yet at some point, despite the dearth of cues in my environment and the negative stigma associated with it, I connected my comfort with women, my attraction to women, my sexual feelings, my sense of being different, with this label. Within the gay and lesbian community, making that personal connection is called 'coming out.'

> The beginning of my journey was coming out to myself. All of my life experiences seemed to come together at once, and I knew I'd discovered the core of myself. I finally saw all that I'd been feeling in a new, sexual light, and found the word for myself: lesbian.
>
> (Barber and Holmes 1994: 1)

One rite of passage all lesbians go through, which may occur at any point in our lives, is coming out. Surveys have found that the process of discovering that one is sexually different may happen to children as young as four as well as to seniors.

(Jay 1995: 8)

That connection with the label can occur upon first seeing or hearing it, as a 'Eureka!' experience, or may require years of struggle and denial. For most lesbians, the experience of coming out is a powerful and exciting one.

I was 37 years old before I ever called myself 'lesbian.' Although I had acknowledged love for a woman and had been in a long-term relationship with a woman both during and after college, I do not recall being aware of the lesbian label until much later in my life. At the time of my first relationship, I do not believe I had ever even heard the word 'lesbian.' If I had, I am sure I did not know what it meant.

Making love to women and being in relationships with women were a part of my actions, but not a part of my conscious reflection. I was in love with a woman and I rationalized my physical attraction as, simply, love. I do not recall any conscious concern about being in love with a woman or making love with a woman. I had also fallen in love with a man, and I described that attraction as love. I do not recall thinking of myself as 'bisexual,' and to the best of my recollection was also unaware of that label. I did not have a conscious awareness of my sexuality, nor did I have an awareness of the political reality of the label; I merely acted on my feelings without reflection. For me, somehow, the issues were separate: love, sex, sexuality and gender. I did not need or use a label to describe how I felt or what I did.

Despite my love for a woman, I married the man that I loved. He was handsome, intelligent and fun to be with and marriage to a man was the accepted and expected 'thing to do.' I was comfortable and safe in my married life. But my attraction to women persisted and I always found ways to spend much of my time with women and in my mid-thirties, I once again found myself falling in love with women.

I have no recollection of the specific moment I began to associate the label 'lesbian' with my own sexuality, but in retrospect it must have been during this time. In my first lesbian relationship during and after college, my lover and I never used the label. In fact, we never discussed our sexuality. But the women I became romantically involved with in my thirties called themselves lesbians and had a personal and political consciousness about the label and about themselves as lesbians. They loved being lesbians, they were happy and confident in their lives and in their love and they embraced the label with delight and passion.

Through my relationships with these women, I became immersed in lesbian culture. I went to lesbian bars and saw rooms filled with all shapes, sizes and colors of 'woman-loving women.' I began to read lesbian literature and poetry and listened intensely to lesbian music. Much of this literature, poetry and music focused on the personal struggle of connecting oneself with the lesbian label that results from our own internalized homophobia and that of others. But much also focused on the exhilaration of coming out to ourselves and on the personal and political empowerment gained from embracing a lesbian identity.

I met many lesbians who were open and positive about their lives and their sexuality and who 'talked about it out loud.' Conversations with these women, characteristic of lesbian social interactions, involved their own coming-out stories and discussions of the fear, consequences and joys of being a lesbian. Some of these lesbians also introduced me to the political power of naming ourselves, and how naming ourselves and developing community empowers us against society's homophobia. Learning about the existence and meaning of the label for others allowed me to create a personal identity for myself as a lesbian and to begin to use the label to describe myself.

The steps between having an awareness of the label, connecting the label to ourselves, and embracing the label as a part of our identity (whether negatively or positively), are difficult steps that hinge on many factors including our age, community, previous experiences and personal circumstances. But no matter what our circumstances, the more deeply we build the connection between ourselves and the label, the greater the potential impact on our lives. Even lesbians who embrace the label for themselves often still remain 'in the closet' to others: family, close friends, co-workers. Homophobia makes it difficult for us to expand our connection with the label so that it is an integrated part of our lives. We may be 'out' to ourselves, but being 'out' to many others carries fears, both real and imagined, that keep many of us in the closet.

For me, the risk of losing my family and friends and jeopardizing my career in teaching caused me to live separate lives. For years I lived one life in the heterosexual world as a married, seemingly 'straight' woman, wife, mother and teacher, and I lived another life as a lesbian. And even after I had come to the point of personally embracing the label as a part of my identity, I still remained in the closet to all but a close circle of friends.

In my first administrative position at Orton College,[1] I had no thought or intention of ever being 'out' as a lesbian. In fact, as the director of educational studies at Orton, I found myself even more closeted than in my previous position as a faculty member at the university at Albany. Although I never reflected on it at the time, there were undoubtedly many reasons why I drifted further into the closet. First, the city where Orton is located is much smaller than Albany and within 30 minutes of the small town where I grew up. I had also been a high school mathematics and computer science teacher, sports coach and referee in this city for over ten years and many people in town knew me. Orton College is also much smaller than the university at Albany, and much more conservative.

I noted the presence of a few gay men and lesbians on the faculty at Orton, but no one ever openly acknowledged their sexuality. With the exception of an annual AIDS conference, I do not recall any conversations in my five years at Orton where the labels 'gay' or 'lesbian' were mentioned. Even the AIDS conferences focused much more on biology and disease than on any of the related sociological, psychological or personal issues.

As I try to reconstruct my sense of the homophobia at Orton, I struggle to distinguish between my own fears and internalized homophobia, and the actual conditions and environment that existed there. On the rare occasions that I asked other lesbian colleagues (that is, colleagues I assumed to be lesbians) to lunch, we always met well off campus and drove in separate cars. In our discussions about campus happenings, we never talked about our sexuality, or about gay or lesbian issues. There was always a level of nervousness about our interactions. Were my lesbian colleagues at lunch really uncomfortable, or was it my own discomfort lens that read the scene that way? Was it my discomfort that made my colleagues uncomfortable? If, in fact, they were lesbian and unwilling to talk about it, what in the environment caused this silence? What cues do we, as gay men and lesbians, go by to determine how open and comfortable we will be? Hearing others acknowledge their sexuality is an important cue and this, at the very least, was absent at Orton.

My responsibilities and pride in the teacher preparation program at Orton translated into a particularly strong concern for its integrity and status in the college and local community. As director, I was in and out of schools routinely, interacting with students and teachers, 're-presenting' the college and our program. For me, the administrative responsibility and resulting ownership of the program intensified my fears of being 'discovered' and labeled lesbian.

I completely avoided the local lesbian bar and went to the bars in Albany, anxiously looking around to see who else might be there. I returned to a pattern of driving three or four hours to Boston, Syracuse or Rochester to be in a 'lesbian space.' Though I had personally embraced the label of lesbian, its potential connection to me outside of my small circle of friends carried too much fear and risk.

Fear of the lesbian label is linked to both personal and professional consequences. Personally, I feared the loss of loved ones – family and friends. Professionally I feared the loss of status, credibility, and intimate interactions with colleagues at work and, perhaps, even the job itself. So, the coming-out process at work, like coming out to ourselves, is primarily the process of getting past the fear and getting to a place where the freedom of being out balances the potential risk.

The most powerful fear for me was the loss of self. When you have spent your whole life in the closet, everyone you know, either personally or professionally, knows you as someone other than who you are. In coming out, you run the risk of losing all control, all ability to predict how everyone in your life will feel about you, interact with you, think of you. Everything about who I was in the world and how people knew me had the potential of changing, and changing negatively. When people know you and love you for who they think you are, will they love you for who you really are?

My fear that someone would discover my sexuality was heightened when I became involved with a lesbian who was a member of ACT-UP (AIDS Coalition To Unleash Power). My other lesbian friends feared she would 'out' me (i.e. that, as a political act, she would intentionally reveal my sexuality to others). Although I in no way shared their fear about her, these conversations heightened my awareness of the issue of 'outing.' I worried about meeting her friends and whom they might know. I worried when she brought me to parties. We made her friends promise they would not disclose whom she was seeing.

While feeling more pressure to remain closeted in my position at Orton, my personal need to be lesbian-identified and connected also intensified. Despite the negative attributes of the lesbian label, for me, as for many lesbians, there was a personal power and excitement that resulted from embracing the label. For me, the power of being lesbian-identified brought a freedom that placed me in direct conflict with the oppression I feared I could experience as a lesbian.

I fell in love with the lesbian from ACT-UP and my label of 'straight wife' grew more tentative daily. My ability to live separate, unintegrated lives grew less viable and less credible personally. As my consciousness of my sexuality increased so did my consciousness of my life-long deception: deception to myself, to my husband and child, and to my family and friends. In earlier years I had struggled with the risk of losing my husband, family and friends. In more recent years I had struggled with the fear of losing my young son Steven. I feared the loss of my job and the respect of my colleagues. But soon the risk of losing Judy outweighed all other fears.

While still closeted at work, I came out to my husband Pete and soon thereafter to my family and closest friends, one and two at a time. Some of my fears had been accurate. A few family members and friends were lost instantly. But to my surprise, the vast majority were amazingly supportive and understanding.

I was euphoric: euphoric in my love for Judy and hers for me, but even more euphoric about discarding the weight of the closet, the weight of the deception and the segregation of my lives. And even though our relationships were clearly changed, I would not 'lose' my husband or son or most of my family and friends.

There was also a personal validation. 'We love you for who you are,' said my mother. 'I love you and want you to be happy,' my husband said. My euphoria was also connected with my sexuality and identity as a lesbian. 'Yes, I can say it out loud, I am a lesbian.' Family and straight friends now validated the lesbian label that was such a part of me. They did not validate what it means to be a lesbian (they still feared and did not quite understand that), rather they validated their love for me, even after hearing me name myself as a lesbian. The contempt and loss of love that I feared did not materialize when I labeled myself 'lesbian' in this piece of my straight world.

I decided to leave Pete and live with Judy, which was made much more difficult by the fact that she had accepted a position at Oklahoma State

University. I resolved to leave my marriage of twenty-two years, share custody of our 5-year-old son, quit the most satisfying and exciting job I had ever experienced, and move 1,600 miles away from my family, friends and the only region of the country in which I had ever lived. I told my colleagues at Orton College in September that I would be leaving in June of the following year.

I had made the next transition in my connectedness with the label. The label was no longer solely how I would describe myself, but how I would allow others to describe me. My resistance to giving others the power to use the label came from the fear of what that power would bring. My initial experiences with giving over that power reinforced my decision as a good one.

Despite these massive personal steps, the overwhelmingly positive support and the liberating sense of freedom I felt, I still had *no* intention of being out at work. Being out at work brings a different kind of fear. There are many lesbians who are out to themselves and perhaps to family and a few friends, but would never consider allowing themselves to live that reality at work. Many of us fear the loss of the job (Goff 1994) or even our careers, especially lesbians in the military (Cammermeyer 1994) or those in religiously affiliated professions (Curb and Manahan 1985). Very few of my friends and associates are comfortably out at work. We fear the hatred and judgment of our peers and colleagues; we fear the loss of respect and dignity, the loss of control of our lives, and so we stay in the closet.

When I was in the closet, thoughts of hearing the label, or being connected to the label at work formulated much of my conscious and unconscious action and inaction. I avoided personal pronouns, names and any real discussions of my life outside of work. When others discussed weekend or evening events, I remained cautiously ambiguous about details, would tell partial stories, or just remain separate. My lesbian friends and I would discuss how we might imagine having photos of our loved ones at our desks, like those of our colleagues, but feared the potential personal and professional consequences. We created 'cover stories' that provided a front, so as to avoid the perception of deviance associated with the label and to retain the heterosexual privilege of our colleagues. And although academia is generally thought to be a more liberal and accepting environment than other work environs, being out in academia remains a difficult decision for many lesbians. Even as academics, we are 'often unable to predict the reactions of colleagues, students, administrators, and friends, and [are] sometimes shocked at either the level of acceptance or the level of heterosexism' (Mintz and Rothblum 1997: 4).

As difficult as it was to leave Orton College, it was made more difficult by my reluctance to fully explain why. I tearfully told my colleagues and students at the college and the local schools that although I really loved my job, I needed to leave for 'personal reasons.' Understandably everyone was confused, and often hurt by my reluctance to share anything further.

Earlier in my life it had been easy to remain in the closet at work. I had discovered that the world of work operates on a tacit assumption of heterosexuality and, since I had the other positive cues and 'trappings' (husband, child, etc.), deceit of omission had been my worst transgression. However, I was so much more conscious now and so my deception seemed far worse.

The people I worked with cared about me and were concerned. They wondered why I would leave a job that I loved and at which I seemed to be so successful. What could be going on in my personal life that would cause such a drastic decision? Several of my superiors and colleagues called me into their offices for 'I don't want to pry ... but how can I help?' sessions. Concerns about a 'mid-life crisis' entered their conversations. Offers of raises, vacations and changes in job responsibilities followed. Although these sessions increased my already clear sense of being very much valued, they evoked the same struggle I had just overcome in my personal life. Could I possibly even consider coming out at work? No.

Throughout the year before I left, I ran the program, worked to hire my replacement, prepared the program for my departure, and flew as often as possible to Oklahoma to see Judy. Weekly I searched the *Chronicle of Higher Education* for postings from Oklahoma. Finally in February, there was a position of division chair in education posted for Hadley University. But how could I ask for letters of reference to Hadley without outing myself? Since everyone knew that Judy had accepted a position in Oklahoma, I feared that it would be all too obvious to ask for a letter for an institution there.

Fearful of homophobic responses from my colleagues at Orton, I strategized about how I could get the high-quality letters of recommendation that I felt I deserved from my superiors and colleagues without coming out to them. I asked them to write general letters for my placement file thinking that I would not have to disclose where I was looking for a position. To my frustration, each of my potential referees told me that letters are more powerful if they are written to a specific institution addressing a specific position. When I pressed that I did not want them to have to write more than one letter, each responded that they wanted to put in the extra effort for me. I considered just using the older letters in my placement file, but knew at some point my colleagues at Orton would need to be contacted.

I eventually devised a plan. I selected fifteen positions from all over the country which closely matched the position requirements for the job at Hadley and asked my referees to send their letters to each of the fifteen. When several of the other fourteen started calling to ask why I had sent references and not applied, I told them I had changed my mind about the particular positions. Worried (but with the letters of recommendation 'safely' in my placement file), I came out to my closest friend and superior at Orton. She reacted so positively and with so much support, that I began to seriously consider being out at Orton.

One of the non-Oklahoma institutions that had received my letters of reference called my dean to find out why I had not applied. Confused, the dean called me into his office for an explanation. He said that I had obviously come upon a brilliant strategy for getting a job: don't apply! Forced with the necessity of either coming out or lying, I came out to Arnold. I was now 'two for two' at work. Maybe I had imagined and overinflated the risks to my professional life as greatly as I had in my personal life. Times were changing. Perhaps what had been reasonable fears twenty years earlier were no longer reasonable.

At about the same time I received a phone call from a former colleague at Newcastle High School. We had been first year teachers together and she had been one of the mentors we had hired at Orton to work with our student interns. She was calling, she said, on behalf of the faculty at Newcastle, to find out 'what the hell was going on.' She told me she had scheduled an appointment with my secretary and that she would see me the following week.

I had the weekend to decide what I was going to say. Just as I had always suspected, once this 'coming out' got rolling, there seemed to be no stopping it. Now I had to decide if I would come out to Linda.[1] 'Then what?' I thought. Would I have to come out to all of my former colleagues? To the whole town? Judy told me, 'You have to decide every day of your life whether or not to come out.'

'Out' is, in fact, a very ambiguous term. Maria De La O calls the expression 'one of the more muddling terms ever invented to describe ourselves' (1995: 271):

> A person can never come out once and for all because she or he will always meet new people. Depending on their overall awareness of gays, lesbians and bisexuals, these people are likely to assume their new acquaintance is heterosexual until they are corrected. Therefore, most of us are always somewhere between in and out.

Linda arrived at the office, obviously quite nervous. I had decided to tell her right away, but she was so nervous I couldn't get a word in. I later discovered the cause of her nervousness. Since I had been so secretive about my reason for leaving Orton, people had feared the worst. Rumors had started and had been mixed with the accurate news that my father was dying of cancer. Linda had come to my office to confirm whether or not *I* was dying of cancer (and had been flying to Oklahoma for treatments!). When she finally gave me a moment to break into her steady stream of self-answered questions, I explained that I had been flying to Oklahoma to visit my lesbian lover, Judy. Ecstatic with the news, she blurted out, 'Oh thank God, you're not dying of cancer!'

Resolved not to pressure Linda into having to keep a secret, and concerned that everyone thought I was dying, I gave her permission to tell 'selected' others. At the end of the next week, I phoned a school superintendent in a nearby town to set up a student placement for the next year. He answered the phone with, 'So, it's Oklahoma.' I responded jokingly, 'Well I had planned to put up a billboard on the Interstate, but I guess that won't be necessary.' 'No,' he responded, 'it won't be. You've been the topic of conversation in at least six of the last meetings I've been to.' At her apartment, Judy and I joked that the billboard should read, 'Yes, it's Oklahoma. Yes, it's a woman!' By the end of the following week, it seemed I was out to everyone in the Capital District. I was gaining perspective on coming out.

I had assumed that I could separate being out personally and being 'closeted' professionally. I saw many lesbians who lived with this separation and assumed that I could as well. However, once I had embraced the label in the personal domain, the momentum of change carried me over into the professional. The label began to weave itself into my professional perception of myself.

I am not sure why I was so quickly able to make the transition from embracing the label personally to embracing it professionally. Perhaps because my personal transition had occurred over such a long period of time. Perhaps because the environment at Orton was not as hostile as I had imagined it to be. Perhaps because Judy's friends provided me with role models. Perhaps because the reactions to my coming out personally had been predominantly positive. Perhaps because my professional status and history provided me with enough privilege to take that risk.

As I continued to work on pulling my personal life together in New York, we awaited news from Hadley University about the position. In March I flew out to interview for what seemed to be the only academic position in Oklahoma. The interview went very well and I was led to believe that the position was mine; it would just be a short time while they 'finalized details.' I was unaware at the time that the major detail to be finalized involved my sexuality.

When I applied and interviewed at Hadley I had not come out, but I did not consciously hide the fact from them. Except for a persistent question of whether or not I would be comfortable teaching at a religiously affiliated institution, the three-day interview had seemed otherwise 'normal.' I was unaware that the committee knew I was a lesbian.

I had predicted that my colleagues at Orton College would connect Judy's departure to Oklahoma with my departure, but I would never have predicted that my future colleagues at Hadley University would connect the arrival of a New York Jewish lesbian at Oklahoma State University a year earlier with my application. Despite the 65-mile distance between the two universities, somehow, they made the connection. Unbeknown to me, my decision to live with an out-of-the-closet lesbian was going to have a significant impact on my professional life.

My frequent calls to the dean at Hadley to determine the status of their decision were met each time with a different diversionary explanation for the delay and pleas to remain available and positive. They had struggled for a month over whether or not to interview me. Then they struggled for two more over whether or not to offer me the position. They called each of my referees back for a third time and asked if I had ever said or done anything to embarrass the institution I was working in. Eventually the search committee convinced themselves and the university community that I should be offered the position. Their struggle and ultimate decision split the university community in ways that I would only gradually come to know about.

My arrival at Hadley was immediately followed by the resignation of two members of the education faculty. At the time I was unaware that the resignations were related to homophobia. In my naiveté, I missed most of the early signs. I explained actions and inactions, strange statements and strange looks as reactions to an assertive New York Yankee female administrator. And although these labels obviously played an important role in how I was initially perceived at Hadley, I discovered later that initial perceptions were also related to my sexuality.

After several weeks on campus, a student from one of my classes began frequenting my office and, after several visits, came out to me as a lesbian. She described how difficult it was to be a lesbian in this town and how she felt even more oppressed as an African American lesbian. I came out to her and invited her to attend the Gay-Lesbian-Bisexual Community Association meetings at Oklahoma State University that my partner Judy co-advised. Eventually we began to discuss the viability of starting a similar club at Hadley. I recall her first burst of laughter at the suggestion. 'You're in the buckle of the Bible Belt, woman! Are you crazy?'

A few more students started visiting my office. I began to press them on what appeared to me to be a real need to have a group of their own on campus. I told them I would 'test out the waters' with several of the faculty and administrators with whom I felt comfortable.

I knew the risk of even asking the question about having a club and I braced myself for a wide range of potential reactions. I was aware of the potential power of the label in the South, but in retrospect the risk of outing myself at work was no longer a powerful issue for me. It seemed much more important to try to meet the needs of the gay and lesbian students who came out to me.

Why was I now willing to take such a formidable risk? In some ways, I imagine it was because no one really knew me. I had the privilege of being an outsider. Much of my fear in New York had come from losing the love and respect of people who had known me much or all of my life. In Oklahoma I knew no one and that gave me the freedom to start over, both personally and professionally.

Judy also played an important role in my development. Her own personal connection with the label was more integrated and evolved than mine. She had a political vision and mission connected to the label that she intentionally used both personally and professionally. She and many of her friends were very visible and 'strong' self-identified lesbians and they collectively served as role models, as a supportive community, and as a source of political discourse around sexual orientation. They defined the label more broadly, and this definition included a lesbian 'perspective' (Penelope 1990: 90), a lens for seeing, interpreting and interacting with a heterosexist world; they fostered a community in order to provide personal and political support and power (Sedgewick 1990). The fact that I chose to live with Judy, an out, 'in your face' lesbian, may have been a signal of my impending readiness.

Judy had come out in her interview at Oklahoma State and for the past year, had been very out on campus without repercussions. Her colleagues had been very supportive of her attempts to get sexual orientation added to the non-discrimination clause at the university and had even joined her at one of the rallies. My professional coming out at Orton had also been relatively untraumatic and I was filled with a satisfaction and a sense of completeness living as an out lesbian in my personal life. I was conceptualizing the lesbian label holistically. The label was helping me to integrate my life.

I explained to a Hadley colleague that several students and I thought there was a need on campus for a gay and lesbian group. The anticipated pregnant pause never came. She responded instantly: 'Well, I think that would be great. It's about time.' Instant and positive responses came from the other faculty and administrators I questioned. I sensed that these issues were not new to them. And when I came out as a lesbian to a select few, they were clearly not surprised.

After much pressing and probing I reconstructed the story of my hiring. I found out about the faculty who were vehemently against my hiring, and the hate campaign they had begun with students, alumni/ae and the community before I arrived. These discoveries provided a context that explained much that was happening around me. I met individually with my faculty and staff to discuss their concerns. For some it was not an issue, while for others it was significant. For example, Ellen's face paled when I explained what I wanted to discuss, but when I pushed her to help me understand her concerns, she spoke frankly. She was worried about how much time I spent in the schools. Not understanding why that would be an issue, I probed further. 'Well you know,' she said, 'all the little girls.' Her eyes dropped to the floor and I realized that her concerns revolved around her belief that I would be preying on young girls.

Ralph's concerns, he said, were not personal. 'We had you people in the military ... and I dealt with you there, I can deal with you now.' He was concerned about the years of hard work he had invested in making the school of education a highly regarded place for preparing teachers. He felt that everything he and his colleagues had worked for was lost upon my arrival and that it would only get worse. What parents would possibly send their children here? What schools would possibly consider hiring a teacher who had prepared here when they learned about our 'gay agenda'? I explained that I had no agenda other than to help prepare excellent teachers and that I simply did not want to be discriminated against on the basis of my sexuality. He laughed. 'You know, I'm part Indian,' he said, 'but you people are as bad as the goddamned Indians. They get their tax-free bingo and then bitch about being discriminated against.' Two weeks later Ralph went to the president's office and declared, 'It's either her or me.' The following week Ralph moved out of his office.

The discussions with faculty and staff were difficult. I did not want to make my sexuality an issue for my colleagues, but I felt I could not be effective as division chair without confronting the issue out loud. Naming it, being open and honest about it, seemed to carry with it a strange kind of respect from even my staunchest adversaries. Some of my new friends explained it as a Western appreciation for 'rugged individualism.'

With my help, the students pushed on with their goal to establish a student group. They decided to call the group 'Perspectives.' Their constitution and application for club status passed the student government with surprisingly little debate. However, the next day the group's formation was a front-page headline in the city's newspaper (this is a city with a population of 55,000!).

When the local paper called to interview me for the story, I told them I thought the campus was generally supportive of the group. When this appeared in the paper, it outraged many members of the campus community and led to a full-day rally to 'Reaffirm Romans 1: 24–27,' a section of the Bible which some interpret as denouncing homosexuality. The newspaper article and the rally began a several-month campaign of hate mail and phone calls, as well as numerous articles and letters to the editor in both the university and city newspapers. Students and faculty were polarized around support for the group, the issue, and me.

One day the student Umbrella Coalition group handed out condoms in support of safer sex. The next day the city paper was again filled with articles and letters to the editor. The weekend edition carried a full-page advertisement denouncing this 'support of homosexuality' by the university. The advertisement was purchased by three local churches and signed by most of their members, including a few colleagues and several students in my classes.

The university bought a full-page advertisement the following day and printed the university motto and mission statement in large, bold print along with an explanation of their support for the rights of gay and lesbian 'persons' and for education around safer sex. The advertisement was signed by the university president and the chair of the board of trustees. The next day the lawn of the president's house was strewn with garbage and an old toilet. Several community members and alumni/ae called to ask for the return of their financial contributions.

The advertisement reinvigorated the debate on campus and in the press. Letters to the editor, some forwarded to me personally, described concerns about bestiality and fears of a local AIDS epidemic. A student who had never taken a class from me wrote a letter to the editor detailing why I was a terrible teacher. The president of the alumni/ae association put forth an extraordinary resolution to the board of trustees: in the future, according to the resolution, all university documents should explicitly state that the university did not desire to be a welcoming place for gays and lesbians. (The resolution failed.)

My fear of the power of the label in the hands of others had become a reality. I had encountered homophobic people earlier in my life, but their fear and hatred had never been personally directed at me. In my embracing the label, the hatred became personalized and I became much more vulnerable to its poison.

I also felt the label was defining who I was, rather than just being an important part of my identity. I grew tired of the constant debate and the emotional rollercoaster triggered by every new event. In my classes I no longer felt as comfortable discussing educational issues related to gays and lesbians, fearing that it would be interpreted as 'promoting a gay agenda.' When a homophobic colleague came up for tenure, I worried that my negative evaluation would be construed as judgement of her views rather than my assessment of her teaching, scholarship and service. When I was out in the community representing the university and our programs, I was constantly paranoid: 'Everyone knows who I am.' On many occasions my paranoia was confirmed by specific comments and questions about my sexuality. I worried that anything I did would result in yet another front-page debate or personal attack.

Throughout my three years at Hadley, my professional self was never really separate from my personal self as a lesbian. Although in many ways that was an empowering change and helped me to more fully integrate my personal and professional lives, it was also oppressive. I was never able to separate myself from the label 'lesbian' and its often negative connotations. Personally and professionally I wanted people to think of me as 'Me,' without the label. 'Yes, I am a lesbian, but there is so much more to me.'

My third year at Hadley University began with much less fanfare than the previous two. I had gained tenure the year before and had become dean of the school of education. I felt like I would be able to fully concentrate on my professional responsibilities. In October of that year I received a letter inviting me to apply for the position of dean at Urbana University in New York. Although I was intrigued with the possibility, I felt like I was just getting started at Hadley. We had hired several new faculty in the school and were building exciting new programs. I was still too drained emotionally to even consider moving and starting over again, and I did not want to give anyone the satisfaction of feeling they had been successful in driving me away. Several months later, however, my need to be closer to my son made me pull the letter from Urbana out of the recycling bin.

Although I assumed there would be much less homophobia in New York than in Oklahoma, I still worried about whether I should be out in my interview. I was dealing with the emotional toll of being out professionally in Oklahoma and I did not want to take the chance in New York. The chance of being closer to my son was too important to risk. So, in my interview I avoided personal pronouns and names, except for my son. I focused my desire for the job around him, and when I was unable to avoid direct questions, I referred to my 'family' in New York and my 'family' in Oklahoma.

During each of the three interview trips to New York, I scoured the campus for signs of support and acceptance. I noted with excitement the domestic partner benefits that were described prominently in their materials, the non-discrimination policy in the student application materials and the bulletin board on the New York campus listing events for the gay and lesbian group (but checked over my shoulder for potential observers before taking any of the free materials). Aware of the close relationships between sexism, heterosexism and homophobia, I noted with delight the many women in positions of authority. I closely questioned the one faculty member I was out to about the level of acceptance on campus and was convinced it 'wasn't an issue.'

I worried about the description of Urbana in a gay and lesbian guide for college campuses. It suggested a potentially homophobic environment, where, at the very best, 'it just wasn't talked about.' For at least some of the Urbana campus, the 'University Culture of Silence' (Mintz and Rothblum 1997: 7) seemed alive and well. But by then the decision to live out personally and professionally was the only thing that seemed reasonable. I had felt the freedom from the oppression of the closet, and the thought of going back in seemed more inconceivable than being out had ever been.

When it seemed that I had a chance of getting the position at Urbana, Judy began her own search for a position in or near New York City. Yet again we had the challenge of finding two academic positions in the same geographic location. When I got the offer at Urbana we were faced with the dilemma of either giving up the offer or living apart for the year or more it might take Judy to find a university position. Resolved not to spend another year that far away from Steven, Judy and I decided that I would move back to New York whether or not she found a teaching position.

I do not recall needing to make a conscious decision to be out both personally and professionally at Urbana. In some ways it would have been easy since I was living alone that first year. But by the time I arrived at Urbana my personal and professional lives were very much integrated, and my lesbian identity was very much a part of both.

My current connection with the label – the meaning I make of it – continues to evolve. I continue to integrate my sense of being a lesbian with my sense of who I am as a woman, a mother, a partner, a friend, an educator, and an administrator. These are the multiple 'speaking subjects' (Alcoff 1988) that form my identity, define who I am, and define my connection with the label. I have a level of personal and professional comfort with the label, as do most of my family, friends and colleagues at Urbana.

I recognize the power that the label can carry for others and I intentionally label myself a lesbian, especially when I feel that defining myself in that way is important for the situation or context. Rarely, I still also sometimes intentionally avoid the label when I feel the situation does not warrant it. In these ways I 'map the tactical positions' (Sandoval 1991) for use of the label.

In many ways, I now perceive the label of 'lesbian' as positional, contextual. This is similar to how Alcoff defines the label 'woman' as a particular position, rather than a particular set of attributes (1988: 324):

> The external position determines the person's relative position, just as the position of a pawn on a chessboard is considered safe or dangerous, powerful or weak, according to its relation to the other chess pieces ... The positional definition ... makes her identity relative to a constantly shifting context.

My connection with the lesbian label has evolved significantly over the thirteen years described here. My initial ignorance of the label was replaced by a passive connection to it, as co-opted by a heterosexist culture. In my passivity, the hegemonic message that homosexuality is bad and evil and lesbians are deviant controlled me. I accepted the dominant culture's definition of 'lesbian.'

As my consciousness of my sexuality emerged, so did my consciousness of the label and its ability to be a tool of both liberation and oppression. I have become conscious and more critical in relation to the label. I still must tactically select those contexts and moments when I call myself lesbian, but the selections are intentional, measured by an assessment of when the potential gain outweighs the potential loss or pain. On occasion, as in this essay, I have reflected on my experiences and my emerging consciousness in writing (McDonald 1993, 1997). For those of us who have crafted narratives of our experiences with the label, the writing of these narratives themselves becomes an act of 'self-emancipation' (Dugan 1997: 205). 'Indeed,' writes Jo Reger (1999: 190), 'central to all [such] narratives is the idea that publicly claiming one's sexuality is a form of political and personal empowerment.'

As my connection with the label took on a more active status, I began to gain control and power over it. The label can be dangerous when you are subject to the hegemony of a heterosexist culture. Yet I have learned that the destructive power of being labeled by others can be neutralized and, often, reversed by my labeling myself. And though the label can still be dangerous, my personal evolution, my environment and geography, and the cultural context of my current position allow me to have more control over it.

I initially separated myself both subconsciously and consciously from the label. At a later point in my life I defined myself almost completely with and through the label. Now I see the label as helping to define *one* of many critical attributes of who I am as woman, partner, mother, educator. I am now more fully aware of the freedom and power which comes from being a visible lesbian. I have realized that 'when we become visible and stay visible, it becomes easier to discard the stereotypes by which we have been characterized' (Hepner 1995: 299). It is those stereotypes, both positive and negative, that make us fear the label, limit us in our connection to the label and limit how we, and others, define and engage with the label and with ourselves.

Note

1   I have used pseudonyms for the names of colleges and for all my former co-workers.

References

Alcoff, L. (1988) 'Cultural Feminism versus Post-Structuralism: The Identity Crisis in Feminist Theory,' *Signs*, 13(3): 8–15.

Barber, K. and Holmes, S. (eds) (1994) *Testimonies: Lesbian Coming Out Stories*, Boston: Alyson Publications.

Cammermeyer, M. (with C. Fisher) (1994) *Serving in Silence*, New York: Viking Press.

Curb, R. and Manahan, N. (1985) *Lesbian Nuns: Breaking Silence*, New York: Warner Books.

De La O, M. (1995) 'Lesbians in Corporate America' in K. Jay (ed.) *Dyke Life* (265–81), New York: Basic Books.

Dugan, P. (1997) 'Degrees of Freedom' in B. Mintz and E. D. Rothblum (eds) *Lesbians in Academia* (203–9), New York: Routledge.

Goff, M. (ed.) (1994) *Out in America: A Portrait of Gay and Lesbian Life*, New York: Viking Studio Books.

Hepner, P.J. (1995) 'Oy veh, the Judge on the Bench is a Dyke' in K. Jay (ed.) *Dyke Life* (299–301), New York: Basic Books.

Jay, K. (ed.) (1995) *Dyke Life*, New York: Basic Books.

Jay, K. and Glasgow, J. (eds) (1990) *Lesbian Texts and Contexts*, New York: New York University Press.

Jay, K. and Young, A. (eds) (1992) *Out of the Closets*, New York: New York University Press.

McDonald, J. (1993) 'A Year of My Life in Enid, America,' *The Herland Voice*, 10(10), Herland Sister Resources, Oklahoma City.

—— (1997) 'Being Out in Academia: A Year of My Life in Enid, America' in B. Mintz and E. D. Rothblum (eds) *Lesbians in Academia* (120–5), New York: Routledge.

Mintz, B. and Rothblum, E. D. (eds) (1997) *Lesbians in Academia*, New York: Routledge.

Morris, J. F., Ojerholm, A.J., Brooks, T.M., Osoiecki, D.M. and Rothblum, E. (1995) 'Finding a Word for Myself: Themes in Lesbian Coming Out Stories' in K. Jay (ed.) *Dyke Life* (36–44), New York: Basic Books.

Penelope, J. (1990) 'The Lesbian Perspective' in J. Allen (ed.) *Lesbian Philosophies and Cultures* (89–108), Albany: State University of New York Press.

Penelope, J. (ed.) (1994) *Out of the Class Closet: Lesbians Speak*, Freedom, CA: The Crossing Press.

Reger, J. (1999) 'Review: Lesbians in Academia: Degrees of Freedom,' *Contemporary Sociology* 28(2): 190–1.

Sandoval, C. (1991) 'U.S. Third World Feminism: The Theory and Method of Oppositional Consciousness in the Postmodern World,' *Genders*, 10: 322–5.

Sedgewick, E. K. (1990) *Epistemology of the Closet*, Berkeley: University of California Press.

Stanley, J. P. and Wolfe, J. S. (eds) (1980) *The Coming Out Stories*, Watertown, MA: Persephone Press.

12 The callings of sexual identity

Peter Maas Taubman

> [O]nce you have discerned the meaning of a label, it may seem to define you
> for others but it does not have the power to define you to yourself.
>
> (James Baldwin 1985: 681)

Rather than use the word 'labeling' in the title of this essay, I have used the
word 'callings.' I have chosen that word because labeling, whose derivation
suggests a material marking attached to an object, implies an objectification
that elides any complicity or involvement on the part of the person labeled in
their own marking. 'Callings' on the other hand, with its etymological connotations of summoning, suggests a response. One may or may not respond
to a calling. In using this concept of 'callings,' a concept I shall momentarily
explain, I hope to open the question of how we participate in the construction of our own identities and how we respond to the labels with which others
mark us.

My aim in this essay is to explore the way in which we are 'called' to
sexual identities. I have tried to touch on some of the questions such an
exploration stimulates. For example, what do we mean by sexual identities? How do we come to assume the sexual identities we take on? How do
various sensations, feelings, fantasies and desires come to be labeled 'sexual,' and what are the processes of inclusion and exclusion that make such
labeling possible? How do these 'sexual' categories affect our thinking
and our epistemological assumptions? What can we, as teachers, do to
challenge harmful organizations of sexuality, gender and sex, organizations that, by labeling and sorting us, affect the most trivial and most profound dimensions of our lives? To the extent that we ignore these
questions, we ignore both the suffering of many of our students and the
limits and narrowness of our own thinking.

Traces

Sexuality exists only as an allusion, as vapor or dust, showing a path along which language has passed, but which it continues to jolt and to erase like so many extremely disturbing childhood memories.

(Deleuze 1990: 242)

When I was 12 years old, I was sent for the last time to dancing school. I had gone before, in the fourth grade, but now I was in the throes of puberty, and wearing white gloves, suit and tie, drenched in perspiration and listening to Miss Hepburn [I have used pseudonyms throughout this chapter] in her black chiffon dress as she clicked her castanets and mocked my awkward attempts at foxtrots and waltzes, I was furious at my parents for making me suffer the torments of being the last picked in multiplication dances or made fun of by supercilious girls whose feet I crashed down upon as we tried to Lindy. The long narrow room in Grace Church became for me a kind of bodily Inquisition, where each of my movements around the rack of the floor confessed my body's heresy and made me inwardly pray for invisibility. At the same time, amid the damp gloves and mixed scent of sweat and childish perfume and in the glare of chandeliers and pale wooden floors, I developed a crush on Lynn Owens, whose lack of attention to me was exceeded only by her quite obvious regard for Raymond Delgado, whom I despised, admired, wanted to be like and with whom that same year I wound up in bed.

I am sleeping over at Del's house, we called him Del, on a pull-out couch. He offers to give me a back rub. His strange grandma lives in the basement. The pillow smells musty. Is it clean? Lower and lower, sliding my jockey shorts off, his hands move around under me. Held breath. My heart will burst. I am embarrassed by the sprouting pubic hair I've grown and worry it will put him off. We lie on top of one another. He smells of Vitalis. A cough. Someone's there. Nothing happens; yet I remember, what? Nothing? What was my intention and desire? Who was that boy and what did he want or want to be?

A few months later, I discovered that Del was having more sophisticated sex with other boys in our prep school, and I do have a vague recollection of discovering him late one afternoon, under a bush on the school's lush grounds, with another boy who would briefly become a sexual partner and later one of my best friends. Their clothes were disheveled, and I felt flushed from jealousy. Many years later I would meet Del at a class reunion. He had married and become a doctor. The other boy remains one of my closest friends, and we have daughters now who are both just 15 years old.

The year I slept over at Del's house was the last year I did really well in school. I liked coming home then, where my grandmother would make me tea, and I would sit in the kitchen doing my homework. I particularly liked the longer social studies projects – ones on Schweitzer and Perry I vividly remember – and how I stayed up late reading Landmark books on these two men, while my parents watched our old Zenith TV in the next room. But that year I was also beginning to sneak copies of my dad's volumes of Havelock Ellis's *The History of Sex* into the bathroom, and my reading of the case histories in those volumes came rapidly to absorb the energy I had brought to my more academic projects. If Freud was correct that our curiosity and drive for knowledge have as their origin curiosity about sex, I seemed to be regressing to the root cause of the desire to know. Jane Hirschfield's (1998: 20) reminder of the dual use of the Biblical 'to know,' and the etymological meanings of the ancient Greek verb *mnaomai* : 'to hold in attention' and 'to woo,' suggest that knowledge and the erotic are not unrelated, but at age twelve I was more intent on knowledge *of* the erotic.

It was also the year I was 12 that one night my parents came home to find me dressed in my mother's clothes. Maybe it was the fact that my grandmother died a few months later, and my parents wanted to be alone with their grief, but I suspect it was actually their panic I was becoming a homosexual that made them send me for two months to a boys' camp in Maine, where I won trophies for baseball, and learned to dress as a 'cool guy' for the one social that summer.

That summer I also stopped reading, except the school's required summer reading, and from then on school became, well, school. Although many of us at the school who were the first to have sex with girls were also the first to have had sex with one another, from ninth grade on, sports, girls and social life called me away from those earlier sensuous experiences, called me to the hurly-burly world of teens and pimples, and cramming for tests, and 'how far did you get?' and scoring touchdowns and girls, called me to the clearly articulated, but ferociously idealized and abstract identities of heterosexual and male. And I answered that call – at times with a vengeance, at times out of fear, and at times in a desultory and ambiguous fashion, like the time I bought an orange mohair sweater and ostentatiously swung my hips when I walked into a party because I figured it looked sexy; after all it looked sexy to me when girls did it. When I was told by a few giggling girls that I walked 'like a dancer,' I got the message and began standing with my feet planted widely apart, a stance, I was informed by Greg Simon, that real men assumed.

I do not think it was either coincidental or unique that one loss and its replacement should have been paralleled by another. I lost an inchoate, fluid, psychosomatically apprehended world, where the smell of Vitalis, the wheezing and coughing of Del's crazy grandma, the blushing of skin and the held breath of anticipation called me to my senses. Its replacement was an abstract world of thrills, gained from resting my hand on top of an anonymous girl's breast buried beneath layers upon layers of clothes, or from the stereotyped fantasies and nightly, routine orgasm, wiped into a tissue, or from the fist fight over whether or not Paul Steinberg had 'fingered' Ruth Palmer, a world that forcefully called me to an abstract gender and sexuality. At the same time I lost my love of reading anything other than pulp fiction, which was excluded from school; its replacement became the drudgery of school, relieved only by shoulder pads, parties and gossip and the desperate search for the right answer and the right move and the right girl.

As sex and gender became normalized in school, so did knowing and the known, and except for the few gay teachers I had, many of whom were the most popular in the school, the teachers were generally quite forgettable. The more firmly specific identities were linked to specific fantasies and styles of being, that is, the more technologies of self-formation were sought and/or applied, the more stylized and ritualized sex, sexuality and gender became. The more I adapted to and adopted particular gestures, ways of acting and talking, and 'appropriate' identities and attitudes towards sex, the more those identities, actions and what was 'clearly' meant by 'sex,' became compulsively repetitious and thus, reproducing themselves, retroactively made it seem as if I was simply expressing some *a priori* heterosexuality rather than, as Judith Butler (1990) would say, performing it and thus constituting it *a posteriori*. The way I French-inhaled my cigarette and French- kissed a girl, tried to feel someone up, winked at a girl at a party, wore my shirt with two buttons opened at the top, came up with a line, all these, it seems to me now, were not the expression of my heterosexuality but the performance of what I took to be 'cool,' and what would in retrospect *constitute* the form of my heterosexuality. The object of that heterosexuality was apparently and by definition female, but, as I shall argue, the cathecting of various girlfriends must be understood not in terms of normal development, but rather in terms of what I shall define as the callings of sexual identities.

At the same time that I was cathecting girls and crafting a style based on ideals of maleness and heterosexuality, the curriculum, books, the world of knowledge other than localized knowledge revolving around sports, social life, sex and sexuality, appeared and indeed was increasingly stylized, abstracted, ritualized, and linked to particular modes of knowing and styles of being that I for one violently de-cathected. As correct answers, grades, exams and the 'correct' meaning of a text increasingly came to constitute the content of classes and the curriculum, as studying increasingly required a passion to outperform someone else, and as knowledge increasingly became 'cultural capital' that might garner privileges in school, the more libidinal everything that went on outside the classroom became. I was a star athlete, had sex on the weekend with my girlfriend, had friends, was popular. Who needed school? I was just a normal guy looking for sex from a sexy girl. And yet there remained other whispers, moods, tracings, while everywhere there were callings.

Callings

What does it mean to say we are 'called' to our sexual identities? Before we even answer that question, we need to ask what sexual identities are: do they relate to gender, to sex roles, to sex, to sexual orientation, to erotic styles, to anatomical or biological categories, or to all of the above? And what do these mean, anyway? The denotative and connotative meanings of 'sex' and 'sexuality' are so complicated and varied today; they become even more so when we add these other terms. It therefore seems appropriate to offer some tentative definitions, if only to give us some provisional landmarks that can guide us as we explore the topic of sexuality and labeling, the callings of sexual identities.

In the 1970s feminists came to theorize 'sex' as the minimal biological raw material, and 'gender' as what resulted when this raw material was subjected to culture. In a gloss of this definition, Madeleine Grumet wrote that gender is 'what we make of [sex], what we make from it,' and that gender is 'not determined but made up in the course of human history' (1993: ix). As she explained:

So over here we have gonads, vaginas, and penises.	And over here we have EVERYTHING ELSE: maleness, femaleness, mothering, patriarchy, madonnas, machismo, equal pay for equal work, women's history month, football, heroes, romance, reading, testing, schooling. The … list goes on and on.

In exposing the artificiality of the link between the signifier of gender and the signified of sex, feminist analyses opened up the possibility of challenging the ways in which the raw material of sex was organized into gender, and the injustice of this organization. Gender, in these analyses, was not the expression of sex, but the result of the historically, culturally and socially contingent ways by which sex was shaped and organized. The political or therapeutic agendas implied by such analyses were threefold. First, if the dominant organization of sex were not established by natural or divine law, then those who did not conform to it were not anomalies of nature or sinners, and thus they deserved equal treatment. Second, if sex was malleable, individuals could be led to conform to culturally appropriate standards of gender or, conversely, those standards could be changed. Third, the organization of sex could be named, challenged and dismantled or reformed.

Although this reformulated distinction between sex and gender opened the way for rethinking what it means to be male or female, there have been problems with this way of defining sex and gender. One of the problems is that generally speaking 'sex' also denotes sexuality, which includes all the erotic ways we relate to one another and ourselves and thus assumes, or at least implies, not only the tripartite division of sexuality into heterosexuality, homosexuality, and bi-sexuality, but also the inextricability of gender from anatomical sex and sex as erotics. One has sex not simply with someone, but with a male or a female, and these designations are often, as the play *M. Butterfly* and the movie *The Crying Game* suggest, more about gender than sex (although as the latter makes clear, the unexpected appearance of an unanticipated anatomical feature can quickly, if perhaps only temporarily, diminish one's desire). But if anatomical sex and gender are not intrinsically linked, that is, if gender does not 'naturally' express sex, then on what basis is erotic orientation or sexuality determined? Is it assigned on the basis of attraction to gender or sex, or the congruence or perhaps incongruence between the two? Who is more heterosexual, the protagonist in *The Crying Game* who falls in love with the gender of the man/woman but is repulsed by his sex, or the male character in *The Ballad of Little Joe* who takes no apparent sexual interest in Joe's masculine gender but falls in love when he discovers her sex? Or is it Gary Cooper's or Marlene Dietrich's character in *Morocco* that is the more heterosexual, when he lusts after her appearance as a man and she, dressed as a man, lures him by passionately seducing and kissing a woman in the audience? If, in fact, part of what defines one's gender is one's sexual orientation (a real man supposedly desires only women and a true woman supposedly desires only men), and if sexual orientation is determined in large part by the sex of the object of one's desire and one's own sex, then sex and gender cannot be quite so clearly separated.

Another problem with uncoupling sex from gender has been raised by Michel Foucault (1980) and, more recently, Judith Butler (1990), who have argued that not only sexuality but also sex in the anatomical and/or biological sense are socially constructed. In other words, the very project of focusing on particular anatomical zones, the search for chromosomal and hormonal distinctions and the zoning and articulation of the body into male and female anatomy, is itself culturally determined. Foucault argued that sex was not the base of some superstructure of gender and sexuality but rather was itself produced by socio/discursive regimes of sexuality. According to Butler's reading of Foucault and Freud, there is no biological stuff that serves as the 'bedrock' or the raw material on which gender is layered or as the pre-discursive 'stuff' that gets socially processed into gender. Rather, sexualities, sex and genders are all produced and deployed in discursive and non-discursive networks. Butler has put it this way (1990: 7):

> Gender is not to culture as sex is to nature; gender is also the discursive/cultural means by which 'sexed nature' or 'a natural sex' is produced and established as 'prediscursive,' prior to culture, a politically neutral surface on which culture acts.

In other words, basing gender and therefore sexuality on 'gonads, vaginas and penises,' as if these were self-evidently the best and most fundamental way to categorize humans, is to found gender on reproduction, which means that heterosexuality is smuggled in as the natural, biological 'stuff' on which gender is based. Foucault and Butler exposed this cultural or social or discursive construction for what it is, culture masquerading as biology.

In order to talk about sex, gender and sexuality yet not fall into the trap of assuming that these, whatever their cultural or historical forms, refer to some stable or *a priori* substance, I want to offer some provisional definitions that denote categories that emerge in the dominant organization of bodies, pleasures, fantasies and desires in the West. I shall refer to the ways we are organized according to our behaviors and appearances into male, female, transgendered and androgynous identities as 'gender'; to the ways our bodies are organized according to anatomy and biology into hermaphrodite, male, transsexual and female bodies as 'anatomical sex'; to the way our desires, fantasies and bodily pleasures and activities are organized according to the sex and/or gender of their object into heterosexual, lesbian, homosexual, and bisexual identities as 'sexuality'; and to the way our erotic life is organized according to standards of pleasure and reproduction as 'sex.' The various identities I shall refer to as 'sexual identities.' The discursive and non-discursive practices that produce gender, anatomical sex, sexuality and sex, I shall call the 'sexual matrix.' When I wish to refer to what comes to form in or is organized by this matrix, I shall refer to psychic and somatic pulsations, energies, movements, intensities, streams, blockages, shocks, irruptions, and flows, and I shall use these terms to suggest some sense of the flux that we are before we are called to these sexual identities within the sexual matrix.

To say we are 'called' to our sexual identities is very different from saying we express some inner essence or some desires that are already inscribed or organized as sexual or, conversely, that there is nothing that exists prior to that inscription and organization. It also suggests something other than a notion of labeling that holds that a hegemonic sexual matrix determines our sexual identities, as we remain passive victims of that matrix. *To be 'called' to an identity requires that one answer the call.* It is one thing to say that our sexual identities result from or express what is already within us and that what they express is our nature or that our sexual identity is completely malleable, determined only by the sexual matrix. It is quite another to suggest that in fact we, you and I as individuals, are 'called' into being, but only if we answer that call. Let me try to explain this notion of 'calling.'

In 'Ideological State Apparatuses,' Louis Althusser presents a sketch of the power of ideology to constitute subjects. He theorizes how the individual becomes a subject through interpellation, that is through being hailed. The example he gives is of an individual being hailed by the police (1994. 133):

> I shall … suggest that ideology 'acts' or 'functions' in such a way that it 'recruits' subjects among the individuals … or 'transforms' the individuals into subjects … by that very precise operation … called interpellation or hailing, and which can be imagined along the lines of the most commonplace everyday police (or other) hailing: 'Hey, you there!'
>
> Assuming that the theoretical scene I have imagined takes place in the street, the hailed individual will turn around. By this mere one-hundred-and-eighty degree physical conversion, he becomes a subject. Why? Because he has recognized that the hail was 'really' addressed to him, and that 'it was really him [*sic*] who was hailed' (and not someone else).

Any ideological formation, including that of the sexual matrix, interpellates subjects as anatomical sexes, genders and sexualities. Even before the individual is born, even conceived, one or both parents and often other relatives have a preference as to the anatomical sex of their child and most certainly as to its sexuality. Even if they assure their friends and themselves that all they wish for is a healthy baby, unconsciously they may harbor preferences, which will be subtly and not so subtly made known to the child. As Althusser writes (*ibid.* 132, my emphasis):

> Before its birth, the child is therefore always-already a subject, appointed as a subject in and by the specific family ideological configuration in which it is expected once it has been conceived ... this familial ideological configuration is, in its uniqueness, highly structured, and ... it is in this implacable ... structure that the former subject-to-be will have to 'find' its place, i.e. become the sexual subject (boy or girl) *which it already is in advance.*

Although he does not talk about the 'boyness' or 'girlness' of the subject, Althusser does say that one becomes a subject in ideology also by performing actions that constitute one as ideological subject. He gives as an example Pascal's advice that if one wants to find faith, one should kneel down and pray, and faith will follow. Thus, for Althusser, two things promise identity – the turning to the hailing and the performing of actions – both of which, at the moment of turning and performing, simultaneously constitute one's identity and configure the identity that turns and performs. The faster one turns to the hailing and the more one masters the actions, the more one is 'subjectified' or achieves an identity.

All this should bring to mind Judith Butler's theory that gender is constituted retrospectively after it has been performed. 'Gender,' she argues, 'is the repeated stylization of the body, a set of repeated acts ... that congeal over time to produce the appearance of substance, of a natural sort of being' (1990: 33). Her argument may be summarized by two statements taken from her work:

> Gender ought not be construed as a stable identity ... from which various acts follow; rather, gender is an identity tenuously constituted in time, instituted in an exterior space through a stylized repetition of acts ... the appearance of substance is precisely that, a constructed identity, a performative accomplishment which ... the actors themselves come to believe and to perform in the mode of belief.
>
> (Butler 1990: 140–1)

> [G]ender is a performance that produces the illusion of an inner sex or essence or psychic gender core; it produces on the skin, through the gesture, the move, the gait ... the illusion of an inner depth.
>
> (Butler 1991: 28)

Because she needs to address the psychic dimensions of who or what is performing gender, in *The Psychic Life of Power* Butler extends Althusser's theory of subject formation and plays with the allegory of the police's hailing to suggest that to become a subject one is always 'in the process of acquitting oneself of the accusation of guilt' (1997: 118). For Butler, following Althusser, we come into being simultaneously as we respond to the hailing and as we repetitively perform those actions that will retrospectively constitute our identity as, for example, male or female, homosexual or heterosexual, under particular discursive or ideological formations. What Butler adds to Althusser are the questions of what makes the subject turn to the hailing, what if anything exists prior to the turn to the hailing and what makes the subject repeat the practices that retrospectively constitute it. In other words, she is questioning the relationship between the social and the psychic.

Rather than follow Butler as she employs Freud's articulation of the role of narcissism and melancholia in the formation of a 'gendered' ego, let me address these questions in another way. In *The Interpersonal World of the Infant* Danny Stern talks about the profound role of what he calls 'selective attunement' in the development of a child's subjectivity. Attunement, according to Stern, is 'the performance of behaviors that express the quality of feeling of a shared affective state' (1985: 142) but is not synonymous with imitation, which would be the robotic mimicking of behaviors.

> An attunement is a recasting, a restatement of a subjective state. It treats the subjective state as the referent and the overt behavior as one of several possible manifestations or expressions of the referent.
>
> (*ibid.* 161)

Attunement occurs throughout a child's development and requires that the parent or caretaker 'read the infant's feeling state' from the infant's actions or expressions, and act in a way that corresponds to or 'fits with' the infant's overt behavior or expression, and that the child behave in such a way as to acknowledge the correspondence between his or her own state and the parental response. For attunement to work, there must be some correspondence between parent and child behaviors. These, according to Stern, can occur in different modalities that are interchangeable. He lists intensity, time, and shape as constituting 'intermodal fluency.' In other words, for there to be successful attunement, the parent must enter into the inner world of the child and respond in the same or interchangeable modalities in such a way that the child's response reveals a 'match.'

> Selective attunement is one of the most potent ways that a person can shape the development of a child's subjective and interpersonal life. It helps to account for [the particularity of any infant]. Attunements are also one of the main vehicles for the influence of parents' fantasies about their infants. In essence, attunement permits the parents to convey to the infant what is shareable, that is, which subjective experiences are

beyond the pale of mutual consideration and acceptance ... It is in this way that the parents' desires, fears, prohibitions, and fantasies contour the psychic experiences of the child. The communicative power of selective attunement reaches to almost all forms of experience. It determines which overt behaviors fall inside or outside the pale ... It includes preferences for people ... And it includes degrees or types or internal states ... that can occur with another person.

(Stern 1985: 207–8)

Selective attunement, then, names a process of subjectification that goes beyond simple mirroring, by pointing out the give and take between child and parent. In other words, depending on the 'fit' between the child's responses and the 'attunement' of the caretaker, a subjectivity is called into being through the process of selective attunement. Not only is the content of that subjectivity called forth, but, given the modalities through which selective attunement occurs, so are the intensity, time, and shape of behaviors or what we could call their style. As that subjectivity is being shaped, then, so too are the child's corporeal and cognitive ways of experiencing the world, and so too are those corporeal and cognitive possibilities that are 'beyond the pale.'

Selective attunement suggests that the Other or parent who is attuning to the child, must enter into that child's intrapsychic world in such a way that the child will respond to, and literally find its 'self' in that attunement. Nevertheless, because Stern presents an uncomplicated version of reading behavior – he sees the signifier of behavior and its emotional referent as self-evidently linked in a direct way – it is not at all clear how much negotiation of meaning between parent and child is actually taking place and how much the parent is reading into the child.

Stern tries to address this concern by theorizing what he calls 'misattunement,' which, he argues, can be dangerous. In misattunement the parent 'steals' the infant's emotional experience, by attuning to it and then changing it 'so it is lost to the child' (1985: 213). He adds (*ibid.* 214):

One of the main features for the infant [of misattunement] is the danger in permitting the intersubjective sharing of experience, namely that intersubjective sharing can result in loss. This is likely to be the point of origin of the long developmental line that later results in older children's need for lying, secrets, and evasions, to keep their own experiences intact.

Through misattunement, or what Stolorow, Brandhoft and Atwood (1995) call 'intersubjective disjunction,' a kind of empathic failure, a child may come to develop what Stern calls a 'false self,' which is the utilization of 'that portion of inner experience that can achieve intersubjective acceptance with the inner experience of another, at the expense of the remaining, equally legitimate, portions of inner experience' (1985: 210). Stern's false self/true self split is not complete or unavoidable, because if selective attunement and verbal relatedness 'fit' with the inner experiences of the infant, then there will be no permanent split. Even Stern admits, however, that such a perfect fit is unlikely. In fact, given parental fears that their child may not be 'normal,' and also that patience and great sensitivity are required for attunement, misattunement may be the norm, particularly when we take into account the unconscious dimensions of attunement and misattunement.

Through selective attunement, misattunement, and what Stern calls 'social referencing' – the way a parent can literally instil feelings in a child, and alter a child's experience (1985: 221, 223) – that which is 'beyond the pale' and that which is 'lost' are split off, and begin to form the unconscious and to shape desire.

While Stern does not specifically discuss gender or sexuality, it is implicit in his theory that the child's gender and sexuality are also simultaneously beginning to form with the inauguration of subjectivity. Thus, as selective attunement, misattunement and social referencing occur, the child is also developing corporeal, affective, cognitive and behavioral styles that may or may not be or come to be consistent with societal norms of gender and sexuality; what Foucault called 'regulatory ideals.' The sexuality called into being is not one that was attuned to the initial flows, pulsations, attractions, fantasies of the child, but one that was in fact consciously and unconsciously infused into, read into, and called forth by the parent at the expense of what will fall beyond the pale. Michael Basch (quoted in Stern 1985: 210) gives one example of what I am talking about:

> How, to use Freudian terminology, could the superego of the parents be conveyed so exquisitely accurately to the infant and the young child? Take for example, masturbatory practices … How, if the parents are psychologically enlightened and determined not to either shame the child or make it feel guilty for those activities, does it get the idea that these activities are beyond the pale of acceptance? Although the parents may say nothing to the child in the way of criticism or censure, they do not share the activity through cross-modal attunement, and that sends the message loud and clear.

Because parents and adults in general carry limited, often conventional and frequently stereotyped ideas and fantasies about sexuality, anatomical sex, sex and gender (Casper *et al.* 1996), and because they also unconsciously convey their own abject erotic life – that which is 'beyond the pale' – to their child, there is little chance that this child's unique modes of corporal expressiveness will be attuned to. As it emerges as anatomically sexed, gendered and sexualized, the template for its shareable interpersonal world is often a result of failed empathy, intersubjective disjunction and misattunement.

What is important to note is that in Stern's account of subject formation, he assumes the 'normal' development of 'appropriate' gender and sexuality, but what he provides is a way to understand how all development creates a split subject, how there can be no 'appropriate' gender and sexuality, unless, of course, all dimensions of the child's psychosomatic world are consciously and unconsciously attuned to – a clear impossibility. Most important, Stern suggests how the sexual identity of the subject is called to form in such a way that it responds to its interpellation. Furthermore, Stern's account provides a way for us to understand how Judith Butler's subject, as described earlier, comes to repeat her or his performance – or perhaps to disrupt it.

Let us return to two of the questions Butler (1997) raised: what makes the subject turn to the hailing, and what if anything exists prior to the turn to the hailing? We can follow Stern and say that it is the initial subjectivizing of the infant through selective attunement that produces a subject who is in some sense split, whose potential self requires in some ways the marginalizing of that which, for whatever reasons, has not been attuned to. Thus, as the infant comes to be subjectivized by the parents, siblings and caretakers, so too the infant's anatomical sex, gender, and sexuality develop through attunement, misattunement and social referencing. As 'the parents' desires, fears, prohibitions, and fantasies contour the psychic experiences of the child,' as 'selective attunement reaches to almost all forms of experience' and 'determines which overt behaviors fall inside or outside the pale,' what preferences the child might have for others, and the 'degrees or types or internal states … that can occur with another person,' the child's sexual identity comes to form (1997: 207–8).

It would take a micro-analysis to detail the ways in which a particular individual's sexual identity is called forth by parents and significant others from the Heraclitean flux of the infant's inner and external worlds. We can say, though, that the sexual identity that begins to emerge has developed at the expense of other pulsations, attractions, pleasures, and may constitute a false self, false in the sense of being partial or of belonging to someone else. It is not that there is some true sexuality or sex or gender waiting beneath the false one. Rather, we can think of what Stern refers to as 'lying beyond the pale' as similar to what Julia Kristeva called the 'abject.' The abject is the excess split off from the sexed body and cannot come into being within the sexual matrix or, in this case, within the attunement of the parent. Kristeva's abject refers to what is disavowed when the subject takes up a position in the Symbolic, or, in other words, when the subject comes to form in a social identity. As Elizabeth Grosz writes (1990: 87):

> What is new about Kristeva's position is her claim that what must be expelled from the subject's corporal functioning can never be fully obliterated but hovers at the border of the subject's identity, threatening apparent unities and stabilities with disruption and possible dissolution. They recur and threaten the subject not only in those events Freud described as the 'return of the repressed' – that is, in psychical symptoms –

they are also a necessary accompaniment of ... socially unacceptable forms of sexual drives.

Thus what Stern refers to as 'beyond the pale' and Kristeva refers to as the 'abject' comes to exist alongside the sexual identity called into being, like a shadow without clear boundaries or a filmy liquid clinging to the borders of that sexual identity and seeping into it, opening up crevices, creating undertows and occasionally streaming through it. What makes the subject turn to a particular interpellation can be either the sexual identity called forth by the parents or significant others, or else the inchoate that remains 'beyond the pale.' For example, one day as I was on my way back from 'having sex' with my girlfriend at her house, at age 15, I was called 'queer' by some kids on a park bench. I ran from them in fear, in my mind confirming their accusation, and I felt marked in a way that crystallized latent feelings or ideas without making me fully identify with being homosexual or 'queer,' yet leading me to respond to the 'calling.' The subject who turned to that interpellation, who responded to that call was already constituted by a sexual identity and its remainder, that which clung to its margins and was 'beyond the pale.'

It seems clear, though, that none of the sexual identities provided within the sexual matrix can or ever could encompass or articulate both that which lies 'beyond the pale' and the sexual identity called forth at a particular moment, whether or not within one's family. Perhaps Stern's work, coupled with that of the other theorists I have alluded to, leads us to the conclusion that there are as many sexual identities (i.e. anatomical sexes, genders, sexualities) as there are people, but the sexual matrix provides only massified, set identities to which we are called. It is within this matrix that the body is born. It is from within this matrix that the callings of sexual identities come.

I have outlined so far how we are 'called to' our sexual identities through interpellation and through intersubjective relationships with parents, and I have tried to sketch a response to the questions Judith Butler has raised about what makes the subject turn to the hailing. I want to focus more now on how we are interpellated within the dominant sexual matrix. In particular I want to focus on how the institution of school normalizes sexual identities.

Normalization is, of course, a concept associated with Michel Foucault, who used it to describe how particular behaviors, attitudes, ideas, feelings, values and particular ways of thinking, talking and seeing the world are articulated, organized and made into the norm against which all else is measured (and generally found aberrant, inadequate, or dangerous). For Foucault the molding of who we are and how we define and think about ourselves is a function of these organizing and normalizing processes – that is, both discursive and non-discursive practices and what he later called 'technologies of the self.' He described how power works positively to create entire discourses in which various selves or identities, what in his early texts he called 'figures,' emerge and are subject to and anchor formal and informal disciplinary procedures.

Clearly, two central locations for constructing norms and 'figures' are the academy, where the disciplines create the objects and figures they study, and the school, where the young are classified, placed in hierarchies and, according to the formal and informal norms of the schools, subjected to a range of formal and informal treatments.

We have all witnessed the normalization, the standardization and the construction of identities in our schools, but the normalization of sexualities and sex is perhaps the least theorized, in part because heterosexuality is so hegemonic and therefore invisible, but also because sex remains, for all its prolixity, framed in terms that render its discussion 'out of bounds' in all but sex education classes or, of course, in the vernacular discussions among students. My daughter currently attends a school in California where at homecoming they choose a prince and princess for every class. She tells me that the winners are not the best looking, but they are the most popular. The boy and girl who win in the senior class are, of course, the king and queen. One need only imagine a teacher or principal extending such a popularity contest by having classes also elect prince and prince or princess and princess and encouraging students to vote on these without regard to anatomy, to get a glimpse of the entrenched and massified ways of thinking about gender and sexuality that support what is passed off as a perfectly normal and 'fun' school ritual. This is an obvious example of how sexuality is organized in schools and there are hundreds of other ways, from the absence in English classes of literature about non-heterosexual love to the intentional omission of the sexuality of famous people studied in history classes. While every schoolchild knows about Catherine the Great's death and Henry VIII's wives, ironically teachers often smugly comment that bringing someone's homosexuality or lesbianism into class is silly, irrelevant and surrendering to the 'thought police.' If we wish other obvious examples of how schools norm sexual identity, we might consider the construction of proms and dances at schools, or the required presentation of teachers' sexuality at faculty parties or school functions to which spouses or 'significant' (read opposite sex) others are invited. We might look at the way sports have, as Brian Pronger (1990) documents in *The Arena of Masculinity: Sports, Homosexuality and the Meaning of Sex*, helped construct sexuality. For example, coaches will call boys 'sissy,' 'faggot,' or 'girl' to motivate them to play harder, yet encourage a kind of homoeroticism by having, for example, football players in a huddle hold hands, or by encouraging rough-housing in the showers. Or to take another example, one that is a bit less obvious, we can consider the ways teachers often try to make their pedagogy relevant by referring to examples from their students' lives, examples that always assume heterosexuality.

Because teaching and learning occur in relationships and because the dynamics of the classroom are intersubjective, teachers, like parents, engage in attuning, misattunement and social referencing all the time. Just as parents and significant others are calling forth sexual identities, so too are teachers and students. Students' gestures, off-beat moves, looks that slide over faces, moods and behaviors may be subjected to the very kinds of misattunement and social referencing that occur in the family. And teachers, too, are themselves subjected to normalizing practices and to the social referencing of their students.

Certainly the threat of being labeled homosexual or lesbian, or some sexuality that is not heterosexual, works to police teachers and students. One need only recall Sherwood Anderson's tale in *Winesburg, Ohio* of Wing Biddlebaum, whose wandering hands and 'feeling for the boys under his charge' targeted him for assault and a near lynching. In an article entitled 'Manly Men and Womanly Women: Deviance, Gender Role Polarization and the Shift in Women's School Employment, 1900–1976,' Jackie Blount (1996) argues that the threat of being labeled lesbian was used after the Second World War to drive single women out of positions of power in the schools.

Heterosexuality is so naturalized in schools that even to talk of creating institutions that are physically and psychically safe for gay and lesbian students and teachers is to risk being fired, stigmatized, ridiculed or positioned at the limit of possible conversation on the subject. To talk about creating curricula or pedagogies or school cultures that *encourage* various sexualities, that investigate and problematize sexual identities, to advocate interrupting the assumed naturalness of any sexual identity including those of the teacher, is to take a position 'off the map.' And yet such a project is urgent. The appalling statistics on suicide, gay-bashing, runaways and health problems among gay and lesbian youth and the continued discrimination against gays and lesbians demand that we make schools safer for gay and lesbian students and teachers (Eggleston, 1997). As the letters and essays that appeared in *Harvard Educational Review*'s special issue, 'Lesbian, Gay, Bisexual and Transgender People and Education' make clear, the psychic and physical toll of being other than heterosexual is high.

The naturalizing of heterosexuality in schools, requiring as it does the de-naturalizing and stigmatizing of homosexuality as well as the bolstering of particular heterosexualities, also results in extremely limited, parochial and rigid images of and norms for what and how boys and girls should appear or 'be,' colluding with media images of sex and sexuality that place students in impossible double binds. Furthermore, the heterosexualities that are in part produced in schools contribute to the epidemic proportions of heterosexual pedophilia, rape, sexual harassment and sexual abuse (Silin 1995). They also contribute to the narrowness and impoverishment of both heterosexual and homosexual sex. One need only read the results of sex researchers like Shere Hite (1984), Blumstein and Schwartz (1983) or Susie Bright (1997) to glimpse just how limited our bodies are. The average length of heterosexual sex is 8 minutes; many married women do not have orgasms; premature ejaculation is common among young men, and impotence is on the rise; many young women do not know where their clitoris is and most young men certainly do not know about their own or female bodies; heterosexual sex is often confined to touching the penis, vagina, clitoris and breasts. One need only look at media depictions of heterosexual, gay and lesbian sex to note the predictability, repetitiveness, stereotypicality and shallowness of sexual fantasies. One need only listen to the vocabulary available to describe or name sex, to hear the limitation and rigidity of male sexuality. Finally, one need only look at media images of gender and anatomical sex to understand the procrustean stylization of the body. Is it any wonder that the gender of the models for female fashion magazines is identical to that of drag queens? It is so easy to imitate.

It is urgent that we address the harsh realities of being a gay or lesbian student in schools today, but we cannot stop at policies and legislation that respond only to the inequities faced by students who are homosexuals. We also have to confront the systemic ways in which sexuality is organized, as well as why we consistently collude with those organizations. Often, in attempts to make schools inclusive of lesbian and gay youth, educators make the assumption that we all know what gays and lesbians 'are,' or that 'we' are not gay or lesbian, or that somehow we can approach lesbian and gay youth as well as straight youth using the same paradigm we bring to programs that work to make schools inclusive of all races, ethnicities and anatomical sexes. But if the categories 'lesbian' and 'gay' and 'heterosexual' involve desire and what people do with their bodies, then to make schools inclusive in the same way as one thinks of inclusiveness for racial groups, for example, would mean making sexual activity, or desire itself, celebrated, judged healthy, or at least explored; would mean bringing sexual activity into the open and discussing it, not only heterosexual activity but homosexual activity too. I fully support such a program, but with the caveat that in so doing we do not leave unproblematized the sexual identities and sex that will emerge.

The organization of sexual identities in schools, however, does not only impoverish all our lives and oppress those who are not identified as heterosexual. It also impoverishes our thinking. If the truth of our being has in modern times been sought in sexuality, yet this sexuality has itself been limited and contingent, then to assume fixed and natural sexual identities, whether normative or alternative, is to censor the pursuit of truth, and, I would argue, to block thinking.

Teaching and thinking

[T]he instinct for knowledge in children is attracted unexpectedly early and intensively to sexual problems and is in fact possibly first aroused by them.

(Freud 1962: 54)

'The term of reason is truly vast' (Lyotard, 1993). Vast enough to be grafted onto the skin of the body? Why not start with the body? It is vast too. Maybe we might ask the body to speak? What if I become a speaking body, a thinking body? Would your body call to me? ... When the body speaks, what will be said? What will we hear? Will 'we' be here?

(Pinar 1997: 106)

If, as several curriculum theorists and educators have argued, we come to know the world as embodied subjects, and if how we know the world is inextricably related to our bodies, then how we know the world is also related to our sexual identities. If that is the case, and if, as I have tried to show, the bodies through which we know the world are partial, fixed, and stereotyped, then we are coming to know the world in partial, stereotypical, fixed and ultimately impoverished ways.

According to Gilles Deleuze (quoted in Grosz 1995: 125):

Thinking is not innate, but must be engendered in thought ... the problem is not to direct or methodologically apply a thought which preexists in principle and in nature, but to bring into being that which does not yet exist ... To think is to create – there is no other creation.

Clearly this is not the kind of thinking that generally occurs in schools. Thinking in schools tends to consist only of accumulating cultural capital, recalling information and memorizing bits and pieces of decontextualized 'knowledge,' the absence of which is interpreted as ignorance. In schools certainty, surety and syllogistic logic are valued over ambiguity, ambivalence and free association. I do not object to such thinking any more than I would or could argue that various sexual identities were less or more valuable than others, or that there were some bodies that were better than others. I am sure it is clear, though, that I think the more we can tolerate a range of bodies, the more we can make schools inclusive, then the better off we shall be. In the same sense, I believe it would be better to encourage the thinking Deleuze describes than to continue solely to impose the normative and normalizing thought so pervasive in schools today.

But how does this thinking relate to sexual identity? My sense is that the more rigidly an individual adheres to a sexual identity, the more compulsively an identity is repeated, the more stereotypic are an individual's fantasy life and desires, the more invested in particular sexual identities, whether normative or alternative, the more stylized the body is, the less thinking, in Deleuze's sense, occurs.

It seems to me that thinking differently involves 'not knowing,' involves the suspension of or at least the putting into question of one's own sexual identity and the discourses that articulate that identity (normative or alternative), and working towards a 'broadening' of the body; whereas to think the same is to repeat, to hold on to a solid sexual identity, to reiterate what one knows – communication in the sense of passing on or putting into circulation only what is already understood and known. As Lacan writes (1990: xxv–xxvi):

> To make oneself understood is not the same as teaching – it is the opposite. One only understands what one thinks one already knows. More precisely, one never understands anything but a meaning whose satisfaction or comfort one has already felt ... one never understands anything but one's fantasies. And one is never taught by anything other than what one doesn't understand, i.e. by nonsense.

Reading this we can see how thinking is not unlike what Elizabeth Bishop (1985) meant when she defined poetry as 'a self-forgetful and perfectly senseless concentration.' This practice opposes truth to knowledge. As Marie Januus says, glossing Lacan's views on truth and knowledge (quoted in Apollon and Feldstein 1996: 199):

> Truth has to do with the unintelligible, the nonsensical, the mute ... whereas knowledge is about answers, the requirement of coherence in discourse, intelligibility ... Knowledge is a form of systematization, bounded and inert; truth by contrast is coextensive with origination, invention and birth ... If the state and the university are not particularly interested in psychoanalysis it has to do with their desire for sense, meaning, the verifiable, and objective – for knowledge that has power precisely because it claims, erroneously to be synonymous with the truth.

The opposition that Lacan makes between truth and knowledge is, I would suggest, analogous to the opposition between Eros and sex. The erotic is 'unintelligible,' and 'nonsensical.' It is 'mute' because it resists the sexual matrix. Thinking and truth are mute in the sense that they can only come to be as new concepts, lightning movements, whose traces will eventually become thought, just as the shock and intensity of new sensations on the body will, because they may never be able to escape the sexual matrix, eventually become sex. Elizabeth Grosz (1995: 240) writes of Deleuze that he 'wants to link the unthought to the body, which can no longer be conceived in terms of being a medium of thought or a blockage to it (as in the Platonic and Cartesian traditions): rather the body is the motive of thought, its source or well.' She quotes Deleuze (*ibid.*):

> The body is no longer the obstacle that separates thought from itself, that which it has to overcome to reach thinking. It is on the contrary that which it plunges into or must plunge into, in order to reach the unthought, that is life. Not that the body thinks, but, obstinate and stubborn, it forces us to think, and forces us to think what is concealed from thought, life. Life will no longer be made to appear before the categories of thought; thought will be thrown into the categories of life. The

categories of life are precisely the attitudes of the body, its postures. 'We do not even know what the body can do'; in its sleep, in its drunkenness, in its efforts and resistances. To think is to learn what a non-thinking body is capable of, its capacity, its postures.

The more partial, fixed or stereotyped the body, the less life there is to plunge into. The more stylized the body, the less we can learn what it is capable of. It is not the body that is the obstacle to thinking, but the body called into form and classified within the sexual matrix.

There is perhaps no final escape from the sexual matrix, any more than there is the possibility of only thinking without thought, or truth without knowledge. I am convinced, though, that to be fully present in our teaching requires each of us to work to attune to our own bodies and to those of our students, to analyze and reconceive the relationships between our sexualized bodies, and to provide ways in our classes for multiple bodies to be and to think. To remain stuck in or collapsed into one sexual identity – that is supported by whatever fantasmatic space and used to sustain whatever desires – is to produce a teaching and a knowledge that are also stuck, repetitive and finally foreclosed. To attune to the shimmer of a student's hand rising against the light or the thick drip of a running nose, to attune to the abject and to what is 'beyond the pale,' to encourage the shock of the new in our students and ourselves, may leave us open to new ways of thinking and being together.

References

Althusser, Louis (1994) 'Ideology and Ideological State Apparatuses (Notes towards an Investigation)' in Slavoj Zizek (ed.) *Mapping Ideology* (100–40), London: Verso Press.

Anderson, Sherwood. (1993). *Winesburg, Ohio*, NY: Signet.

Apollon, Willy and Feldstein, Richard (1996) *Lacan, Politics, Aesthetics*, Albany, NY: State University of New York Press.

Baldwin, James (1985) *The Price of the Ticket. Collected Nonfiction 1948–1985*, New York: St Martin's Press.

Barreca, Regina and Morse, Deborah Denenholz (eds) (1997) *The Erotics of Instruction*, Hanover and London: University Press of New England.

Bishop, Elizabeth. (1985). *The Collected Prose*, Boston, MA: Noonday Press.

Blount, Jackie M. (1996) 'Manly Men and Womanly Women: Deviance, Gender Role Polarization, and the Shift in Women's School Employment, 1900–1976,' *Harvard Educational Review*, 66(2): 318–38.

Blumstein, Philip and Schwartz, Pepper (1983) *American Couples*, New York: William Morrow and Co.

Boldt, Gail Masuchika (1996) 'Sexist and Heterosexist Responses to Gender Bending in an Elementary Classroom,' *Curriculum Inquiry*, 26(2): 113–32.

Bright, Susie (1997) *Susie Bright's Sexual State of the Union*, New York: Simon & Schuster.

Bruner, Jerome (1996) *The Culture of Education*, Cambridge, MA: Harvard University Press.

Butler, Judith (1990) *Gender Trouble. Feminism and the Subversion of Identity*, New York and London: Routledge.

—— (1991) 'Imitation and Gender Insubordination' in Diana Fuss (ed.) *Inside/Out: Lesbian Theories. Gay Theories* (13–31), New York and London: Routledge.

—— (1993) *Bodies That Matter: On the Discursive Limits of 'Sex,'* New York and London: Routledge.

—— (1994) 'Gender as Performance: An Interview with Judith Butler,' *Radical Philosophy*, 67: 32–9.

—— (1997) *The Psychic Life of Power: Theories in Subjection*, Stanford, CA: Stanford University Press.

Casper, Virginia, Cuffaro, Harriet, Schultz, Steven, Silin, Jonathan, and Wickens, Elaine (1996) 'Toward a Most Thorough Understanding of the World: Sexual Orientation and Early Childhood Education,' *Harvard Educational Review*, 66(2): 271–93.

Chodorow, Nancy (1978) *The Reproduction of Mothering: Psychoanalysis and the Sociology of Gender*, Berkeley: University of California Press.

David-Menard, Monique (1989) *Hysteria from Freud to Lacan: Body and Language in Psychoanalysis* tr. Catherine Porter, Ithaca and London: Cornell University Press.

Deleuze, Gilles (1990) *The Logic of Sense* tr. Mark Lester with Charles Stivale, New York: Columbia University Press.

—— (1994) *What Is Philosophy?*, New York: Columbia University Press.

Deleuze, Gilles and Guattari, Felix (1977) *Anti-Oedipus: Capitalism and Schizophrenia*, New York: Viking Press.

Eggleston, Verna (1997) *Newsletter* November 1997, Herrick-Martin Institute, New York.

Foucault, Michel (1970) *The Order of Things* tr. Alan Sheriden, London: Tavistock.

—— (1980) Introduction to *The History of Sexuality* vol. 1 tr. Robert Hurley, New York: Vintage/Random House.

Freire, Paulo (1997) *Pedagogy of the Oppressed* tr. Myra Bergman Ramos, New York: Continuum.

Freud, Sigmund (1962) *Three Contributions to the Theory of Sex* tr. A. A. Brill, New York: E. P. Dutton.

—— (1963) *Dora: An Analysis of a Case of Hysteria*, New York: Collier Books.

Freud, Sigmund and Breuer, Joseph (2000) *Studies in Hysteria* tr. James Strachey, New York: Basic Books.

Fuss, Diana (ed.) (1991) *Inside/Out: Lesbian Theories. Gay Theories*, New York and London: Routledge.

—— (1995) *Identification Papers*, New York: Routledge.

Grosz, Elizabeth (1990) 'The Body of Signification,' in John Fletcher and Andrew Benjamin (eds) *Abjection, Melancholy and Love: The Work of Julia Kristeva*, New York and London: Routledge.

—— (1994) *Volatile Bodies: Toward a Corporeal Feminism*, Bloomington and Indianapolis: Indiana University Press.

—— (1995) *Space, Time, and Perversion: Essays on the Politics of Bodies*, New York and London: Routledge.

Grumet, Madeleine (1988) *Bitter Milk: Women and Teaching*, Amherst, MA: University of Massachusetts Press.

—— (1993) 'Preface' to Louis Castenell and William Pinar (eds) *Understanding Curriculum as Racial Text: Representations of Identity and Difference in Education*, Albany, NY: State University of New York Press.

Harvard Educational Review 66:2.

Hirschfield, Jane (1998) *Nine Gates: Entering the Mind of Poetry: Essays*. NY: Harpercollins.

Hite, Shere. (1984). *The Hite Report: A Nationwide Study of Female Sexuality*. NY: Bookthrift Co.

Irigaray, Luce (1992) *Elemental Passions* tr. Joanne Collie and Judith Still, New York: Routledge.

Krohn, Alan (1978) *Hysteria: The Elusive Neurosis*, New York: International Universities Press.

Lacan, J. (1977) *Ecrits: A Selection* tr. Alan Sheriden, New York: W. W. Norton & Co.

—— (1981) in Jacques-Alain Miller (ed.) *The Four Fundamental Concepts of Psychoanalysis* tr. Alan Sheriden, New York: W. W. Norton & Co.

—— (1988a) 'Freud's Papers on Technique 1953–1954' in Jacques-Alain Miller (ed.) *The Seminar of Jacques Lacan* Book I tr. John Forrester, New York: W. W. Norton & Co.

—— (1988b) 'The Ego in Freud's Theory and in the Technique of Psychoanalysis 1954–1955' in Jacques-Alain Miller (ed.) *The Seminar of Jacques Lacan* Book II tr. Sylvana Tomaselli, New York: W. W. Norton & Co.

—— (1990) *Television* tr. D. Hollier, R. Kraus, and A. Michelson, New York: W. W. Norton & Co.

—— (1992) 'The Ethics of Psychoanalysis 1959–1960' in Jacques-Alain Miller (ed.) *The Seminar of Jacques Lacan* Book VII tr. Dennis Porter, New York: W. W. Norton & Co.

—— (1993) 'The Psychoses 1955–1956' in Jacques-Alain Miller (ed.) *The Seminar of Jacques Lacan* Book III tr. Russell Grigg, New York: W. W. Norton & Co.

Males, Michael (1996) *The Scapegoat Generation: America's War on Adolescence*, Monroe, ME: Common Courage Press.

Miller, Jacques-Alain (1995) 'Context and Concepts' in Richard Feldstein, Bruce Fink and Marie Jaanus (eds) *Reading Seminar XI: Lacan's Four Fundamental Concepts of Psychoanalysis*, Albany, NY: State University of New York.

Moi, Toril (1989) 'Patriarchal Thought and the Drive for Knowledge' in Teresa Brenan (ed.) *Between Feminism and Psychoanalysis* (189–205), New York: Routledge.

Perloff, Marjorie (1996) *Wittgenstein's Ladder: Poetic Language and the Strangeness of the Ordinary*, Chicago, IL: University of Chicago Press.

Phelan, Shane (ed.) (1997) *Playing with Fire: Queer Politics, Queer Theories*, New York and London: Routledge.

Pinar, William (1994) *Autobiography, Politics and Sexuality. Essays in Curriculum Theory 1972–1992*, New York: Peter Lang.

—— (1997) 'Regimes of Reason and the Male Narrative Voice' in William Tierney and Yvonna Lincoln (eds) *Representation and the Text: Re-Framing the Narrative Voice* (81–114), Albany, NY: State University of New York Press.

Pronger, Brian (1990) *The Arena of Masculinity: Sports, Homosexuality and the Meaning of Sex*, New York: St Martin's Press.

Rabinow, Paul (1983) *The Foucault Reader*, New York: Pantheon.

Rich, Adrienne (1986) 'Compulsory Heterosexuality and Lesbian Experience' in *Blood, Bread and Poetry: Selected Prose 1979–1985* (23–75), New York: Norton.

Rubin, Gayle (1975) 'The Traffic in Women: Notes on the "Political Economy" of Sex' in Rayna Reiter (ed.) *Toward an Anthropology of Women* (157–210), New York: Monthly Review Press.

Salvio, Paula (1995) 'On the Forbidden Pleasures and Hidden Dangers of Covert Reading,' *English Quarterly*, 27(3): 8–15.

Sedgwick, Eve Kosofsky (1990) *Epistemology of the Closet*, Berkeley: University of California Press.

Silin, Jonathan (1995) *Sex, Death and the Education of Children: Our Passion for Ignorance in the Age of Aids*, New York: Teachers College Press.

Stern, Daniel (1985) *The Interpersonal World of the Infant: A View from Psychoanalysis and Developmental Psychology*, New York: Basic Books.

Stolorow, Robert, Atwood, George and Brandchaft, Bernard (eds) (1995) *The Intersubjective Perspective*. NY: Jason Aronson.

Tierney, William and Lincoln, Yvonne (1997) *Representation and the Text: Re-Framing the Narrative Voice*, Albany, NY: State University of New York Press.

Wittig, Monique (1992) *The Straight Mind and Other Essays*, Boston, MA: Beacon Press.

Globalizing

13 Labeling whiteness

Decentering strategies of white racial domination

Peter McLaren, Aimee M. Carrillo-Rowe, Rebecca L. Clark, and Philip A. Craft

The term 'whiteness' has become a voguish buzzword in academia, having secured at least a temporary place of honor in the lexicon of the new multiculturalists. Increasingly, this itinerant and unstable term has been put on exhibit at the wine-and-cheese salons of postmodernist academics where the concept of 'white trash' has suddenly taken on new scholarly dimensions. A burgeoning fascination with the social construction of whiteness has spawned a giddy rush of conferences, books, articles, and courses dedicated to its analysis and critique. Recently, in an attempt to lend legitimacy to white studies, following the recent surge of interest in critical race theory, Temple University Press has issued a collection of essays entitled, *Critical White Studies* (Delgado and Stefancic 1997). But what exactly is 'whiteness'? Is it multiculturalism's latest effort at rhetorical camouflage? Is it a *foramen magnum* to a new way of understanding racism? A *force majeure* in advancing new theories of subjectivity? Is it simply an academic ruse that will enable white theorists to steal some of the limelight in the ongoing culture wars? Is it a mere quasi-theoretical residue of more complex analyses of racialized identity? Will the topic of whiteness be of interest to a wider public? Can whiteness be addressed pertinently, in a way that delves deeper than the out-of-context cut-and-paste treatises we have come to expect from crackpot 'race' theorists in the media? (After all, such pundits of the airwaves more often than not reduce race and ethnicity to little more than a market-driven, self-serving saturnalia of ill-defined ethnic celebrations – for example, Cinco de Mayo or Black History Month – while acting as stand-alone moralists and unashamedly extolling the commodity character of racial traits.) More importantly, is this label at all useful, or does its racial specificity merely replicate the logic of racism by reifying and dialectically reinitiating 'chromatic' differences, as its critics claim?

We intend to demonstrate –albeit in abbreviated form – that the term 'whiteness' serves as a useful vehicle for contesting and altering the existing and persistent racial power relations within the United States. While traditional discussions of race focus on non-whites, analyses of whiteness examine white people, the dominant racial group, who have heretofore escaped public and academic scrutiny of their racist, sexist and heterosexist practices.

Labeling whiteness provides a sociopolitical optic through which the practices that produce structural privilege and exploitation can be examined and addressed. Using whiteness as a label broadens and deepens more traditional explanations of racism by mapping racist characteristics that are specific to the dominant racial group in this nation: white people.

Largely because public opinion in the United States defines racism 'psychodynamically' as interpersonal acts of hatred and because there has been a decline in overt forms of racial violence, the dominant white society has all too often, jumped to the conclusion that the problem is almost completely resolved. To support this argument one need only cite California's recent abolition of affirmative action measures and its elimination of bilingual education. Another strong indicator of the unacknowledged presence of white supremacy is the manner in which whiteness has become institutionalized as the key marker or measure against which identity is defined. For an example of the hereditary invisibility of whiteness, we need look no farther than Senate majority leader Trent Lott, a politician from Mississippi well known to the general public for his conservative ideals and his role in the impeachment proceedings of president William Jefferson Clinton. Although Lott has been described in a recent issue of *The Nation* as one of 'the pinstriped mafiosi of the culture wars' (Shapiro 1999: 4), he continues to be invoked by the mainstream media as a principled actor in the cause of family values. Despite his past participation in and alleged continuing relationship with Mississippi's white supremacist Council of Conservative Citizens (CCC), Lott is frequently portrayed by the mainstream media as a courageous example of moral impeccability and national leadership.

With white supremacy so invisible in today's society – with the exception of a smattering of stories about growing numbers of militia groups throughout the United States – is it any wonder that racial injustice rages on? Recent analyses of whiteness address some of the numerous oversights that result from this conceptually truncated definition of racism by interrogating it instead as an institutionalized system of economic, political, social, and cultural relations that ensures that one racial group maintains power and advantage over all others. While there is nothing inherently 'white' about racism, the status of white people in the United States as the dominant 'race' demands that we specifically examine the structural relationship between racism and white privilege. It is precisely this structural relationship between white people and racial domination that needs to be 'marked' and examined because, as we will argue, it is a relationship that has nourished a specific form of social and political invisibility in mainstream United States culture.

In order to explore how and why the study of whiteness provides a useful conceptual framework for interrogating racism, we first examine how 'whiteness' functions. In so doing, we identify three strategies through which white people are assured continued racial privilege, strategies that we consider related to the remarkably 'unmarked' character of whiteness.

We follow with an examination of the conjunctural relationship among whiteness, capitalism, and neo-imperialism. We suggest that within the spatial boundaries of the United States, whiteness cannot be reduced to racism, but must be considered as a function of those colonial legacies and contemporary imperialist and racist practices through which white power and social position is hegemonically secured. We conclude with a sketch of possible tactical maneuvers aimed at decentering whiteness in our own daily practices.

Defining whiteness

> [T]he vision of a world of intelligent men [*sic*] with sufficient income to live decently and with the will to build a beautiful world ... will not be easy to accomplish ... but the quickest way to bring the reason of the world face to face with this major problem of human progress is to listen to the complaint of those human beings today who are suffering most from white attitudes, from white habits, from the conscious and unconscious wrongs which white folks are today inflicting on their victims.
>
> (Du Bois 1968: 172)

> If whiteness is never articulated, then it is people of Color, as a group, who can be scrutinized and blamed in order to exalt the perfection of that which is natural and left unexamined.
>
> (Hurtado 1996: 139)

We cannot talk intelligently about 'whiteness' unless we introduce the dynamics of political economy. Too often critical race theory, critical pedagogy, and whiteness studies decapitate or degut the study of race from the history of capitalist social relations. According to Alex Callinicos (1993), racial differences are invented within specific political economies associated with the mode of production. Racism occurs when the characteristics which justify discrimination are held to be inherent in the oppressed group. The institutionalized forms of this type of oppression are peculiar to capitalist societies; they arise in the circumstances surrounding industrial capitalism and the attempt to acquire a large labor force. Racism is no mere epiphenomenon of a determinant social process, but a fundamental component of that process. Callinicos points out three main conditions for the existence of racism as outlined by Marx: economic competition between workers; the appeal of racist ideology to white workers; and efforts of the capitalist class to establish and maintain racial divisions among workers. Capital's constantly changing demands for different kinds of labor can only be met through immigration. Callinicos remarks that 'racism offers for workers of the oppressing "race" the imaginary compensation for the exploitation they suffer of belonging to the "*ruling* nation"' (1993: 39). He also underscores the profound manner in which Marx grasped how racial divisions between 'native' and immigrant workers could weaken the working class.

What George Lipsitz refers to as 'the possessive investment in whiteness' has always been influenced by its origins in the history of United States racist practices, involving the demonization of the *faex populi* (the lower orders), slavery, segregation, and the wholesale extermination of indigenous peoples. In North America, slavery took on distinctive racial formations that reduced African Americans to permanent, hereditary, chattel-bond slaves. According to Lipsitz (1998: 3):

> White settlers institutionalized a possessive investment in whiteness by making blackness synonymous with slavery and whiteness synonymous with freedom, but also by pitting people of color against one another. Fearful of alliances between Native Americans and African Americans that might challenge the prerogatives of whiteness, white settlers prohibited slaves and free blacks from traveling in 'Indian country.' European Americans used diplomacy and force to compel Native Americans to return runaway slaves to their white masters. During the Stono Rebellion of 1739, colonial authorities offered Native Americans a bounty for every rebellious slave they captured or killed. At the same time, British settlers recruited black slaves to fight against Native Americans within colonial militias. The power of whiteness depended not only on white hegemony over separate racialized groups, but also on manipulating racial outsiders to fight against one another, to compete with each other for white approval, and to seek the rewards and privileges of whiteness for themselves at the expense of other racialized populations.

If we wish to get at the roots of whiteness, we need to focus on the social, political, economic, and historical actualities that sustain it. And while we do not have space here to cut a large clearing in the dense thicket of capital's relationship to whiteness, we can still explore a few possibilities. Our principal claim is that we cannot discuss whiteness in abstraction from material circumstances or the practices of exploitation that capitalism provokes in its train. We support the claim that whiteness and capitalism interweave and that whiteness is fundamentally linked to the practice of Anglo-European and United States colonialism. Its concrete historical facticity can be traced to the trans-Atlantic slave trade. Following Theodore W. Allen (1994, 1997), Jonathan Scott (1998), and McLaren and Muñoz (2000), we proceed on the prevailing assumption that whiteness is, first and foremost, a 'sociogenic' (having to do with social forces and relations) rather than a 'phylogenic' (having to do with phenotype or skin color) phenomenon. We start from the premise that the concept of a separate white race did not exist prior to the seventeenth century. For instance, in colonial Virginia, roughly between 1676 and 1705, there existed little distinction in status between 'black' and 'white' bond-laborers who were essentially *ejusdem generis*. Whiteness was a false totality imperiously imposed on the heterogeneous population of the colony so that the Anglo-American continental plantation bourgeoisie could keep the colonial tobacco monoculture from being diversified or threatened by rebellious landless laborers (as in the famous case of the Bacon Rebellion). Whiteness was a status position introduced by the seventeenth-century Anglo-American and United States ruling class – largely the oligarchy of owners of large colonial plantations – who for purely political and economic purposes endowed indentured Europeans (who at the time were *de facto* slaves) with civil and social privileges that greatly exceeded those of their fellow African bondsmen and granted those with white skin an inscrutable unity (Allen 1994; Scott 1998).

Within New England's progressive system of equitably distributed small land holdings, freedom for bond-laborers (6,000 Europeans and 2,000 African Americans) would effectively have created a condition of economic *écroulement*, ending the plantocracy's super-exploitation of the African and European bond-laborers. Freedom for these 8,000 bond-laborers would have transformed the colony into a diversified smallholder economy. This would have been ultimately disastrous for the tobacco monoculture, which essentially depended upon chattel or bond labor. The chattelization of labor thus became a necessity for strengthening Virginia's tobacco monoculture. However, the small landholders of colonial Virginia had begun to oppose changes in Virginia land policy that allocated the best land to wealthy capitalist investors, and laws that forbade them to trade with the Indians. More and more landless laborers began to fight against their chattel bond-servitude. In the Bacon Rebellion Africans and Europeans fought side by side against the plantation bourgeoisie, who would routinely punish runaway laborers by adding years to their servitude, and who ordered severe restrictions on corn-planting and a ban on hunting for food in the forests so that the rebelling chattel bond-laborers would starve to death (Allen 1994; Scott 1998).

The aim of the Anglo-American continental plantation bourgeoisie was to prepare the ground for a system of lifetime hereditary bond-servitude. But the 'confederation' of African American slaves and European bond-laborers made their military power too strong for the colony elite to defeat with its small force of only 500 fighters. Indentured Anglo-Americans were consequently recruited into the middle classes through anomalous white-skin privileges. White-skin privilege was an acknowledgement of loyalty to the colonial land- and property-owning class. Africans were not brought into the middle class because there were simply too many laboring-class Europeans who had no social mobility and were thus a constant threat to the plantocracy. The white race had to be invented in order to diffuse this potential threat to ruling-class hegemony.

In summary, the invention of the white race was a political and economic maneuver designed to secure control by the plantocracy. It was primarily a means of preventing Anglo-Americans who existed in a state of chattel bond-servitude from joining forces with African bondsmen and overthrowing the plantocracy. That is, whiteness was an historical process of homogenizing the social statuses of Anglo-European tenants, merchants and planters into membership in the white race. Racial oppression was systematically put into place and European Americans were brought into the white 'middle class.' This saved the ruling class the money that it would have cost them to put down constant rebellions. Whiteness in this sense was a type of hideous abstraction, a dead 'second nature' invented by capitalism in order to falsely resurrect the putative natural superiority of the plantation bourgeoisie and the necessity of lifetime servitude for those who were not admitted into the white race.

With the rise of the abolitionist movement, racial typologies, classification systems, and criteriologies favoring whiteness and demonizing blackness became widespread in order to justify and legitimize the slavery of Africans and ensure the continuation of lifetime chattel bond-servitude. As Euro-Americans were called to imperialistically impute their categories and criteriologies everywhere, African Americans were forced to subordinate their lives to historically specific external criteria – imprinted with Eurocentric discourses of superiority – designed to usurp their autonomy and to separate their labor from a free collective exercise of will. Whiteness as an affirmation of power did not emerge from some transcendent intertwining with the immanent, but is thoroughly sinewy and historical; whiteness has no absolute, but only historical relevance as a specific mode of oppression. Today 'whiteness' has become naturalized as part of the national envelope of 'commonsense' reality.

Within this historical context, whiteness can be conceptualized as a social location that offers white people a structurally privileged position in current US society in relation to people of color. This social location constitutes a particular 'standpoint' or racial referent against which white people interpret themselves, others, and the world , a standpoint that can be maintained only by burying the historical memory of slavery, sealing it in a vault of silence, a shimmering alabaster monument to the Great White Lie. In talking about whiteness we need to outlaw transhistorical categories. Whiteness is a context-specific social construction, a fictional identity that facilitates and ensures that social privilege is maintained for those who are positioned as white. Accordingly, as well as being a social location or a standpoint, whiteness is also a set of *strategies* that operate to maintain white supremacy. There is no *Aufhebung* of whiteness, no logic of totality or dialectics of transformation that can contain it within the social universe of capital.

McLaren (1997) and McLaren and Muñoz (2000) articulate whiteness as an essentially mystifying and self-naturalizing discourse intrinsic to capitalism, a sociohistorical form of consciousness born at the nexus of capitalism, colonial rule, and the emergent relationships among dominant and subordinate groups. Wherever whiteness operates, the bourgeoisie appropriate the right to speak on behalf of everyone who is non-white, while denying voice to 'others' in the name of 'civilization.' Whiteness is born in a context where increased wealth for the few means impoverishment or marginalization for the many. Whiteness demarcates ideas, feelings, knowledge, social practices, cultural formations, and systems of intelligibility that are invested in by white people as 'white.' Whiteness is also a refusal to acknowledge how white people are implicated in relations of social domination and subordination and instances of economic exploitation. Whiteness, in this sense, as we mentioned before, appears ubiquitous and stable yet at the same time can be considered as a form of historical amnesia. Whiteness constitutes the selective tradition of dominant discourses about race, class, gender, and sexuality. Whiteness is not a unified, homogeneous culture but a *social position*, one that 'unvoices' or 'unpeoples' the Other. As Ignatiev (1998: 199, 233) comments:

> There is nothing positive about white identity. As James Baldwin said, 'As long as you think you're white, there's no hope for you.' Whiteness is not a culture. There is Irish culture and Italian culture and American culture; there is youth culture and drug culture and gear culture. There is no such thing as white culture. Shakespeare was *not* white; he was English. Mozart was not white; he was Austrian. Whiteness has nothing to do with culture and everything to do with social position. Without the privileges attached to it, there would be no white race, and fair skin would have the same significance as big feet.
>
> The problem with white people is not our whiteness, but our possessive investment in it. Created by politics, culture, and consciousness, our possessive investment in whiteness can be altered by those same processes, but only if we face the hard facts openly and honestly and admit that whiteness is a matter of interests as well as attitudes, that it has more to do with property than with pigment. Not all believers in white supremacy are white. All whites do not have to be white supremacists. But the possessive investment in whiteness is a matter of behavior as well as belief.

Referring to California as the 'Mississippi of the 1990s,' George Lipsitz criticizes the University of California regents for abolishing affirmative action, a practice he refers to as a 'possessive investment in whiteness.' He argues (1998: 229):

> The violent upheaval in Los Angeles in 1992 reflected only a small portion of the rage, despair, and cynicism permeating California as a result of the racialized effects of the transformation from a national industrial economy to a global postindustrial economy. The possessive investment in whiteness plays an insidious role in these realities: it occludes the crisis that we all face as a result of declining wages, environmental hazards, and social disintegration, while it generates racial antagonism as the only available frame for comprehending how individuals imagine themselves as a part of society.

Whiteness is not an essential category. For example, we oppose the belief that race is genetically determined, and can be sorted neatly by phenotype. Rather, we insist that whiteness as an *ideology* functions as an ongoing social, historical, cultural, and political practice in which meanings are secured that ensure the reproduction of white racial supremacy. It is absolutely important that we recognize that there are material benefits involuntarily accrued by persons with perceived white racial status, and that the meaning of whiteness and who counts as white entails a social, discursive process. Recent scholarly attention devoted to the topic of whiteness delineates several social practices on which the maintenance of a system of racial domination by whites depends. We outline three here.

The definition of difference

First, through their dominant racial position, white people have been able to construct themselves as 'central' because of their ability to construct 'others' as marginal and different, with difference from whiteness judged as inferior. White people have been able to secure a privileged 'standpoint' manifested in their ability to define cultural common sense, because whiteness has been consciously and unconsciously measured *against* racialized 'others.' This means that the category 'white' is not construed as racialized, while other 'races' serve to define the 'outer limits' of whiteness. Whiteness, in this sense, functions through defining what is different. *And difference never designates neutrality.* As soon as difference is marked, it is evaluated according to the overarching standards of whiteness and is always found to be lacking. Within a logic of hierarchy, where one race dominates the other, difference cannot, by definition, ever be equal to whiteness if white people are to maintain their dominant social position. Hence, we must remain skeptical about a great deal of contemporary rhetoric that advocates 'embracing difference.' Without a critical examination of how whiteness functions through difference as superiority, such claims to equality are premature and serve only to prolong racial disparities. For example, anti-affirmative action bills such as Proposition 209 in California and I–200 in Washington – which effectively terminate financial aid to women and ethnic minority groups – gain support by co-opting the rhetoric used in Civil Rights efforts to 'end discrimination.' In the case of these anti-affirmative action bills, the supposed 'victim' in whose interest we are to 'end discrimination' happens to be white and male. Claims that white men are victimized by what they see as 'racial favoritism' in affirmative action policies are only credible if we assume that differences are equal, that is, that white males experience the same kind of economic disadvantage and discrimination on the basis of skin color and phenotype as people of color who are also 'different'.

The significance of difference

The ability of white people to arrange social perception highlights our second point, that whiteness is really a type of social contract, a social construction and organization which works only if social subjects accept both that racial differences exist and that they provide a valid means to interpret or understand ourselves and others. Because racial differences are visible to social subjects as a text to be read, they take on a semblance of reality or facticity. Differences seem factual because we trust our eyes to provide us with 'accurate' information about our world. We see differences, as Du Bois would say, of 'skin, hair and bone' (1968). But what is important is not that differences merely *exist*, but that such differences are associated with certain meanings or endowed with a special significance (a significance always populated with the intentions of others). How do we make sense of the differences we see? The differences that make a difference? Culture – ranging from the popular (movies, books, newspapers) to the institutional (schools, families, government) – has been described as the 'terrain' upon and through which social meaning occurs. As social subjects, we make sense of the world through the values and norms expressed through the cultural production of knowledge. But culture is also the quilting point where nature intersects with labor, and in this regard it is important to consider how people are reduced to the commodification of their labor-power to be bought and sold in the expanding capitalist marketplace. Race 'matters' to us because we are ideological subjects and whiteness, as a dominant ideological formation and social position, informs and deforms our actions and our interactions in and on the world – whether we realize it or not.

The inferiority of difference

Third, it is important to recognize that whiteness is a category that operates and 'succeeds' precisely because it remains itself 'unmarked' . Because whiteness externalizes and labels difference as inferior, its 'gaze' is always directed outward. In other words, white people reserve for themselves the privilege of 'officially' defining racial understandings within the mainstream culture. This outward 'gaze' that white people project on others serves to maintain the white center as 'unmarked.' This allows whiteness to escape the scrutiny of and definition by people of color. People of color have, of course, historically theorized whiteness both academically and culturally in an attempt to call a halt to the historical dialectic of white oppression, but the dominant position of white people ensures that this discussion is not publicly sanctioned in schools, the press, the entertainment industry, or government. Because whiteness is the ideology of the center, those who operate within its precincts are not obliged to examine the power and privilege that their whiteness affords them. Not engaging in or 'not hearing' criticisms against whiteness has been an insidious strategy for neutralizing challenges to the system initiated by people of color. While not a direct rebuttal of attacks on the racial status quo, this strategy functions as a 'trick' of whiteness. Typically, dismissals of racial critique may be brief, but the subtext, according to Hurtado (1996: 152), reads as follows:

> I will listen to you, sometimes for the first time, and will seem engaged. At
> critical points in your analysis I will claim I do not know what you are talking

about and will ask you to elaborate *ad nauseam*. I will consistently subvert your efforts at dialogue by claiming we 'do not speak the same language.'

This trick prompts the erasure of whiteness as a category.

Because whiteness resists labeling, it is also able to resist linkages to racial domination, colonialism, imperialism, racialized labor exploitation, and violent assimilation. For example, contemporary discourses on immigration define the 'problem of illegal immigration' around 'illegal aliens' who are constructed by means of racist terminology as a threat to the integrity of the nation. This outward gaze in the direction of the 'other' protects white subjects from a critical self-examination of the racism evident within these discourses, because such racism is naturalized within an ideology that cloaks difference in the mantle of inferiority. In addition, the policies and practices of imperialism directed by the First World against the so-called 'Third World' is effectively erased from our view. As long as whiteness instantiates a universal center and the basis for all forms of 'truth,' white racial domination will continue. Hence, labeling and thus exposing the socially 'invisible' matrix of privileges and strategies of the white dominant class as 'whiteness' is a necessary, albeit insufficient, counter-strategy in the fight for social justice.

Linking whiteness to the neo/colonial

> Operationally, the maintenance of boundaries between 'politics' and 'non-politics' and the casting of certain 'political' acts into the 'non-political' domain, are themselves political acts, and reflect the structure of power and interest. These acts of labeling in the political domain, far from being self-evident, or a law of the natural world, constitute a form of continuing political 'work' on the part of the elites of power: they are, indeed, often the opening salvo in the whole process of political control.
>
> (Hall 1996)

In the previous section we demonstrated why we need a chromatic analysis of contemporary relations of inequality. In this section, we argue that we are not 'just' talking about race when we talk about whiteness. Rather, we expand our concept of whiteness beyond the confines of a discussion of race as discourse and social position to include social relations linked to transnational capitalism.

President Clinton introduced the nationally televised 'Town Meeting on Race' with the following argument: the United States has shown an ability to overcome adversity (in war, economic depression, natural disasters, etc.) and it should utilize that ability in addressing the issue of race. He cited the nation's strong and prosperous economy as evidence of the continued innovation and determination of the population and the hard work of the country's citizens. His justification for the town meeting was his commitment to the idea that open discussion of 'racial issues' would help the country move beyond its racialized history and would promote, in turn, continued prosperity and leadership in the world economic and political order. Clinton's position with respect to 'racial issues' – we quote this term to highlight the absence of the word 'racism' in much of the town meeting – is representative of a larger problem underlying current efforts to address unequal relations of power and racial injustice within the contemporary conjuncture of neo-liberalism and global capitalism, of which the Clinton administration is the world's leading representative. Clinton is certainly not the main agent of whiteness; rather, his appeal arises, at least in part, out of his powerful articulations of whiteness. Our point is not to foreground Clinton as 'the problem,' but to examine our own attachments to his political strategies. In analyzing absences in Clinton's introduction of the 'Town Meeting on Race,' the following section focuses on how whiteness centers and privileges those perceived as white, gazing outward to define and defend differences and transcend those differences by remaining unmarked.

In his town hall remarks, Clinton willfully ignored the processes through which the United States has been able to secure 'the strongest economy in the world.' He did not mention the country's history of transnational labor exploitation, advocacy for unbalanced trade negotiations, or its role in creating unfair development loans and structural adjustments through global lending agencies such as the World Bank and the International Monetary Fund. Many scholars have analyzed the role of United States corporate and governing bodies in a variety of development policies that continue to organize privilege and oppression on a massive scale. Others have tied those policies, more specifically, to racial ideologies. Yet the commonsense understanding about Third World economic crises that was largely exhibited in President Clinton's remarks at the town hall meeting focuses blame and responsibility on those so-called 'Third World' countries, while celebrating the United States as a leader in global politics and capitalist production. This inability to implicate the United States capitalist elite in analyses of global capital flows and ruptures stems, in our view, from an inability to recognize the ways in which whiteness constitutes relations of power in our neo/colonial present.

Clinton's focus on 'racial issues' remained almost exclusively on United States history and the country's *internal* cultural politics. Clinton's approach to race assumes it is a cultural or 'lifestyle' issue that involves the exercise of prudent citizenship skills and does not challenge dominant class arrangements and institutional class interests. In its imposed ignorance, Clinton's conception of race suggests that 'culture' is somehow autonomous from social relations of production. As a result of his magisterial incomprehension of, or motivated neglect with respect to, the racialized characteristics of development economics, transnational capitalism, and neo-colonial relations, Clinton cordoned off the possibility of a larger analysis of the role of whiteness in organizing social formations at both national and global levels. Further, by restricting the concept of racism to irresistible impersonal forces and attitude formations that occur within the cultural borders of the United States, Clinton foreclosed an important opportunity to analyze racism in relation to broader social forces such as global systems of trade and production, as well as international political relations and 'orientalist' ideologies. His perspective tramples historical context under the heel of bourgeois humanism, an approach that has more to do with opinion polls than scientific social analysis.

Deploying spatial borders around the politics of race (so that racial antagonisms in the United States are assumed to be about black–white histories, while inequalities around the world are assumed to be about the underdeveloped nature of Second and Third World countries) remains one of the most powerful and pervasive strategies for resecuring privilege based on race and class. Gayatri Spivak emphasizes the possible repercussions of critical work that neglects the position of the United States within larger systems of power: 'To simply foreclose or ignore the international division of labor because that's complicit with our own production, in the interests of the black–white division as representing the problem, is a foreclosure of neo-colonialism operated by chromatist race-analysis' . We present our analysis of 'whiteness' as part of a counter-strategy against the frequent reductionist discourses linked to identity politics that increasingly fleck the landscape of multicultural education, and the often apolitical discourse that informs the pedagogy of development studies.

Dominant development models operate from the misguided and exceedingly Eurocentric assumption that Western nations are more advanced in economic, political, and cultural formation than so-called 'Third World' countries. Although development models have earned the counter-attacks of leftist scholars who consistently point to the massive influences of industrialized nations on the economies of the Third World, many of these scholars have neglected to interrogate further the assumption that industrialized nations have 'healthy,' 'prosperous,' and 'model' economic and cultural systems. In part, this lacuna in critical scholarship has resulted from too little attention being paid to the mutual imbrication of whiteness and transnational relations. However, by focusing one's critique on the mechanisms of whiteness that variously constitute global systems of exploitation – mechanisms that we expose as largely dependent upon myths of the Third World 'Other' as inferior – we contend that new and fecund possibilities will emerge for unsettling the reigning assumptions of developmental models. Exploring global economic histories and development policies through the optic of whiteness studies can address the complexities of power relations and their racialized modalities across modernity.

If destabilizing the Eurocentric and orientalist models in development economics is a prime necessity, the same type of decentering has also to take place when analyzing the internal cultural politics of the United States, a politics that implicitly persuades public opinion in the direction of supporting a market economy as the only sane and responsible position. We agree with Ellen Meiksins Wood's observation that 'wherever market imperatives regulate the economy and govern social reproduction, there will be no escape from exploitation.' There can, in other words, be no such thing as a truly 'social' or democratic market, let alone a 'market socialism' (1999: 119). Woods' perspective is worth quoting at length (1999: 121):

> Today it is more obvious than ever that the imperatives of the market will not allow capital to prosper without depressing the conditions of great multitudes of people and degrading the environment throughout the world. We have now reached the point where the destructive effects of capitalism are outstripping its material gains. No third world country to-day, for example, can hope to achieve even the contradictory development that England underwent. With the pressures of competition, accumulation, and exploitation imposed by more developed capitalist economies, and with the inevitable crises of overcapacity engendered by capitalist competition, the attempt to achieve material prosperity according to capitalist principles is increasingly likely to bring with it only the negative side of the capitalist contradiction, its dispossession and destruction without its material benefits – certainly for the vast majority.

Revealing that a discourse of 'whiteness' exists at the very heart of reigning constructions of race and citizenship displaces the assumption of the nation as a taken-for-granted boundary separating ideological systems and histories. Prevailing forms of racial analysis in the United States displace a global frame that could articulate the hegemonizing role of 'whiteness' in organizing new forms of capital accumulation and new modes of oppression with resepct to specific social collectivities as well as differentiated forms of exploitation linked to both different social sectors and the differential composition of the labor force. In effect, nation-centered expositions of racial politics allow celebratory claims about the economic prosperity of the United States to stand unfettered by doubt and discrimination and unburdened by challenges from more critical perspectives. In failing to respond adequately to causal claims about the economic success of the United States in relation to the stagnated economies of Asian Pacific, South Asian, and South American countries (causal claims that link success to the hard work, initiative, and the innovation of United States corporations and entrepreneurs), dominant models of multiculturalism give ballast to prevailing development explanations of inequality in the United States and worldwide. Dominant explanatory frameworks on poverty, for instance, argue that poverty is exacerbated by low-income groups' 'dependency' on the welfare state, declines in the moral character of the poor, and a massive breakdown of 'family values.' Viewing the nation-state as a concept-metaphor populated by changing meanings and functions, rather than as a final organizer of various forms of cultural politics, provides a working context for initiating heuristic critiques of whiteness that partake of a discursive, material and political effectivity and are productive of a re-visioning of experiences of people and groups in their local and global relation to capital. The key point here is that material relations of production are not liquidable from racialized social practices. It is the exploitation of human labor, not consumer culture, that remains the dominant mechanism in capitalist society (Cleaver 1999). And while to a certain extent it is true that the labor force has been outstripping the relative growth rate of jobs (via downsizing and layoffs), we still need to consider the redistribution of work from waged to unwaged in the informal sector. If we truly want to fight racism, we need to fight capitalism and we need to push beyond this struggle in order to bring about the abolition of capital itself.

Deconstructing whiteness

> Mujeres, a no dejar que el peligro del viaje y la immensidad del territorio nos asuste – a mirar hacia adelante y a abrir paso en el monte. [*Women, let's not let the danger of the journey and the vastness of the territory scare us – let's look forward and open paths in these woods.*] ... Caminante, no hay puentes, se hace puentes al andar. [*Voyager, there are no bridges, one builds them as one walks*].
> (Anzaldúa, in Moraga and Anzaldúa 1981: v)

> Humility is not thinking less of yourself, but rather, thinking of yourself less.
> (Anon.)

Deconstructing whiteness essentially involves submitting it to the type of critical examination that it has long avoided, inverting the white hegemonic gaze, in order to reveal the strategies by which racial inequality is tenebrously secured. This entails analyzing the relations of production, the privileges, and the affective energies that enable a possessive investment in whiteness. This also suggests that deconstructing whiteness is not so much the rejection of racialized social practices as a rigorously honest appraisal of the ways in which white individuals benefit from and contribute to preserving social inequality.

Because they have suffered the vicissitudes of history in perilously unambiguous ways, it has been the particular charge of people of color to contest racism, to prove that it exists in multifarious formations and practices, to translate it to the theater of mundane and everyday practices of ordinary citizens, and to do something about it – particularly now, when the rotting corpse of civil rights has been disinterred and reanimated by Republican lawmakers eager to bring about a new conservative restoration (i.e. calling for civil rights for white people). Examining and challenging whiteness is, however, not just an ambitious political project but a deeply personal one. It is also a project in which white people especially need to participate, because, as Hurtado says, 'it takes psychological work to maintain privilege; it takes cognitive training not to empathize or feel for your victims – how individuals get socialized to accomplish the abnormal should be at the core of a reflexive theory of subordination' (1996: 130). Thus the deconstruction of whiteness promises more than 'equality;' it offers freedom from the contract that binds both oppressor and oppressed.

Hamani Bannerji registers a signal insight when she maintains that 'there is no better point of entry into a critique or a reflection than one's own experience' . Such a move enjoins us to focus on whiteness as a product of the constitution of the subject under capitalism by way of the phenomenon of lived experience rather than to relegate whiteness solely to the category of 'race.' Individual experience is a productive site for the interrogation of whiteness precisely because it is framed by the specular structure of ideology that sutures or chains the subject into the flow of discourse or to 'structures of meaning.' Hence, Bannerji advocates that we engage in 'textual mediation,' by which she means a critical examination of the relationship between individual experience and social relations in our daily lives. Because white people occupy a privileged structural location, mediated self-reflexivity entails a critical examination of how ideological and institutional structures ensure the continued, unearned, and race-based privilege white people enjoy at the expense of people of color. The insidious nature of whiteness is precisely that it disguises itself as 'natural,' especially to white people who, voluntarily or not, consciously or not, continue to benefit from a social position marked by whiteness. White people in particular need to be vigilant, to take an active role in decentering whiteness, and to call for its mystifications to be done away with. They can begin by examining their own affective investments in whiteness and how such investments add ballast to the hegemonic relations of white supremacist capitalist patriarchy.

Because the very structure of whiteness presents it as an excess of recognizability, as beyond symbolization, as too-real in the sense that it has the power to create itself, decentering whiteness is destined to provoke a profound defensiveness on the part of many white people, and here we do not refer simply to the reactionary charges of political correctness by conservative politicians but to generalized feelings of victimization on the part of the white population. The vexing question that remains to be uncoiled in all of this is not the *meaning* of whiteness, but why discourses of whiteness reverberate so much as to go unnoticed and why representations of whiteness continue to remain so zealously unproblematized. A provisional answer would be that discourses and representations of whiteness go unnamed and unmarked and yet remain powerful sites for investment because their continued deployment is functionally advantageous for the prevailing structures of capitalism and for the advancement of white people. The characteristics we attribute to whiteness are a function of the 'social capital' (the informal and formal rules that govern human interaction) within which they are embedded. White identity does not operate out of a contextualizing transcendence, but involves the exercise of privilege determined – at least in part – by the social relations prevailing at the time. Although the middle class is shrinking in the United States, the promise of escaping poverty by joining the white race has continuing appeal for Euro-Americans, just as it did when the colonial plantocracy promised chattel bond-laborers that by becoming part of the white race they could rise above the economic and social status of African slaves. A fraught example of the conspiracy of whiteness occurred recently when some of us attended a reading group with several white communication scholars. The focus of the group was a study of whiteness by Nakayama and Krizek. The article concludes with an 'invitation to communication scholars to begin to mark and incorporate whiteness into their analyses and claims – an invitation to become reflexive' (1995: 305). Many members of the reading group perceived this 'invitation' as threatening and expressed exasperation at the 'angry' tone of the article. Instead of engaging the 'invitation,' they wondered if *all* essays *had* to address race, and if their work was irrelevant if they failed to do so. They wanted to know *how much* engagement with whiteness would be *enough* to absolve them of their whiteness. The request seemingly threatened the relevance of their scholarly training, since they had no formal background in anti-racist education. When it came to the 'critical point' in the discussion where white scholars were asked to deconstruct whiteness, suddenly no one knew what the authors were talking about, and they proceeded to attack the authors of the article for not being specific enough, or for not clarifying their theoretical citations.

Because whiteness is based fundamentally on exclusion, there is a fear associated with decentering whiteness that white people will be excluded from a 'post-whiteness' world. This attendant fear of exclusion is often accompanied by anger and operates out of a perception of 'individual justice' that is fundamental to the ideology of whiteness. Many white people believe that the American ideals of 'liberty' and 'justice' mean that they have a right to be anywhere they want to, and to do anything they want. Confusedly clinging to such a perception, white people feel that anything that is for 'people of color only,' that puts any restrictions on unlimited white access, constitutes an 'injustice.'

However, the practice of social justice exclusively for white people has deep historical roots. As Cheryl Harris (1993) has detailed, US law has conflated property rights with legal rights from its inception. But property ownership, like freedom and access to social resources, is deeply racialized. For instance, the democratization of the nineteenth-century United States, in which political participation was extended to non-property-owning white men, was *de facto* a political strategy of the elite to gain support for slavery in exchange for the promise of economic opportunity. Thus a true democracy, a socialist democracy (socialist because it includes everyone), would have to transcend historical conceptions of liberty that are founded on racial injustice. In their efforts to move towards dismantling whiteness, white people therefore need to relinquish their own need for inclusion so as to let new possibilities for inclusion develop.

Another pervasive defensive strategy on the part of white people that arises in anti-racist discussions is their impulse to discuss race only in a 'safe space.' While having safe spaces in which to question one's identity formation is important, this insistence by white people on safety has often functioned to disavow responsibility for discussing and disinvesting in whiteness.

In a country where the word 'crime' has become almost completely interchangeable with 'African Americans', 'Latinos', 'inner cities', and 'illegal immigrants,' it is impossible to extricate the term 'safety' from a racialized understanding. Because our sense of safety has been thoroughly racialized, 'safety' needs to be a focal point for a dismantling of whiteness. This rhetoric of 'safety,' usually accompanying campaigns against violence, can be found in almost any public high school in the United States. Rather than address the reasons for violence among high school students, teachers often emphasize, for example, Eurocentric notions of 'decency' and 'civility' in order to frame how youth must conduct themselves, and with what language they may discuss their experience of oppression. Among students of color, it is often their very claims of oppression and racism, both in and out of the classroom, both verbally or visually (through graffiti, clothing, music, colors, haircuts, and especially violence), that make white people feel threatened and unsafe. It is through a mainstream and racially determined definition of safety that counter-voices raised in opposition to social injustice are largely silenced.

Inverting the white gaze means moving beyond a 'closet' critique of whiteness; it entails a fundamentally painful process, especially for those white people who pride themselves on their liberal values of equality and social justice but fail to see how their own assumptions undermine such values. Marking whiteness as hegemonic involves partaking in the discomfort that accompanies the inversion of the white gaze – a discomfort which this hegemony imposes on its 'others.' For female or working-class white people in particular, this means recognizing that they occupy a contradictory space *vis-à-vis* oppression that isn't easily resolved.

Conclusion

> Labels are invented and maintained by institutions on an ongoing basis, as part of an apparently rational process that is essentially political. Although the whole process has at times devastating effects on the labeled groups – through stereotyping, normalizing, fragmentation of people's experience, disorganization of the poor – it also implies the possibility of counterlabeling.
> (Escobar 1995: 110)

Critical work on whiteness should specify the ways in which unmarked racial tropes, cultural formations, and social relations of production, and social and institutional practices organize both our social and political structures as well as the microprocesses of our daily lives. In arguing that whiteness is a *learned* set of ideologies, behaviors, and practices, we mean to emphasize the profoundly contextually specific processes through which whiteness is reproduced and transformed. In conclusion, we argue for the specific ways in which labeling whiteness can contribute to redefining the content of this ideological formation. In doing so, we argue that the racism that contemporary forms of whiteness enable may be successfully challenged.

First, the label 'whiteness' aims to reconfigure the 'unmarked' aspect of this racial location by redefining its contents. As we argued earlier, whiteness 'succeeds' as a dominant discourse that privileges white people because it is conflated with universal Western ideals. Because 'white' is delinked from the idea of a racial formation, other 'races' thus serve to define the outer limits of whiteness. This means that, as a hegemonic discourse embedded in a set of capitalist social relations and practices, whiteness secures power for whites by *universalizing* whiteness. Universalized conceptualizations of whiteness function to center the white racial formation, because the universal is privileged as the standard of measure for 'appropriate' ways of life, behavior, rules for society, *et cetera*. The move to label whiteness seeks therefore to *specify* whiteness and is designed precisely to counteract its universalizing functions. To articulate whiteness as a specific set of qualities and strategies serves to unhinge it from its universal social location. This, we argue, undermines the ability of discursive practices inscribed as 'white' to define what is deemed 'appropriate' and 'commonsensical.' In the process, whiteness may no longer be conflated with propriety and the strategies by which it has maintained this definitional power can be unmasked and challenged.

As elaborated above, the second and related point we wish to foreground is that whiteness is a category that 'succeeds' precisely because it is 'unmarked' (Frankenberg 1993; Kincheloe and Steinberg 1997). The outward gaze of whiteness serves three vital functions in maintaining white privilege: it externalizes difference; it defines difference from whiteness as inferiority; and it resists self-examination and critique. Each of these functions of white hegemony is enabled by the outwardly directed gaze of whiteness. Because labeling whiteness 'inverts the gaze' of the white center and provokes an examination of that center, white people are presented with a proactive framework for examining the modes through which white privilege is secured. The very process of marking these three functions of the outward gaze of whiteness is an important step in the direction of dismantling whiteness. As we point to the specific discursive strategies through which whiteness remains centered and unexamined, we invert the outward gaze and *label* whiteness as a strategic discourse of privilege. This is the first and necessary step in examining the meanings that get attached to whiteness and in raising our awareness of how this discourse serves to insulate white people from acknowledging their own privilege, even where they want to.

Next we argue that whiteness functions within an international context by means of neo-imperialist practices and ideologies that must be examined with respect to the inscription and marking of whiteness. This focus is consistent with deconstructionist moves to examine the silences produced within the discourses of the white Western logic of phallocentrism and its metaphysical search for 'truth,' in which the white heterosexual Christian male figure is continually reinscribed as the standard measure of 'mankind.'

We must recognize that the task of labeling whiteness is but one step in a much larger project of defetishizing whiteness, of showing how the givenness of whiteness is not a natural fact but is socially and historically constituted and conjuncturally embedded within capitalist social relations of production. We want to emphasize that because whiteness is ideological, and not 'natural,' because it is socially constituted, fluid, changing, and not permanently fixed, then it can be transformed. As we have mentioned in the previous section, due to the complex and contradictory nature of this particular ideological formation, this represents very challenging work. If whiteness secures power for white people by means of its capacity to remain unmarked and to maintain its outward gaze, then redressing these conditions will not be easy. Attempting to resist and transform these relations may even feel 'wrong' and 'gravely uncomfortable,' particularly to white people themselves. We must begin to recognize such feelings as productive of change, as evidence of success, and as a positive indicator for a more just future.

We conclude, along with Lipsitz (1998), that free market policies reinforce rather than ameliorate the possessive investment in whiteness. We also support the observation by Howard Winant that at a time where we are witnessing growing diasporic movements – as former colonial subjects immigrate to the Western metropoles, challenging the majoritarian status of European groups – we need to focus our attention on the racialized dimensions of capital and the mobilization of white racial antagonisms. Whiteness is being implicated on a global basis in the internationalization of capital, which can only lead to the internationalization of racial antagonisms.

We want to underscore the fact that North American workers have, for the most part, embraced ideologies of whiteness and in doing so have failed to turn their partial consciousness of the economic depravations of capitalism into a revolutionary political project aimed at transforming the current social division of labor. Their whiteness has been purchased at the faultline that separates them from the ownership of the conditions for the realization of their labor. The baptism of workers in the Sacred White Trust denies them an opportunity to create both strategic as well as tactical alliances with people of color. As workers assume the mantle of whiteness, they become at the same time fully integrated into the process of self-expanding profit-making. Whiteness in this instance serves as a 'cover' for the collusion of corporate and financial groups in the promotion of financial integration, deregulation, trade liberalization, and the internationalization of production. We believe that the more surplus labor becomes regulated at a global level, with consequent urgent 'adjustments' to entitlements and welfare spending in the quest for national competitiveness, the more implications arise for the racialization of capital (Cole, Hill, Rikowski and McLaren 2000).

The globalization of trade is similarly fraught with dangers, often related to indigenous cultures and local networks of production and subsistence. The corporate drive to reduce the cost of production and to create new markets invariably leads to plant closures and, whenever unionized labor poses a threat to profit, to frequent and rapid shifts to 'emergent economies.' Globalization is leading to increased global poverty among unskilled and skilled workers, at a time when capitalist reification is extending into spheres of life previously unsubjected to capitalist exploitation or rationalization. Global institutions such as the World Trade Organization and the World Bank and the International Monetary Fund frequently exercise their power in order to undo national and regional legislation designed to create some barriers over environmental, labor, and social issues (De

Angelis 1999). The current internationalization of labor that occurs in the wake of these conditions depends upon the structural fragmentation of the working class. The division of workers within an income hierarchy that offers the most economic mobility and security to white workers is functionally advantageous to capital because it keeps the working class racialized and decentered. The figuration of racial and ethnic specificity remains entombed within the governing discourses and tropes of globalization and the enthralling media apparatuses that promote them. Furthermore, the sacrosanct character of the unfettered free market is divinely invoked to overwrite the voices of indigenous peoples and the demands of the minoritized racial and ethnic groups who constitute those most marginalized by globalization. Within the fractal geometry of today's capitalist production, the threat to the white working class is so great that whites are doing everything in their power to maintain their advantage, from attempts at dismantling affirmative action and bilingual education, to militarizing the border, to demonizing Mexican immigrants when they are permitted to enter the country. The social function of the economic rationale of neo-liberalism is to keep white workers from creating alliances with aggrieved communities of color. It is in the interests of capital to keep 'race' and 'class' separate.

It is also functionally advantageous for capital if corporations expropriate the residual power that workers once had in the Keynesian era: the power to negotiate conditions of work, wage, and social entitlements through trade unions or political parties (Taylor 1999). The social process of recomposing civil society through social movements is a forbidding possibility for the corporate barons of globalization, that international cadre of renovated carpetbaggers and overworlders who remain bent on keeping working people vulnerable and dependent. Because capitalism takes the form of a self-constituting reality, the continuing rationalization of the labor process involves attempts to prevent the working class from conceptualizing the social totality. Identity politics is one way to promote the sectionalism necessary to mystify the relationship between the globalization and racialization of labor, and the universal objective of human emancipation. What is needed is not identity politics but a revolutionary multiculturalism that is able to confront the relationship between the reification of everyday labor and the possessive investment in whiteness.

Read in this light, revolutionary multiculturalism, with its enthrallment with open-endedness, its resistance to fixity, and its quest for flexible identities, offers us a serious challenge to certain trajectories of postmodernist theory. Revolutionary multiculturalism calls attention to the bourgeois outlawry, fashionable philistinism, and aristocratic brigandism that characterize those forms of postmodern criticism that betray a civil inattention to issues of relations of production and a motivated amnesia towards history (McLaren 1997).

A limited praxis – a praxis that does not take into account the totality of social relations – only reproduces the given social order or dialectical contradictions in their inversion. Especially at this less than quiescent political moment, revolutionary or critical praxis must do two things: it must critique the resulting ideological explanations, and it must transform those relations which constitute the social contradictions. In so doing, it reveals what a pedagogy of liberation looks like, one that moves from the liberal humanist notion of 'traditional democratic freedom' to the Marxist-humanist concept of freeing oneself and others from a relationship of dependency to capital.

A nagging question facing the left around the globe can be pitched as follows: how can the left protagonize a process of structural change that goes beyond state intervention and its goal to achieve internal redistribution and a tacit acceptance of the neo-liberal model of free market integration into the global economy? One cannot of course ignore the important contributions of organized left parties such as the Sandinista National Liberation Front in Nicaragua, the Workers Party in Brazil, the Farabundo Liberation Front in El Salvador, the Party of the Democratic Revolution in Mexico, the Broad Front in Uruguay, the National Solidarity Front in Argentina, the Fuerzas Armadas Revolucionarios de Colombia – Ejército del Pueblo (FARC), the Causa-R in Venezuela, the Communist Party in Cuba, and the Communist Party in Chile. But one also has to recognize and emphasize the importance of grass-roots social movements that operate outside of state structures and organized left parties, such as Christian-based communities, solidarity groups, the Landless Workers of Brazil, and revolutionary groups such as Mexico's Zapatistas (Robinson 1998/99). How can these new social movements mediate between the state and the popular masses? How can these struggles be made within a transnational space that can challenge and contest the hegemony of the transnational elite and their local counterparts? How can a transnationalism from below – from the civil society as distinct from the political society – occur that is capable of challenging the power of the global elite? How can relations of capitalist exploitation be engaged so that the ideologies of racial superiority, of unmarked whiteness, that support them can finally be overcome and thrown into the dustbin of history? These are questions that cannot be ignored or pushed aside in our universal struggle for a world unfettered by racism and unmarked by exploitation.

References

Allen, Theodore W. (1994) *The Invention of the White Race* vol. 1, 'Racial Oppression and Social Control,' London and New York: Verso.

Allen, T. (1997) *The Invention of the White Race, Volume Two: The Origin of Racial Oppression in Anglo-America*, London and New York: Verso.

Bannerji, H. (1995) *Thinking Through: Essays on Feminism, Marxism and Anti-Racism*, Toronto: Women's Press.

Callinicos, Alex (1993) *Race and Class*, London: Bookmarks.

Cleaver, Harry (1999) 'Work is Still the Central Issue,' unpublished paper.

Cole, Mike, Dave Hill, Glenn Ritowski, and Peter McLaren. (2000) *Red Chalk*. London: The Tufnell Press.

Du Bois, W. E. B. (1968) *Dusk of Dawn: An Essay Toward an Autobiography of a Race Concept*, New York: Schocken Books.

De Angelis, Massimo (1999) 'Globalization, Work, and Class: Some Research Notes,' unpublished paper.

Delgado, Richard and Stefancic, Jean (eds) (1997) *Critical White Studies: Looking Behind the Mirror*, Philadelphia: Temple University Press.

Escobar, A. (1995) *Encountering Development: The Making and Unmaking of the Third World*, Princeton, NJ: Princeton University Press.

Ferguson, J. (1996) *The Anti-Politics Machine: 'Development,' Depoliticization, and Bureaucratic Power in Lesotho*, Minneapolis: University of Minnesota Press.

Frankenberg, R. (1993) *White Women, Race Matters: The Social Construction of Whiteness*, Minneapolis: University of Minnesota Press.

Hall, S. (1996) 'Gramsci's Relevance for the Study of Race and Ethnicity,' in D. Morley and K. H. Chen (eds) *Stuart Hall: Critical Dialogues in Cultural Studies*, New York: Routledge.

Hall, S (1996) 'The problem of ideology: Marxism without Guarantees,' in David Morley and Kuan-Hsing Chen (eds) *Stuart Hall: Critical Dialogues in Cultural Studies*, New York: Routledge.

Harris, C. (1993) 'Whiteness as Property,' *Harvard Law Review* 106(8): 709-91.

Hurtado, A. (1996) *The Color of Privilege: Three Blasphemies on Race and Feminism*, Ann Arbor: University of Michigan.

Ignatiev, N. 1998. 'The New Abolitionists,' *Transition* 73: 199-203.

Kincheloe, Joe and Steinberg, Shirley (1997) *Changing Multiculturalism*, London: Open University Press.

Lipsitz, George (1998) *The Possessive Investment in Whiteness*, Philadelphia: Temple University Press.

Lowe, L. (1996) *Immigrant Acts: On Asian American Cultural Politics*, Durham and London: Duke University Press.

McLaren, Peter (1995) *Critical Pedagogy and Predatory Culture*, London and New York: Routledge.

—— (1997) *Revolutionary Multiculturalism*, Boulder: Westview Press.

McLaren, Peter and Muñoz, Juan (2000) 'Unsettling Whiteness' in Carlos Ovando and Peter McLaren (eds) *The Politics of Multiculturalism and Bilingual Education: Students and Teachers Caught in the Crossfire*, New York: McGraw-Hill.

Moraga, C. and Anzaldúa, G. (1981) *This Bridge Called My Back: Writings by Radical Women of Color*, New York: Kitchen Table.

Morrison, T. (1992) *Playing in the Dark: Whiteness and the Literary Imagination*, New York: Vintage Books.

Nakayama, T. and Krizek, R. (1995) 'Whiteness: A Strategic Rhetoric,' *Quarterly Journal of Speech*, 81: 291–309.

Robinson, William (1998/1999) 'Latin America and Global Capitalism,' *Race & Class*, 40(2 & 3): 111–31.

Saxton, A. (1990) *The Rise and Fall of the White Republic*, New York: Verso.

Scott, Jonathan (1998) 'Before the White Race Was Invented,' *Against the Current*, 72: 46–9.

Shapiro, Bruce (1999) 'The Guns of Littleton,' *The Nation*, 268(18): 4–5.

Spivak, G. (1987) 'French Feminism in an International Frame' in G. Spivak (ed.) *In Other Worlds: Essays in Cultural Politics*, New York: Routledge.

—— (1990) *The Post-Colonial Critic: Interviews, Strategies, Dialogues*, New York: Routledge.

Taylor, Graham (1999) 'Labor and Subjectivity: Rethinking the Limits of Working Class Consciousness,' unpublished paper.

Tsing, A. L. (1993) *In the Realm of the Diamond Queen: Marginality in an Out of the Way Place*, Princeton, NJ: Princeton University Press.

Winant, Howard (1994) *Racial Conditions*, Minneapolis: University of Minnesota Press.

Wood, Ellen Meiksins (1999) *The Origin of Capitalism*, New York: Monthly Review Press.

14 Labeling resentment

Re-narrating difference

Cameron McCarthy and Greg Dimitriadis

Friedrich Nietzsche conceptualized 'resentment' as the specific practice of identity displacement in which the social actor consolidates his identity by a complete disavowal of the merits and existence of his social other. One thus becomes 'good' by constructing the 'other' as evil. Nietzsche writes (1967: 39):

> Picture 'the enemy' as the man of ressentiment conceives him – and here precisely is his deed, his creation: he has conceived 'the evil enemy,' 'the Evil One,' and this in fact is his basic concept, from which he then evolves, as an afterthought and pendant, a 'good one' – himself!

A sense of self is thus only possible through an annihilation or emptying out of the other. Indeed, though all processes of identity-construction are relational, processes of resentment are explicitly nihilistic and reactive. The world is conceived of as 'hostile' and all one's energies are directed 'outward' towards the annihilation of the other. In this fashion, one's own identity becomes pure, good, and coherent.

We see these processes linked, as well, to the question of 'labeling'. Labeling is the largely unavoidable process by which we separate out and name, order and understand the world. Labeling, in and of itself, is neither oppressive nor destructive. However, when labeling is linked to resentment, to the emptying out and annihilation of the other, it is profoundly dangerous indeed. Unfortunately, this kind of labeling proliferates in much public discourse today, informing a whole range of sites and social subjects. We see such labeling as inextricably linked to the ways in which race and racial difference are being coded and recoded in the public imagination.

Specifically, disoriented white people, both working-class and professional, confronted with the panoply of 'difference' that marks the contemporary moment, have produced their own sense of 'whiteness' by explicitly marking the other as 'different.' Whiteness – the unspoken norm – is made pure and real only in terms of a growing and largely undefined 'other,' of that which it is not. 'Its fullness,' as Michelle Fine and Lois Weis note, 'inscribes, at one and the same time, its emptiness and presumed innocence' (1998: 156–7).

We see this process of the emptying out of the other, of resentment, as undergirded by several key discourses made available in popular culture and academic circles today. In a time of ever-widening economic and cultural anxiety, when we see this problem of the production of quietude as occupying more and more public, discursive space, these discourses seek to manage the extraordinary complexities which so mark contemporary cultural life by re-narrating coherent social identities. We shall limit our discussion to four such discourses of resentment, discourses that 'label' in new ways that produce coherent racial identities.

First, we would like to call attention to the discourse of *origins*, as revealed in, for example, the Eurocentric/Afrocentric debate over curriculum reform. Labels operate here to allow social combatants to order and understand the past in easy ways. Discourses of racial origins rely on the simulation of a pastoral sense of the past in which Europe and Africa are available to American racial combatants without the noise of their modern tensions, contradictions, and conflicts. For Eurocentric combatants such as William Bennett (1994) or George Will (1989), Europe and America are a self-evident and transcendent cultural unity. For Afrocentric combatants, Africa and the diaspora are one 'solid identity,' to use the language of Molefi Asante (1993). In a time of constantly changing demographic and economic realities, proponents of both Eurocentrism and Afrocentrism are themselves proxies for the larger impulses and desires for stability that prevail among the middle classes in American society. The immigrants are coming! Jobs are slipping overseas into the third world! Discourses of Eurocentrism and Afrocentrism travel in a time warp to an age when the gods stalked the earth.

The discourse of racial origins provides imaginary solutions to groups and individuals who refuse the radical hybridity that is the historically evolved reality of the United States and other major Western metropolitan societies. The dreaded line of difference is drawn around glittering objects of heritage and secured with the knot of ideological closure. The university itself has become a playground of the war of simulation between these labels. Contending paradigms of knowledge become embattled as combatants release the levers of atavism, holding their faces in their hands as the latest volley of absolutism circles in the air.

For example, Michael Steinberg tells the story of his first job (he was hired during the 1980s) as 'the new European intellectual and cultural historian at a semi-small, semi-elite, semi-liberal arts college' in the Northeast. Steinberg says that during a departmental meeting he unwittingly contradicted the hegemonic hiring practices of his new institution by 'voting for the appointment to the history department of an African Americanist whose teaching load would include the standard course on the Civil War and Reconstruction.' Several minutes after the meeting, one of the white academic elders of this Northeastern college informed Steinberg a) that his function as a European intellectual was 'to serve as the guardian of the intellectual and curricular tradition;' b) that he should 'resist at all costs the insidious slide from the party of scholarship to the party of ideology;' and c) that if he 'persisted in tipping the scales of the department from tradition to experimentation and from scholarship to ideology,' he would be digging his own grave insofar as his own, 'traditionally defined academic position would be the most likely to face elimination by a newly politicized institution' (1996: 105). Unwittingly, Steinberg had been thrown pell-mell into a war of position over origins; within the context of this war, the resources of the history department he had just entered were under the strain of the imperatives of 'difference.'

A second resentment discourse at work in contemporary life and popular culture is the discourse of *nation*. Here, too, the label of 'nation' allows social combatants to understand the world – and their place in the world – in dangerously facile ways. This discourse is foregrounded in a spate of recent advertisements by multinational corporations such as IBM, United and American Airlines, MCI and General Electric. These advertisements both feed on and provide fictive solutions to the racial anxieties of the age. They effectively appropriate multicultural symbols and redeploy them in a broad project aimed at the coordination and consolidation of corporate citizenship and consumer affiliation.

The marriage of art and economy, as Stuart Ewen (1988) defines advertising in *All Consuming Images*, is now commingled with the exigencies of ethnic identity and nation. One moment, the semiotic subject of advertising is a free American citizen abroad in the open seas sailing upon the Atlantic or the translucent aquamarine waters of the Caribbean sea. In another, the free American citizen is transported to the pastoral life of the unspoiled, undulating landscape of medieval Europe. Both implicate a burgeoning consumer culture underpinned by the global triumph of consumer capitalism.

Hence the General Electric 'We Bring Good Things to Life' advertisement (which is shown quite regularly on CNN and ABC), in which GE is portrayed as a latter-day Joan of Arc fighting the good fight of American entrepreneurship overseas, bringing electricity to one Japanese town. In the ad GE breaks through the cabalism of foreign language, bureaucracy and unethical Japanese rules to procure the goal of the big sell. The American nation can rest in peace as the Japanese nation succumbs to superior US technology.

Third, there is the discourse of *popular memory and popular history*. This discourse suffuses the nostalgic films of the last decade or so. Films such as *Dances with Wolves* (1990), *Bonfire of the Vanities* (1990), *Grand Canyon* (1993), *Falling Down* (1993), *Forrest Gump* (1994), *A Time to Kill* (1996), *The Fan*

(1997), *Armageddon* (1998), and *Saving Private Ryan* (1998) all foreground a white middle-class protagonist who appropriates the subject position of the persecuted social victim at the mercy of myriad forces – from 'wild' black youth in Los Angeles (in *Grand Canyon*), to Asian store-owners who do not speak English well (in *Falling Down*), to a black baseball player, living the too-good life in a moment of corporate downsizing (in *The Fan*). All hearken back to the 'good old days' when the rules were few and exceedingly simple for now-persecuted white men.

These films are steeped in nostalgia, enmeshed in the project of rewriting and relabeling history from the perspective of bourgeois anxieties and the feelings of resentment by which these are so often driven. History becomes a range of empty signifiers to be ordered and reordered in easy and ultimately destructive ways. This project is realized perhaps most forcefully in the wildly successful *Forrest Gump*. A special-effects masterwork, this film literally interpolates actor Tom Hanks into actual and recreated historical footage of key events in US history, renarrating the later part of the twentieth century in ways that blur the line between fact and fiction. Here, the peripatetic Gump steals the spotlight from the civil rights movement, the Vietnam War protesters, the feminist movement, and so forth. Public history is overwhelmed by personal consumerism and wish-fulfilment. 'Life,' after all, 'is like a box of chocolates. You never know what you're gonna get.' You might get Newt Gingrich. But who cares? History will absolve the American consumer.

Finally, we wish to call attention to the conversationalizing discourses of the *media culture*. From the television and radio talk shows of Oprah Winfrey and Jenny Jones to the rap music of Tupac Shakur to pseudo-academic books like *The Bell Curve*, *The Hot Zone* and *The Coming Plague*, to self-improvement texts like *Don't Sweat the Small Stuff ... and It's All Small Stuff*, popular culture psychologizes and seemingly internalizes complex social problems, managing the intense feelings of anxiety which are so much a part of contemporary cultural life. Television talk shows, for example, reduce complex social phenomena to mere personality conflicts between guests, encouraging them to air their differences before encouraging some kind of denouement or resolution. Histories of oppression are thus put aside as guests argue in and through the details of their private lives, mediated, as they often are, by so-called experts. Racial harmony becomes a relative's acceptance of a 'biracial' child. Sexual parity is reduced to a spouse publicly rejecting an adulterous partner. Psychologistic explanations for social phenomena reign supreme, supported by a burgeoning literature of self-improvement texts, which mostly posit poor self-esteem as the pre-eminent societal ill of today. These popular texts and media programs are pivotal in what Deborah Tannen (1998) calls *The Argument Culture*, in which the private is political, and politics is war by other means. This discourse works to label complex social phenomena as psychological problems, eliding, once again, broader anxieties and tensions.

Identities are thus being formed and re-formed – 'produced,' following Edward Said – in this complex social moment, where the global 'tide of difference' is being met by profound renarrations and relabelings of history. It is precisely this kind of rearticulation and recoding that one of us has called 'nonsynchrony' (McCarthy 1998). We have tried above to draw attention to how these complicated dynamics operate in debates over identity and curriculum reform, hegemonic cultural assertions in advertising, popular film, and in the conversationalizing discourses of contemporary popular culture. We have also tried to show how these discourses are linked to a popular culture industry that has radically appropriated the new to consolidate the past. This is the triumph of a nostalgia of the present, as 'difference' comes under the normalizing logics and disciplinary imperatives of hegemonic power. Diversity, as such, can sell visits to theme parks as well as it can sell textbooks. Diversity can sell AT&T and MCI long-distance calling cards as well as the new ethnic stalls in the ethereal hearths of the shopping mall. And sometimes, in the most earnest of ways, diversity lights up the whole world and makes it available to capitalism.

Educational policy and the pedagogy of resentment

Importantly and most disturbingly, we wish to note, this kind of diversity is also increasingly informing educational policy on both the right and left, as evidenced by several key debates now circulating in the public sphere. The process of labeling and emptying out the 'other,' so explored throughout, has thus come to take on a salience in the realm of public policy.

Indeed, these debates have had very real material effects on the dispossessed, for example those quickly losing the (albeit meager) benefits of affirmative action (California's Proposition 209), bilingual education (California's Proposition 227 – the so-called 'English for the Children' initiative), and need-based financial aid. The idea of high-quality (public) education as the great potential equalizer – a good in and of itself – is now being lost to the bitter resentments at the heart of contemporary culture.

How the discourse of resentment has (explicitly) propelled the conservative agenda here is fairly obvious. A new and seemingly beleaguered middle class is looking to recapture its once unquestioned privilege by advocating 'color-blind' hiring and acceptance policies (in the case of affirmative action) while forging a seemingly unified – and, of course, white Anglo – cultural identity through restrictive language policies (in the case of bilingual education). Indeed, the consolidation of seamless and coherent subjects so at the heart of contemporary cultural media flows (as explored above) has enabled and encouraged the overwhelming public support and passage of such bills as California's Propositions 209 and 227 – in the case of the latter, by a two-to-one margin.

These resentments run deep and operate on numerous levels here – hence the tensions now erupting between African Americans and Latinos *vis-à-vis* many such bills. A *Time* magazine article entitled 'The Next Big Divide?' explores burgeoning conflicts between African Americans and Latinos in Palo Alto over bilingual education, noting that these disputes

> arise in part from frustration over how to spend the dwindling pot of cash in low-income districts. But they also reflect a jostling for power, as blacks who labored hard to earn a place in central offices, on school boards and in classrooms confront a Latino population eager to grab a share of these positions.
>
> (Ratnesar 1997: 1)

It has been suggested, in fact, that efforts to institute black 'ebonics' as a second language in Oakland were prompted by competition for shrinking funds traditionally allotted to bilingual (Spanish) programs. Resentment, spawned by increasing competition for decreasing resources, is key to unraveling the complexities of these struggles.

Perhaps more importantly, however, the discourse of resentment is also informing more 'liberal' responses to these issues and bills. The importance of public education in equalizing the profound injustices of contemporary American society is increasingly downplayed in favor of discourses about self-interest and the rigid feelings of resentment which undergird them. Affirmative action, to this way of thinking, is a 'good' because education will keep dangerous minorities off 'our' streets by subjecting them to a lifetime of 'civilizing' education, crafting them into good subjects for global cultural capitalism. Further, the story goes, affirmative action really helps middle-class women more than blacks or Latinos, so it should – quite naturally – remain in place.

These discourses inform the debate on bilingual education as well, a debate that has similarly collapsed liberal and conservative voices and opinions. Indeed, bilingual education, many argue, should be supported (only) because it will prepare young people for an increasingly polyglot global cultural economy, hence keeping immigrants and minorities off public assistance, allowing them to compete in an increasingly 'diverse' (in the sense developed above) global community. Cultural arguments are also elided from within these positions, for, as many so eagerly stress, bilingual education really helps immigrants learn English and become assimilated faster – a bottom line supported by an ever-flowing spate of quantitative studies.

Market logics are all-pervasive here and are deeply informed by self-interest and resentment. These forces have shown themselves most clearly in recent decisions to provide less need-based financial aid for higher education to the poor, apportioning the savings to attract more so-called qualified middle-class students (Bronner 1998). Competition for the 'best' students – seemingly without regard for race, class, and gender – has become a mantra for those wishing to further destroy educational access for the dispossessed. Indeed, why, many argue, should poor minorities take precious spots away from the 'better' qualified wealthy? The resentment of the elite has now come full circle, especially and most ironically in this moment of unmatched economic wealth. As Jerome Karabel, professor of sociology at UC Berkeley (the site of key roll-backs in affirmative action) comments, 'College endowments are at historically unprecedented heights, so the number of need-blind institutions should be increasing rather than decreasing' (*ibid.*, 16). As we all know, these are not lean, mean times for everybody; we live in an era of unbridled wealth. This has been won largely for the elite, and obtained, at least in part, through 'divide and conquer' strategies founded on the triumph of resentment and its ability to dictate public policy.

Conclusion

Resentment, in sum, is produced at the level of the popular, at the level of the textual through the proliferation of labels which allow us to order and understand the world by emptying it of its complexity. Yet its implications run deep and cross a myriad contexts, including that of public policy, which is increasingly defined by the logic of resentment. Thus those of us on the left, those wishing to help keep the promise of public education a real one, must question the terms on which we fight these battles. We must question whether our responses will further reproduce a discourse with such devastating and wholly regressive implications. As Foucault reminds us, we must choose what discourses we want to engage in, the 'games of truth' we want to play. Indeed, what will be our responses to the burgeoning trend of eliminating need-based financial aid policies? What game will we play? And towards what end?

Such questions are crucial and pressing, as this moment is replete with both possibility and danger. This period of intense globalization and multinational capital is witness to the ushering in of the multicultural age – an age in which the empire has struck back, and first-world exploitation of the third world has so depressed these areas that there has been a steady stream of immigrants from the periphery seeking better futures in the metropolitan centers. With the rapid growth of the indigenous minority population in the US, diversity now has a formidable cultural presence in every sphere of cultural life. Clearly, as Appadurai reminds us (1996), social reproduction and integration have been inextricably complicated by globalization and the new and unpredictable flows of peoples, as well as of money, technology, media images and ideologies, that this has engendered. All, he stresses, must be understood both individually and in tandem if we are to understand the emerging cultural landscape and its imbrication in a multifaceted global reality.

Indeed, if this is an era of the 'post,' it is also an era of difference – and the challenge of this era of difference is the challenge of living in a world of incompleteness, discontinuity and multiplicity. It requires generating a mythology of social interaction that goes beyond the model of resentment which seems so securely in place in these times. It means that we must take seriously the implications of the best intuition in the Nietzschean critique of resentment as the process of identity formation that thrives on the negation of the other – the dominant response from those facing a new and complex global and local reality. The challenge is to embrace a politics that calls on the moral resources of all who are opposed to the power block and its emerging global contours.

This age of difference thus poses new, though difficult, tactical and strategic challenges to critical and subaltern intellectuals as well as to activists. A strategy that seeks to address these new challenges and openings must involve as a first condition a recognition that our differences of race, gender, and nation are merely starting-points for new solidarities and new alliances, not terminal stations where we deposit our agency and identities or extinguish hope and possibility. Such a strategy might help us better to understand the issue of diversity in schooling and its linkages to the problems of social integration and public policy in modern life. Such a strategy might also allow us to 'produce' new discourses, especially and most importantly at this fraught and exceedingly fragile moment of historical complexity.

References

Appadurai, A. (1996) *Modernity at Large: Cultural Dimensions of Globalization*, Minneapolis: Minnesota.

Asante, M. (1993) *Malcolm X as Cultural Hero and Other Afrocentric Essays*, Trenton: Africa World Press.

Bennett, W. (1994) *The Book of Virtues*, New York: Simon & Schuster.

Bronner, E. (1998) 'Universities Giving Less Financial Aid on Basis of Need,' *New York Times*, 21 June 1998: A1+.

Ewen, S. (1988) *All Consuming Images: The Politics of Style in Contemporary Culture*, New York: Basic Books.

Fine, M. and Weis, L. (1998) *The Unknown City: Lives of Poor and Working-Class Young Adults*, Boston: Beacon Press.

McCarthy, C. (1998) *The uses of culture: Education and the limits of ethnic affiliation.* New York: Routledge.

Nietzsche, F. (1967) *On the Genealogy of Morals* tr. W. Kaufman, New York: Vintage.

Ratnesar, R. (1997) 'The Next Big Divide?' *Time*, 1 December 1997: 52.

Steinberg, M. (1996) 'Cultural History and Cultural Studies' in C. Nelson and D. P. Gaonkar (eds) *Disciplinarity and Dissent in Cultural Studies* (103–29), New York: Routledge.

Tannen, D. (1998) *The Argument Culture: Moving from Debate to Dialogue*, New York: Random House.

Will, G. (1989) 'Eurocentricity and the School Curriculum,' *Baton Rouge Morning Advocate*, 18 December 1989: 3.

Knowing

15 The 'magic' of 'science'

The labeling of ideas

Randall Styers

Science is the big game in town. It stands as the determinative feature of developed modern economies, operating through an elaborate network of educational and research institutions, government and defense funding, and business, technological and industrial interests. Much of this social capital has been amassed, of course, as a result of the dazzling technical prowess of modern science – a prowess which enables remarkable prediction of the operations of nature, intricate and controlled interventions in the material world, the lengthening of human life, and a proliferation of products and investment opportunities. Modern science aspires to the heavens, even as it penetrates and informs the most obscure reaches of the body and psyche.

Yet beyond these technical capacities, science has also filled a crucial role in the self-representations of the modern world. Science – and scientific rationality – have served as the definitive markers of precisely what it means to be modern. Science has been championed as the defining characteristic that separates us from our primitive and unenlightened forebears; it shows us who we are; it offers the allure of limitless potential and progress. Indeed, as many cultural historians have underscored, one of the most intriguing aspects of the emergence of modern science is that science began to fill these ideological functions in the West's self-representations long before scientists could boast extensive achievements.

But this story of scientific rationality and progress has not been without its detractors. While there has been a long tradition of Western thinkers championing modernity and eagerly trumpeting the powers of science, from at least the era of Rousseau and early Romanticism there have also been vocal critics more skeptical of the modern world and its direction. Philosophers and social theorists have engaged in heated disputes over the nature of modernity and the consequences of the modern race to the future. And because of the central role of science in the representational and ideological schemes of the modern world, these disputes have often taken the form of debates over the origin and essence of science, its capacity to stand as the bell-wether of truth, its effects both intended and unforeseen. Critics of modernity have repeatedly turned their sights against the pretensions and presumptions of science and cold scientific rationalism. They have challenged many of the consequences of science, from destructive and dehumanizing technological developments, to the reordering of social and economic systems, to the implications of science for human self-perception and identity.

It is at this point that the politics of labeling enters the narrative. Throughout these polemics over the nature and effects of modernity, scholars and critics of many different persuasions have found it extraordinarily important to demarcate the nature of science. Yet science – perhaps we should say 'science' – is nothing if not multifarious. An amorphous family of practices and phenomena, science is dispersed throughout the social field, assuming enormously divergent forms. Is it to be best understood as a world-view, or a form of logic, or a method of inquiry and observation, or a body of results, or a set of academic disciplines and broader social institutions? Given its indeterminate contours, science – this most central component of modernity, this most crucial, and contested, ideological marker – has proved notoriously difficult for historians and philosophers to define.

In the face of this difficulty, 'magic' has emerged as a surprisingly important feature of historical and philosophical accounts of science. One of the most long-standing and recurrent methods used in theoretical texts to define and explain modern scientific rationality has been to contrast science with a foil, to demarcate the boundaries of science by juxtaposing it with the definitively non-scientific. Since the emergence of the Western social sciences as academic disciplines in the latter decades of the nineteenth century, 'magic' has been regularly invoked as this foil. Throughout the theoretical literature of these disciplines, magical thinking has been traditionally configured as the archetype of non-modern (or pre-modern, or anti-modern) thought. Particularly in the context of European and American colonialism, this broad new category was invoked as a central analytical tool in the effort to explain non-European cultures, and magic came to play a major role in accounts of cultural development, particularly accounts of the emergence and nature of science.

Through the course of this theoretical tradition, many scholars have echoed the sentiment of the venerable late Victorian James George Frazer, that magic is 'the bastard sister of science' (Frazer 1963: 57). This filiation has served many thinkers as a means of bringing the nature of science into sharp relief: we can identify science through the contrast with what it is *not*, that is, pre-scientific magic. And at the same time, other scholars have invoked this purported filiation between science and magic to offer a more nuanced assessment of science's pedigree: perhaps if science bears some family resemblance to this rather dubious sibling, it should be placed in more organic relation with other forms of human thought and rationality.

This process of invoking an 'other,' in order either to consolidate and reify an identity or to problematize it, is hardly unique to debates over science. In recent decades philosophers and cultural analysts from a range of perspectives have worked to map the dualistic systems of thought which have shaped

Western modernity and to excavate the ways in which these binary logics have defined the modern imagination. But the debate over the nature and pedigree of science – over the relation between science and magic – offers a particularly vivid demonstration both of the operations of dualistic thought and of the politics of labeling.

Debates over the relation between science and magic have emerged in numerous contexts in the social sciences, philosophy and history. Many anthropologists and sociologists of the late nineteenth and early twentieth centuries sought to uncover the essence of science by discovering its origins, and in their efforts often invoked magic. In competing theories, a number of influential social theorists attempted to formulate various essential distinctions between the two categories (so as to establish that science was *sui generis* and originated independently of magic), while others argued that magic and science were fundamentally continuous or related forms of practice (with science evolving in a relatively organic fashion out of magical thought). Over time, as social scientists turned from the search for origins to other themes, such fanciful conjecture concerning the pre-history of science began to subside. But magic remained a central component in later theoretical disputes over such issues as the nature of 'primitive' thought, human cultural commensurability, and the ability of modern scientific rationality to comprehend and explain irrational modes of thought. These debates regularly turned on competing notions of the fundamental nature of science and scientific rationality, on the fixity with which science is to be demarcated in relation to other systems of thought and practice.

One arena in which these disputes concerning the relation of science and magic has been particularly contentious has been in the history of science. Intellectual and social historians have long sought to account for the emergence of scientific thought in Europe in the early modern period and to explain the relation of this new science to prior modes of thought, particularly medieval and Renaissance traditions of hermetic magic and occultism. Did modern science emerge in a 'revolution,' or should it be better understood as continuous in significant respects with prior traditions of inquiry? Is modern scientific rationality a new and distinctive form of thought, or does it share important links with earlier forms of occultism and natural magic?[1]

This historical debate turns on the question of labeling. How is science to be defined? How is it related – or juxtaposed – to this foil, magical thinking? Indeed, the dogged persistence of this dispute among historians of science points us to a consideration of the significant political stakes that underlie it. The account offered by an historian concerning the emergence of science is shaped by the labels and categories used to formulate that account, and those labels and categories themselves are often shaped in complex fashion by the historian's own evaluation of science, perspective on the role of science in the modern world, and fundamental assessment of modernity itself.

We have before us a vivid example of the politics at work in the construction of historical and analytical categories. For generations of historians under the sway of Enlightenment theories of social evolution and progress, there was widespread acceptance of the claim that modern scientific thought represented a fundamental and decisive break with prior schemes of inquiry. This view emerged with increasing clarity in the writings of Bacon, Voltaire and Condorcet, and it became particularly prominent in the latter half of the nineteenth century in the work of historians such as Jacob Burckhardt. Historians of this perspective, though perhaps acknowledging that early modern science benefited from the thought or method of classical antiquity, insisted that the new science stood in sharpest contrast to the benighted stagnation of the Dark Ages and the medieval period.[2]

In these accounts, the Scientific Revolution was sparked by the emergence of a form of rationality which ignited in direct opposition to all forms of medieval and Renaissance occultism and magic (see Cohen 1994: 116). Floris Cohen provides a succinct summary of this view: 'the emergence of early modern science comes down to a general process of purification, to which the three undistinct sisters "magic, mysticism, and superstition" contributed in an essentially negative way by allowing themselves to be gradually eliminated by science' (*ibid.* 118). In this traditional perspective, the advent of science was truly a revolution. Such historical accounts invoke Europe's benighted past to heighten, by contrast, the revolutionary luster of the new rationality. Thus, the early modern witchcraft persecutions (contemporaneous, of course, with the emergence of early modern science) are configured as the final great paroxysm of the superstitions of the Dark Ages, and Renaissance traditions of high magic and hermetic occultism are depicted as a brief outbreak of folly soon to be quashed by the enlightened insight of heroic scientific innovators.

The triumphalism of this account of the thoroughgoing antipathy between incipient scientific thought and the occultism and magic of the Renaissance is well captured in Preserved Smith's 1930 work, *A History of Modern Culture*. Smith here asserts that in Europe and America, belief in witchcraft was destroyed by 'the spirit of science with its revelation of a new world of law and of reason in which there is no place for either magic or devil,' adding: 'The noxious germ of superstition can no more flourish in a world flooded with the light of science than can the germ of tuberculosis flourish in the beams of the sun, even though a few germs linger on and develop sporadically' (vol. 1: 451).[3] Smith concludes that even if superstition and magic were not thoroughly extirpated by Enlightenment rationalism, they suffered 'a decisive defeat':

> The devil ... and his army of spirits still skulked in the backward parts of the world, in lonely country houses or in the chambers of the inquisitors or in the alchemical laboratories of the idle and uneducated rich ... yet, a vast change in public opinion had taken place. The sun had pierced the clouds, but not wholly dispelled them.
>
> (vol. 2: 545)[4]

Smith is joined in the basic outlines of his account by many prominent philosophers and historians of science. Thus, for example, in their accounts of the history of science Bertrand Russell and Karl Popper both argue that modern science represented a decisive break from the prior forms of Renaissance occultism and magic.[5] Throughout the many versions of this story of revolutionary progress, we see various efforts to insulate the new forms of scientific inquiry and rationality from contamination by what has preceded them. And yet the ignorance, superstition and depravity of the past can be used in these accounts to heighten the contours of science, to bring it into sharper and more flattering relief.

But through the course of the twentieth century, a dissenting view gained prominence which challenges fundamental aspects of this traditional perspective. A number of historians have come to argue that, far from being discontinuous with earlier modes of inquiry, early modern science actually emerged as a more organic or continuous development from those systems of thought. Advocates of this thesis of continuity have stressed the formative roles played by natural magic in the emergence of early modern scientific thought. Historians such as Pierre Duhem came to underscore the role of medieval natural philosophy and Christian theology in the emergence of modern science.[6] Other historians – Lynn Thorndike the most influential among them – built on this perspective to examine the emergence of modern Western science within the context of the broader social and intellectual *milieu* of the early modern period and to argue that there were important links between Renaissance magic and early scientific thought.[7]

In the 1960s Frances Yates elaborated a developed account of the argument that the neo-platonic magic and hermetic occultism of the Renaissance played a significant role in the emergence of early modern science.[8] While Yates acknowledged that there were important differences between hermetic magical thought and 'genuine science,' she argued that various strands of hermetic thought served to 'stimulate the will towards genuine science and its operations' by encouraging new attitudes toward the natural world (1991: 447–9).[9] Yates concluded that the 'hermetic attitude toward the cosmos ... was I believe, the chief stimulus of that new turning toward the world and operating on the world which, appearing first as Renaissance magic, was to turn into seventeenth-century science' (1967: 272).

Yates' thesis has attracted a number of prominent supporters. Subsequent historians have highlighted the contributions of hermetic and natural magic traditions (and various other forms of spiritualism) to the rise of science, and have offered nuanced appraisals of the relation between hermeticism and modern modes of thought.[10] Yet despite this support, Yates' thesis has remained controversial among historians of science, who continue to debate her claim that hermetic magic and other occult traditions had a positive role in the emergence of modern science.[11]

These debates over Renaissance natural magic and occultism among historians of science offer a vivid demonstration of the politics of labeling. If modern science is configured as a distinctive, *sui generis* phenomenon, this definition leads to historical accounts in which science is rigorously contrasted to the various modes of inquiry which preceded it. Renaissance magic is left with only a negative role in the story of the origins of science, as an antithetical mode of thought which was decisively superseded. If, on the other hand, science is not reified as *sui generis*, it is possible for the historian to formulate an account in which modern scientific inquiry shares important commonalties with prior modes of investigation, or evolves from them in a more organic fashion. Renaissance magic might then be seen as, for example, displaying new forms of attentiveness toward the material world which could contribute to the emergence of new scientific modes of thought. The definitions of these categories of analysis – science and magic – and the ways in which these labels are deployed play a decisive role in shaping the various historical accounts.

These processes through which labels and categories of analysis are constructed and deployed, and the politics which can animate them, come into clearer focus if we turn to a particular text. One of the most prominent opponents of Yates' thesis of the continuity between Renaissance magic and early modern science is Brian Vickers. In his introduction to the essays collected in the 1984 anthology *Occult and Scientific Mentalities in the Renaissance*, Vickers rejects the fundamental premises of Yates' argument, even in milder versions which would assert only that the occult had a minor 'formative influence' on the new science (1984a: 5).[12] Vickers' arguments here are notable particularly because of the extraordinary lengths he goes to in order to formulate and maintain a rigid and fixed boundary between scientific thought and all forms of occultism as two mutually incompatible traditions. As his arguments build, Vickers demonstrates the rhetorical power of using this occult 'other' to reify and idealize the nature of science. His arguments are worth surveying in the present context not so much because of the originality of his claims, but rather because of the vivid manner in which he sets out this compendium of arguments. Vickers provides a valuable example of the power of labeling to promote a distinctively moralizing theoretical project.

Vickers begins by rejecting any historical model in which modern science might be seen as emerging out of an occult or magical view of nature or in which the occult work of various early modern scientists (most notably Newton) might be harmonized with their non-occult science. It is erroneous, he asserts, either to seek any connection between these two distinct systems of thought or to claim 'that the occult sciences in the Renaissance were productive of ideas, theories, and techniques in the new sciences' (1984a: 44).[13] Vickers proceeds to offer a catalog of what he sees as the fundamental distinctions which must be drawn between science and magical occultism.

The first important difference is that occult science is marked by resistance to change. In Vickers' view, the scientific mentality depends on an ability to abstract and to integrate the results of this abstraction (leading, in turn, to an awareness of the very processes of theorizing itself) (Vickers 1984a: 7, 36 citing Horton 1970: 160). He quotes the anthropologist Robin Horton on the key difference between 'African traditional thought' and Western science:

> in traditional cultures there is no developed awareness of alternatives to the established body of theoretical tenets; whereas in scientifically oriented cultures, such an awareness is highly developed. It is this difference we refer to when we say that traditional cultures are 'closed' and scientifically oriented cultures 'open.'
>
> (Horton 1970: 153, quoted in Vickers 1984a: 34)

In Vickers' view, the closed system of the occult is 'self-contained, a homogeneity that has synthesized its various elements into a mutually supporting relationship from which no part can be removed' (1984a: 34–5). Thus, the occult system (like 'African' and all other 'traditional' systems) is fundamentally conservative, blind to alternatives and improperly holistic in the synthetic sweep of its world-view.

Next, Vickers asserts that magical thought fails to acknowledge the proper boundaries between language and reality, between human minds and materiality, between humanity and the non-human world. Whereas the scientific world-view 'draws a clear distinction between the literal and the metaphorical,' in the occult tradition metaphors are mistaken for realities and 'abstract ideas are given concrete attributes.' Magical occultism thus demonstrates a tendency to think in nebulous images rather than in appropriate forms of abstraction (Vickers 1984a: 9–10; see also Horton 1970: 156). As Vickers states:

> Much of occult science, if I may sum up the conclusions of my own researches, is built out of purely mental operations, the arrangement of items into hierarchies, the construction of categories that become matrices for the production of further categories. Far from being a science of nature, or even of man, it comes to seem more and more like a classification system, self-contained and self-referring.
>
> (1984a: 12–13)[14]

In distinction to the occult approach to knowledge, modern science 'has dismissed such ideas because they would imply that reality did not exist independently of language and that human whim could control the world.' The scientific world-view is based on a recognition that 'ideas and reality exist on different levels' (Vickers 1984a: 35–6). Modern science is thus superior to magical thinking on two counts: because science views human thought (and 'whim') as fundamentally immaterial, and because science maintains important analytical boundaries between humanity and other parts of the natural world.

Vickers also finds that science and magical occultism differ in their responses to the failure of their predictions. Again he quotes Robin Horton:

> In the theoretical thought of the traditional cultures, there is a notable reluctance to register repeated failures of prediction and to act by attacking the beliefs involved. Instead, other current beliefs are utilized in such a way as to 'excuse' each failure as it occurs, and hence to protect the major theoretical assumptions on which prediction is based.
> (Horton 1970: 162, quoted in Vickers 1984a: 36–7)

Thus, traditional and occult minds lack the fundamentally scientific ability to question one's basic beliefs on the basis of predictive failures. In Vickers' view, it is this recognition of success and failure that allows the scientific tradition to modify or even discard its theories, because a scientist knows that theory is always provisional and subject to change (1984a: 37).

The progressivism of science stands in sharp contrast to the stasis of the occult, and the two modes of thought thus demonstrate radically divergent attitudes toward the past. Whereas traditional and occult thought holds the past in relatively high regard (with the past often seen as a golden age of pure knowledge or simplicity), the scientific view is dramatically different:

> The scientific tradition ... sees the first age as ... a state of deprivation out of which we have painfully emerged, thanks to inventors, technologists, scientists. As Horton puts it: 'Where the traditional thinker is busily trying to annul the passage of time, the scientist' is 'trying frantically to hurry time up. For in his impassioned pursuit of the experimental method, he is striving after the creation of new situations which nature, if left to herself, would bring about slowly if ever at all.'
> (Vickers 1984a: 38, quoting Horton 1970: 169)

This scientist has 'his' eyes on the future, envisioning and striving for new creations which dawdling nature 'herself' might neglect. Yet despite this enthusiastic affirmation of the instrumental capacities of the masculine scientific will, Vickers immediately stresses that a further distinction between science and the occult is to be found in the fundamental humility of science. While occult sciences 'claimed to be omniscient, able to account for all phenomena, and were, as a result, strictly irrefutable,' modern science has demonstrated a willingness 'to admit the limits of its knowledge, to state clearly what it does not know.' In fact, this mature acknowledgment of limits further facilitates scientific innovation (1984a: 39).

Vickers next turns to anthropologist Ernest Gellner's account of 'The Savage and the Modern Mind' to trace a further set of differences between occult and scientific thought. The occult system, he explains, lacks abstraction; it relies too much on the concrete properties of objects, rather than employing a more general, second-order focus on the properties of explanation itself. And again, while the occult persists in using 'anthropomorphic, socioreligious, or ethical categories' and characterizations, modern science is 'socially neutral' and 'ill suited for the underpinning of moral expectations, of a status- and value-system' (Vickers 1984a: 41–2, quoting Gellner 1973: 171). Science is superior to magic and occultism because science disclaims parochial social interests.

Further, in its effort to account for the world in 'homocentric, symbolic, and religious terms,' the occult seeks to form 'totalities in which everything mutually coheres.' Science, on the other hand, 'depends on a classification of knowledge and language into various types' and into separate components, and then applies different criteria of validity to these respective domains. Thus, Vickers explains, 'primitive thought systems are able to tolerate logical contradictions that would be unthinkable to a modern European' (1984a: 42–3). Europeans avoid these contradictions, it appears, by segmenting the world and various forms of knowledge into differentiated components and by keeping these differences firmly in mind.

As he concludes, Vickers cites Gellner for two last distinctions between occult and scientific thought. First, according to Gellner, traditional societies are unable to distinguish between concepts 'which have an empirically operational role, and those whose reference is transcendent;' they use 'concepts that are, so to speak, semioperational, which have both empirical and transcendent reference' (Gellner 1973: 176, quoted in Vickers 1984a: 43). In contrast, the scientific tradition has worked to define a boundary between the testable and the non-testable and then to inhibit improper crossing of this boundary. Again science is superior to magic because of its superior forms of differentiation and boundary maintenance.

Finally, according to Gellner, in traditional thought systems the network of fundamental beliefs is widespread and mutually reinforcing to the point where challenges to one belief reverberate throughout the system. Thus, in a traditional system the notion of 'the sacred or the crucial' is 'more extensive, more untidily dispersed, and much more pervasive' than in the modern world-view, where this notion is 'tidier, narrower, as it were economical,' less 'diffused among the detailed aspects of life' (Gellner 1973: 178, quoted in Vickers 1984a: 43–4). Science surpasses magic because the scientific world-view has successfully delimited the realm of the sacred. With the sacred cordoned away into a more 'economical' zone, the world is rendered more readily subject to scientific manipulation.

There are, of course, many aspects of Vickers' account of the difference between magical occultism and modern science which are relevant for our purposes here. Perhaps the most striking feature of his enterprise is the constant collapsing of labels and categories. On the one hand, we have 'the occult,' 'traditional thought,' 'traditional belief-systems,' 'African thought,' 'African magic,' members of 'primitive societies.' On the other, we have 'modern science,' 'scientific thought-systems,' 'Western science,' 'Western modes of thought,' 'the Western scientific tradition.'

In keeping with a lengthy tradition in European and American social thought, Vickers configures a sharp Manichean division between the scientific and the magical, the rational and the irrational, the modern and the non-modern, a division in which all the related categories seamlessly align. This aspect of Vickers' argument is particularly apparent in his deployment of 'evidence' from anthropological studies of 'primitive' cultures to further his claims concerning early modern European history. It would appear from the structure of his argument that there is little relevant difference in world-view between the high magicians of the European Renaissance and Robin Horton's 'Africans' or Ernest Gellner's 'savages.' The differences among these diverse peoples (chronological, geographical, cultural) are all obliterated as Vickers contrasts them with the scientific modern Westerner. And yet the principal effect of this rhetorical structure is not so much to submerge the identities of these magical thinkers as actually to consolidate the identity of this modern Westerner (appropriately rationalized and scientific), a figure who emerges in heightened contrast to all that has gone before and all that exists elsewhere.

Vickers uses this bifurcation of two antithetical modes of thought not only to consolidate the identity of this modern thinker, but also to consolidate a single form of proper scientific thought. (Note, of course, that the innumerable differences that exist both among various forms of science and among various forms of magic all disappear.) The singular nature of scientific thought can then be used to bolster his claim that modern science is ontologically distinct from all preceding forms of 'traditional' thinking. Through this process, the way in which Vickers defines science largely determines the results of his argument.

Yet this rigid contrast between science and magic serves even more significant functions in Vickers' argument. This abstractly reified notion of science has little definition or content until it is brought into contrast with its magical foil. It is actually by means of his extended account of magic that Vickers is able to demarcate the precise contours of science and to explain its nature. He here provides a vivid example of the use of magic for the purpose of giving shape to a concept of science. Echoing innumerable earlier theories of magic in philosophy and the social sciences, Vickers explains to us that magic (of whatever cultural provenance) demonstrates a uniform and consistent set of features (it is resistant to change, closed, unresponsive to failure, traditionalist, inflexible, arrogant, morally biased, etc.). In fact, magic epitomizes everything that science is not – or should not be.

This leads to a further aspect of Vickers' argument which is worth underlining. While he has explained to us that modern science is 'socially neutral' and ill-suited to serve as a tool in ethical or moral debates (Vickers 1984a: 41–2), the same cannot be said of Vickers' own account. In fact, his catalog of the contrasts between science and magic is characterized by a strident and often moralizing tone. Science should, in his view, relativize the content of its theories (recognizing that this content is always contingent), but science's own relativizing method appears to be beyond question. Vickers uses the discussion of magical occultism as an opportunity to formulate and promote a distinctive set of scientific values and ideals, and he spells out those ideals and gives them rhetorical force through the deployment of magic as a foil. Indeed, his account of magical thought demonstrates an overriding concern with policing human relations toward nature and technology. He offers a range of normative declarations concerning the proper mode of scientific inquiry, the appropriate shape of human engagement with the material world, and normative limits on human manipulation of nature.

As an example of Vickers' moralizing, let me turn to one final issue raised in his discussion of the distinctions between science and magic. On the one hand, Vickers valorizes the capacity of the scientific will to intervene in the natural world in order to reshape that world to human intentions and desires. Yet on the other he underscores the fundamental humility of science in recognizing the limits of human knowledge and human power (1984a: 39). Science is more effective – and, it appears, more moral – than magic because science acknowledges limits which magic arrogantly disregards.

Vickers is alone neither in his ambivalence on this issue (is science assertive, or is it submissive?), nor in ultimately accenting what he sees as the fundamental humility of science. While many theorists valorize modern science as a tool of profound, liberating power which immeasurably enlarges 'the bounds of human empire' (Randall 1940: 224), many also join Vickers in stressing its fundamental humility. As a particularly vivid example, W. C. Dampier echoes this theme when he states that the spirit of magic is fundamentally opposed to that of science because the scientific spirit is shaped by 'a slow, cautious and humble-minded search for truth.' As Dampier explains, magic is arrogant and willful in ways far removed from the quiet path of science: 'Science, with clearer insight than is possessed by magic, humbly studies nature's laws, and by obeying them gains that control of nature which magic falsely imagines itself to have acquired' (Dampier 1943: 57, 376).

There is, of course, an element of irony in this claim that science is fundamentally humble, not only in light of the enormous social and economic capital of the scientific establishment, but also because of the innumerable ways in which scientific 'humility' has licensed unimaginable transformation – and destruction – of the natural world. Yet this rhetorical contrast between humble science and willful, malignant magic is a recurrent trope in the literature of the social sciences. Practitioners of magic (primitive, non-modern or anti-modern) are regularly depicted by historians and theorists as dominated by improper and inordinate desires which lead them to magical irrationality. In contrast, science is characterized as respectful of the appropriate bounds on both reason and desire.

These aspects of Vickers' account lead us back to a consideration of the more fundamental issues that underlie the disputes over the relation between science and magic. Debate continues among historians and philosophers of science concerning the relation between modern science and earlier magical traditions and modes of thought (Lindberg 1992: 357–60; see also generally Cohen 1994). As Floris Cohen has highlighted, these disputes often turn on broader questions concerning the role of science in shaping the modern world. Should the scientific revolution be seen as 'the beneficial triumph of rational thought about nature,' or as 'the agent chiefly responsible for the destructive handling of nature'? (Cohen 1994: 170.) Does science epitomize the triumph of the rational control of nature, or does it rather represent the victory of a dehumanizing reductivism? Does science teach us an appropriate humility in the face of nature's laws, or is it the pinnacle of human hubris?

On the one hand, as Cohen explains, there are historians holding the traditional, Enlightenment-inspired view which sees early modern science as replacing a premodern fear of nature with 'the quiet certainty that we know, and can predict, nature's operations.' Scholars in this tradition not only see science as a profoundly liberating force, but also view it as decisively distinct from earlier forms of inquiry (Cohen 1994: 176). These scholars are thus eager to police sharp boundaries between the labels 'science' and 'magic.' A rigid separation of these categories is essential in maintaining the distinctive and singular nature of modern science.

On the other hand, there are theorists and social critics more ambivalent in their assessment of the consequences of science. These scholars have been less persuaded by the Enlightenment reifications of scientific rationality and more inclined to stress the relations or continuities between science and various forms of magical thinking. They have even at times invoked magic as an alternative to the dominant rationalist modes of relation to nature. Thus, Cohen argues (1994: 182), historians such as Frances Yates emphasize the links between early modern science and magical thought because this very relation can demonstrate that prominent early scientists recognized that the new technical insights of science came at a high price, as alternative perspectives on human identity and the human relation to nature were suppressed. Historians of this perspective encourage a more porous use of the labels, 'magic' and 'science.' Greater continuity between the two categories undercuts the reification of science and opens up a conceptual terrain with more resources for the critique of the modern world.

At the core of the scholarly debates over the role of hermetic magic in the emergence of early modern science are competing visions of what science is and what science has meant in giving shape to modernity (Cohen 1994: 176). And this same dynamic reappears throughout the many contexts in which philosophers and historians of science invoke magic in their accounts of the nature and history of science and scientific rationality. Throughout this theoretical tradition, scholars have positioned magic at (or beyond) the boundary of modern rationality. Magic is thus configured as a definitive marker of the non-modern, the emblem of all that is non-scientific. With magic so defined, scholarly debates over magic come to serve as a crucial site for contesting the nature of modernity itself.

Magic has thus played an invaluable role in the theoretical literature on science. This category has been regularly invoked as the foil against which science is juxtaposed, and by means of magic the contours of science have been demarcated and its nature – and limitations – debated. Through the deployment of these labels, that deployment in itself a potent form of rhetorical magic, science has been produced as an object of study.

Notes

1 See Lindberg 1992: 355–68. For a valuable overview of the historiography of the scientific revolution, see Cohen 1994.
2 See Lindberg 1992: 355–7. For a vivid example of this view, see Singer 1958: xxiii, speaking of the Middle Ages: 'it is always necessary to remember that the knowledge of the day was not only perverted and corrupted in quality but that it was also extremely small in extent.'
3 Smith continues (1930 vol. 1: 451): 'The greatest triumphs of science have been not its material achievements, wonderful as these are, but the diffusion of the bright light of knowledge and the consequent banishment of ghosts and bugaboos created by man's fear of the dark.'
4 Note, of course, that Smith's new 'public' appears to exclude the 'backward,' the rural, Catholic inquisitors and the idle wealthy.
5 See, for example, Russell 1945: 527, 536; Popper 1983: 212; and Popper 1994: 199.
6 See for example Duhem 1985; and Lindberg 1992: 357.
7 See for example Thorndike 1923–58, and 1905.
8 See for example Yates 1991 and 1967. See also Cohen 1994: 110–11, 169–83.
9 For a critique of Yates' arguments concerning the ways in which this influence was manifested, see Cohen 1994: 285–96, concluding that the most plausible connection suggested by Yates between hermetic thought and the emergence of the new forms of science is that hermetic magic perceived the natural world as subject to human manipulation in a manner which set the stage for scientific experimentation.
10 See, for example, Rattansi 1972; Hansen 1975; Debus 1978; Webster 1982; Merkel and Debus 1988; and Nebelsick 1992.
11 For an overview of Yates' subsequent writings on this theme and the critical debate concerning Yates' thesis, see Copenhaver 1990.
12 For examples of essays in *Occult and Scientific Mentalities in the Renaissance* (Vickers 1984) more hospitable to the notion that occult traditions might have played a role in the formulation and spread of new scientific knowledge, see Mordechai Feingold, 'The Occult Tradition in the English Universities of the Renaissance: A Reassessment,' 73–94; Richard S. Westfall, 'Newton and Alchemy,' 315–36; and Lotte Mulligan, '"Reason," "Right Reason," and "Revelation" in Mid-Seventeenth-Century England,' 375–401.
13 See also Vickers 1984a: 8, 13–15, 22–3, 31–44; and Vickers 1984b, arguing that the occult and experimental scientific traditions must be differentiated with respect to goals, methods and assumptions.
14 See also Vickers 1984b: 95–6.

References

Cohen, H. Floris (1994) *The Scientific Revolution: A Historiographic Inquiry*, Chicago and London: University of Chicago Press.

Copenhaver, Brian P. (1990) 'Natural Magic, Hermeticism, and Occultism in Early Modern Science' in David C. Lindberg and Robert S. Westman (eds) *Reappraisals of the Scientific Revolution* (260–301, Cambridge: Cambridge University Press.

Dampier, William Cecil (1943) *A History of Science and its Relations with Philosophy and Religion* (3rd edn), Cambridge: Cambridge University Press; New York: Macmillan.

Debus, Allen (1978) *Man and Nature in the Renaissance*, Cambridge: Cambridge University Press.

Duhem, Pierre (1985) *Medieval Cosmology: Theories of Infinity, Place, Time, Void, and the Plurality of Worlds* tr. Roger Ariew (ed.), Chicago: University of Chicago Press.

Frazer, James George (1963) *The Golden Bough: A Study in Magic and Religion* (abridged edn), New York: Collier Books/Macmillan.

Gellner, Ernest (1973) 'The Savage and the Modern Mind' in Robin Horton and Ruth Finnegan (eds) *Modes of Thought: Essays on Thinking in Western and Non-Western Societies* (162–81), London: Faber & Faber.

Hansen, Bert (1975) 'Science and Magic' in David C. Lindberg (ed.) *Science in the Middle Ages* (483–500), Chicago: University of Chicago Press.

Horton, Robin (1970) 'African Traditional Thought and Modern Science' in Bryan R. Wilson (ed.) *Rationality*, New York: Harper & Row.

Lindberg, David C. (1992) *The Beginnings of Western Science*, Chicago and London: University of Chicago Press.

Merkel, Ingrid and Debus, Allen G. (eds) (1988) *Hermeticism and the Renaissance: Intellectual History and the Occult in Early Modern Europe*, Washington, DC: Folger Shakespeare Library; London and Toronto: Associated University Presses.

Nebelsick, H. P. (1992) *The Renaissance, the Reformation and the Rise of Science*, Edinburgh: T. & T. Clark.

Popper, Karl R. (1983) excerpt from *Postscript to the Logic of Scientific Discovery* (1956) in W. W. Bartley III (ed.) *Realism and the Aim of Science*, Totowa, NJ: Rowman and Littlefield.

—— (1994) in M. A. Notturno (ed.) *The Myth of the Framework: In Defense of Science and Rationality*, London and New York: Routledge.

Randall, John Herman, Jr (1940) [1926] *The Making of the Modern Mind: A Survey of the Intellectual Background of the Present Age* (revised edn), Cambridge, MA: Riverside Press.

Rattansi, P. M. (1972) 'The Social Interpretation of Science in the 17th Century' in Peter Mathias (ed.) *Science and Society 1600–1900* (1–32, London: Cambridge University Press.

Russell, Bertrand (1945) *A History of Western Philosophy*, New York: Simon & Schuster.

Singer, Charles (1958) *From Magic to Science: Essays on the Scientific Twilight*, New York: Dover Publications Inc.

Smith, Preserved (1930) *A History of Modern Culture* 2 vols, New York: Henry Hold and Co.

Thorndike, Lynn (1923–58) *A History of Magic and Experimental Science* 8 vols, New York: Columbia University Press.

—— (1905) 'The Place of Magic in the Intellectual History of Europe' in Faculty of Political Science of Columbia University (ed.) *Studies in History, Economics and Public Law* 24: 1–110, New York: Columbia University Press.

Vickers, Brian (1984) 'Introduction' in *Occult and Scientific Mentalities in the Renaissance*, Cambridge: Cambridge University Press.

—— (1984) 'Analogy versus Identity: The Rejection of Occult Symbolism, 1580–1680' in *Occult and Scientific Mentalities in the Renaissance* 95–163, Cambridge: Cambridge University Press.

Webster, Charles (1982) *From Paracelsus to Newton: Magic and the Making of Modern Science*, Cambridge: Cambridge University Press.

Yates, Francis A. (1967) 'The Hermetic Tradition in Renaissance Science' in Charles S. Singleton (ed.) *Art, Science, and History in the Renaissance* (255–74), Baltimore: Johns Hopkins University Press.

—— (1991) [1964] *Giordano Bruno and the Hermetic Tradition*, Chicago and London: University of Chicago Press.

16 Addicting epistemologies?[1]

Glenn M. Hudak

Do not be idolatrous about or bound to any doctrine, theory, or ideology, even Buddhist ones.

Do not think the knowledge you presently possess is changeless, absolute truth. Avoid being narrow-minded and bound to present views. Learn and practice nonattachment from views in order to be open to receive others' viewpoints. Truth is found in life and not merely in conceptual knowledge.

Do not force others, including children, by any means whatsoever, to adopt your views, whether by authority, threat, money, propaganda, or even education.

(Thich Nhat Hanh 1993)

And if you are sure that you are a guide to the blind,
a corrector of the foolish,
a teacher of children,
having in the Law the embodiment of knowledge and truth,
you, then, that teach others,
will you not teach yourself?

Romans 2: 19–21, New Oxford Annotated Bible (NSRV)

And how do we professional educators – academics – teach ourselves? In her recent writings the African American educator Lisa Delpit discusses her journeys into 'understanding other worlds, journeys that involved learning to see, albeit dimly, through the haze of my own cultural lenses' (1995: 9). She discusses the insights she gained as she explored other cultures, particularly the lives of Native Alaskans. Her goal is an attempt to gain understanding of what it means to be 'multicultural' – to be different and yet connected; to bridge the gap with another culture. What is most astonishing about Delpit's journeys is her struggle with research epistemologies such as 'the narrow and essentially Eurocentric curriculum' (*ibid.* 181) found in many teacher-education programs, a curriculum which tends to objectify non-Western cultures and to assume an air of superiority towards them. Indeed, Delpit writes (*ibid.* 92) that one lesson she received during her stay with Native Alaskans was on:

learning to be part of the world rather than trying to dominate it – on learning to see rather than merely look, to feel rather than touch, to hear rather than listen: to learn, in short, about the world by being still and opening myself to experiencing it. If I realize that I am an organic part of all that is, and learn to adopt a receptive, connected stance, then I need not take an active, dominant role to understand; the universe will, in essence, include me in understanding.

Notice Delpit's emphasis on 'stillness,' on being 'receptive,' on being 'connected,' on being 'part of all that is' as a way of knowing and understanding, a way which does not intend to control, or to cling to, or to dominate others. It is an epistemology that amplifies freedom, respect, and love; it is also an epistemological stance that amplifies a non-Western perspective on learning.

As I read Lisa Delpit, various loose ends in my thinking began to tie together: like Delpit I too am concerned with the ways in which we train future teachers to teach other people's children. Like Delpit, I too have found that the ways in which we academics, with our rational, dualistic, Cartesian epistemologies serve most often to create disconnection rather than connection, disequilibrium rather than balance, fragmentation rather than wholeness, pathology rather than health – both between ourselves as faculty and with the students we teach. And finally, like Lisa Delpit, I too have found much inspiration, insight, and understanding in non-Western epistemologies. For me, Buddhism has been particularly helpful, especially the work of the Zen Buddhist Thich Nhat Hanh.

Indeed, it is because her observations appear compatible with Zen Buddhist thought that I have begun this essay with the above insights from Lisa Delpit; they help to situate my interest in Thich Nhat Hanh's *Cultivating The Mind of Love* (1996). Though I have been a student of Buddhist thought for over two and a half decades, it has always remained something of a puzzle for me to work out how to integrate Buddhist epistemology into my workplace – academia. As such, my aim in this essay has been to cast a wide net, so to speak, in hopes of getting a good catch. My logic is intentionally circular, rather than linear. I begin by circling around something very basic to all academics in educational research – our relationship with words and concepts.

Admittedly, without words and concepts it would be extremely difficult for us academics to do our jobs. However, my observation has been that we tend to become possessive of our ideas – of our words and concepts – and that this sense of ownership serves most often to reinforce precisely what we as progressive educators claim we are ideologically committed to eradicating. That is, a good deal of the 'turf' issues and power struggles among faculty are related to an obsessive clinging to ideas as if they were the final truth. In contradistinction, this essay represents no more than a sort of rumination – something to be read with morning coffee – on academia and Zen Buddhism, inspired simply by the poetic insights of Thich Nhat Hanh.

Thich Nhat Hanh is a Vietnamese Zen Buddhist master who currently lives in France. He served as chair of the Buddhist peace delegation to the Paris peace talks during the war in Vietnam and was nominated for the Nobel Peace Prize by Dr Martin Luther King Jr. He is the author of over seventy books. In *Cultivating the Mind of Love*, Nhat Hanh writes in alternating chapters of love and of Buddhist epistemology. The chapters on love present vignettes of Nhat Hanh's own falling in love with a Buddhist nun, many years ago in his youth. He writes (1996: 21):

> monks do not usually share stories like this, but I think it is important to do so. Otherwise, how will the younger generation know what to do when they are stuck? As a monk, you are not supposed to fall in love, but sometimes love is stronger than your determination.

The chapters on love do not attempt to explain what love is in an analytical way. Rather, as a 'dharma talk' (Buddhist teachings), they are intended to be heard, listened to, with our whole being. This mode of listening is very like Delpit's sense of 'being still and opening myself,' being completely receptive to the experience of those around us. For as Nhat Hanh writes (*ibid.* 3), we must learn to listen with the whole of our being, not just with our intellects:

> Seeds of love and understanding buried deep within [our] consciousness [are] touched, and I could see that [you are] listening not just to my talk but [yours] as well ... When you listen to a Dharma Talk, just allow the rain of the Dharma to penetrate the soil of your consciousness. Don't think too much; don't argue or compare. [My emphasis.]

'Don't think too much.' It sounds strange to us in academia to hear Nhat Hanh say that thinking, the intellect itself, can get in the way of our direct experience of reality. For him there is a difference between mediated and unmediated realities. Hence dharma talk is like the Zen saying, 'The finger that points to the moon is not the moon.' The finger, the words, the concepts all point beyond themselves to what lies beyond the horizon of language, beyond words and concepts and notions. Likewise the interconnectedness between ourselves and the world – that is, love – lies beyond the concept of the word 'love.' Love is not simply a state of understanding, but rather the direct realization of our connection with the universe.

Love and liberation from suffering both lie in a realm beyond language; they are directly experienced and immediate – not concepts. Nhat Hanh's concern is not with gaining an intellectual understanding of love, but rather to evoke the poetic experience of it through his writing. To this end the chapters on love include love poetry and other heartfelt moments in his struggle with being in love. However, his intent is not discursive; it is not simply to discuss the issue of falling in love, nor is it simply to instruct us on Zen Buddhist epistemology. Instead he suggests through the form of the text (this alternating of chapters) that the ways in which we cling to another person when we claim to have fallen in love are similar to the ways in which we cling to words and concepts. In either case, we are prevented from directly experiencing the world around us, from being connected to it. Instead, our grasping of concepts, the *idea* of 'love,' militates against our actually realizing the very love, the very connectedness with the universe that we so desire in our lives.

There is a strong pedagogical undercurrent within the text, instructing, pointing to human liberation – living in love and freedom. For Thich Nhat Hanh, learning is not the accumulation of knowledge, but the letting go of concepts and ideas that mediate or stand in the way of our encounters with the world. In *Cultivating the Mind of Love* he writes (1996: 53–4):

> Notions and concepts can be useful if we learn how to use them. Zen master Lin Chi said, 'If you see the Buddha on your way, kill him.' He means if you have an idea of the Buddha that prevents you from having a direct experience of the Buddha, you are caught by that object of your perception, and the only way to free yourself and experience the Buddha is to kill your notion of the Buddha. This is the secret of the practice. If you hold onto an idea or a notion, you lose the chance. Learning to transcend your mental constructs of reality is an art. *Teachers have to help their students learn how not to accumulate notions.* If you are laden with notions, you will never be emancipated. Learning to look deeply to see into the true nature of things, having direct contact with reality and not just describing reality in terms of notions and concepts, is the practice.

This pericope tells us that Zen Buddhist epistemology is not anti-language, anti-word. Rather, concepts and notions can be helpful if used skillfully, if they aid our initial understanding of reality. The cautionary note is that our concepts can prevent us from direct perception of the Buddha himself. This is an interesting note in that for Buddhists, killing is prohibited. One wonders if metaphorical 'killing' is the exception to the rule. Or is there another intent here? Even the prohibition 'no killing' is itself a *notion*, and if we become infatuated, fixated with these precepts, then once again we become disconnected from our environment. Here we perceive the reality of 'no killing' through words, not through the direct experience of being connected with the universe. Hence the only way to free ourselves and experience reality is to kill all notions, including the notion 'to kill all notions.' This task can become painfully regressive as we willfully attempt to extinguish the meta-dialogues in our heads telling us to be silent.

Though concepts and notions serve a pedagogical function, to teach and instruct, it is wrong to view reality as equivalent to signs – to notions and concepts. In an earlier work, Nhat Hanh writes (1995: 140):

the ultimate dimension of reality has nothing to do with concepts. It is not just absolute reality that cannot be talked about. Nothing can be conceived or talked about. Take, for instance, a glass of apple juice. You cannot talk about apple juice to someone who has never tasted it. No matter what you say, the other person will not have the true experience of apple juice. Things cannot be described by concepts and words. They can only be encountered by direct experience.

For Nhat Hanh, the idea is for us to use concepts and notions skillfully, without getting caught by them. To explain his point he refers to Wittgenstein's famous analogy of language as a 'ladder.' That is, we can use words to climb to a certain point, and when we arrive, we no longer need the ladder. Thich Nhat Hanh refers to Buddha's teachings as a 'raft,' to remind us that all teachings are constructs that aid us to 'cross' various rivers of life. After the crossing, we must learn to 'let go' of all true teachings of the Buddha (and not to mention all teachings that are not true). There is more to the universe than can be captured in conceptual, intellectual understanding.

Indeed, educational theorist Dwayne Huebner writes of the 'spirit' as that sense of 'moreness' found in everyday life, arguing that language paradoxically communicates 'more' than it is able to express. Huebner elaborates this point in his article 'Education and Spirituality' (1996: 15–16):

> there is more than we know, can know, ever will know. It is this 'moreness' that takes us by surprise when we are at the edge and the end of our knowing … Call it what you will … One knows of that presence, that 'moreness,' when known resources fail and somehow we go beyond what we were and are and become something different, something new … It is this very 'moreness' that can be identified with the 'spirit' and the 'spiritual.' Spirit is that which transcends the known, the expected, even the ego and the self. It is the source of hope. It is manifested through love and the waiting expectation that accompanies love.

Huebner's sense of the spiritual-as-moreness suggests the possibility of there being more to heaven and earth, in a manner of speaking, than language; that the spirit exists as a moment of waiting, patiently, possibly in silence. Indeed, Huebner suggests that the spirit transcends knowledge, in that we begin to live by love and faith. Living by love and faith does not negate knowledge or communication; rather this is a moment of transcendent living: living beyond the expectations of 'even the ego and the self,' as Huebner puts it. For as soon as we claim to know something, there is always something more and unexpected that can occur, something that lies beyond our horizon of awareness – beyond, possibly, language.

From Huebner and Nhat Hanh we learn that living fully as human beings entails a letting go of conceptual frameworks to such an extent that we become able to experience that sense of 'moreness' in everyday life.

However, while the 'spiritual' discussions reflected in such work as theirs move towards this letting go of concepts, trends within the educational research community reflect a move towards the greater accumulation of ideas, as something to be possessed, as cultural capital to be exchanged within the marketplace of the university. A simple observation here: while nothing is monolithic, I can bear witness that life in the academy is at times far from peaceful, particularly with regard to the politics connected with 'turf issues.' Challenge someone's epistemology, ideology, or words and sparks are likely to fly, even if the challenges are initially intended to be helpful!

Now my point is not to belabor conflicts in the academy; rather to make the observation that as academics, we spend a good deal of time writing and speaking. Words and ideas are the basic tools of the trade, so to speak. Our words perform many functions, among which they are a form of capital which we use as a means to establish our place in the academic hierarchy, to publish or perish, to merit pay increases, et cetera. We therefore invest much time, effort, and personal sacrifice in our writing and our thinking, not only to connect with others but also to satisfy the conditions of our job. It is no great mystery that we can become protective of what we write or say.

But it is one thing to become protective, to guard against unfair attacks, and yet another to become infatuated with our words, meaning that, to a certain degree, we have fallen in love with them. Our words and ideas take on the role of a loved one; they are our lovers. We love our words, which is fine; they are our creations. However, the pathology occurs when we cling to them like a jealous lover, reifying them to such an extent that it becomes virtually impossible for us to see, hear, or touch ourselves or others. Nhat Hanh writes (1996: 41–2):

> Because of our tendency to use notions and concepts to grasp reality, we cannot touch reality as it is. We construct an image of reality that does not coincide with reality itself ... In Western philosophy the term 'being-in-itself' is very close to the Buddhist term 'suchness,' reality as it is, free from conceptions or grasping. You cannot grasp it, because grasping reality with concepts and notions is like catching space with a net.

Likewise, as Delpit observed (1995: xiv):

> we educators set out to teach, but how can we reach the worlds of others, when we don't even know they exist? Indeed, many of us don't even realize that our own worlds exist only in our heads and in the cultural institutions we have built to support them.

When we are seduced by our own words, we hear what we want to hear and see what we want to see; reality is in our heads.

This sense of how epistemologies, ways of knowing, can disconnect us from each other within the academic context of teacher education is further illustrated by some of the arguments presented in Jennifer Gore's book *The Struggle for Pedagogies* (1993). Gore uses a Foucault-style analysis to try to come to terms with the ways in which so-called progressive pedagogies, specifically derived from Marxist and feminist thought, have generated their own hierarchies within the academy. That is, here we have progressive thought used against itself to create yet another repressive structure in schooling. Gore underscores Foucault's claim that all knowledge can become dangerous – that is, knowledge can be used, transformed, transmuted, for strategic purposes within a field of power. Simply to evoke Marxist or feminist (or Buddhist) thought provides no immunity against using these notions or concepts for larger political purposes or advantages. For Gore (and for Foucault) there is therefore no such thing as inherently liberating pedagogical thought; knowledge comes without fixed guarantees. Hence questions of liberation must be addressed by looking at the larger political picture and how a specific knowledge form is circulated, say, within the school. Here Gore comes very close to Nhat Hanh's concern about being attached to concepts or notions as a fixed sort of truth – the Law. She writes (1993: 11):

> My concern is that when discourses of critical or feminist pedagogy present themselves as fixed, or final, or 'founded' form, that form soon protects them from rethinking and change. It turns what was once 'critical' in their work into a kind of norm or law – a final truth, a final emancipation … As a teacher educator practicing critical and feminist pedagogy, I wanted to believe that what I am doing is right – it is certainly more difficult to live with uncertainty.

It is worth noting how Gore's desire to do right, to have certainty in one's actions, especially when teaching future teachers about other people's children, can lead to the constitution of laws, norms, final truths that again act as laws controlling what we see, hear, and understand.

Indeed, Delpit, Nhat Hanh, and Gore all suggest that embedded in our notions of liberating epistemologies there is simultaneously a double play at work in our thinking. Namely, liberation, from a commonsense perspective, implies a freedom from suffering, from oppression. And at the same time this movement away from suffering implies a sort of certainty – that is, liberation will cure suffering. More specifically, if for example we employ a Marxist or feminist epistemology, the intention is that we shall be working towards alleviating social and economic injustices; these epistemologies promise to cure injustice. Along similar lines of thinking, we can say that Zen Buddhism promises to cure suffering by transcending the cycle of birth and death.

Notice how uncertainty itself can become normalized, static, once we begin to tack on to liberation epistemologies a *telos* – a specific grand purpose – and that *telos* is to cure. And notice further, once a liberation epistemology becomes a cure, then like some precious drug it becomes possible to barter this cure as a possession within current relations of power. So, for example, we, the teachers of teachers, may become experts on liberation, on how to cure suffering; as such we may gain prominence in society, earn a healthy salary, gain respect from our peers and, in short, live a comfortable, secure (certain!) lifestyle. What began for us as a 'raft' to cross the river of suffering becomes a comfortable upper-middle-class lifestyle. To this point, J. Krishnamurti writes (1953: 11), 'if we are being educated only to be scientists, to be scholars wedded to books, or specialists *addicted* to knowledge, then we shall be contributing to the destruction and misery of the world.' The point of education is to humanize the world, not simply to study it.

When liberating epistemologies become cures, it is possible, within the current play of capitalist power relations, to become addicted to that knowledge – to become dependent not only on the content of knowledge, but also on the contextual lifestyle that can be construed around the 'expert' who possesses that cure. Here liberation becomes its own enemy. If you meet 'liberation' on the street, kill it!

So liberation can be an addicting epistemology. However, as Eve Sedgwick notes, within the contemporary play of signifiers, any activity can be labeled as addicting. 'What is startling,' Sedgwick writes (1993: 132), 'is the rapidity with which it has now become commonplace that, precisely, any substance, any behavior, even any affect may be pathologized as addictive.' We may have come to the point in American culture where liberation epistemologies and theologies in postmodern societies embrace Jacques Derrida's (1995) notion of the *pharmakon*. That is, within the context of a consumer-oriented society it becomes difficult to distinguish liberation, the cure, from liberation, the poison.

Consider the way in which 'media Buddhism' appears to consume older, more 'authentic' notions; even for Buddhism, in the postmodern culture of media America the line between remedy and poison is thinly drawn. Consider some recent American media rage over Buddhism. In an October 1997 issue of *Time* magazine, Buddhism hit the cover page. The article refers to two current movies, *Seven Years in Tibet* and *Kundun*. We are told of the plight of Tibetans in China. Of how celebrities are using money and influence to push for Tibetan independence. Of how Zen Buddhists in San Francisco run two well-respected AIDS hospices. Of how Thich Nhat Hanh's book, *Living Buddha, Living Christ* has sold over 100,000 hardcover copies. Of how large numbers of middle Americans meditate, chant, and observe Buddhist teachings. In short, the article tells how Buddhism is once again 'fashionable.' (Buddhism was fashionable both at the turn of the century and in the 1950s with the Beat movement.) These efforts to help others are of course commendable; but the postmodern moment here lies in the way in which the media, within a capitalist discourse, are framing Buddhism as a 'phenomenon.'

Indeed, it is becoming increasingly difficult to distinguish Thich Nhat Hanh the engaged Buddhist monk, who struggled to bring peace to

Vietnam, from Thich Nhat Hanh the media image in *Time* magazine. As boundaries blur, the multiplex of possibilities makes one dizzy, for everything has the potential to become infused with meaning, even in locations once thought of as devoid of spirit, such as suburban shopping malls.

As Thich Nhat Hanh suggests, words and concepts need to be used skillfully and without attachment, for the point that must be stressed is that all concepts can aid as well as obscure in our journeys to connect with others. Indeed, as Eve Sedgwick points out, even 'addiction' can become its own poison, a mode of hegemonic thinking, a label used to contain, control the behaviors of others. Here Sedgwick and Nhat Hanh come very close to contemporary postmodern thought on language and literacy. Knoblauch and Brannon write of language as an endless play of signifiers, 'proliferating meanings without ever delivering on the promise that they point to something beyond the tangles of language' (1993: 167). Language is conceived as a sort of 'leaky' system, forever composing and subverting the world, a sort of 'joker' who seems at first glance to be stable, to have a presence, but turns out under scrutiny to be a tricky, mysterious, slippery character. If, for instance, we attempt to pin down the meaning of a term, instead of coming up with a single definition we are referred to yet more terms. Language is utterly interdependent: each word is related to another to such a degree that it is virtually impossible to understand one word without understanding the larger sociolinguistic universe of which it is a part. The interdependence of the system is what makes it difficult to experience the 'moreness' that lies beyond this universe.

And so? What does all this mean for us, the teachers of teachers within the context of the academy? It means that language, words and concepts, are all tricky. Language can illuminate as well as conceal. Nothing new here! But it also means that we academics tend to place a great deal of import on language, so great as to become addicted to our own words. When we become addicted, we become dependent on our words, fixated by them, and when we are thus fixated we no longer experience others and their humanity afresh. Paradoxically, also, we no longer experience our words as wondrous. The cure always has the potential to poison; the language that reveals can also blind us to others. Indeed, Delpit writes, 'the answers, I believe, lie not in a proliferation of new reform programs but in some basic understanding of who we are and how we are connected and disconnected from one another' (1995: xv). And who are we? Though as humans we are constituted within language, Nhat Hanh, Huebner, and Delpit remind us that there is always 'more' to reality and to how we are connected to one another and the world. So the answer to many educational problems is probably not more reforms, if by 'reforms' we mean more technical solutions, more concepts that obscure reality. Rather, it is about gaining a basic realization of what it means to be human and to share the earth with others in a loving way.

Thich Nhat Hanh reminds us of the Buddhist notion of 'sangha.' The Sangha is a Buddhist community, in which 'the Sangha contains the Buddha and the Dharma. A good teacher is important, but sisters and brothers in practices are the main ingredient for success. You cannot achieve enlightenment by locking yourself in a room' (1996: 71). Sangha is about a community in common pursuit; it is about right relationship with oneself and the world. Whether or not we are in a postmodern era, where liberating epistemologies such as Zen can be both cure and food for media consumption, does not alter Nhat Hanh's assertion that we must look beyond the words and concepts, beyond the Law, to our first love and make "eye-to-eye" contact with the world around us if there is to be a significant transformation in the quality of our teaching, learning, and living.

Note

1   This essay originally appeared in *Education Researcher*, December 1998.

References

Delpit, L. (1995) *Other People's Children*, New York: New Press.

Derrida, J. (1995) 'The Rhetoric of Drugs' in E. Weber (ed.) *Points ... Interviews 1974–1994*, Stanford: Stanford University Press.

Gore, J. (1993) *The Struggle for Pedagogies*, New York: Routledge.

Huebner, D. (1996) 'Education and Spirituality,' *Journal of Curriculum Theorizing*, 11(2): 13–34.

Knoblauch, C. H. and Brannon, Lil (1993) *Critical Teaching and the Idea of Literacy*, Portsmouth: Boynton/Cook Publishers.

Krishnamurti, J. (1953) *Education and the Significance of Life*, New York: Harper & Row.

Nhat Hanh, T. (1993) *Interbeing*, Berkeley: Parallax Press.

—— (1995) *Living Buddha, Living Christ*, New York: Riverhead Books.

—— (1996) *Cultivating the Mind of Love*, Berkeley: Parallax Press.

Sedgwick, E. (1993) *Tendencies*, Durham: Duke University Press.

Afterword

The Politics of Labeling in a Conservative Age

Michael W. Apple

One of the most insightful American sociologists of the century – Erving Goffman – declared in 1961 that it was very important to pay critical attention to the labels that institutions employ to deal with their 'clients.' Even though the labeling process is supposedly there to help people, it is shot through with moral meanings and significances that often have negative effects. Labels too often function to confer a lesser status on those labeled. They create categories of deviance that have an essentializing quality to them. The person receiving the label is 'this and *only* this.' Goffman saw that the person to whom the 'deviant' label is applied is usually viewed as morally inferior, and her or his 'condition' or behavior is quite often interpreted as evidence of her or his 'moral culpability.' 'Different,' then, means 'inferior' (Goffman 1961).

For students this is especially dangerous, since although reforms are put in place to 'help' students, these reforms may have hidden contradictions. They may enable schools themselves to participate in the creation and use of categories that differentially stratify students in terms of class, race, gender, 'ability,' and so on. The 'helping' language of schools at times makes it hard to see the very real hidden social effects of the social and psychological labels commonsensically used by educators (Apple 1990).

These points about labeling, social stratification, and the hidden effects of school reforms are significant in general. However, they become of even greater import during times of crisis and when theories of what schooling is for and who it will benefit most are being reconstructed in dangerous ways. This situation is now upon us. And we cannot understand what this means for the politics of labeling unless we directly situate it in the larger politics of school reforms currently under way.

Schooling and the conservative restoration

We have entered a period of reaction in education. Our educational institutions are seen as total failures. High drop-out rates, a decline in 'functional literacy,' a loss of standards and discipline, the failure to teach 'real knowledge' and economically useful skills, poor scores on standardized tests, and more – all of these are charges leveled at schools. And all of these, we are told, have led to declining economic productivity, unemployment, poverty, a loss of international competitiveness, and so on. Return to a 'common culture,' make schools more efficient, more responsive to the private sector – do this and our problems will be solved.

Behind all this rhetoric is an attack on egalitarian norms and values. Though hidden in the rhetorical flourishes of the critics, in essence 'too much democracy' – both cultural and political – is seen as one of the major causes of 'our' declining economy and culture. Similar tendencies are quite visible in other countries. The extent of the reaction is captured in the words of Kenneth Baker, former British secretary of education and science in the Thatcher government, who evaluated nearly a decade of rightist efforts in education in the words 'The age of egalitarianism is over' (Arnot 1990). He was speaking decidedly positively, not negatively.

The threat to egalitarian ideals that these attacks represent is not usually made quite this explicitly, since they are often couched in the discourse of 'improving' competitiveness, jobs, standards, and quality in an educational system that is seen as being in total crisis.

It would be simplistic, however, to interpret what is happening as no more than the result of efforts by dominant economic elites to impose their will on education. Many of these attacks do represent attempts to reintegrate education into an economic agenda. Yet they cannot be fully reduced to that, nor to being only about the economy. Cultural struggles and struggles over race and gender coincide with class alliances and class power.

Education is a site of struggle and compromise. It also serves as a proxy for larger battles over what our institutions should do, whom they should serve, and who should make these decisions. And yet by itself it is one of the major arenas in which resources, power, and ideology specific to policy, finance, curriculum, pedagogy, and evaluation in education are worked through. Thus, education is both cause and effect, determining and determined. No one essay could hope to give a complete picture of this complexity. What I hope to do instead is to provide an outline of some of the major tensions surrounding education and the politics of labeling in the United States as the country moves in conservative directions.

A key word here is 'directions.' The plural is crucial to my arguments, since there are multiple and at times contradictory tendencies within the rightist turn.

While my focus will largely be internal, it is impossible to understand current educational policy in the United States without placing it in its international context. Though some of these other nations are still mired in an economic crisis, we are nervous: behind our own stress on higher standards, more rigorous testing, education for employment, a much closer relationship between education and the economy in general, and so on, lies the fear of losing in international competition and the loss of jobs and money to Japan and, increasingly, the 'Asian Tiger' economies, to Mexico and elsewhere. In the same way, the equally evident pressure in the United States to reinstall a (selective) vision of a common culture, to place more importance on the 'Western tradition,' on religion, on the English language, and similar emphases are all deeply connected to cultural fears about Latin America, Africa, and Asia. This context provides a backdrop for my discussion.

The rightward turn – what I have elsewhere called the *conservative restoration* (Apple 1996, 2000) – has been the result of the successful struggle by the right to form a broad-based alliance. Part of the reason why this new alliance has succeeded so well is that it has been able to win the battle over common sense. That is, it has creatively stitched together different social tendencies and commitments and has organized them under its own general leadership in issues dealing with social welfare, culture, the economy and, as we shall see in this essay, education. Its aim in educational and social policy is what might best be described as 'conservative modernization' (Dale 1989b).[1]

There are four major elements within this alliance. Each has its own relatively autonomous history and dynamics; but each has also been sutured into the more general conservative movement. These elements include neo-liberals, neo-conservatives, authoritarian populists, and a particular fraction of the upwardly mobile new middle class. I shall pay particular attention to the first two of these groups here since they – especially the neo-liberals – are currently in leadership in this alliance to 'reform' education. However, in no way do I want to dismiss the power of the latter two groups.

Neo-liberals

Neo-liberals are the most powerful element within the conservative restoration. They are guided by a vision of the weak state. Thus, what is private is necessarily good and what is public is necessarily bad. Public institutions such as schools are 'black holes' into which money is poured – and then seemingly disappears – but which do not provide anywhere near adequate results. For neo-liberals, there is one form of rationality that is more powerful than any other – economic rationality. Efficiency and an 'ethic' of cost–benefit analysis are the dominant norms. All people are to act in ways that maximize their own personal benefits. Indeed, behind this position is an empirical claim that this is how *all* rational actors act. Yet rather than being a neutral description of the world of social motivation, this is actually a construction of the world around the valuative characteristics of an efficiently acquisitive class type (Apple 1996; Honderich 1990).

Underpinning this position is a vision of students as human capital. In the neo-liberal view, the world, primarily an economic world, is intensely competitive, and students – as future workers – must be given the requisite skills and dispositions to compete efficiently and effectively.[2] Students who are not seen as important to these economic goals are 'inferior products' and are not worth large expenses. Further, any money spent on schools that is not directly related to these economic goals is suspect. In fact as 'black holes,' schools and other public services, as currently organized and controlled, waste economic resources that should go into private enterprise. Thus, not only are public schools failing our children as future workers, but like nearly all public institutions they are sucking the financial life out of this society. Partly this is the result of 'producer capture.' Schools are built for teachers and state bureaucrats, not 'consumers.' They respond to the demands of professionals and other selfish state workers, not to those of the consumers who rely on them.

The idea of the 'consumer' is crucial here. For neo-liberals, the world in essence is a vast supermarket. 'Consumer choice' is the guarantor of democracy. In effect, education is seen as simply one more product, like bread, cars, and television (see Apple 1990). By turning it over to the market through voucher and choice plans, education will become largely self-regulating. Thus, democracy is turned over to consumption practices. In these plans, the ideal of the citizen is that of the purchaser. The ideological effects of this are momentous. Rather than democracy being a *political* concept, it is transformed into a wholly *economic* concept. The message of such policies is one of what might best be called 'arithmetical particularism', in which the unattached individual – as a consumer – is deraced, declassed, and degendered (see Ball 1994; Apple 1996).

The metaphors of the consumer and the supermarket are actually quite apposite here. In real life, there are indeed individuals who can go into supermarkets and choose among a vast array of similar or diverse products, just as there are those who can only engage in what can best be called 'postmodern' consumption – who stand outside the supermarket and can only consume the image.

The entire project of neo-liberalism is connected to a larger process of exporting blame for the decisions of dominant groups away from these groups on to the state and on to poor people (Apple 1995). After all, it was not the government who made the decisions to engage in capital flight and to move factories to those nations that have weak or no unions, fewer environmental regulations, and repressive governments. And it was not working-class and poor communities that chose to lose those jobs and factories, with the concomitant loss of hope – and the collapse of schools and communities into crisis – that were among the results of these decisions. And it was neither of them who chose to lay off millions of workers – many of whom had done rather well in school – due to mergers and leveraged buy-outs.

With their emphasis on the consumer rather than the producer, neo-liberal policies need also to be seen as part of a more extensive attack on government employees. In education in particular, they constitute an offensive against teacher unions who are seen to be much too powerful and much too costly. While perhaps not conscious, this needs to be interpreted as part of a longer history of attacks on women's labor, since the vast majority of teachers in the United States – as in so many other nations – are women (Apple 1988).

There are varied policy initiatives that have emerged from the neo-liberal segments of the new hegemonic alliance. Most have centered around either creating closer linkages between education and the economy, or placing schools themselves into the market. The former is represented by widespread proposals for 'school to work' and 'education for employment' programs, and by vigorous cost-cutting attacks on the 'bloated state.' The latter is no less widespread and is becoming increasingly powerful. It is represented by both national and state-by-state proposals for voucher and choice programs (Chubb and Moe 1990). These include providing public money for private and religious schools (although these are highly contested proposals). Behind this is a plan to subject schools to the discipline of market competition. Such 'quasi-market solutions' are among the most divisive and hotly debated policy issues in the entire nation, with a close watch currently being kept on important pending court cases concerning funding for private and/or religious schools through voucher mechanisms (see Wells 1993; Smith and Meier 1995; Henig 1994).

Some proponents of 'choice' argue that only enhanced parental 'voice' and choice will provide a chance for 'educational salvation' for minority parents and children (Whitty 1997; see also Chubb and Moe 1990). Moe, for instance (quoted in Whitty 1997: 17), claims that the best hope for the poor to gain the right 'to leave bad schools and seek out good ones' is through an 'unorthodox alliance.' Only by allying themselves with Republicans and business – the most powerful groups supposedly willing to transform the system – can the poor succeed.

There is, however, increasing empirical evidence that the development of 'quasi-markets' in education has led to the exacerbation of existing social divisions surrounding class, race, and 'ability.' There are now increasingly convincing arguments that while the supposed overt goal of voucher and choice plans is to give poor people the right to exit public schools, among the ultimate long-term effects of such plans may be an increase in 'white flight' from public schools into private and religious schools, and the creation of conditions in which affluent white parents may refuse to pay taxes to support public schools that are suffering more and more from the debilitating effects of the fiscal crisis of the state. The end result is more educational apartheid, not less (Apple 1996). That many of these private schools do not have the same obligation as the public schools do to teach students of various needs and handicapping conditions (and may not want to admit such students because they may lower the overall test scores of the school), means that the implications for these students is significant as well.

In his own review of evidence from the US experience, Whitty argues that while advocates of choice assume that competition will enhance the efficiency and responsiveness of schools, as well as giving disadvantaged children opportunities that they currently do not have, this may be a false hope.

These hopes are not now being realized and are unlikely to be realized in the future 'in the context of broader policies that do nothing to challenge deeper social and cultural inequalities' (1997: 58). As Whitty goes on to say (*ibid.*): 'Atomized decision-making in a highly stratified society may appear to give everyone equal opportunities but transforming responsibility for decision-making from the public to the private sphere can actually reduce the scope for collective action to improve the quality of education for all.'

This position is ratified by Henig (1994: 222):

> the sad irony of the current education reform movement is that, through over-identification with school choice proposals, the healthy impulse to consider radical reforms to address social problems may be channeled into initiatives that further erode the potential for collective deliberation and collective response.

When this is coupled with the fact that such neo-liberal policies in practice may reproduce traditional hierarchies of class, race, gender, and 'ability,' this should give us serious pause (see Apple 1996; Whitty 1997; Whitty *et al.* 1998).

There is a second variant of neo-liberalism. This one *is* willing to spend more state and/or private money on schools, if and only if schools meet the needs expressed by capital. Thus, resources are made available for 'reforms' and policies that further connect the education system to the project of making our economy more competitive. Two examples can provide a glimpse of this position. First, in a number of states, legislation has been passed that directs schools and universities to make closer links between education and the business community. In the state of Wisconsin, for instance, all teacher education programs must include identifiable experiences on 'education for employment' for all of its future teachers; and all teaching in the public elementary, middle, and secondary schools of the state must include elements of education for employment in its formal curricula.[3]

The second example is seemingly less consequential, but in reality it is a powerful statement of the reintegration of educational policy and practice into the ideological agenda of neo-liberalism. I am referring here to Channel One, a for-profit television network that is now broadcast into schools (many of which are financially hard pressed, given the fiscal crisis), enrolling over 40 percent of all middle and secondary school students in the nation. In this 'reform,' schools are offered a 'free' satellite dish, two VCRs, and television monitors for each of their classrooms by a private media corporation. They are also offered a free news broadcast for these students. In return for the equipment and the news, all participating schools must sign a three- to five-year contract guaranteeing that their students will watch Channel One every day (Apple 2000).

This sounds relatively benign. However, not only is the technology 'hard wired' so that *only* Channel One can be received, but broadcast along with the news are *mandatory advertisements* for major fast food, athletic wear, and other corporations that students – by contract – must also watch. Students, in essence, are sold as a captive audience to corporations. Since, by law, these students must be in schools, the US is one of the first nations in the world to consciously allow its youth to be sold as commodities to those many corporations willing to pay the high price of advertising on Channel One to get a guaranteed (captive) audience.[4] Thus, under a number of variants of neo-liberalism not only are schools transformed into market commodities, but so too now are our children (Apple 2000; see also Molnar 1996).

As I noted, the attractiveness of conservative restorational politics in education rests in large part on major shifts in our common sense – about what democracy is, about whether we see ourselves as possessive individuals ('consumers'), and ultimately about how we see the market working. Underlying neo-liberal policies in education and neo-liberal social policies in general is a faith in the essential fairness and justice of markets. Markets will ultimately distribute resources efficiently and fairly according to effort. They will ultimately create jobs for all who want them. They are the best possible mechanism to ensure a better future for all citizens (that is, all consumers).

We must of course ask what this economy that reigns supreme in neo-liberal positions actually looks like. In the positive picture that neo-liberals paint, if we would only set the market loose on our schools and children, then technologically advanced jobs would soon replace the drudgery and the under- and unemployment that so many people now experience. But the reality is something else again. As I demonstrate in a much more complete analysis in *Cultural Politics and Education* (Apple 1996: 68–90), markets are as powerfully destructive in people's lives as they are productive.

Let us take as a case in point: the paid labor market, to which neo-liberals want us to attach so much of the education system. Even with the growth in proportion in high-tech-related jobs, the kinds of work that are and will be increasingly available to a large portion of the American population will not be highly skilled, technically elegant positions. Just the opposite: the paid labor market will increasingly be dominated by low-paying, repetitive work in the retail, trade, and service sector. This is made strikingly clear by one fact. There will be more cashier jobs created by the year 2005 than jobs for computer scientists, systems analysts, physical therapists, operations analysts, and radiology technicians *combined*. In fact, it is projected that 95 percent of all new positions will be found in the service sector. This sector broadly includes personal care, home health aides, social workers (many of whom are now losing their jobs because of cutbacks in social spending), hotel and lodging workers, restaurant employees, transportation workers, and business and clerical services. Further, of the top ten individual occupations that will account for the most job growth in the next ten years, eight are: retail salespersons, cashiers, office clerks, truck-drivers, waitresses/waiters, nursing aides/orderlies, food preparation workers, and janitors. It is obvious that the majority of these positions do not require high levels of education. Many of them are low-paid, non-unionized and part-time, with low or no benefits.

And many are dramatically linked to, and often exacerbate, the existing race, gender, and class divisions of labor (Apple 1996). This is the emerging economy we face, not the overly romantic picture painted by neo-liberals who urge us to trust the market.

Neo-liberals argue that making the market the ultimate arbiter of social worthiness will eliminate politics and its accompanying irrationality from our educational and social decisions. Efficiency and cost–benefit analysis will be the engines of social and educational transformation. Yet among the ultimate effects of such 'economizing' and 'depoliticizing' strategies is actually to make it ever harder to interrupt the growing inequalities in resources and power that so deeply characterize this society. Nancy Fraser illuminates the process in the following way (1989: 168):

> In male dominated capitalist societies, what is 'political' is normally defined contrastively against what is 'economic' and what is 'domestic' or 'personal.' Here, then, we can identify two principal sets of institutions that depoliticize social discourses: they are, first, domestic institutions, especially the normative domestic form, namely the modern restricted male-headed nuclear family; and, second, official economic capitalist system institutions, especially paid workplaces, markets, credit mechanisms, and 'private' enterprises and corporations. Domestic institutions depoliticize certain matters by personalizing and/or familializing them; they cast these as private-domestic or personal-familial matters in contradistinction to public, political matters. Official economic capitalist system institutions, on the other hand, depoliticize certain matters by economizing them; the issues in question here are cast as impersonal market imperatives, or as 'private' ownership prerogatives, or as technical problems for managers and planners, all in contradistinction to political matters. In both cases, the result is a foreshortening of chains of in-order-to relations for interpreting people's needs; interpretive chains are truncated and prevented from spilling across the boundaries separating the 'domestic' and the 'economic' from the political.

For Fraser, this very process of depoliticization makes it very difficult for the needs of those with less economic, political, and cultural power to be accurately heard and acted upon in ways that deal with the true depth of the problem, because of what happens when 'needs discourses' get retranslated into both market talk and 'privately' driven policies.

For our purposes here, we can talk about two major kinds of needs discourses. There are first *oppositional* forms of needs talk. They arise when needs are politicized from below and are part of the crystallization of new oppositional identities on the part of subordinated social groups. What was once seen as largely a 'private' matter is now placed into the larger political arena. Sexual harassment, race and sex segregation in paid labor, and affirmative action policies in educational and economic institutions provide examples of 'private' issues that have now spilled over and can no longer be confined to the 'domestic' sphere (Fraser 1989: 172).[5]

A second kind of needs discourse is what might be called *reprivatization* discourses. They emerge as a response to the newly emergent oppositional forms and try to press these forms back into the 'private' or the 'domestic' arena. They are often aimed at dismantling or cutting back social services, deregulating 'private' enterprise, or stopping what are seen as 'runaway needs.' Thus, reprivatizers may attempt to keep issues such as, say, domestic battery from spilling over into overt political discourse and will seek to define it as purely a family matter. Or they will argue that the closing of a factory is not a political question, but instead is an 'unimpeachable prerogative of private ownership or an unassailable imperative of an impersonal market mechanism' (Fraser 1989: 172). In each of these cases the task is to contest the possible breakout of runaway needs, while depoliticizing the issues.

In educational policy in the United States there are a number of clear examples of these processes. In the state of California, for instance, a recent binding referendum that prohibited the use of affirmative action policies in state government, in university admission policies, and so on was passed overwhelmingly as 'reprivatizers' spent an exceptional amount of money on an advertising campaign that labeled such policies as 'out of control' and as improper government intervention into decisions involving 'individual merit.'[6] Voucher plans in education – where contentious issues surrounding whose knowledge should be taught, who should control school policy and practice, and how schools should be financed are all left to the market to decide – offer another prime example of such attempts at 'depoliticizing' educational needs. The claim that too much money is being spent on children in 'special education' and that this is both draining resources and wasting taxpayers' money on such students – with its implication of 'biological inferiority' (see Selden 1999) – once again shows how the needs of the private sector take precedence over social needs related to general and individual well-being. All of these show the emerging power of reprivatizing discourses.

A distinction that is useful here in understanding what is happening in these cases is that between 'value' and 'sense' legitimation (Dale 1989a). Each signifies a different strategy by which powerful groups or states legitimate their authority. In the first (value) strategy, legitimation is accomplished by actually giving people what may have been promised. Thus, the social democratic state may provide social services for the population in return for continued support. That the state will do this is often the result of oppositional discourses gaining more power in the social arena and having more power to redefine the border between public and private.

In the second (sense) strategy, rather than providing people with policies that meet the needs they have expressed, states and/or dominant groups attempt to *change the very meaning* of the sense of social need into something that is very different. Thus, if less powerful people call for 'more democracy' and for a more responsive state (for instance, for sufficient money for a serious and responsive education for children who are labeled as in need of 'special services'), the task is not to give 'value' that meets this demand, especially when it may lead to runaway needs. Rather, the task is to change what actually counts as 'democracy.' In the case of neo-liberal policies, democracy is now redefined as guaranteeing choice in an unfettered market. In essence, the state withdraws. The extent of acceptance of such transformations of needs and needs discourses shows the success of the reprivatizers in redefining the borders between public and private, and demonstrates how a people's common sense can be shifted in conservative directions during a time of economic and ideological crisis.

Neo-conservatism

While neo-liberals are largely in leadership in the conservative alliance, the second major element within the new alliance is neo-conservatism. However, whereas neo-liberal emphasis is on the weak state, neo-conservatives are usually guided by a vision of the strong state. This is especially true surrounding issues of knowledge, values, and the body. And whereas neo-liberalism may be seen as based in what Raymond Williams would call an 'emergent' ideological assemblage, neo-conservatism is grounded in 'residual' forms (Williams 1977); it is mainly, though not totally, based in a romantic appraisal of the past, past in which 'real knowledge' and morality reigned supreme, where people 'knew their place,' and where stable communities guided by a natural order protected us from the ravages of society (see Apple 1996; Hunter 1988).

Among the policies being proposed under this ideological position are national curricula, national testing, a 'return' to higher standards, a revivification of the 'Western tradition,' and patriotism. Yet underlying some of the neo-conservative thrust in education and in social policy in general is not just a call for 'return.' Behind it as well – and this is essential – is a fear of the 'other.' This is expressed in its support for a standardized national curriculum, its attacks on bilingualism and multiculturalism, and its insistent call for raising standards (see for example Hirsch 1996).

That the neo-conservative emphasis on a return to traditional values and 'morality' has struck a responsive chord can be seen in the fact that among the best-selling books in the nation has been William Bennett's *The Book of Virtues* (1994). Bennett, a former secretary of education in a conservative Republican administration, has argued that, for too long a period of time, 'we have stopped doing the right things [and] allowed an assault on intellectual and moral standards.' In opposition to this, we need 'a renewed commitment to excellence, character, and fundamentals' (1988: 8–10). Bennett's 1994 book aims at providing 'moral tales' for children to 'restore' a commitment to 'traditional virtues' such as patriotism, honesty, moral character, and entrepreneurial spirit. Not only have such positions entered the common sense of society in quite influential ways, but they have provided part of the driving force behind the movement toward 'charter' schools. These are schools that have individual charters that allow them to opt out of most state requirements and develop curricula based on the wishes of their clientele (see Whitty 1997). While in theory there is much to commend such policies, all too many charter schools have become ways through which conservative religious activists and others gain public funding for schools that would otherwise be prohibited such support.

Behind much of this is a clear sense of loss – a loss of faith, of imagined communities, of a nearly pastoral vision of like-minded people who shared norms and values and in which the 'Western tradition' reigned supreme. It is more than a little similar to Mary Douglas's discussion of purity and danger, in which what was imagined to exist is sacred and 'pollution' is feared above all else (Douglas 1966). We/they binary oppositions dominate this discourse and the culture of *the other* is to be feared.

This sense of cultural pollution can be seen in the increasingly virulent attacks on multiculturalism, itself a very broad category that combines multiple political and cultural positions (see McCarthy and Crichlow 1994): in attacks on the offering of schooling or any other social benefits to the children of 'illegal' immigrants and even in some cases to the children of legal immigrants; in the conservative English-only movement and the definitions of 'ability' and literacy that underpin it; and in the equally conservative attempts to reorient curricula and textbooks toward a particular construction of the Western tradition.

In this regard, neo-conservatives mourn the 'decline' of the traditional curriculum and of the history, literature, and values it is said to have represented. Behind this is a set of historical assumptions about 'tradition,' about the existence of a social consensus over what should count as legitimate knowledge (Apple 1990), and about cultural superiority. Yet it is crucial to remember that the 'traditional' curriculum whose decline is lamented so fervently by neo-conservative critics 'ignored most of the groups that compose the American population, whether they were from Africa, Europe, Asia, Central and South America, or from indigenous North American peoples' (Levine 1996: 20). Its primary and often exclusive focus was on quite a narrow spectrum of those people who came from a small number of northern and western European nations, in spite of the fact that the cultures and histories represented in the United States were 'forged out of a much larger and more diverse complex of peoples and societies' (*ibid.*). The mores and cultures of this narrow spectrum were seen as archetypes of 'tradition' for everyone. They were not simply taught, but taught as superior to every other set of mores and culture.

As Lawrence Levine reminds us, the nostalgic yearnings of neo-conservatives are fueled by a selective and faulty sense of history. The canon and the curriculum have never been static. They have always been in a constant process of revision, 'with irate defenders insisting, as they still do, that change would bring with it instant decline' (Levine 1996: 15; see also Apple 1990, Kliebard 1995). Indeed, even the inclusion of such 'classics' as Shakespeare within the curriculum of schools in the United States came about only after prolonged and intense battles, equals of the divisive debates over whose knowledge should be taught today. Thus, Levine notes that when neo-conservative cultural critics ask for a 'return' to a 'common culture' and 'tradition,' they are oversimplifying to the point of distortion. What is happening in terms of the expansion and alteration of official knowledge in schools and universities today

> is by no means out of the ordinary; certainly it is not a radical departure from the patterns that have marked the history of [education] – constant and often controversial expansion and alteration of curricula and canons and incessant struggle over the nature of that expansion and alteration.
>
> (Levine 1996: 15).

Of course, such conservative positions have been forced into a kind of compromise in order to maintain their cultural and ideological leadership as a movement to 'reform' educational policy and practice. A prime example is the emerging discourse over the history curriculum – in particular the construction of the United States as a 'nation of immigrants.' In this hegemonic discourse, everyone in the history of the nation was an immigrant, from the first Native American population who supposedly trekked across the Bering Strait and ultimately populated North, Central, and South America, to the later waves of populations who came from Mexico, Ireland, Germany, Scandinavia, Italy, Russia, Poland, and elsewhere, to finally the recent populations from Asia, Latin America, Africa, and other regions. While it is true that the United States is constituted by people from all over the world – and that is one of the things that makes it so culturally rich and vital – such a perspective constitutes an erasure of historical memory. For some groups came in chains and were subjected to state-sanctioned slavery and apartheid for hundreds of years. Others suffered what can only be called bodily, linguistic, and cultural destruction (Apple 1996).

This said, however, the multi-ethnic perspective does mean that while the neo-conservatives keep pressing for their goals of national curricula and national testing, their efforts are strongly mediated by the necessity for compromise. Because of this, even the strongest supporters of neo-conservative educational programs and policies have also had to support the creation of curricula that at least partly recognize 'the contributions of the other.'[7] This is partly due to the absence of an overt and strong national department of education and to a tradition of state and local control of schooling. The 'solution' has been to have national standards developed 'voluntarily' in each subject area (see Ravitch 1995). Indeed, the example I gave above about history is one of the results of such voluntary standards.

Since it is the national professional organizations in these subject areas – such as the National Council of Teachers of Mathematics – that are developing such national standards, the standards themselves are compromises and thus are often more flexible than those wished for by neo-conservatives. The very process acts to provide a check on conservative policies over knowledge. However, this should not lead to an overly romantic picture of the overall tendencies emerging in educational policy. Since leadership in school 'reform' is increasingly dominated by conservative discourses surrounding 'standards', 'excellence', 'accountability', and so on, and since the more flexible parts of the standards have proven too expensive to actually implement, standards talk ultimately functions to give more rhetorical weight to the neo-conservative movement to enhance central control over 'official knowledge' (Apple 2000) and to 'raise the bar' for achievement. The social implications of this in terms of creating even more differential school results are increasingly worrisome (Apple 1992, 1999) and will undoubtedly lead to even more labeling of students, especially since human and monetary resources to actually meet the new 'bar' will be increasingly scarce.

Yet it is not only in such things as the control over legitimate knowledge that neo-conservative impulses are seen. The idea of a strong state is also visible in the growth of the regulatory state where this affects teachers. There has been a steadily growing change from 'licensed autonomy' to 'regulated autonomy,' with teachers' work being ever more highly standardized, rationalized, and 'policed' (Dale 1989a). Under conditions of licensed autonomy, once teachers are given the appropriate professional certification they are basically free – within limits – to act in their classrooms according to their own judgment. Such a regime is based on trust in 'professional discretion.' Under the growing conditions of regulated autonomy, teachers' actions are now subject to much greater scrutiny in terms of process and outcomes. Indeed, there are states in the US that have not only specified the content that teachers are to teach, but have also regulated the only appropriate methods of teaching it. Not following these specified 'appropriate' methods puts the teacher at risk of administrative sanctions. Such a regime of control is based not on trust, but on a deep suspicion of the motives and competence of teachers. For neo-conservatives it is the equivalent of the notion of 'producer capture' that is so powerful among neo-liberals. For the former, however, it is not the market that will solve this problem, but a strong and interventionist state that will see to it that only 'legitimate' content and methods are taught. And this will be policed by state-wide and national tests of both students and teachers.

It has been claimed that such policies lead to the 'deskilling' of teachers, the 'intensification' of their work, and the loss of autonomy and respect (see Apple 1988, 1995). This is not surprising, since behind much of this conservative impulse is a clear distrust of teachers and an attack both on teachers' claims to competence and, especially, on teachers' unions.[8]

The mistrust of teachers, the concern over a supposed loss of cultural control, and the sense of dangerous 'pollution' are among the many cultural and social fears that drive neo-conservative policies. However, as I noted earlier, underpinning these positions as well is often an ethnocentric, and even racialized, understanding of the world. Perhaps this can be best illuminated through the example of Herrnstein and Murray's *The Bell Curve* (1994). In a book that sold hundreds of thousands of copies, the authors argue for a genetic determinism based on race (and to some extent gender). For them, it is romantic to assume that educational and social policies can ultimately lead to more equal results, since differences in intelligence and achievement are basically genetically driven. The wisest thing policy-makers can do would be to accept this and plan for a society that recognizes these biological differences and does not provide 'false hopes' to the poor and the less intelligent, most of whom will be black. The implications of all of this for the politics of labeling – and for *who* gets labeled as what – should be clear. Obviously *The Bell Curve* has reinforced racist stereotypes that have long played a considerable part in educational and social policies in the United States (see, for example, Omi and Winant 1994; Selden 1999).

Rather than seeing race as it is – as a fully *social* category that is mobilized and used in different ways by different groups at different times (Omi and Winant 1994) – positions such as those argued by Herrnstein and Murray provide a veneer of seeming scientific legitimacy for policy discourses that have been discredited intellectually many times before (Kincheloe and Steinberg 1996). The sponsored mobility given to this book, which reports that the authors received large sums of money from neo-conservative foundations to write and publicize the volume, speaks clearly not only to the racial underpinnings of important parts of the neo-conservative agenda but also to the power of conservative groups to bring their case before the public.

The consequences of such positions are found not only in educational policies, but in the intersection of these with broader social and economic policies, where they have been quite influential. Here too we can find claims that what the poor lack is not money but an 'appropriate' biological inheritance, coupled with a decided lack of values regarding discipline, hard work, and morality (Klatch 1987). Prime examples here include programs such as 'Learnfare,' where parents lose a portion of their welfare benefits if their children miss a significant number of school days, and 'Workfare,' where no benefits are paid if a person does not accept low-paid work, no matter how demeaning or even where childcare or healthcare are not provided by the state. Such policies reinstall the earlier 'workhouse' policies that were so popular – and so utterly damaging – in the United States, Britain, and elsewhere (Apple 1996).

I have spent much of my time in this final essay documenting the growing power of neo-conservative positions in educational and social policy in the US. Neo-conservatism has forged a creative coalition with neo-liberals, a coalition that – in concert with other groups – is effectively changing the landscape in which policies are argued out. Yet, even given the growing influence of neo-liberal and neo-conservative policies, this coalition would be considerably less successful if it had not also brought authoritarian populist religious fundamentalists under the umbrella of the conservative alliance. It is to this group that we shall now turn.

Authoritarian populists

Perhaps more than in any other major industrialized nation, it is not possible to fully understand educational politics in the United States without paying a good deal of attention to the 'Christian Right.' It is exceptionally powerful and influential, beyond its numbers, in debates over public policy in the media, education, social welfare, the politics of sexuality and the body, religion, and so on. Its influence comes from the immense commitment by activists within it, its large financial base, its populist rhetorical positions, and its aggressiveness in pursuing its agenda. 'New Right' authoritarian populists ground their positions on education and social policy in general in particular visions of Biblical authority, 'Christian morality,' gender roles, and the family. The New Right sees gender and the family, for instance, as an organic and divine unity that resolves 'male egoism and female selflessness.'

As Hunter puts it (1988a: 15):

> Since gender is divine and natural ... there is [no] room for legitimate political conflict ... Within the family women and men – stability and dynamism – are harmoniously fused when undisturbed by modernism, liberalism, feminism, and humanism which not only threaten masculinity and femininity directly, but also [do so] through their effects on children and youth ... 'Real women,' i.e., women who know themselves as wives *and* mothers, will not threaten the sanctity of the home by striving for self. When men or women challenge these gender roles they break with God and nature; when liberals, feminists, and secular humanists prevent them from fulfilling these roles they undermine the divine and natural supports upon which society rests.

In the minds of such groups, public schooling is thus in itself a site of immense danger. In the words of conservative activist Tim LaHaye, 'Modern public education is the most dangerous force in a child's life: religiously, sexually, economically, patriotically, and physically' (quoted in Hunter 1988: 57). This is connected to the New Right's sense of loss surrounding schooling and the family (*ibid.*):

> Until recently, as the New Right sees it, schools were extensions of home and traditional morality. Parents could entrust their children to public schools because they were locally controlled and reflected Biblical and parental values. However, taken over by alien, elitist forces schools now

interpose themselves between parents and children. Many people experience fragmentation of the unity between family, church, and school as a loss of control of daily life, one's children, and America. Indeed, [the New Right] argues that parental control of education is Biblical, for in God's plan, the primary responsibility for educating the young lies in the home and directly in the father.

It is exactly this sense of 'alien and elite control', the loss of Biblical connections, and the destruction of 'God-given' family and moral structures that drives the authoritarian populist agenda. It is an agenda that is increasingly powerful, not only rhetorically, but in terms of funding and in conflicts over what schools should do, how they should be financed, and who should control them. This agenda includes, but goes beyond, issues of gender, sexuality, and the family. It extends as well to a much larger array of questions about what is to count as 'legitimate' knowledge in schools. And in this larger arena of concern about the entire corpus of school knowledge, conservative activists have had no small measure of success in pressuring textbook publishers to change what they include and in altering important aspects of state educational policy on teaching, curriculum, and evaluation. This is crucial, since in the absence of an overt national curriculum the commercially produced textbook – regulated by individual states' purchases and authority – remains the dominant definition of the curriculum in the United States (see Apple 1988, 1996, 2000).

The power of these groups is visible, for example, in the 'self-censorship' in which publishers engage. For instance, under conservative pressure a number of publishers of high school literature anthologies have chosen to include Martin Luther King's 'I Have a Dream' speech, but only after all references to the intense racism of the United States have been removed (Delfattore 1992: 123). At the level of state curriculum policy, this is very visible in the textbook legislation in, say, Texas which mandates texts that stress patriotism, obedience to authority, and the discouragement of 'deviance' (*ibid.* 139). Since most textbook publishers aim the content and organization of their textbooks at what will be approved by a small number of populous states that in essence approve and purchase their textbooks statewide, this gives such states as Texas (and California) immense power in determining what will count as 'official knowledge' throughout the entire country (Apple 1988, 2000; Cornbleth and Waugh 1995).

Thus, in concert with neo-conservative elements within the conservative alliance, authoritarian populist religious fundamentalists have had a substantial influence on curriculum policy and practice. For them, only by recentering issues of authority, morality, family, church, and 'decency' can schools overcome the 'moral decay' so evident all around us. Only by returning to irredentist understandings of Biblical teachings and fostering (or mandating) a climate in schools where such teachings are given renewed emphasis can our culture be saved (Delfattore 1992; Reed 1996).

Though a number of states and school systems have been able to create mechanisms that deflect some of these pressures, the bureaucratic nature of many school systems and of the local and regional state in general has actually brought about conditions in which parents and other community members who might otherwise disagree with the New Right ideologically are convinced to join in with its attacks on the content and organization of schooling (Apple 1996).

While authoritarian populist struggles over curriculum and texts have been growing rapidly, this mistrust of public schools has also fueled considerable and intense support for neo-liberal policies such as voucher and choice plans. The New Right, as a largely populist assemblage, has some very real mistrust of the motives and economic plans of capital. After all, such rightist populists have often themselves experienced the effects of downsizing, layoffs, and economic restructuring. However, even given these partial insights into the differential effects of global competition and economic restructuring, they see in proposals for educational marketization and privatization a way in which they can use such 'reforms' for their own purposes. Either through reduced school taxes, through tax credits, or through the allocation of public money to private and religious schools, they can create a set of schools organized around the more moral 'imagined communities' (Anderson 1991) that they believe to have been lost.

This search for the reconstitution of 'imagined communities' points to one of the effects of reprivatization talk on the politics surrounding educational policy: in the process of denying the legitimacy of oppositional claims, reprivatization discourses may actually tend to politicize the issues even more, with these issues increasingly becoming a part of public contestation, rather than remaining 'domestic.' This paradox – that reprivatization talk may actually lead to further public discussion of breakaway needs – does not always lead to victories by oppositional groups such as feminists, racially subjected peoples, or other disempowered groups, however. Rather, such politicization can in fact lead to the growth of new social movements and new social identities whose fundamental aim is to push breakaway needs back into the economic, domestic, and private spheres. New, and quite conservative, coalitions can be formed.

This is exactly what has happened in the United States, where a set of reprivatizing discourses 'in the accents of authoritarian populism' has made creative connections with the hopes and especially the fears of a range of disaffected constituencies and has united them into a tense but very effective alliance supporting positions behind reprivatization (Fraser 1989: 172–3). And this could not have been done if rightist groups had not succeeded in changing the very meaning of key concepts of democracy in such a way that the Christian Right could comfortably find a place under the larger umbrella of the conservative alliance.

The professional new middle class

Although I shall only speak very briefly about them here because of both space limitations and their limited power, there is a final group that provides some of the support for the policies of conservative modernization. This is a fraction of the professional new middle class that gains its own mobility within the state and within the economy on the basis of technical expertise. These are people mainly with backgrounds in management and efficiency techniques who provide the technical and 'professional' support for accountability, measurement, 'product control,' and assessment that is required by the proponents of neo-liberal policies of marketization and neo-conservative policies of tighter central control in education.

Members of this fraction of the upwardly mobile professional new middle class do not necessarily believe in the ideological positions that underpin the conservative alliance. In fact in other aspects of their lives they may be considerably more moderate and even politically 'liberal'. However, as experts in efficiency, management, testing, and accountability, they provide the technical expertise to put in place the policies of conservative modernization. Their own mobility is wholly dependent on the expansion of such expertise and of the professional ideologies of control, measurement, and efficiency that accompany it. Thus they often support such policies as 'neutral instrumentalities,' even when these very policies may be used for purposes – such as stereotyping and inappropriate labeling – other than those supposedly neutral ends to which this class fraction is committed.[9]

However, this group is not immune to ideological shifts to the Right. In the climate of fear generated by attacks on the state and on the public sphere from both neo-liberals and neo-conservatives, this class fraction is decidedly worried about the future mobility of its children in an uncertain economic world. It may thus be drawn to parts of the conservative alliance's positions, especially those coming from neo-conservative elements which stress greater attention to traditional 'high status' content, greater attention to testing, and a greater emphasis on schooling as a stratifying mechanism. This can be seen in a number of states where parents of this class fraction are supporting charter schools that will stress academic achievement in traditional subjects and traditional teaching practices. It remains to be seen where the majority of members of this class group will align themselves in future debates over policy. Given their contradictory ideological tendencies, it is possible that the Right will be able to mobilize them under conditions of fear for the future of their jobs and children (see Wright 1985; Wright 1989).

Conclusion

Because of the complexity of educational politics in the United States, I have devoted most of this essay to an analysis of the conservative social movements that are having a powerful impact on debates over policy and practice in education and in the larger social arena. I have suggested that the conservative restoration is guided by a tense coalition of forces, some of whose aims partly contradict others.

The very nature of this coalition is crucial. It is more than a little possible that the conservative modernization that is implied in this alliance can overcome its own internal contradictions and can succeed in radically transforming educational policy and practice. Thus, while neo-liberals call for a weak state and neo-conservatives demand a strong state, these very evident contradictory impulses can come together in creative ways. The emerging focus on centralized standards, content, and tighter control paradoxically can be the first and most essential step on the path to marketization through voucher and choice plans.

Once statewide and/or national curricula and tests are put in place, comparative school-by-school data will be available and will be published in a manner similar to the 'league tables' on school achievement published in England. Only when there is standardized content and assessment can the market be set free, since the 'consumer' can then have 'objective' data on which schools are 'succeeding' and which schools are not. Market rationality, based on 'consumer choice', will insure that the supposedly good schools will gain students and the bad schools will disappear.

When the poor 'choose' to keep their children in underfunded and decaying schools in the inner cities or in rural areas (given the decline and expense of urban mass transportation, poor information, the absence of time, and their decaying economic conditions, to name but a few of the realities), it is they, the poor, who will be blamed individually and collectively for making bad 'consumer choices.' Thus, just as the children of the poor will continue to bear the brunt of being labeled as the 'other,' so too will their parents be blamed as uncaring and 'bad consumers.' Reprivatizing discourses and arithmetical particularism will justify the structural inequalities that will be (re)produced here. In this way, odd as it may seem, neo-liberal and neo-conservative policies that are seemingly contradictory – policies ultimately supported by authoritarian populists and even by many members of the professional middle class – may mutually reinforce each other in the long run (Apple 1996).

Yet, while I have argued that the overall leadership in educational policy is exercised by this alliance, I do not want to give the impression that these four elements under the hegemonic umbrella of this coalition are uncontested or are always victorious. This is simply not the case. As a number of people have demonstrated, at the local level throughout the United States there are scores of counter-hegemonic programs and possibilities. Many schools and school districts have shown remarkable resiliency in the face of concerted ideological attacks and pressures from conservative restorational groups. And many teachers, community activists, and others have created and defended educational programs that are both pedagogically and politically emancipatory (see, especially, Apple and Beane 1995, 1999; Smith 1993).[10]

Having said this, however, it is important to note the obstacles that remain to creating optimum conditions for large-scale movements to defend and build progressive policies. We need to remember that there is no powerful central ministry of education in the United States. Teachers' unions are relatively weak at a national level (nor is there any guarantee that teachers' unions always act progressively). There is no consensus about an 'appropriate' progressive agenda in educational policy here, since there is a vast multiplicity of compelling (and unfortunately at times competing) agendas involving race/ethnicity, gender, sexuality, class, religion, 'ability,' and so on. It is therefore structurally difficult to sustain long-term national movements for more progressive policies and practices.

Because of this, most counter-hegemonic work is organized locally or regionally. However, there currently are growing attempts at building national coalitions around what might best be called a 'decentered unity' (Apple 1996). Organizations such as the National Coalition of Educational Activists and around 'Rethinking Schools' are becoming more visible nationally.[11] None of these movements has the financial and organizational backing that stands behind the neo-liberal, neo-conservative, and authoritarian populist groups. None has the ability to bring its case before the 'public' through the media and through foundations in the ways that conservative groups have been able to do. And none has the capacity or the resources to quickly mobilize a large base of nationally directed membership to challenge or promote specific policies in the ways that the members of the alliance can.

Yet despite all these structural, financial, and political dilemmas, the fact that so many groups of people – politically progressive teachers, community activists, disability activists, and many more – have *not* been integrated under the alliance's hegemonic umbrella, but have instead created scores of local examples of the very possibility of difference, shows us in the most eloquent and lived ways that educational policies and practices do not go in any one unidimensional direction. Even more importantly, these multiple examples demonstrate that the success of conservative policies is never guaranteed. This is crucial in a time when it is easy to lose sight of what is necessary for an education worthy of its name for *all* children. While it may not be very nice to state that the forces of the conservative alliance do not have the best interests of all children at heart, it would not be wrong to label their ideological/educational projects with the words 'damaging' and 'misguided.'

Notes

1   Because of the size and complexity of the United States, I cannot focus on all of the policy issues and initiatives now being debated or implemented. For further descriptions, see the chapters on policy research in Pink and Noblit (1995).

2   Given the current emphasis on this by neo-liberals, it may be the case that while Bowles and Gintis's *Schooling in Capitalist America* was reductive, economistic, and essentializing when it first appeared in 1976, oddly enough it may be more

accurate today. For criticism of their position see Apple (1988, 1995) and Cole (1988).

3 Many times, however, these initiatives are actually 'unfunded mandates.' That is, requirements such as these are made mandatory, but no additional funding is provided to accomplish them. The intensification of teachers' labor at all levels of the education system that results from this situation is very visible.

4 I have engaged in a much more detailed analysis of Channel One, including the politics of the news, in Apple (2000).

5 See also the discussion of how gains in one sphere of social life can be 'transported' into another sphere in Bowles and Gintis (1986) and Apple (1988).

6 At the time of writing, the referendum is being challenged in the courts. Its institutionalization has been suspended until its constitutionality is determined.

7 This is often done through a process of 'mentioning' (Apple 2000) where texts and curricula include material on the contributions of women and 'minority' groups, but never allow the reader to see the world through the eyes of oppressed groups. Or as is the case in the discourse of 'we are all immigrants,' compromises are made so that the myth of historical similarity is constructed at the same time as economic divides among groups grow worse and worse.

8 On the relationship between this and gender, see Acker (1995).

9 Basil Bernstein (1990) makes an important distinction between those fractions of the new middle class that work for the state and that group who work in the private sector. They may have different ideological and educational commitments. See also Bourdieu (1996).

10 Also of considerable interest here is the work in progress of Jeannie Oakes on detracking.

11 See, for example the journal *Rethinking Schools*. It is one of the very best indicators of progressive struggles, policies, and practices in education. Information can be obtained from Rethinking Schools, 1001 E. Keefe Avenue, Milwaukee, Wisconsin 53212, USA

References

Acker, S. (1995) 'Gender and Teachers' Work' in M. W. Apple (ed.) *Review of Research in Education*, 21, Washington: American Educational Research Association.

Anderson, B. (1991) *Imagined Communities*, New York: Verso.

Apple, M. W. (1988) *Teachers and Texts*, New York: Routledge.

—— (1990) *Ideology and Curriculum* (2nd edn), New York: Routledge.

—— (1992) 'Do the Standards Go Far Enough?' *Journal for Research in Mathematics Education*, 23: 412–31.

—— (1995) *Education and Power* (2nd edn), New York: Routledge.

—— (1996) *Cultural Politics and Education*, New York: Teachers College Press.

—— (1999) *Power, Meaning, and Identity*, New York: Peter Lang.

—— (2000) *Official Knowledge* (2nd edn), New York: Routledge.

Apple, M. W. and Beane, J. A. (eds) (1995) *Democratic Schools*, Washington, DC: Association for Supervision and Curriculum Development.

—— (1999) *Democratic Schools: Lessons from the Chalk Face*, Buckingham: Open University Press.

Arnot, M. (1990) 'Schooling for Social Justice,' unpublished paper, University of Cambridge, Department of Education.

Ball, S. (1994) *Education Reform*, Philadelphia: Open University Press.

Bennett, W. (1988) *Our Children and Our Country*, New York: Simon & Schuster.
—— (1994) *The Book of Virtues*, New York: Simon & Schuster.
Bernstein, B. (1990) *The structuring of pedagogic discourse*, Philadelphia: Taylor and Francis.
Bourdieu, P. (1996) *The State Nobility*, Stanford: Stanford University Press.
Bowles, S. and Gintis, H. (1976) *Schooling in Capitalist America*, New York: Basic Books.
—— (1986) *Democracy and Capitalism.* New York: Basic Books.
Chubb, J. and Moe, T. (1990) *Politics, Markets, and America's Schools*, Washington: Brookings Institution.
Cole, M. (ed.) (1988) *Bowles and Gintis Revisited*, New York: Falmer Press.
Cornbleth, C. and Waugh, D. (1995) *The Great Speckled Bird*, New York: St Martin's Press.
Dale, R. (1989a) *The State and Education Policy*, Philadelphia: Open University Press.
—— (1989b) 'The Thatcherite Project in Education,' *Critical Social Policy*, 9: 4–19.
Delfattore, J. (1992) *What Johnny Shouldn't Read*, New Haven: Yale University Press.
Douglas, M. (1966) *Purity and Danger*, London: Routledge & Kegan Paul.
Fraser, N. (1989) *Unruly Practices*, Minneapolis: University of Minnesota Press.
Goffman, E. (1961) *Asylums*, New York: Doubleday.
Henig, J. (1994) *Rethinking School Choice*, Princeton: Princeton University Press.
Herrnstein, R. and Murray, C. (1994) *The Bell Curve*, New York: Free Press.
Hirsch, E. D., Jr (1996) *The Schools We Want and Why We Don't Have Them*, New York: Doubleday.
Honderich, T. (1990) *Conservatism*, Boulder: Westview Press.
Hunter, A. (1988) *Children in the Service of Conservatism*, Madison: University of Wisconsin Institute for Legal Studies.
Kincheloe, J., Steinberg, S. and Gresson, A. (eds) (1996) *Measured Lies: The Bell Curve Examined*, New York: St Martin's Press.
Klatch, R. (1987) *Women of the New Right*, Philadelphia: Temple University Press.
Kliebard, H. (1995) *The Struggle for the American Curriculum* (2nd edn), New York: Routledge.
Lauder, H. and Hughes, D. (1999) *Trading in Futures.* Buckingham: Open University Press.
Levine, L. (1996) *The Opening of the American Mind*, Boston: Beacon Press.
McCarthy, C. and Crichlow, W. (eds) (1994) *Race, Identity, and Representation in Education*, New York: Routledge.
Molnar. A. (1996) *Giving Kids the Business*, Boulder: Westview Press.
Omi, M. and Winant, H. (1994) *Racial Formation in the United States*, New York: Routledge.
Pink, W. and Noblit, G. (eds) (1995) *Continuity and Contradiction*, Cresskill, NJ: Hampton Press.
Ravitch, D. (1995) *National Standards in American Education*, Washington: Brookings Institution.
Reed, R. (1996) *After the Revolution*, Dallas: Word Publishing.
Selden, S. (1999) *Inheriting Shame: The Story of Eugenics and Racism in America*, New York: Teachers College Press.
Smith, G. (1993) *Public Schools that Work.* New York: Routledge.
Smith, K. and Meier, K. (eds) (1995) *The Case against School Choice*, Armonk, NY: M. E. Sharpe.
Wells, A. S. (1993) *Time to Choose*, New York: Hill and Wang.

Whitty, G. (1997) 'Creating Quasi-Markets in Education' in M. W. Apple (ed.) *Review of Research in Education*, 22, Washington: American Educational Research Association.

Whitty, G., Power, S. and Halpin, D. (1998) *Devolution and Choice in Education*, Buckingham: Open University Press.

Williams, R. (1977) *Marxism and Literature*, New York: Oxford University Press.

Wright, E.O. (1985) *Classes*, New York: Verso.

Wright, E.O. (ed.) (1989) *The Debate on Classes*, New York: Verso.

Index